LOCALITY AND PRACTICAL JUDGMENT

LOCALITY
AND
PRACTICAL JUDGMENT
Charity and Sacrifice

Stephen David Ross

Fordham University Press
New York
1994

Library of Congress Cataloging-in-Publication Data

Ross, Stephen David
    Locality and practical judgment : charity and sacrifice / Stephen
David Ross.
        p. cm.
    Includes bibliographical references and index.
    ISBN 0–8232–1556–3 : $35.00
    1. Finite, The.   2. Practical judgment.   3. Practice (Philosophy)
I. Title.
BD411.R675   1994   93–47206
128—dc20   CIP

FTW
AFF 8920

PUBLICATION OF THIS BOOK
WAS AIDED BY A GRANT FROM
THE HENRY AND IDA WISSMANN FUND

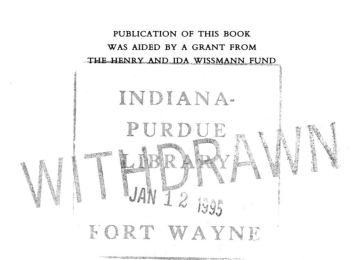
Printed in the United States of America

CONTENTS

PREFACE

LOCALITY, THE PRINCIPAL THEME of the ensuing discussion, is the condition that human life and practice are always *in medias res*, in the midst of things, caught up among them when activities are initiated and terminating among them when activities cease. What such activities are in the midst of are their milieux or "locales": human life is situated among manifold environments, located in manifold surroundings. Locality is incessant and inexhaustible. It follows that what occurs in human experience is always local: located and locating. This generic condition of human life is an expression of a far more general locality: the condition that any being is both located and locating, that its nature and identity, its properties and conditions, are functions of the locales in which it is located and the constituents located within it. At such a generic level, locality is equivalent with inexhaustibility, with multiplicity and excess, with heterogeneity. The function, the work, that beings do in their multiple and heterogenous locations is their ergonality.[1]

Such a position is not altogether new. It is related to the American naturalist and pragmatist traditions and to the views of many twentieth-century European philosophers; it bears affinities with historicism and existentialism, each emphasizing aspects of human finiteness.[2] What is new in the view presented here is the systematic development of locality in application to practical experience. Locality pertains not only to finite beings but also to their conditions and limitations. Even the limits have limits; even the conditions are conditioned. The consequence of this doubly reflexive locality is inexhaustibility. Inexhaustibility is equivalent with multiple locality. Transcendence, excess, belong to every limit, but every limit and every transcendence is local. This is locality's answer to Hegel, preserving his insights into the divided nature of determinateness but rejecting the infinite side of Spirit.

Where my view of locality differs from historicism is in the latter's emphasis on history and time. Every being is located inexhaustibly in many locations and is locatable in many others, including unknown and still to be established locations. History and time, past, present, and future, compose only some of the inexhaustible locations for beings and for human beings. Where locality differs from existentialism lies in the sense of despair that the latter takes to inhabit our discovery that humanity is not God: the infinite constantly throws its shadow over human finiteness; finite being is absurd. To the contrary, I believe that reason belongs inexorably to finiteness. There is, moreover, a transcendence inherent in locality that, if not equivalent to infinity, is equivalent to inexhaustibility.[3] There are laughter and joy amid the despair. What may be added is that these are as inseparable from tears as truth is from error. For there are profound dangers inherent in finiteness, namely, that human life and practice will recurrently contribute to human misery. Nevertheless, there is no shadow to the infinite, no unqualified universality, that surrounds the locality of human practices.

In this part of the trilogy, I examine what Aristotle called *praxis*, the practical judgments that compose human activities. The discussion ranges from everyday activities to ethics and politics and to wisdom; from language and discourse to technology. Understood as practical judgments, these are largely the topics that constitute the focus of Heidegger's analytic of the ontological structures of *Dasein*, the center of his analysis of finiteness, even as he repudiates ethics.[4] Here, we approach being in terms of locality, inexhaustibility, and ergonality, and human being in terms of judgment. Practical judgment is one of a multiplicity of modes of judgment. When sufficiently interrogative and self-critical, it composes practical reason, one of many modes of reason. Judgment and reason are inexhaustibly local and divided.

What follows is the elaboration of a generic theory of locality and inexhaustibility in relation to human experience, and especially to practical judgment. Dewey's theory of valuation as problem solving comes close to locality and inexhaustibility, but may lack their darker side, the memories of catastrophe within every practice.[5] The existentialists understand the locality of human experience from the other side, that of finiteness and despair, but may fail to express the complexity of the relation between finiteness and inexhaustibility.[6] Recent Continental writers, from Heidegger and Gadamer to Derrida, Foucault, and Irigaray, similarly emphasize the finiteness of practice without systematically exploring the importance of locality and inexhaustibility to finiteness.

Yet the weaknesses of our theoretical tradition have not been matched by equivalent defects in the texture of our practical and literary experiences. There we find, amid God's laughter and tears, a continuing if submerged tradition of charity and sacrifice. These notions, I will argue, express the presence of inexhaustibility in practice, manifestations of the inexhaustibility and locality in being.

That practice is always local includes the corollary that every practice is complexly divided within itself and located in many other local practices. A local practice comprises multifarious exceptions to every principle, but emphasizes the importance of ideals; a local practice takes the specificity of particular circumstances and individual cases into account, but recognizes that exceptions are typically self-aggrandizing and abusive. A local practice is, then, modeled after political practices in which adherence to rule is both necessary and impossible. This aporetic formulation is intended to emphasize locality, not to suggest irrationality. To the contrary, there are forms of reason urgently concerned with confronting the tensions in human experience that offer no universal reconciliation. Such rationality belongs to practical judgment primarily and to politics in particular. Politics in this sense is the predominant paradigm of practical reason.

Notes

1. With this discussion of practical judgment I conclude my trilogy in philosophical anthropology concerned with the locality, inexhaustibility, and ergonality of being, and, especially, of human being. The other works of the trilogy are *Inexhaustibility and Human Being: An Essay on Locality* (New York: Fordham University Press, 1989) and *The Limits of Language* (New York: Fordham University Press, 1994).

See *Inexhaustibility and Human Being* for a detailed analysis of locality in relation to human being, and my *Transition to an Ordinal Metaphysics* (Albany: State University of New York Press, 1981) and *Philosophical Mysteries* (Albany: State University of New York Press, 1982) for earlier formulations of locality in terms of ordinality. More recently, I have reformulated the themes of locality as sonant categories: "A *locus*, located and locating, in spheres of relevance: a *locale* composed of its *ingredients*; an ingredient composing other locales.

An ingredient, one among many other ingredients composing a locale:

as one, a *unison* with many *resonances*, the other ingredients relevant to
it in that locale.

A unison including many other unisons: a *superaltern unison* located
in a *superaltern locale*.

An ingredient with a superaltern unison in a superaltern locale *belongs*
there, otherwise it *departs*. Every ingredient belongs to and departs from
any of its locations in *harmony* and *disharmony*.

An ingredient together with other alternatives ingredient in a locale:
such an ingredient works there in *polyphony*, otherwise in *stillness*, lacking possibilities. Every ingredient echoes stilly and polyphonically in any
of its locations" (*The Ring of Representation* [Albany: State University
of New York Press, 1992], pp. 12–13 [slightly revised]). In *Inexhaustibility*, these categories are expressed as locus-constituent, unison-
ramifications, belonging-departing, situality-availability. The sonant
categories express heterogeneity in the music of language.

2. See especially John Dewey, *Experience and Nature*, 2nd ed. (New
York: Dover, 1929) and his essays in *Experience, Nature, and Freedom*,
ed. Richard Bernstein (Indianapolis: Bobbs-Merrill, 1960); see also Rich-
ard Rorty, *Philosophy and the Mirror of Nature* (Princeton: Princeton
University Press, 1979), and *Consequences of Pragmatism* (Minneapolis:
University of Minnesota Press, 1982).

3. See the works cited in note 1; also my "The Inexhaustibility of
Nature," *The Journal of Value Inquiry*, 7, No. 4 (Winter 1973), 241–53,
and "Skepticism, Holism, and Inexhaustibility," *Review of Metaphysics*,
35, No. 3 (March 1982), 529–56.

4. Martin Heidegger, *Being and Time*, trans. J. Macquarrie and E.
Robinson (New York: Harper & Row, 1962).

5. See John Dewey, *Theory of Valuation* (Chicago: The University of
Chicago Press, 1939); and *Human Nature and Conduct* (New York:
Holt, 1922). For a view of Dewey's instrumentalism which lacks all
plausibility except the sense that instrumentality is not critical enough
of its own tenets, see Max Horkheimer, *Eclipse of Reason* (New York:
Continuum, 1974).

6. For perhaps the most effective treatment of practice from an exis-
tentialist point of view, see Simone de Beauvoir, *The Ethics of Ambiguity*
(New York: Philosophical Library, 1948).

LOCALITY AND PRACTICAL JUDGMENT

1

LOCALITY AND JUDGMENT

THE GENERAL THEMES OF THE VIEW OF PRACTICE I will develop here are expressed in the triangle of locality, inexhaustibility, and ergonality. Each requires exploration. Yet it is possible to interpret them in more colloquial terms as preliminaries to the ensuing approach to practice.

(a) *Mediateness*. Locality defines a condition of immersedness, betwixt and between. Every human activity and every natural being is located *in medias res*. This notion is to be distinguished from that of mediation. The latter, except in local, qualified terms, presupposes reconciliation, the conciliation of differences. Mediateness presupposes the triumph of neither reconciliation nor incommensurateness, but grants each local relevance. They are relevant somewhere, but not everywhere, and represent the functions, the work, that inhabit any locale. Mediation, reconciliation, unification, and transcendence are all possible and important, in their particular circumstances, conjoined with local incommensurateness, negativity, exclusion, and limitation. What is involved is taking absences and divisions seriously, as expressions of limits and as prospects for transcendence, manifesting the limits of limits. Locality and inexhaustibility express the inexpugnability of incommensurate differences amid the continuing local presence of possibilities of mediation. What incommensurateness means, explicitly, is the absence of a common measure among local spheres of relevance and influence. It is the mark of locality's excess, heterogeneity.

(b) *Local Mediation*. Unification, mediation, and reconciliation are always local possibilities, but there is no ideal or total mediation. There is no reconciliation of all differences, no underlying commonality behind practical divisions, no total synthesis of divided moments, no total history. Each presupposes a common measure over inexhaustible local differences. Human beings differ in their personal, social, and historical circumstances. These differences, along with inexhaustible differences in our natural surroundings, are the source and medium of practical activities. Differences between experienced satisfactions and dissatisfactions engender practice; differences between envisaged prospects and the conditions from which practical difficulties emerge make practice intelligible; differences between human beings, individual and social, and between conditions, past, present, and future, make practice inescapable; differences between ethics and politics, politics and science, thought and action, enable practice to be effective; and differences in human experience mark both the individuality of human being and the local nature of every understanding and practice. Locality entails that difference is required for determinateness, but differences express excess.

One of the consequences of distinguishing mediateness from mediation, emphasizing that the latter is always present as a local possibility, is rejection of a comprehensive world order. There is no totality, either behind differences or as a prospect among them, no supreme unification, though there are multiple connections, relations, and conjunctions. The totality of such local relations is inexhaustible and excessive. The image that captures this sense of local interconnections replaces Hegel's image of circles upon circles—the good infinite[1]—without his notion of the bad infinite, but with snarls of entanglement.[2]

(c) *Entanglement.* Human and natural conditions, especially those that typify human being, are entangled among themselves indissociably. The image of entanglement opposes both those forms of differentiation that lend themselves to enumerative analysis and holistic forms of synthesis and reconciliation. Entanglement expresses influences and relations without presupposing a common measure; it expresses heterogeneity and excess. Enumeration presupposes such a measure. It follows that reason must be distinguished in all practical circumstances from enumeration: we cannot in principle enumerate all the beings in a room, all that belong to a given locale, all the factors relevant to a given course of action, all the qualities of an artistic masterpiece. Each involves a complex entanglement of discourse, power, desire, and knowledge. Moreover, these entanglements are "dense" and "specific":

practical influences are materially effective and inexhaustibly complex, differentially and reflexively.

We have, then, as generic principles: practice begins and ends in the midst of things, locally; practice along with every ingredient of human experience begins, ends, and functions locally; but nevertheless, practice is intelligible to the extent that local transcendence is always possible.

(d) *Local Transcendence.* Practice is intelligible only insofar as it can be effective, insofar as it has the power to transform human surroundings, insofar as it does work. Every condition of human life is both an initiating origin of practice and open to modification through practice. These modifications, inclusive of the forms of thought and production that define them, are all profoundly transcendent, departures from and modifications of their locating conditions. Such transcendences are always local. They exceed any local conditions.

No understanding of human being or nature can be intelligible without an account of transcendence. The philosophic tradition has emphasized transcendence, without, perhaps, recognizing its locality. There is no overarching universality, no absolute exteriority—the one presupposing a common measure; the other denying any measure. Fundamental to locality, inexhaustibility, and ergonality is the continuing presence of potential measures and transcendences, expressions of the presence and function of limits, and of the limits of every limit. Every limit exists to be transcended, but every transcendence is itself limited. Local transcendence is a direct expression of the indeterminateness that pertains to every determination, and conversely.

LOCALITY

Mediateness entails that practices are always densely entangled among other practices, traditions, expectations, purposes, and desires, and are themselves entangling spheres of subpractices and activities. In this double sense, mediateness is a specification of locality: every human practice is located within—densely entangled among—multifarious other practices and is a sphere of locations for other practices and judgments. Every practical judgment, every human condition and event, is multiply located and locating, inexhaustibly. This is the generic expression of locality: *Every being is located and locating, in multiple ways, and is characterized in its identity and its ingredients by its locations.* This generic characterization of identity by location is ergonality. This generic locality entails the inexhaustibility of human being and the dense entanglements of practical judgments, both expressions of heterogeneity. Identities are functions of location; locations and identities are inexhaustibly complex and entangled.

Inexhaustibility, locality, and ergonality are not independent conditions, somehow conjoined, but complexly implicate each other. Locality—multiple locatedness—is implicit in inexhaustibility. Reciprocally, inexhaustibility is entailed by the dense entanglements of locality. Ergonality expresses the implications of locality and inexhaustibility for identity, which is always multiple and local, always densely entangled. Multiple locality—locating and being located—is understood in terms of density and entanglement, which together express inexhaustibility. I am describing the effectiveness of inexhaustible powers and influences, and the constitution of identities by multiple location—ergonality and heterogeneity.

Locality and inexhaustibility express finiteness, limitation. The two sides of inexhaustibility are the presence of limits, but also the limits of limits, therefore the openness of every being, every locus, to transformation and modification. These two sides are inseparable, complementary: every being has limits but every being transcends its limits, confronts the limits of limits; every limit is transcendable but never all limits. Complementariness is not reciprocity but excess—the limits of limits, the excess of excess, transcendence of transcendence.

The complementariness emerges from the generic conditions of locality. Limitation here is qualification: a being is limited, qualified, restricted, and influenced by other beings; but those other beings and the limits they impose are themselves qualified and limited by the locales to which they belong and in which they work. It follows that under certain circumstances, certain limits both define and constrain; under other circumstances, in other contexts or locales, limits are surmountable. These reciprocal conditions are inseparable; limitation is inseparable from latitude, determinateness from indeterminateness, and conversely, entailing surplus, transcendence, excess. Identity is determinateness and excess.

The complementarity of determinateness and indeterminateness is a manifestation of locality and equivalent to inexhaustibility. Being and human experience, but also practice and judgment, are all profoundly characterized by and inextricably related to multiple forms of determinateness and indeterminateness. This complex relation is the generic expression of the dense entanglements of human locales. It may be expressed in terms of locality. Every being, especially every human judgment, is local: located within dense entanglements of other conditions and judgments and itself a sphere of densely entangled locations. The sense of restrictiveness suggested by local being is complemented by the openness and excesses demanded by local transcendence. The complementarity of determinateness and indeterminateness is the generic expression of the complementarity of limitation and openness that pertains to locality, inexhaustibility, and ergonality.

The presence and relevance of limits manifests the principle that the identity of any being, any locus, is a function of its locations and relations. I understand this functional trait as ergonality. It may be expressed in the following language, leading to four sets of categories. Every being is located and locating, a locus of ingredients located within it and an ingredient itself in another inclusive locale. The term "ingredient" represents a locus in a location; the term "locale" represents a locus as a sphere locating its ingredients; the term "locus" is the expression of the complementarity of locale-ingredient.[3] A locus, then, is both locale and ingredient, locating many ingredients and multiply located as an ingredient in many other locales. This multiple locality is equivalent with inexhaustibility, the complementarity of determinateness and indeterminateness. Here, determinateness pertains to locating—a locus in relation to its ingredients—and being located—ingredients composing their locales—while indeterminateness pertains to the heterogeneous multiplicity of locations. I add that this indeterminateness is intrinsic and profound. There is no wholly determinate location for any or all loci—for example, a world locale. A world locale would locate but would not itself be located. There is similarly no collection of all possible worlds. Possibility pertains to particular locations. The categories themselves, and the local theory, do not compose an all-inclusive sphere of locations. Here, metaphysics may be regarded as one of many modes of reason, divided by science and art, but also by practice, none of which has unqualified authority over the others. Heterogeneity pertains everywhere and expresses multiple location.

The reciprocity of determinateness and indeterminateness, heterogeneity, has been expressed generically in terms of multiple location. But it is possible to express it in terms relating to a particular locus: how it is heterogeneous, excessive, multiply determinate and indeterminate. I am speaking of "what" a locus is, an identity that I understand to be constituted by location and transcendent of any location. If a locus is multiply located, and if its nature and identity vary with its locations, its functions and work, then in any location there may be found expressions of what it is in that location, how it is multiply influential there, and how it exceeds that location. We may then speak of the "unison" of a locus as its unitariness in a location: what-it-is-unitarily-in-that-location. To belong in a location is to function unitarily, to possess a unison in that location. Such a unison is a function of certain of that locus's ingredients, those that compose its unitariness, but not all its ingredients. This functional unitariness is then its unison while the multiplicity of its other ingredients, its other relations, involving variations and influences throughout its location, are its "resonances," its ramifications. Every locus is composed in any location of a unison and multiple resonances, and the two together compose its ingredients in that location.

I have begun to develop the notion of ergonality in this discussion: "what" a being is, in any sense of that term, is a function of location. Every sense of being, every identity or property of a being, is variable with and a function of location—though not always variable with every location. The local categories here are not kinds of being, genera of being, properties of beings, but functional distinctions relevant to location. Functionality (or ergonality) is a corollary of inexhaustibility and locality. It is an expression of relationality, of the constitution of identity by place and work. An additional corollary for practice is that a practical judgment is a function of its locales and has different unisons and resonances for different locations. Such functional variation is among the most important ways in which the future bears a continuing relevance to the past, defining new locations in which past events that continue to be relevant to the future bear different unisons and resonances. It follows that every practical judgment, with its different locales, in particular, its different futures, varies in its unisons and resonances. What we do influences the future to the point of introducing new locations for past judgments. In this way, practice transforms the past, one of its greatest dangers and achievements.

To speak of multifarious unisons as functions of different locations may seem to neglect the stability of things for a particular location. If every unison varies with location, in what sense may we speak of "a" being or locus? Locality and ergonality entail that nothing can include all a locus's ingredients or even all its unisons, and nothing can be pervasive throughout all of its locations; a locus has no unqualified or all-inclusive identity. There is in this sense no unqualified common measure of all the functions and locations of a being—a manifestation of its inexhaustibility. Yet there is a sense in which any unison is stable over multiple locations. This notion may be expressed in terms of superaltern and subaltern unisons. These again are functional determinations.

To be determinate in the ways it is determinate—for it is also indeterminate, in manifold ways—a locus possesses a unison in any of its locations, that which defines its unitariness in that location, its stability relative to certain resonances. Every unison represents functional stability over a range of variations. Every unison is a superaltern unison stable over a range of subaltern unisons. This is true wherever we can speak of "a" locus or ingredient. The notion involved is identity over variation: one locus, the same over many variations and departures. A locus's resonances vary with variations within a locale as well as with variations among locales. Unisons vary with different locales, but each unison is stable unitarily over some range of subaltern locations, however local. Nevertheless, no superaltern unison can include all the unisons of a locus; it has no overarching identity. The notion of a superaltern unison expresses the meaning to be given to a common measure. Incommensurateness means, then, the absence of a common measure over all the relevant loci in a locale, the absence of an comprehensive identity.

Superaltern and subaltern unisons are not different kinds of unisons, but reciprocal functions wherever unitariness and multiplicity are interrelated. Every locus is unitary in certain respects and multiple in others. Unity and multiplicity are complementary in the sense that every unit is multiple, divisible, at least in certain respects if not others, and every multiplicity is "one" multiplicity, "that" multiplicity. Moreover, the unitariness conjoined with multiplicity is itself multiple, since "one" locus is always multifarious, and unitariness belongs to a locus over many subaltern locations.

A striking example of superaltern unisons is found among different traditions or forms of life, different cultural conditions, throughout history. Over time, one tradition is succeeded by others, yet the succession is no more an abandonment of that tradition or history than its continuance. We speak of Western culture, over many nations and centuries, of the Western tradition that continues despite changes, however massive. The point is that change and stability are inseparable, that identity and similarity are inseparable from difference and departure. There are different epochs, different traditions and subtraditions, different cultures and subcultures. Every tradition is divided within itself into subtraditions; every culture is divided within itself; every form of life contains diverse forms of life. Every practice is divided into diverse subpractices. There is no total history. Here, one "is" many in the sense that unitariness and multiplicity are functional determinations relative to certain specific contexts and locations.

It follows that every unison is a superaltern unison over many other unisons, just as a tradition is divided into hostile and antagonistic subtraditions, and a subaltern tradition is divided within another, longer tradition that continues despite differences among the subaltern traditions. Identity here is a functional relation between a superaltern unison of a locus and multiple subaltern unisons, and is always in relation to some locale. In this same sense, any history is both a single story of one time and one people and many stories of many times and many peoples. The multiplicity is not abolished by the inclusiveness of the larger story, but is an expression of the functional limits of any superaltern unison. To be a locus, to be at all, is to possess not only a unison and resonances, many unisons and many resonances, but also a superaltern unison that defines an identity over many variations—effectively, many identities and superaltern unisons. This multiplicity conjoined with stability is inexhaustibility. Being is functional, multifarious, inexhaustible.

The notions of locale and ingredient, united in the idea of locus, and the notions of unison and resonances, including superaltern and subaltern unisons, express the most generic conditions of being-something. And there is no other sense of being than that of being-something, being something determinate and local, where locality joins multiplicity and excess. Determinateness pertains to things as expressed through the local categories, except that every pair of categories expresses indeterminateness no less than determinateness, and in at least two ways. A locus is defined by its ingredients, but not every variation in a ingredient changes the locus into "another" locus. In this sense, given a locus, its ingredients are indeterminate in certain respects; given any ingredients, a locus is similarly indeterminate in certain respects. Given a unison of a locus, its resonances are indeterminate; given one superaltern unison, other such unisons are indeterminate; and so forth. Inexhaustibility entails that every locus transcends any of its determinations inexhaustibly, and is expressed by the transcendence within each pair of one category by the other as well as by the transcendence of each pair by other pairs. In this sense again, local being is multifarious and inexhaustible: there is no unequivocal sense of being-determinate and only an empty sense of being in general, that of being-a-locus.

Some practical applications of these categories are immediate; others represent the focus of later discussions. One of the immediate implications is that the consequences that pertain to practical activities as the basis of their validation are among their resonances as well as their unisons, and that the unisons and resonances of practices are densely entangled. Practices emerge within established historical conditions and give rise to the establishment of other conditions. Yet what is established and what is novel do not simply war with each other, but jointly compose the traditions within which practical judgments function. Among the practical implications of locality and inexhaustibility is that a practical judgment that belongs to history is confronted by multiple perils of future temporality: the dangers of an unknown and as yet unachieved future, which is manifested in the consequences of practical events; the twofold dangers of the indeterminatenesses of practical intentions, that every intention is effectively divided, a consequence of its dense entanglements, and that every intention is threatened by its future, by belonging to traditions that are only partly instituted; the dangers of producing a future that has the capacity to transform the past by making it conform to a tradition that is not yet present; the dangers inherent in the alterities that belong to every human situation.

These dangers inherent in practical judgments are specifications of more generic local conditions. Practice strives for mediation and reconciliation; mediation gives way to mediateness due to the multiple locations of every locus. No synthesis, no reconciliation can be more than local, proximate, qualified, and incomplete. There is no ideal reconciliation or synthesis, no common measure, in relation to which these incomplete practical movements fall short. To the contrary, in its best political forms, practice is the only ideal historical synthesis possible—ideal in the sense that the judgments involved are rational, and entail unending criticism and interrogation, but not in the sense that they conform to transcendent external standards. Here, balance, harmony, and reconciliation of differences, all essential to ethics and politics, even for successful everyday practices, are local achievements without comprehensive ideality. In this sense, ideals and universal principles—essential for rational practices—are always local. So are the expression and revelation of differences, also essential for rational practices.

Other local categories are important in relation to practice. Given a superaltern unison, a locus stable over different unisons and locations, we may speak of that locus as "belonging" to a generic location inclusive of different subaltern locations. Belonging here is a stronger condition than that of being an ingredient relevant to a locus, and refers to the sphere of stability of an ingredient or locus in a location. It is equivalent to the condition that a unison of a locus in a particular location be a superaltern unison. That range of unisons over which a locus has a stable superaltern unison is where that locus "belongs" (relative to that unison), where its identity is "stable."

Yet no superaltern unison can be unqualified or all-inclusive for any locus. A given superaltern unison cannot include all the unisons of a given locus: this is the sense in which the "identity" of a locus is proximate and qualified. Where a superaltern unison is functionally stable over a range of subaltern unisons, the locus "belongs"; where that unison is variable over a range of subaltern unisons, the locus "departs." Belonging and departing are themselves functions of location: every locus belongs to some range of ingredients and locations, and departs from some other range.

These categories pointedly express some of the perils of the future and of heterogeneity. What belongs to one tradition may find itself continuing to be relevant to a future tradition, but in alien and antagonistic ways, changing in its functions and qualities. A given cultural practice may be unintelligible in certain ways from the standpoint of another practice, though the changes described do not produce irrelevance. We import practices from other cultures; they remain the same with differences in identities, in unisons, and resonances. They belong to both cultural traditions, but not in the same ways and respects. Their belonging to one is effectively a departing from the other. Democratic practices vary greatly from one society to the next, from one tradition to the next. There is no particular way in which a complex practice can belong to different societies and traditions without major variations and departures. A complex practice cannot be imported from one culture to another without grave risks.

Another pair of local categories is important for understanding practical effectiveness and power. The relation is not of a locus to its ingredients—involved in the categories above—but of an ingredient to the other ingredients that compose a locale. There are relations of influence among ingredients: given one subset of ingredients, others are effectively settled. This is the notion inherent in all conceptions of power, including causality. Among the resonances of a locus in a location are determinative powers, those that open alternatives and those that preclude them. The relation of ingredients in a locale that diminishes the range of alternatives may be called "stillness"; the relation that expresses alternatives may be called "polyphony." Given a subset of ingredients, some other ingredients are settled, still. But given any subset, there are other ingredients that compose alternatives available in that locale. The subset here defines options polyphonically. Stillness and polyphony define the qualifications and conditions that pertain within any locale among its ingredients. In any location, a locus defines a sphere of conditions expressive of its powers. These may be divided into those that leave room for variations and alternatives, and those that do not.

Perhaps the most important properties of practical judgments are their obtrusiveness in human life and experience—the effects and consequences of human practices upon life and its surroundings—coupled with the irresistible sense we have that individual agents are largely impotent, unable to greatly affect the course of events. These two properties appear to clash, but they manifest the reciprocal workings of stillness and polyphony. In every locale, there are influences and determinations, consequences and causal relations; but, there are also alternatives and latitude. Moreover, the consequences and effects are themselves divisible into stillnesses and polyphonies: even the stillnesses have alternatives and the alternatives are both settled in certain ways and open in other ways. The ideas of stillness and polyphony bear a historical relation to traditional understandings of actuality and possibility. In every locale, for every being, there are always influential determinations but also relevant possibilities, the generic conditions of latitude, novelty, and, where pertinent, freedom. Here, actualities as stillness are functional, expressive of the determinations inherent in situations and conditions, inseparable from the latitude, the polyphonic alternatives, that also belong to every situation and condition.

The local categories compose a generic account of local being. In this sense, there is no unequivocal characterization of being, or nature, but many, divided into multiple categories, each category itself divided into multiple subcategories. This multifariousness of being is an expression of inexhaustibility. The various categories are expressions of locality. More important, the categories define the complementariness of determinateness and indeterminateness in two important ways. Each category is complemented by another, and, as a pair, jointly expresses the complementarity of determinateness and indeterminateness. Locale-ingredient, unison-resonances, belonging-departing, stillness-polyphony, each corresponds on one reading to determinateness and indeterminateness respectively. Every locus possesses a unison and diverse resonances undetermined by that unison; every locus departs in manifold ways not subsumed under any superaltern unison; every locale contains settled determinations and admits a range of latitude, diverse polyphonies. I add that every locus is multiply located with multiple determinations and indeterminations; that what is indeterminate in one location is determinate in another, and conversely: what belongs in one location departs in another and conversely; what is still in one location is polyphonic in another and conversely. All are expressions of ergonality.

In the senses described here, expressed in the local categories, practice is inexhaustible, densely entangled among the activities and situations of human experience, determinative in profoundly important ways but threatened constantly by uncertainties and departures. In the sense described by the categories, human practical experience, along with human experience in its multifarious other forms, belongs to its natural surroundings; no intruder, it influences and is influenced by what surrounds it. But belonging here is always accompanied by departures, stillnesses by polyphonies, and our natural surroundings are as strange as they are friendly, as encouraging as they are forbidding. Every being, every locus, is influential and influenced; no locus can incorporate another locus into itself without loss or departure: every locus transcends any other locus, any location, inexhaustibly. That is one of the implications of locality.

It follows that practice cannot avoid the dark side of power and the consequences of intrusion. In every practice, in every judgment, are ramifications beyond the agent's control, transcendences that cannot be anticipated, a plenitude in nature and experience that escapes our presence. There are genuine differences that cannot be overcome, not in principle, but because of their contingencies. And there is no intelligible meaning to an ideal overcoming, a mediation of all differences. To the contrary, overcoming is local, transforming mediation into mediateness. Thought and practice, human experience, are local: functioning in locales, milieux are themselves milieux within which particular experiences and practical judgments are located.

JUDGMENT AND HUMAN BEING

Locality, inexhaustibility, and ergonality are generic conditions of being and nature. We turn from them to the generic conditions of human being. The departure is unavoidable if we are to make a transition from local being to local practice. Human beings, individually and collectively, if not human beings alone, engage in practice, seek to influence their surroundings. And we cannot assume that human being is intelligible independent of human practice or of its natural surroundings. To the contrary, if practice is influential, it transforms human life and experience. More radically still, practice institutes and transforms human being itself, as well as nature.[4] This understanding is an implication of the materiality and power of practice, conjoined with its inexhaustibility.[5] To be effective, practice must be influential, materially and transcendentally. As inexhaustible, its influences and powers must be capable of transforming every aspect of human experience, even humanity itself and nature.

Locality, inexhaustibility, and ergonality express multiple relatedness and relevance. To be relevant here is to be influential, to work upon other things. To be is to be influenced and influential—dimensions of locality. In such a view of nature and being may be found the generic conditions of power and efficacy: to be is to exercise powers and to respond to powers, inseparably. What is required in moving from such generic relatedness and power to practical experience is the capacity for such influence to be subjected to selection and discrimination. What is required further is that these human capacities be understood as multiply located and as functions of their different locations, influencing them and being influenced by them. What is required, then, given the far-reaching efficacies of human practice and experience, is either the rejection of any "essence" to human being, or, a view of that essence as inclusive, thoroughly pervaded by locality, relatedness, and transcendence.

There is a long Western tradition in which human being is defined in terms of a distinguishing essence, ranging from reason and consciousness to tool-making, language, and even, negativity. That such essences always presuppose dualism, promoting the human subject to an indefensible and unintelligible uniqueness, incompatible with inexhaustible transcendence, is only one of this tradition's weaknesses. More important is that every such defining term—consciousness, instrumentality, language, and negativity—tends to breach its boundaries, along with practice, to become virtually all-inclusive. The movement to such inclusiveness is a manifestation of inexhaustibility. What is omitted is the reciprocal movement. For human being is local, expressive of the ways in which it is influenced by the local conditions in which it lives and produces. If we are to define a local and inexhaustible essence to human being, it must engage in two reciprocal directions, the one expressive of human inexhaustibility, the other expressive of human locality.

What, then, is the scale of human practice? To what extent is practice intelligible only as contrasted with theory and art? The Western tradition has wavered in its answer to these questions, from a synthetic impulse to unify all forms of reason into one to a more disjointed conception of the multiplicity of forms of life and production. The Plato of the Theory of Ideas[6] holds that all knowledge is effectively of the Good, that no one knowingly does what is wrong or injurious to oneself; therefore, that there is a unified and determinate knowledge of the Good independent of the divided precariousness of practices. The Plato of the dialogues[7] distinguishes knowledge of virtue—which cannot be separated from true opinion[8]—from *epistēmē* and *technē*. In his *Treatise*, Hume argues that reasoning concerning matter of fact cannot affect the will, so that moral decisions cannot follow from matters of fact. Yet Hume is also skeptical concerning knowledge of matters of fact, so that science, ethics, and art all depend on universal tendencies of human nature that have no adequate foundation in reason. It remained for Kant, whose view of the autonomy of the cognitive faculties establishes distinct spheres of theory and practice as well as art, to address the complexities involved in how such distinct spheres may be conjoined and to acknowledge that the autonomy required by each is a requisite for the others. Particularly striking about Kant's analysis is that the spheres of practical reason, or freedom, and of the understanding, or causal law, entirely overlap. They have the same territory but neither conflict nor interact. "Understanding and reason exercise, therefore, two distinct legislations on one and the same territory of experience without prejudice to each other."[9] This suggestion has seemed unintelligible to many readers, that freedom and causality might overlap without conflict. Yet Kant's view contains profound insights into the heterogeneity of reason.

At one extreme, practice includes whatever a human being does, therefore, all human production and expression. Here, science and philosophy, along with art, are subaltern forms among more inclusive forms of practice. Such a view is incompatible with locality, for practice has been made all-inclusive at the expense of its conditions. At the other extreme, then, we may be struck by the important distinctions in the tradition and in everyday experience between theory and practice, among saying, doing, and making, among diverse disciplines, the sciences, the social and behavioral sciences, and the arts. From this point of view, practice is one of many distinct forms of life. Yet this view may also be incompatible with locality, defining absolute junctures in the fabric of human experience. Both extremes require important qualifications. To add to the confusion, there is the ambiguity in English of "practices" that are not practical, such as science and art, forms of life that are not predominantly concerned with outcomes, though they have their work.

There is a modest dialectical rejoinder to the extremes: in response to synthetic tendencies to unify all forms of human life into one, we may emphasize the plurality of faculties or disciplines, the differences between them; in response to a plurality of autonomous spheres, each with authority over its own territory, we may emphasize both how the spheres interact and how authority belongs to human life in general, or to nature, not to a particular discipline that cannot establish its own authority. To this we may add the distinction between a practice, or form of life, and *praxis*, concerned with influences and results.

Such responses are valuable, but they neglect important insights. Practice is indeed a universal form applicable throughout human experience, and beyond. Whatever a human being produces can be said to be what that human being "does," including speaking, thinking, and building. Equally, however, anything a human being does can be said to be what that human being "thinks," including speaking, working, and fabricating. And the same can be said of human production: what a human being does is what a human being produces. Practice, thought, production, but also consciousness, meaning, valuation, are all terms that, on the one hand, possess a universal purview, inclusive of everything human, and, on the other, are intelligible only in their contrasts.

The discussions of practice that follow will move uneasily between two great poles: one, human life and experience—including natural being—in general, as spheres of activity and process, and, more generally, as locales of relevance and relation; the other, the specific undertakings that we understand in terms of acts and their consequences. A far-reaching affinity will recur throughout the ensuing discussion, between natural events as processes and activities, profoundly imbued with temporality, but in which natural beings are not intrinsically or altogether historical beings, and human practices as activities and processes, profoundly immersed in history, with past, present, and future, but in which human being is not altogether a temporal or practical being. What is at issue is the continuity between the locality and inexhaustibility of nature and the locality and inexhaustibility of humanity, expressed in its transcendence of any of the categories that define it.

Aristotle suggests that we regard human activities in terms of a triad of functions, colloquially describable as saying, doing, and making. In such terms, practice may be distinguished from science and art. Yet practice lends itself to expansion to include not only all the human functions, including science and art, but also all forms of power, all forms of production, whatever influence a being exercises upon its surroundings. To this we may add Dewey's insight that experience is a matter of doing and undergoing, of acting and being acted upon.[10] Locality entails that relevance is generic and reciprocal. In such terms, activity always entails two sides inseparably, that of the agent and that of the recipient, suggesting that experience is equivalent with practice.

What is required is a generic term that mediates between locality and inexhaustibility and the human functions Aristotle describes; a term, moreover, that preserves the dividedness and reflexiveness inherent in these functions, and makes clear the relations among them. The term in the Western tradition, after Aristotle and Kant, that describes these properties is "judgment." We may call the Aristotelian functions forms of judgment. Whatever a human being produces, as a human being, that is the result of selection and that offers itself for validation is a judgment. There are diverse modalities of human judgment. Human judgments are not the only judgments there are.

Judgment here is divided into diverse modalities, corresponding at least to saying, doing, and making: to propositional, practical, and fabricative judgment. I would include a fourth, syndetic judgment, concerned with unification, conjunction, and differentiation.[11] The notion of judgment here is Aristotelian as well as Kantian, much closer to *phronēsis* than to *epistēmē*. Indeed, the traditional conception of *epistēmē*, concerned with propositional and certain truth, is incompatible with locality, inexhaustibility, and ergonality. Judgment is not rule-governed, but utilizes rules; judgment does not demand universality but employs it. Practical judgment is fully epistemic as practice—not as thought or propositional utterance—insofar as practice can be understood to be influenced by its conditions and validated by its future. The presence of alternative possibilities of judgment and of diverse forms of validation and criticism marks judgment to be epistemic. Rehabilitating the traditional term without its connotations, we may say that judgment is epistemic in providing the only productive activities possible in local human experience that can be associated with knowledge. Here, knowledge is intrinsically divided, locally. Diverse modes of validation manifest the diversity of modes of judgment. We may distinguish propositional truth, for example, from influence over the future and the fabrication of sovereign works, not only as distinct from each other but unintelligible as forms of validation relative to each other.

If we assume that knowledge and judgment are always one, then the question is why are they always divided. Given diverse modes of judgment, the question is how the modes are interrelated. For judgments are multimodal and intermodal, especially at the most complex levels of human functioning. Some works of science portray a majestic vision of natural order; some works of literature portray a sublime vision of human understanding. The question of the morality of art intrudes upon our most formalistic interpretations. Any judgment may be interpreted to possess any modality.

Such multimodality is a consequence of local transcendence. Multimodality and intermodality are implications of the generic principle that every being is limited and qualified, insofar as it is local, but every limit is limited and local. The defining limits of a mode of judgment exist to be transcended. A rigid view of modalities of judgment or of disciplines of thought would entail that the boundaries of understanding from within a discipline would be fixed and determinate. Local transcendence entails that every limit exists to be breached; nevertheless, there are local limits and conditions, and they are vital in human experience and its surroundings. Local transcendence also entails the inventions and departures without which no form of judgment could be effective and rational.

Mediateness has other implications. Judgments are in the midst of things. One consequence, already noted, is that the modality of a judgment is itself located amid other modalities, and that the limits of any mode exist to be breached. The result is intermodality. A further consequence is that human judgments are located in the midst of other human activities, within the spheres of human functioning and reception that they influence and that are influenced by them. Human judgments belong to spheres of human doing and undergoing, to the spheres of experience that delineate their qualities and properties. They belong, that is, to locales of influence and relevance.[12]

I have divided practice into two forms. What is meant by "a" practice, a "form of life" or *Lebenswelt*, is expressed by the notion of a human locale. Judgment is influential within and influenced by its locales and milieux. In the narrower sense in which practice is distinguished from science and art, we have multifarious modes of judgment, including practical judgment. The predominant concern of the discussion here is with practice in this latter sense, with the proviso that the senses of practice cannot be sharply separated. The reason is that a judgment is constituted a judgment, with a particular modality, in relation to its defining locale, while, reciprocally, a human locale is defined by the role it plays in constituting a milieu for judgment. Human locales and human judgments are inseparable notions. Judgment here defines what it is generically to be human: whatever a human being produces as a human being is a judgment. Part of what is meant is that whatever a person produces can be interpretated as falling under different modes of judgment, interpretable or judgeable as a proposition, an action, or a fabrication. Part of what is also meant is that human beings inhabit locales defined by the judgments they produce and that influence them. To be human is to inhabit locales constituted by judgments; to be human is to judge; but, judgments are intelligible only in relation to locating locales. To be human is to judge in many modes, concurrently or sequentially, in multiple locations. But human beings are not the only judges.

Practice here is a mode of judgment—practical judgment—interpreted in terms of a theory of judgment that provides a generic perspective on human being continuous with a generic perspective on nature. The indeterminateness and openness of human being are manifested in the indeterminateness of the modalities of human judgment: there is no fixed number and no settled distinction among the different modes. The notion of human judgment then expresses the generic tendencies of human discourse and of thought in order to inhabit and to transgress their boundaries—a manifestation of their heterogeneity. Similarly, human experience and judgment, framed by their natural surroundings, are expressed in two important ways: the generic conditions of human being are expressions of far more generic natural conditions, and while everything a human being produces "as a human being" is a judgment, not everything human is a judgment, but may belong to human locales that compose the conditions for judgment, and creatures who are not human also judge. There is unbreakable continuity between human experience and its natural surroundings, not only because what human beings do transforms those surroundings, sometimes profoundly, but also because natural locales deeply influence human life and judgment.

With this view of judgment, divided into diverse modalities, but emphasizing multimodality and intermodality, we situate human being generically amid locality and inexhaustibility. To be human is to judge, where human judgment is divided into diverse modes and open indefinitely to local transcendence and variation. The mediateness and heterogeneity of human being are expressed doubly, in the locality of human experiences and judgments and in the dividedness of judgments into different modes. The entanglements and transcendences of human experience are also expressed doubly, in the intermodality and multimodality of judgment and in the transformations produced by such judgments in human and natural locales. Every human locale is influential and effective, but also open to influence by judgments through time. The fundamental temporality of human experience finds its expression in the inescapable historicality and temporality of judgment. All judgments require the future for their influence and validation. All judgments are effective only as profoundly temporal. Within this inescapable temporality is the importance and inescapability of practical judgment. In this far-reaching sense, there could be no judgment and no human experience without practical judgments among other modes of judgment.

PRACTICAL JUDGMENT

To be human is to judge in many modes, sequentially and concurrently. It follows that practice is situated, as practical judgment, among many other modes of judgment, human and natural. It is a form of doing, not thought—though thought is indisputably a form of practice in the sense that it has consequences and is a consequence of other undertakings. Practical judgment here is typified by consequences, by temporality: a practical judgment belongs to time and is validated in terms of consequences, but not consequences alone. Propositional judgments—for example, reports of scientific experiments or weather reports—always have consequences, but are validatable as true or false in factual terms. Propositional validation does not depend on consequences in this sense although without its future, no propositional judgment can be validated. Even predictions—of the weather, for example—are not judged true or false in virtue of the consequences of the predictive acts, but in virtue of the states of affairs that are the basis of the predictions. Nevertheless, insofar as they direct human activities, weather reports are more typically practical than propositional judgments. Fabricative judgments—works of art, for example—also have consequences, but are validated in terms of contrasting and configurational more than consequential properties.[13] Where we think of practice in terms of the style of life that an agent achieves, independent of its consequences, we are thinking of fabricative rather than of practical judgment. We are observing the intermodality of judgment. Even so, the distinctiveness of the modes of judgment does not entail their autonomy.

That scientific reports have important consequences, that great works of art change the shape of human experience, does not vitiate distinctions among the modes of judgment, but may be understood as a manifestation of intermodality and multimodality. Scientific reports and works of art are practical judgments insofar as they are produced in human experience with determinate consequences. By way of contrast, true propositions would be true if they had no consequences (if no one heard them), and masterpieces of art may molder in the basements of museums, without significant influence or outcome.[14] Nevertheless, claims and works always have consequences, and these are in many cases important. Furthermore, some consequences are important for propositions and works, as verification requires predictive consequences and political works issue in activities and events. Still further, practical judgments are typically validated within the modes of propositional and fabricative judgment. Nevertheless, we understand the materiality of judgments to express their temporality and practicality, that every judgment is a consequence of its past and has consequences.[15]

The diversity of judgmental modalities is an expression of locality: every judgment is local in being interpretable only from within certain locales while it is also located in others. Intermodality and multimodality are expressions in relation to judgment of the locality of locality, that every limit exists to be surmounted—itself locally. Every judgment is a practical judgment in the sense that it may be regarded as something done and that there exist locales in which it may be judged in terms of consequences and results. Nevertheless, a judgment is a practical judgment rather than a propositional or fabricative judgment insofar as it is interpreted (or subsequently judged) in terms of such consequences and results. In this sense, practice belongs to space and time uniquely, demands its future quite differently from the other modes of judgment. Nevertheless, every judgment demands its future for its validation, for no judgment is self-validating. A judgment offers itself for validation, but its validation belongs to other, subsequent judgments. This process of judgment upon judgment is "semasis."[16]

Practice is associated with practical judgment in the specific sense of consequences and results in which practical judgment is distinct and in the generic sense in which any judgment may be interpreted as practical. There is, then, practice compared with theory and art: the first validated in terms of consequences; theory and art validated in terms of evidence and argument in the one case, in terms of the sovereignty and structure of its works in the other. But in addition, all human activities and productions—all human judgments—are practical in wielding powers and influencing outcomes, including those common milieux or locales that define the contexts and modalities of judgment.

Every judgment is epistemic in the sense that it involves selection and validation. But not every judgment is valid, and even when valid, a judgment may not be based on ongoing interrogation. Every judgment is then epistemic, but may not be rational. This formulation appears more felicitous with respect to propositional judgments than to practical and fabricative judgments: a propositional judgment is true of some state of affairs and based on evidence or proof. Moreover, even a true statement may be based on inadequate evidence. In the case of practical judgment, however, the act itself is the judgment, validated in terms of consequences, outcomes, and remembrances. A practical judgment is not valid "about" any state of affairs, but it is valid in the ways it belongs to and transforms states of affairs. It may be thought of as a form of knowing "how" rather than knowing "that," provided that we think of art as neither of these, but as knowing "through." These distinctions obscure the far more important point that knowledge here is based on judgmental processes, on semasis, that what is known is less important than the processes of interrogation that pertain to judgments. In this sense, not every judgment has an object, especially in practical and fabricative judgment. Nevertheless, every judgment is situated in wider locales of judgment, its surroundings, in virtue of which it may be judged.

Every judgment belongs to some or many locales—a consequence of locality. These locales are milieux, human environments, with the qualification that every such locale typifies both action and thought within it—in that sense is "perspectival."[17] Judgments not only belong to, are located within, diverse locales, but are the judgments they are in virtue of those locales. Judgments either reinforce or transform their environing locales; reciprocally, transformations in locales influence the judgments within them, even past judgments that appeared to be settled. In this sense, nothing, past, present, or future, is ever entirely settled; this is an expression of the indeterminateness that, together with determinateness, manifests inexhaustibility.

In two very important and general senses, practice tends to usurp the province of the other modes of judgment: the openness of the future to judgment is a manifestation of inexhaustibility; the dynamic side of practice is a manifestation of power, expressing influence and relevance, generic conditions of locality. These natural extensions of practical judgment are the source of its unique temporality. Yet to accept the generality of indeterminateness and power is not to collapse the distinctions among the modes of judgment. Practical judgment expresses openness to an unsettled future as no other mode of judgment can. More accurately, practice profoundly depends on future consequences. Practical judgment is temporal both as judgment and in the particular ways that pertain to consequences and results.

Some of these complex temporal entanglements have been expressed in the tradition in non-temporal terms; for example, the timelessness of propositional or logical truths, the atemporality of sublime works of art. Yet propositional truth is temporal in the triple sense that our natural surroundings change, that supporting evidence, theory, and languages change, and that confirmation is a function of future judgments. Similarly, works of art insistently manifest their own times and utilize materials of tangible temporality. What may be recognized in such claims of atemporality is that, like other modes of judgment, practice belongs to time and history, to the march of human events and to the succession of material conditions; but in a sense unique to it, taking into account the relevance of future events and conditions to the validation of practical judgments. When all forms of human experience are called practical (as against theoretical or beautiful), it is always in part to emphasize the irresistible temporality of human experience and the importance of the future. We understand that every judgment may be interpreted as a practical judgment, with its consequences relevant to it, but not every judgment depends on consequences for its validation. Nevertheless, all judgments are situated in time and demand future judgments for their validation.

We have, then, that judgment and practice belong insistently to human time and history, but that practical judgment is uniquely historical while no judgment is practical alone. Here, practice is the mode of judgment that most profoundly addresses the temporality of human experience and the dangers of the future. Failure belongs to practice as it does not belong to propositional and fabricative judgment—to science and art. A false proposition cries out for modification, for further experimentation and formulation, but is not a failure. It neither pertains to a scientist personally nor carries the weight of blame and reproach. Only in terms of science as practice does such failure apply—to scientists who practice fraud and deceit, who manipulate data and falsify results, whose mistakes produce pain and suffering. Falsity in propositional judgment is a stimulus to further interrogation, but neither involves failure nor justifies despair. Similarly, invalidation in art and other forms of fabricative judgment involves failure only in the sense that we consider their future in locales for which art is a form of practice.

Practice involves the future and its human implications directly: they establish the terms of its achievements. And while not every consequence is important, and not every disadvantageous result is the mark of failure, even the notion of importance here peculiarly belongs to practical judgment: what is relevant to human beings and their surroundings in terms of the influence of past events and actions upon them. In all these ways, then, failure inhabits practice as it does not inhabit other judgmental modalities. It is, of course, a mistake to be so captivated by one side of practice, the terror of failure, as to neglect its other sides. Not only are practical judgments frequently valid: they may under certain conditions constitute a form of reason, promote joy and happiness. Where practical judgments succeed, in contexts of terror and despair, they are among the greatest of human achievements. Yet while complacency is to be avoided in any of the modes of judgment—and is the greatest enemy of the self-criticism that is required for rationality—only in practical affairs is the absence of complacency based on a tragic sense of inadequacy. This is a natural result of the omnipresence of failure in practical judgments. Failure belongs inescapably to every practical judgment.

Failure is the defining characteristic of practical judgment, the shadow that haunts the qualities and fulfillments of human practical life. We may add that such failure belongs to practical human experience intrinsically, that failure cannot be eliminated, but may at best be ameliorated. The other forms of judgment do not involve failure similarly, but they are interpretable as practical judgments. In this sense, practice is the form of judgment that is most profoundly involved with the nature and qualities of lived experience and human achievements, qualities manifested in the continuing pressure of failure in all human events and activities.

PRACTICAL QUERY

That practical judgment may be neither propositional nor certain, that when it provides knowledge it may have no object, that possibilities of failure cannot be avoided in practical activities, does not entail that practice is neither epistemic nor rational. Every mode of judgment is selective and validational.[18] What is required is to examine the types of activities and judgments that pertain to reason and to apply them specifically to practice.

I have elsewhere, in the context of a discussion of foundationalism, characterized a distinction between "external" and "internal" theories of knowledge.[19] Foundationalism holds that knowledge is legitimate only when based on uniquely determinate grounds—defined in terms of external objects that can be adequately known or in terms of the internal processes whereby knowledge is acquired. I reject such foundationalism on the basis of mediateness: even in our most rational activities, we are always in the midst of finite circumstances, and there are no determinate foundations.

Mediateness requires us to emphasize internal epistemic activities without foundations. Yet it is natural, in relation to inquiry, to insist on both an internal and external description, since propositional knowledge always takes an object, is grammatically transitive. Put another way, we may insist on an internal account of knowledge as derived from empirical conditions, but reject narrow views of experience and of inquiry as neglecting practice on the one hand and truth on the other. Experience is as practical as it is epistemic, is influenced as much by practice as it influences practice, is surrounded by influential external conditions. What is known through propositional judgment is always the truth that pertains to some locales, however limited or local they may be. Locality and inexhaustibility follow from such an external movement in relation to the inexhaustibility of propositional judgments.

Practical judgment, though as epistemic as any other mode of judgment, is not transitive, and where valid does not always take an object or accommodate an external account of what is known or judged. Practice is validated by its future but does not refer to it. Nevertheless, there is a corresponding, if less immediately plausible, external and foundational basis for practical judgment: norms and principles that lie outside specific and historical human practices. Platonic Ideas are one example; a priori principles of reason are another. Both neglect mediateness and make human activities subservient to indefensible foundations—indefensible in having no locations themselves. The view of practical judgment emphasized here is entirely internal—norms and principles of practice as well as theory are derived from the lived processes of human experience, including human environments and their histories. Nevertheless, the conditions and milieux of human experience compose important exteriorities in relation to practice: the surroundings within which a practical judgment transpires, the locales it transforms, its capacity to transcend any initiating conditions. The local transcendence of conditions is one of the generic traits of inexhaustibility.

Practical judgments are epistemic and validative, but not always rational. We may ask what could make everyday and frequently unreflective practices rational. From an internal point of view only one kind of answer is acceptable. Practical reason is located in the activities and undertakings involved in practical affairs carried on with the greatest intelligence and self-criticism. We may define *query* as that form of semasis, judgment upon judgment, in which invention and validation are predominant. Query is the genus of which inquiry is the species, generalized to include practice and fabrication, ethics and art, but also philosophy and perhaps newer forms such as psychoanalysis. Here, reason is divided into modes along with the modes of judgment, typified by the diverse methods and forms appropriate to interrogation and validation. Science is paradigmatic of propositional query, ethics and politics of practical query and rational practice, art of fabricative query, and philosophy, especially in its systematic and metaphysical works, the predominant form of syndetic query.[20] Here, reason as query is located among the activities that human beings undertake. It is to be identified not with formal canons of argument or method, but with unceasing interrogation and criticism, especially interrogation of one's most sacred tenets, with unstinting self-criticism, and with the inventions necessary to the development of judgmental alternatives.

The most important features of query, its inventiveness and interrogativeness, have the consequence that established modes of judgment do not altogether determine the modes of reason, any more than that modes of practical experience determine the modes of thought. Science, ethics, art, and philosophy correspond to the predominance in query of one of the modes of judgment. But that there should be these four modes of reason—four and only four—immediately raises the question of why and what might be done about it. The question is one of limits; the answer returns us to transcendence, the principle that every limit exists to be transgressed. The local transcendence of a form of reason leads us to other, newer forms of reason. Thus, interrogation and invention in query lead to multimodality and intermodality, to new forms of thought and practice.

Thus, there is no one form of propositional query, Science, but multifarious sciences. And given many sciences—biology, chemistry, physics—there are other sciences at their junctures: biophysics, biochemistry, chemical physics. There are in addition conjunctions of physical with social and behavioral sciences—psychobiology, sociobiology, geophysics. And there are traditional fields of philosophy—epistemology, metaphysics, and ethics—and newer, interdisciplinary fields—philosophy of science, of law, of art. More striking still, there are novel forms of thought—psychoanalysis, structuralism—that offer themselves as forms of reason in virtue of their reflexive interrogativeness, but that demand novel ways of understanding and interpreting. The most striking and remarkable of the properties of these newer forms of query is that they undergo major transformations from within and without under the pressures of interrogation. In the sense in which a form of judgment is indefinitely open to interrogation and criticism, especially from within, in terms of its own methods and forms of validation, psychoanalysis is a form of query, perhaps one of the most pervasive and fundamental contemporary forms whereby we understand the structure of human experience. It is not, however, propositional query alone, not primarily a science, but has become a generic discourse of contemporary human thought.

The principle here is that query is not restricted to the established modes of judgment—propositional, practical, fabricative, and syndetic—but, under the pressure of intermodality and multimodality, engenders new forms of reason and truth. There is no Science, but many sciences; more important, what a science is undergoes modification with the development of other sciences and under the pressures of its own self-critical methods as well as from the standpoint of other interrogative perspectives. We may add another condition of query, a corollary of local mediation, that the interrogation and invention required in query lead to intermodality and multimodality. Judgment admits of intermodality; query demands it. Yet multimodality and intermodality take diverse forms and a given form of query may express intermodality negatively, by defining firmer limits as well as by opening itself to richer forms of validation.

We see such negative intermodality in the almost inevitable question, in the modern epoch, of whether a given discipline or subdiscipline is a science. To the extent that a discipline defines itself narrowly as a science, it carries only that authority and acceptability available to it under the pressures of criticisms from within and without—effectively situated among manifold intermodalities. To the extent that science is granted sole legitimacy among the forms of reason, it inevitably takes on as wide a range of multimodalities and intermodalities possible—an excessive range. There are then at least two questions of the relation between science and non-science. One is a question of multiple forms of legitimacy and validation; science is but one of the generic modes of query, situated among many others. This is question of the limits a discipline may impose to achieve more valid results—in a particular mode of validation. This sense of disciplinariness does not preempt the force of validation.

The second sense, however, contains the covert desire to control all the forms of legitimate validation, casting non-science to perdition. It presupposes further that all forms of validation are commensurate. It violates locality, mediateness, and inexhaustibility. There are multiple modes of judgment because there are multiple modes of selection and validation. The multiplicity here is marked by the unintelligibility of one mode of judgment from the standpoint of another. And this unintelligibility obtains despite the continual interrogative pressure to overcome every boundary and limitation. What the pressure generates is not the transformation of art and practice into science, or their overcoming into a higher synthesis that takes precedence over each of them, but new forms of query, even of judgment, that are synthetic, multimodal and intermodal, without precedence or supervening authority.

What makes practice query is that it develops its own forms of selection and validation, and that the inventiveness and interrogativeness associated with such forms is unterminating, as much as possible unrestricted by arbitrary determinants, intermodal and multimodal. The fact is, however, that questions can be answered only from within established methods of judgment. Thus, every form of query develops singular methods and limits to become more effective while every such form subjects itself continuously to criticism and interrogation in order to enforce its claim to rationality. In practice, the tendency is for the former requirement to take precedence, leading to a multiplicity of effectively closed forms of thought. The tendency in human life in general, including most of the forms of query, is for established forms to hold sway over newer forms, imposing imperial standards of doctrine over less orthodox, intrusive forms; and for a new form, once established, to impose its imperial will upon older and newer forms. The language describing this territoriality is political, not reflective. In this sense, practical query—we may acknowledge here the will to power—invades and presumes upon the territories of all the other modes of judgment and query.

This great principle of imperialism and inertia, in practice and reflection, in science and art as well as morality, does not altogether hold sway over human history, either thought or practice. Disciplines are invaded by new forms of reason from within and from without. Reason demands its victims, demands the fall of tyrants. The march of query through history is not an unbroken triumph, but is an ebb and flow, with victims on all sides, the results of the struggles essential to rational interrogativeness. Again, the picture we are offered is one in which the story of query, in its different modes, is told in terms of practical query, battles and triumphs. Even the history of reason, divided into many forms, falls prey to the rhetoric of practice, conflict and victory.

NOTES

1. G. W. F. Hegel, *The Science of Logic*, trans. William Wallace (Oxford: Oxford University Press, 1873), pp. 24–25: "Each of the parts of philosophy is a philosophical whole, a circle rounded and complete in itself. In each of these parts, however, the philosophical idea is found in a particular specificality or medium. The single circle, because it is a real totality, bursts through the limits imposed by its special medium, and gives rise to a wider circle. The whole of philosophy in this way resembles a circle of circles. The Idea appears in each single circle, but, at the same time, the whole Idea is constituted by the system of these peculiar phases, and each is a necessary member of the organization."

2. These images of entanglement and materiality constituting the practicality of human experience can be found in Michel Foucault; see especially, *The Archaeology of Knowledge*, trans. A. M. Sheridan Smith (New York: Random House, 1972).

3. See my *Inexhaustibility and Human Being*, chap. 1. See also note 1 of the Preface, above.

4. Traces of such understandings can be found in Foucault and Derrida: "For the entire modern *episteme*—that which was formed toward the end of the eighteenth century and still serves as the positive ground of our knowledge, that which constituted man's particular mode of being and the possibility of knowing him empirically—that entire *episteme* was bound up with the disappearance of Discourse and its featureless reign,

with the shift of language towards objectivity, and with its reappearance in multiple forms. . . . Man had been a figure occurring between two modes of language; or, rather, he was constituted only when language, having been situated within representation and, as it were, dissolved in it, freed itself from that situation at the cost of its own fragmentation: man composed his own figure in the interstices of that fragmented language" (Michel Foucault, *The Order of Things: An Archaeology of the Human Sciences* [New York: Vintage, 1973], pp. 385–86).

"What seems to announce itself now is, on the one hand, that grammatology must not be must not be one of the *sciences of man* and, on the other hand, that it must not be just one *regional science* among others.

"It ought not to be *one of the sciences of man*, because it asks first, as its characteristic question, the question of the *name of man*" (Jacques Derrida, *Of Grammatology*, trans. Gayatri Spivak [Baltimore: The Johns Hopkins University Press, 1974], p. 83).

5. "What political status can you give to discourse if you see in it merely a thin transparency that shines for an instant at the limit of things and thoughts? Has not the practice of revolutionary discourse and scientific discourse in Europe over the past two hundred years freed you from this idea that words are wind, an external whisper, a beating of wings that one has difficulty in hearing in the serious matter of history" (Foucault, *Archaeology of Knowledge*, p. 209)?

6. While a theory of Ideas can be found in the Platonic dialogues, too many passages in the dialogues call that theory into question, and irony is too common to claim that Plato promulgated such a theory without qualification. Far more important, the dialogues together express an interrogative sense of philosophy and dialectic incompatible with the normative spirit inherent in unchanging Ideas.

7. The Plato I find far more congenial and important makes the dialogue form central to philosophic activity: unceasing interrogation and validation, the process of query.

8. *Meno*, read with the appropriate ironies, explicitly denies that there is a knowledge of virtue superior to true opinion. This entails that we are never in a position, in relation to practice, whereby determinate principled or theoretical knowledge can overcome the uncertainties of the future. See my *Learning and Discovery* ([London and New York: Gordon and Breach, 1982], chap. 1) for a detailed reading of *Meno*. See also my *Metaphysical Aporia and Philosophical Heresy* [Albany: State University of New York Press, 1990].

9. Immanuel Kant, *Critique of Judgment*, trans. J. H. Bernard (New York: Hafner, 1951), p. 11.

10. "'Experience' is what James called a double-barrelled word. Like its congeners, life and history, it includes *what* men do and suffer, *what*

they strive for, love, believe and endure, and also *how* men act and are acted upon, the ways in which they do and suffer, desire and enjoy, see, believe, imagine—in short, processes of *experiencing*" (*Experience and Nature*, p. 8).

11. See my *Transition to an Ordinal Metaphysics* and *Ring of Representation* for a discussion of syndetic judgment in relation to philosophy.

12. I have called such human locales "perspectives"—not points of view, but locales of relevance. See my *Transition to an Ordinal Metaphysics* and my *Perspective in Whitehead's Metaphysics* (Albany: State University of New York Press, 1983).

13. See my *A Theory of Art: Inexhaustibility by Contrast* (Albany: State University of New York Press, 1982) and "The Sovereignty and Utility of the Work of Art" (*Journal of Aesthetics and Art Criticism*, 40, No. 2 [Winter 1981], pp. 145–154) for a discussion of the contrasts involving utility in art. See Charles Sanders Peirce, "Logic as Semiotic: The Theory of Signs,"[*Philosophical Writings of Peirce*, ed. Justus Buchler (New York: Dover, 1955), pp. 98–119] for a discussion of the configurational properties of signs.

14. This is the basis of Dewey's claim that "the actual work of art is what the product does with and in experience" (*Art as Experience* [New York: Minton, Balch, 1934], p. 3). See the discussion of this view in my *Theory of Art*, p. 98.

15. See note 2, above.

16. To avoid the historical entanglements of traditional theories of meaning, for example, semiotic and structuralist, I employ the term *semasis* to describe the play of judgment upon judgment, including language. See my *Inexhaustibility and Human Being*, chap. 3. See also Ferdinand de Saussure, *Course in General Linguistics*, trans. Wade Baskin (New York: McGraw-Hill, 1966).

17. See note 12, above.

18. For an epistemology insufficiently general to include practice, though with applications in that direction, see Nelson Goodman, *Languages of Art: An Approach to a Theory of Symbols*, 2nd ed. (Indianapolis: Hackett, 1976); and his *Ways of Worldmaking* (Indianapolis: Hackett, 1978). Goodman's theory, an epistemology of symbols, might be extended to include practice, but only where practices and actions are understood to be referential symbols. This does not seem sufficient to include the relation of practice to its future, which is not one of reference.

19. See my *Inexhaustibility and Human Being*, chap. 2.

20. See note 11, above.

2

PRACTICE

WITH APPROPRIATE QUALIFICATIONS, we may say that practice composes the locales in which human beings live, in their day-to-day as well as more refined activities. The major qualification is that propositional judgment and scientific query, along with fabricative judgment and artistic query, are pervasive forms of human life and activity even in the respects in which they are not forms of practice. Any judgment may be judged as practical; but this pervasiveness of practice does not replace the equally pervasive condition that the modes of judgment and query, together with other locales of nature and experience, contain heterogeneous differences, that the modality of a judgment and its associated forms of validation are unintelligible as judgments and validations from the standpoint of other modes. We must avoid the tendency to reduce multiple modes of judgment and query to one predominant form, even to that of practice.

The sense that we live in our practical judgments possesses an almost irresistible force. One reason is the tendency to interpret intermodality in terms of domination and subordination,[1] so that the pervasiveness of practice indicates its domination over heterogeneous forms of human being. A second reason is a concern to counter the imperial tendency of propositional thought to dominate over other forms of judgment in the name of truth and science. A third reason is a confusion of scale in relation to practical judgment, so that practice expresses not one of many modes of judgment but, generically, the active side of human being. All these reasons work against recognition of the inescapable heterogeneity of modes of judgment and reason. Yet there is a positive side to the sense that life is somehow more intimately related to practice than to assertion or to fabrication: the irresistible temporality of practical judgments. Practice not only demands its future, as does every judgment, but it is validated by it. Neither assertion nor fabrication, even as science and art, requires its future in the same way—though without its future neither could be validated.

Practical judgments manifest more vividly than any other mode of judgment the historicality of human life. Practical judgment points to history in the double sense that all judgments are located within history, with a past and future that qualify their judgment and interpretation, but more directly in the case of practice that history is composed of judgments that had their futures and produced their consequences. History is not the story of human practical judgment alone, nor is human being incorporated entirely within its history; nevertheless, history tells stories of human practices and events, of antecedents and consequents, in this sense interpreting human events in terms of practice. The stories of scientific discoveries and artistic styles and works are historical in part, but cannot be expressed as history. No autobiography can explain the truth of a scientific theory or the intensity of an artistic work. These are unintelligible as forms of validation from the standpoint of practical judgment, and history is primarily a tale of practical judgments, of undertakings and culminations. One of the pervasive tensions within history is manifested here: history includes all judgments and all of human being, but cannot do so without distortion, since it transforms every judgment into a practical judgment. The insistent temporality of history forces it to insist on practicality.

An additional feature of human life and being that belongs to practice as it does not to other modes of judgment are the dense entanglements of human activities. They are embedded in inexhaustible milieux and traditions, form intricate patterns and establish complex relations, in which oppositions and conflicts, differences and resistances, are as present as positivities. I am speaking of powers and influences divided inexhaustibly over multiple sites and expressions. I am emphasizing that oppositions and voids express density and heterogeneity as thoroughly as positivities exercise influence, that in this sense propositional judgments and artistic works are attenuated in relation to their validation. Another way of putting this is that failure pertains to practice as it does not pertain to science and art, relating densely and materially throughout practical experience.

The emphasis on difference and specificity is Hegelian: no being can be determinate except in terms of differences and oppositions.

What is rejected is that side of Hegel in which differences are more fully realized in their mediation. What is accepted in its place is mediation, that every difference calls for and may attain local mediation. This demand for local mediation is the pervasive source of judgment. But it is realized in multifarious modes, inexhaustibly, and in no comprehensive, higher synthesis, even one that preserves the differences inherent within it as moments in its historical realization. What is rejected is the transformation of all differences into moments of the whole, the suggestion that locality presupposes totality and finiteness infiniteness. What is rejected also is the sense that heterogeneous human events and practices, and natural beings, join together without waste and dissipation. To the contrary, there are always irrelevant contingencies, variations, and departures, from the standpoint of any mediation or reconciliation. Life and nature are filled with irrelevance and triviality as well as with influence and importance. These together compose heterogeneity.

Waste and triviality, contingency and variation, belong to practical judgments as they do not belong to propositional and fabricative judgments—though there is waste everywhere. The point parallels the unique relevance of history and time to practice: waste and triviality are the materials of failure and sources of frustration in practice. This understanding of the negative, inhibiting side of natural things and its importance for practical experience, is the recurrent motif of the ensuing discussions. I add that this darker side of the inexhaustibility of being and practice contains within it a positive side, the joy and hope of practical judgment.

CONSEQUENCES

All judgments have consequences; all judgments have ramifications. Though these conditions of judgment appear parallel, they are very different. Even the most natural qualification, that consequences are a species of the ramifications of judgments, is unacceptable, despite the importance of the insight associated with it. All judgments, all human experiences, belong to time and to history; however, neither time nor history can be all-inclusive. Ideals and forms do not belong to time, or, if they do, some of their subaltern ingredients do not, at least in the same ways and respects. The reason is that some structural elements of ideals and forms—an example is mathematical patterns—do not vary with historical events. It follows that such elements belong to the unisons of the patterns while historical events belong to their resonances. Time does not pertain to the unisons of all things: were it so, it would be an all-inclusive superaltern locale for all loci, and there is no such locale. Rather, time is divided, fragmented, dispersed. Temporal events belong to the unisons of some loci and the resonances of others. It follows that some ingredients of such unisons are irrelevant to temporal occurrences. Examples are deductive relations, formal metrics, structural conditions, probably certain physical constants and natural laws. It does not follow that we can precisely determine what is in this sense not influenced by the passing of time, for anything may be modified in some locale, if only imaginatively.

This argument about the limitations of time is a specification of a more general argument. There are three general arguments against the all-inclusiveness of any principle or category. One is that everything is local, limited in some way. It follows that irrelevance is a condition of every locus: no being is relevant to every other. The second is that every inclusive locale is itself located, but an all-inclusive locale can have no location. The third, the generic form of the argument concerning the limits of time and history, is that in order for loci to differ at all, they must differ in some of their ingredients.[2] It follows that even where two different loci belong to the same locale, some of their ingredients do not. Some differences remain unmediated: that is what local mediation means. Wherever certain differences are mediated, others remain heterogeneous. Difference depends on heterogeneity. Moreover, heterogeneity is local: what is incommensurate in one perspective may not be incommensurate in another. Determinateness and indeterminateness are functional, ergonic.

It does not follow from the limits of time that any loci are timeless without qualification, only that different loci bear different kinds of relations to time and history. Every judgment is temporal in a variety of ways: each is entangled in inherited conditions, past traditions, and particular circumstances; each is open semasically to further judgment and looks to the future for its validation; each transpires, begins and ends, in time. Every judgment succeeds other judgments and conditions and is succeeded by other judgments and conditions. Every judgment pertains to temporal events among its ramifications and is influenced by temporal events among its conditions. But only practical judgments are validated by their temporal descendants, by their consequences and antecedents.

Space and time pertain to human being generally and to judgment specifically. There can be no judgments without temporal and spatial locations. I add that practical judgment is doubly spatial and temporal, uniquely, in the sense that it is intelligible only in relation to other temporal and spatial locations, validated by them. It is not that a disembodied, unextended being might think true thoughts or produce great works of art disengaged from space and time,[3] but that there are works whose temporality is mute while their spatiality is intense—in the plastic arts—and there are works whose spatiality is dim while their temporality is intense— in music. There are also mathematical theories that are not validated in relation to spatial and temporal events—though we, as the creatures who produce these theories, require space and time for judgment and experience. Space and time here are conditions of all human judgments, but are uniquely relevant to practical judgment. Practical judgment is that mode of judgment reflexively constituted by the spatiality and temporality of judgment and experience.

Hegel defines time as the primary form whereby Absolute Spirit alienates itself from itself to become concrete.[4] Spirit rests on its past and future. Such a view is plausible only where Spirit is understood in practical terms, that is, in terms of as yet unrealized possibilities in relation to desire.[5] Here, the time that pertains to natural events is to be distinguished from the time that pertains to Spirit—one of antecedents and consequences. All judgment demands its future, giving birth to practical judgment. That time might be abolished, with Spirit, with desire and all forms of alienation, would bring with it the abolition of all practical judgment. This is utopian and unintelligible.

Traditionally, time is one of the primary forms under which the universe has been regarded as an object of thought. It is, for example, in Kant's first *Critique*, the transcendental schema underlying all the other schemata.[6] From the standpoint of locality, such a generic perspective is unintelligible. Every being—including human beings and their judgments—is local, located and locating.

Locality is a pervasive condition of being. It is natural that it should be manifested in certain pervasive forms—pervasive but local and contingent—such as space and time. These are among the most generic of pervasive forms, but they are still local, not only because there are other forms of locality that are neither temporal nor spatial, but because there are other forms of space and time than are manifested in physical or practical terms—in works of mathematics and art—and because different beings and judgments bear different relations to time and space.

Human beings are spatial and temporal beings because their judgments require space and time for production and validation. Space and time here are pervasive and far-reaching but not all-inclusive forms of locality with fundamental importance to human judgments. However, given the generic temporality and spatiality of judgment, practical judgment is constituted uniquely by the reflexive importance of space and time to its validation. Put another way, that judgments are generically spatio-temporal gives rise to the condition whereby practical judgments are uniquely spatio-temporal. I add intermodality: every judgment may be interpreted as a practical judgment; every judgment has consequences though certain judgments are validated independently of their consequences (and although their validation is one of their consequences). The temptation is then nearly irresistible to assign a unique primacy to time and space, and thereby to consequentiality and practical judgment. I have rejected such primacy. Rather, I hope to understand how practicality and consequentiality pertain specifically to human activities, practically and more generally.

In his third *Critique*, Kant distinguishes purposiveness from purpose in terms of the representation of the existence of the beings in which we have an interest.[7] Such a distinction requires us to distinguish sharply between external and internal representations, as if only the former were concerned with interest and existence. Internal representations are effectively fictive, having no exterior legitimacy. What I believe Kant may have intended was a distinction between representation and practice, where the former is understood to include the possibility of practice but does not require or entail it. That is, every judgment, every work of art, movement, thought, or imaginative contrivance, has consequences and may be evaluated in terms of such consequences, but the consequences of such judgments are not relevant to them in every mode of judgment—are not relevant, for example, in terms of science or art. It follows that the temporality of representation or judgment in general is to be distinguished from the temporality of practical judgment in particular.

Kant argues in his first *Critique* that space, and especially time, are intrinsic forms of the unity of the manifold. Such a view gives primacy to sensation and perception as the forms of conception, and makes a creative mathematical imagination largely incomprehensible. This forced him to regard mathematical propositions as synthetic *a priori*, though the evidence he offers suggests instead that mathematical synthetic truths are neither strictly *a priori* nor *a posteriori*. What is implicit in Kant's insight is the intimate relation as well as the difference between mathematics as a form of thought and as a form of practice. The insight is carried into his understanding of time as the transcendental schema, though he omits an equivalent understanding of space. We may substitute for his view that space and time are intrinsic forms of the manifold the notion that they are forms of location intrinsic to judgment. In this sense, space and time are the pervasive forms in which judgments can transpire and be validated. It follows that space and time are the pervasive forms in which consequences obtain and are relevant, in which judgments succeed and pertain to judgments. Practical judgment here is the mode of judgment that manifests this semasic successiveness. We may add that, through intermodality, the conditions of practical judgment pervade all the modes of judgment including our understanding of natural conditions.

Practical judgment, validated by its consequences, belongs to space and time in uniquely intimate and far-reaching ways. Every being is located somewhere, but not always spatio-temporally. Every judgment is located in space and time, but not explicitly in relation to its consequences. Every human practical judgment is located specifically and successively in space and in time; more particularly, it is located in relation to human bodies. A practical judgment's temporal location defines the relevance of other events as antecedents and consequences. Its spatial location defines its relation to an agent and the agent's body; this is fundamental to the exercise of practical powers. Moreover, space and time function jointly in relation to practice: to be spatially located in relation to other events a practical judgment must exhibit consequences; in order to have consequences, a practical judgment must be spatially

related to other events. I add that the space and time referred
to here are local conditions of influence and power. There are
imaginative forms of spatiality and temporality in works of art
that are not referable to practical judgments. In this sense, art
opens new worlds to our imaginations with new forms of space
and time.[8]

We may characterize the relation of practical judgment to time
and space more generically. A fundamental condition of practice
is that it never occurs all at once; it always requires time and space
for its successive occurrences. What is essential is the divisibility
of acts into regions and occurrences, integral to the density and
materiality of practice. Whitehead argues, in *Process and Reality*,
that since every act or event must have a predecessor and a succes-
sor, no act of becoming can be infinitely divided. Yet he finds
himself required to discuss such acts of becoming in terms of two
forms of division, one genetic or successive, the other coordinate
or extensive.[9] The alternative is that divisibility and indivisibility
are complementarily related, that every event is divisible in certain
respects and indivisible in others. With respect to practice, the
divisibility of agency is a generic property, following from the
fact that there is no totalizing act, only local acts that accomplish
their tasks divisibly. In a local practice, every act is divided inexhaustibly by its locales and ingredients. Such divisions are not
only by time and event, but by place and situation, and by other
locations—by agents, circumstances, history, and so forth. This
is heterogeneity.

Time is one of the pervasive, though limited, forms of location,
the dividedness that implicates any being elsewhere and elsewhen,
influenced by other places and other times. Heidegger calls it "ekstatic," out of itself. I add that space is also ekstatic. Otherwise,
we commit what Whitehead calls the fallacy of simple location.[10]
The reflexive locality of time and space lies in the ineradicable
contingency of the particular form of locatedness that they express. Nevertheless, locality is generic; spatiality and temporality
are more specific. Practice is the specific form of judgment that
pertains doubly to the pervasiveness of temporality: directed toward its future from its past, it has a future to which it is relevant
and is judged by that future.

This inherent successiveness and divisibility of practical judgments may explain the recurrent tendency to express the density

and historicality of science and art in terms of their practicality, effectively neglecting the plurality of modalities of judgment and the incommensurateness of different modalities of validation. In both cases, we express as practice the contrasting divisibility and sedimentation of human activities. We emphasize, then, the locality but also the divisibility of science and art by local milieux as well as by history and geographical location. In this sense, we regard science and art as themselves consequences of large-scale human practices and regard certain subsequent human events as consequences of science and art—technology as a particular Western way of thinking, for example. In both cases, science and art are regarded primarily as forms of practical judgment and query, far too limited a view and incompatible with locality and inexhaustibility. The questions "where" and "when" are relevant to any judgments, in any mode, but they may be digressive in relation to art and science while they are unavoidable in relation to practice. One of the most pernicious features of the Western ethical tradition has been its attempt to mask this feature of local practice behind timeless universal principles, transforming practice into fabrication or propositional rules, obscuring the terror that immersion in an unknown and uncontrolled heterogeneous future brings before us.

History

The nature of history is to be found in our understanding of practice, for the stories in history are almost entirely of practical judgments, antecedents and consequences. The reason for this is that history typically relates to time as practice, in terms of the conditions and outcomes of human events. Where history concerns itself with positions and theories, or with works and insights, more than with deeds, it converts them into acts and events—their happenings and influences—or produces a new discipline only peripherally related to history: art history or the history of ideas.

It is a common view that history includes the entire story of humanity. Such all-inclusiveness is impossible, for there is no complete story of human being—or, for that matter, of any being. Every being is inexhaustible, human being conspicuously so. Its inexhaustibility is expressed in a multiplicity of disciplines, modes of judgment, forms of life, and locations. History here either becomes inexhaustible itself, effectively equivalent with human being, with indeterminate boundaries, or, it composes manifold stories of inexhaustibly diverse locales for human being.

No story is the story of being in general or human being in particular, not just because the stories are ours and we can always tell others, but because what we tell the stories of is inexhaustible. In this sense, history is situated precariously between two extremes: as one among many other disciplines and cultural forms that compete with it in narrating the stories of human being; and, impossibly, as overcoming its limits to include every human story. History strives for all-inclusiveness but finds itself restricted to practical judgment.

Analogously, the historicality of practical judgments is divided into a generic historicality that pertains to every judgment and the particular historicality that pertains to practice. The suggestion that all the modes of judgment are practice blurs this distinction, but not without the double plausibility that though every judgment is indeed a practical judgment—or may be interpreted as one—and not a practical judgment alone, every judgment is historical in important and far-reaching ways, though not only in the ways that pertain uniquely to practical judgments.

As a discipline, as a form of knowledge, history is selective and exclusive: it cannot include everything and still be epistemic, for disciplinary intelligibility requires exclusion. Yet history is also inexhaustible, and one of the forms of inexhaustibility represented in historical understanding is that there are multiple forms of selection and exclusion, so that what is included in one account is excluded from another, and conversely. History is always divided into multiple histories, of different kinds and emphases. Certain judgments—of a private or individual nature—may not belong to political or military history, but to social or domestic history. Biography is a primary form of history, and may include the most private and personal judgments, but not, then, the political and military events that shaped the course of national events, except from within its personal perspective.

All judgments belong to history in terms of what may be explained and understood and in terms of their insistent temporality. Moreover, they belong to history intrinsically, in that their natures and modalities are determined by other events to which they are related. In this sense, judgmental modality is variable with different locales. Moreover, many of the forms of historical understanding await establishment, so that every judgment awaits a future—many futures—whereby its nature and validation will be determined. It follows that judgment, semasis, and validation are multiply implicated in historical events. In this sense, historicality has the double meaning of temporality and exteriority. The latter may be reinterpreted not as history but as publicness, as shared locales. Every judgment, every event, every human occurrence, has a public as well as a private side—the two are inseparable—and is a function of public and private ingredients.

Every judgment, including practical judgment, is insistently temporal and has public as well as private determinants. Historicality refers here to the multiple forms of determination that inhabit the multiple locales of human being. Historicality, then, is an exemplification of inexhaustibility, of the reciprocity of determinateness and indeterminateness. For history and temporality inseparably determine and open locales and judgments, and every aspect of human life is determinate and indeterminate, in part due to its historical locations.

I have discussed, to this point, the form of historicality that pertains to judgment generically, and not to practical judgments in particular. Practical judgments differ from judgments in general, not in having consequences—every event has consequences—but in being judged by their consequences. Practical judgments are historical along with other judgments in being situated within and emergent from historical situations, sedimented in traditions and forms of life, directed toward an open future to which they contribute. But, in addition, practice forms and is formed by the future, profoundly and thoroughly. Time, the future, transforms the past; past events are modified by the traditions to which they belong, including an indeterminate future; practical judgments look to future consequences for their validation.

One result of this historicality of practice is that it is tormented by an unknown and nonexistent future as no other mode of judgment can be. The danger in practice is that it needs its future but can never control it. Inversion follows: what cannot be controlled expresses the already-present forms of domination and control, the powers already inherent in established practices. In return, practice always contributes to the uncertainties of the future as much as to their resolution.

The particular way in which practice is historical pertains to the density and specificity of practical entanglements. They belong to the specific determinants of history, as determinants themselves and as influenced by other determinants, and especially in the ways that they depend on what succeeds them for their validation. The specificities of human events are practical; conversely, the determinants of practices include the definite and specific consequences that follow from them. What follows is a rejection of abstract and timeless practical determinants. What follows also are the reciprocal limitations of our practical judgments and their future.

LATITUDE

In the Western tradition, philosophical and jurisprudential, agents are not responsible for what they do involuntarily. They are not held to blame for what is out of their control. It follows that an agent is able to undertake a practical judgment only to the extent that it is situated among diverse competing judgments and that the agent has the power to choose among them. Practical judgment thus presupposes what in the Western tradition has been called freedom or autonomy, but in the context of locality may be described as latitude: the presence of relevant alternatives. In the language of locality, every situation contains settlements and alternatives, stillness and polyphony, without which judgment in general, and certainly practical judgment, would be unintelligible.

Stillness and polyphony pertain to all the modes of judgment and query, for they are generic conditions of locality—of locales and ingredients, human and non-human, not simply judgments. Every situation, locus, or perspective contains settled ingredients and alternatives; these represent the reciprocity of determinateness and indeterminateness inherent in locality. Nothing in any locale can be settled or determinate in all ways, only in certain ways, from certain points of view. Nothing in any locale can be indeterminate in all ways. One of the forms of determinateness of relations among the ingredients of a locus may be expressed in terms of stillness; one of the forms of indeterminateness may be expressed in terms of polyphony. The complementarity of the categories entails that what is still in one locale is polyphonic in another, and conversely. Each is the other's excess.

Possibilities pertain to judgment generically, not to practical judgment alone. Among the forms they take in relation to propositional judgment are the unavoidability of errors, whether careless, systematic, or the result of ignorance, the presence of alternative formulations of any given assertion, and the insecurity of the future—especially, possibilities of new discoveries and new theoretical developments as well as changes in the social organization of science. The Western Enlightenment tradition has repeatedly sought to eradicate these forms of latitude in propositional knowledge, a tendency variously described as a quest for certainty[11] and a "mirroring of nature."[12] Given such descriptions, it may be argued that the shortcoming lies in the very notion of mirroring,[13] or that the notion of certainty is incompatible with ongoing and self-critical inquiry. More generally, however, error is unavoidable in propositional judgment; in science, because of locality. Every judgment, every validation, is local, relevant to certain assumptions and conditions and not to others. Specifically, error pertains to every propositional judgment as an exemplification of the latitude inherent in judgment and the indeterminateness inherent in inexhaustibility. I add that error is but one side of the latitude in scientific query. Science requires inexhaustibility for its intelligibility.[14] Error belongs to propositional judgment and therefore to truth as its other side, its double, not its opponent. For it is within the latitude inherent in such judgment that new discoveries emerge. Error is the other face of discovery. In this sense, to eliminate error would be to annihilate scientific query. Similarly, the presence of alternative formulations of any propositional truth and the insecurities of a changeable scientific future are not simply defects of finiteness, but are conditions of any scientific rationality, inherent in its capacity to disclose new truths and understandings.

A propositional knowledge that could achieve certainty and eliminate error, that could eliminate all forms of extraneous latitude in propositional judgment, would be incompatible with the continuing openness of science to new forms of interrogation and validation. There is, almost irresistibly, throughout the Western tradition, an emphasis upon achieving a state of knowledge in which prior contingencies are eradicated. This tendency is striking in Hegel and Marx, despite their emphasis upon the differential contradictions in history. A theory of scientific knowledge in which inquiry will effectively come to an end is self-contradictory. The principle that query requires here is one of latitude.

Similarly, latitude pertains intrinsically to artistic creation: there could be no art that does not presuppose the relevance of possibilities. I am speaking of the creative imagination, expressed by Kant in his principles of genius.[15] That art might simply imitate events and things is unintelligible. That there could be a fabricative judgment without choices, selections, decisions among alternatives, even more strongly, without novelties and departures, is equally unintelligible. Technology as well as art, every form of fabrication, presupposes inexhaustible possibilities and alternatives.

Yet the Western tradition has considered alternatives primarily in relation to practical rather than propositional and fabricative judgments. One reason is the rejection of latitude as incompatible in principle with propositional knowledge. A second is that art has frequently not been taken seriously within the tradition as a form of judgment or rationality. Even in Kant, though art is referred to the subjective side of judgment, to the delight present in the free employment of the cognitive faculties, it is intelligible only in relation to a freedom whose possibility is established in relation to practical reason, not to art. Without overstating the case, fabricative judgment has typically been regarded in the Western philosophic tradition as epiphenomenal, while ultimate questions belong to the spheres of practice and truth. Whether this be true or not, the issue of freedom in the Western tradition has nearly always been a question of practice and responsibility.

Can one be a practical agent without judging in relation to inexhaustibly multifarious alternatives? The answer is clearly negative in terms of locality. It is similarly negative in relation to any form of judgment and query. In relation to practice, however, the answer is especially decisive. It is this theme that is emphasized in the ethical tradition's concern with autonomy. We can, Kant argues, think of ourselves in relation to practice only as autonomous agents. The reason, from the side of locality, is that we are always located in milieux pervaded by alternatives as well as determinants, polyphonies as well as stillness. Latitude belongs to every being and situation. An additional reason, from the side of practice, is that consequences pertain to practical validation only in relation to alternative courses of action. Practical judgment is intelligible only in relation to alternative possibilities of practice.

What degree of latitude, what range of alternatives, is to be found in any given situation? There is no generic answer, for there is another side to latitude in practice, its functional complement, determinateness in relation to indeterminateness. There is latitude in every locale, complemented by settled, effectively unalterable conditions—in that locale, for they are alterable, available for modification, in other locales. Thus, to the latitude relevant in every human practical situation, we add the intimidating, over-powering density of determinate human and environing conditions. Density and heterogeneity joined with latitude provide an indeterminateness without measure.

There is latitude in every situation and locale, accompanied by dense and specific historical conditions. Density and specificity pertain to practical milieux as thoroughly as do relevant alternatives. This complementarity is historicality: the inexhaustible presence of known and unknown, established and yet-to-be-established determinants and contingencies, joined with unending alternatives for practice and decision. This inexhaustibility of determinants, complemented by latitude and indeterminateness, reflects the indeterminateness of history, its incompleteness without its future—its inexhaustible futures. What a present undertaking means awaits an unknown and unsettled future; every undertaking emerges within a partly settled past, pointing to an indeterminate future—a future that is required to complete the past and one that has been produced by it.

The consequences are that every practical judgment emerges within indeterminate conditions, not only in the sense that not every contingency, not every factual determination, is settled, but also in the sense that every norm and principle is open to modification, that new circumstances and new principles and rules emerge, new determinations. Indeed, we may go further and maintain that the indeterminateness and contingency of practical milieux contribute profoundly to their density and specificity. The principle can be formulated in terms of power. Power is generic only when divided within and upon itself.[16] Similarly, the inexhaustible determinants of historical conditions, their specificity and density, do not war with, but are enhanced by the inexhaustible relevance of alternatives and possibilities. This is a condition of ergonality, the material work that natural things do. Every present practical judgment is deeply influenced by prior practices and judgments permeated by alternatives, by indeterminateness. This indeterminateness does not undo the influences, but opens them to inexhaustibility and specificity: the specificity and density of programs and projects, each containing multiple possibilities of other projects and programs.

We may see here why the traditional view of autonomy and freedom does not suffice, even in Kant. In his view, we are both autonomous agents and causally influenced beings. This is because we are both noumenal and phenomenal selves. What is missing from Kant is a sense of how these selves participate together in practice. If they are not mediatable altogether into one self, they are nevertheless mediatable in interaction. But the relation is deeper: it is that whatever a practical agent does is intelligible only within milieux interpretable in terms of stillness and polyphony. This is as true for evil agents as for good, for irresponsible agents as for responsible ones, for immoral as well as moral acts. Latitude is required for judgment, in any mode, therefore for any form of practice, required by locality and inexhaustibility. Such a principle does not conflict with our powerful conviction that only autonomous agents should be praised or blamed: only certain forms of autonomy may be relevant to praise and blame. But practice cannot be intelligible in the context of settled conditions without alternative possibilities.

Among the most powerful trends in contemporary life and thought are the discovery and acknowledgment of new forms of influence and domination, ranging from censorship and repression in Freud, to ideology in Marx, to hidden patterns of domination and oppression in Foucault. Only the latter seems to recognize that these discoveries are not incompatible with alternatives, with latitude, but require them to be effective, in the sense in which power is permeated by resistances. Were this not so, then power would be solid, indivisible, unable to adapt to changing conditions. Power can be distributed generally only where resistances are themselves forms of power. Moreover, history recurrently brings before us the truth that forms of resistance become oppressive once they have been established, requiring and producing yet other forms of resistance. Similarly, ideology is divided by, not incompatible with, truth and ideality.[17] All these heterogeneities follow from the fact that practical judgments enter history. They have consequences and are consequences of prior practices.

The generic condition is that every milieu, every locale, therefore every tradition, is divided within itself by resistances, departures, variations, and heterogeneities. We may think of practice itself as a milieu, densely situated among other milieux, but divided in every context by alternatives, frequently opposing, subject in every case to diverse and specific influences, also frequently opposing. No matter how enveloping the milieu, there are relevant alternatives; no matter how liberating the practice, there are densely specific and heterogeneous determinants. To this we may add the specificity of the consequences that defines the success and failure of practical judgments, and we find ourselves again before the peculiar admiration and terror that practice evokes. Practical judgments are of utmost importance, yet they are confronted at every turn by failure and indeterminateness.

EXCLUSION AND DIFFERENCE

Anything whatever, to be determinate, must be exclusive, differential, must exclude some alternatives and include others. Nothing can embrace everything. This exclusionary principle is at the heart of Hegel's dialectic, though it is compromised in his view of Absolute Spirit to the extent that it may be thought to reconcile all contingencies and mediate all differences. It is at the center of Whitehead's theory of actuality, though it is compromised by his emphasis on cosmology.[18] Negativity, difference, and exclusion belong fundamentally to locality. For to be located in one place is not to be located in another; to be located determinately always involves irrelevance and negativity. The entire project of philosophy may be understood to pursue a thought of heterogeneity without instituting oppressive and authoritarian exclusions, yet where exclusion is unavoidable.

The generic principles of locality and inexhaustibility pertain specifically to practical judgments, but these in addition manifest exceptional forms of exclusion and negativity, in relation to power and desire. Power works by exclusion and has worked historically by prohibition.[19]

We have, then, two generic differential conditions of exclusion in relation to practice: one, the determinateness that depends on local relations; the other, the exclusions that manifest the workings of power. Practice requires both conditions, but depends on the second, even as it is a historical source of domination and oppression. Power works by exclusion and is required within practice for its efficacy. Exclusion belongs to any established sphere of practice. Historically, power's exclusions have taken the form of prohibitions, excluding and prohibiting selected forms of heterogeneity.

A third form of difference has frequently been thought to apply to practical judgments intrinsically. It presupposes that practices are based on rules, and rules are interpretable as systems of differentiation. This form of differentiation is sometimes derived from a structuralist view of language, that linguistic and other semasic systems are differentiated into basic elements out of which all complex strings are generated.[20] Such a form of differentiation is closely related to notions such as simplicity, elementariness, and complexity by aggregation. It offers too restricted a sense of differentiation in relation to practice.

The important contrast between this sense of differentiation and my understanding of exclusion involve the former's mechanical view of aggregation and the generic conditions that being is divided by differences as well as similarities and that power works by exclusion. Difference here expresses heterogeneity and excess, local expressions of indeterminateness. There is indeterminateness in nature generally, but, especially urgently in relation to human practices. This is true in two explicit senses. One is a corollary of the purposiveness inherent in practical judgment: the results it seeks to establish, the consequences toward which it strives, belong as potentialities to the locales in which practice transpires. In this sense, practical judgment presupposes latitude as part of its intelligibility, presupposes heterogeneity, in alternative courses of action and consequences as well as the differential exclusions implicated in power. Here, in addition, indeterminateness belongs to the determinate conditions of practice in the sense that it looks to an open, indeterminate future emerging from established differential circumstances.

The second sense of indeterminateness is derived from the density, specificity, and historicality of practical judgments, their locations in human milieux, individual and social, private and public. Locality entails heterogeneity in the sense of multiple location and the dividedness of any particular location. In particular, practice transforms itself, its circumstances and goals, in its workings. Here, indeterminateness is the result of the determinations inherent in practical powers.

The ramifications of heterogeneities in practice express themselves in the tensions of historicality and ideality. Notions such as bias, prejudice, and ideology express one side of historicality, complemented by the truth that without such historicality, without its contingent heterogeneities, ideality would be unintelligible and impossible. Heterogeneity and difference always have two sides.[21]

Among the recurrent types of differences in practice are different times and places, different historical circumstances, different contingencies, different goals and purposes, different agents, and different spheres of practice, public and private. The Western philosophic tradition has paid close attention to individual agents, emphasizing differences in interests and gratifications. Yet differences in circumstances and capabilities, understandings and values, may be more profound and pervasive. We understand and desire things differently—if also very similarly. The differences involved produce ineliminable tensions within every reconciliation. We have returned to our understanding of mediateness. Some differences are incompatibilities, heterogeneous; not so much in pairs, where mediation is desired and expected, as in larger aggregates (social institutions are a good example) where pair by pair mediations do not produce larger resolutions. Without such differences, practice would be impossible.

The second major form of exclusion in practice is given by the workings of power. Power here is not intimidation or oppression—though it traditionally works by oppression and prohibition—but is constructive and ubiquitous.[22] Practice involves exclusion because there can be no practice without the exercise of power. Power here is equivalent with the dense and material influences inherent in practical experience.

DENSITY AND SPECIFICITY

Closely associated with inexhaustibility, virtually identical with it, are denseness and specificity: expressions of multiple locatedness, intimately and profoundly related to the historicality and entanglements of practice. To say, for example, that human circumstances, along with every locale but more explicitly, are complex and inexhaustible entanglements of knowledge, power, discourse, and desire is to describe them as dense and specific, heterogeneous. Density and specificity refer to the inexhaustibility of determinants and of the determinants of determinants—the density of human and natural conditions—and to the material influences of concrete events upon each other. Density and specificity speak against abstractness—the substitution of principles and ideals for determinate relations—and enumerativeness, against unqualified mediation and equivalence. They are far-reaching ramifications of inexhaustibility.

To say that human events and conditions, including every form of understanding of such events and conditions, every form of discourse and representation, every form of practice, every form of influence upon events and conditions, are complexly entangled among each other entails that human relations are inexhaustibly influential, in inexhaustible detail, and that while such entanglements frequently produce large-scale structures and processes, there is no total vision, no encompassment of all major influences and entanglements. Density and specificity are the features of local contingencies neglected in universalization. They are the residue or surplus inherent in mediateness contrasted with mediation, the inexhaustible and complex ways in which things are always *in medias res.*

The natural question from the standpoint of such inexhaustible mediateness is how we are to understand understanding itself from within indeterminate and densely entangled relations. What standards of knowledge and practice are possible if problems are never conclusively resolved? Answers to this question from the standpoint of practical judgment compose the focus of the ensuing discussions. From the standpoint of knowledge and reason in general, two answers may be given, both in terms of query. One is that query is an unending process of interrogation and validation: reason belongs to the continuing process of interrogation and criticism, and as soon as that process terminates, in any conclusions or methods that are taken to be beyond the scope of further challenge, rationality terminates as well. This answer follows Peirce's definition of truth: "The opinion which is fated to be ultimately agreed to by all who investigate, is what we mean by the truth, and the object represented in this opinion is the real."[23] I add the qualification that consensus is not always possible. Within the unterminating interrogative processes of science and art, some forms are recurrent, others are remarkably stable, still others bear close family resemblances over long periods of time, while others vary profoundly.[24] This view of reason as query depends on the density of the conditions of human experience.

The second answer is that it is because query is densely and materially entangled among the affairs of human life and history, enabling it to be successful where and when it is, that the resources required for interrogation and validation belong to dense and specific judgments and experiences. Query requires the openness of indeterminateness and the resources of densely entangled conditions of human life and practices for its validation and effectiveness.

Density and specificity pertain to human life in general, to all the forms of judgment and query, to propositional knowledge and science for example, not to practical judgment alone. Yet practice involves specific and dense determinants in unique ways, again because of its particular relations to antecedents and to consequences. In science, the density and specificity of particular circumstances serve as a continuing source of further difficulties, but do not undermine the rationality of prior investigations. Only when measured against an absolute criterion of reason and truth, inappropriate to science and everyday life, does the continuing presence of error and the need for further inquiry suggest that propositional query is intrinsically suspect. Epistemological skepticism rests on the assumption that indeterminateness in propositional judgment and query is failure. The error is equivalent to supposing that science either reaches unqualified and wholly determinate truths or is effectively a form of practice. Thus, the density and specificity of things on the one hand and of science on the other do not undermine science but contribute to its rationality.

The density and specificity of our surroundings and of history make science possible and present it with inexhaustible prospects of interrogation, defining its rationality. The density and specificity of human experience and its surroundings, but particularly of the materials transmuted by imagination into art, define artistic query. Nothing is irrelevant in principle to a work of art; nothing within a given work can be regarded as extrinsic, only within a given interpretation. Every variation in line, every detail of expression, every specification of materials or style, belongs to the work and may contribute to its majesty and power.[25] It follows that such density and specificity play a positive, originative role in works of art, whereby they manifest inexhaustibility, and in no way threaten failure, implicitly or explicitly.

By way of contrast, inexhaustibility in the form of density and specificity menaces practice even as it makes it possible, confronts it with the threat of failure from every side. On the one hand, practical judgments are validated in terms of their consequences, which are themselves specific and dense. It follows that any influence achieved through practice is always tenuous and marginal, pervaded by indeterminateness. Multifarious consequences that are only dimly foreseeable and only weakly controllable follow from any overt act. Moreover, these are not simply multifarious in infinite succession, fading off into the remote future, but are densely specific in the complex ramifications of any practical locale. Some of this understanding is expressed in Dewey's principle of the continuum of means and ends, that in any situation multifarious consequences follow, diverse ends are achieved, only some of which can be intended.[26] The consequences of any practice are densely and specifically inexhaustible, threatening every practical situation with profound loss of control.

On the other hand, practical judgments are situated within established milieux that are themselves dense and specific, with complexly entangled, covert forms of influence and power. Without such entanglements, no practice could be efficacious; because of such entanglements, every practice is historically determined, ideological. There is no pure and untrammeled reason, no transparency to vision, only continuing immersion and situatedness. Here, density and specificity are the forms of locality in relation to practical judgments. Here also, density and specificity are the defining conditions of practical judgment.

Propositional query seeks general principles but is surrounded by specificity and density, imposing an unending process of adjustment and reconciliation. Fabricative query is permeated through and through by density and specificity, but incorporates them as means to its accomplishments. Practical query is tormented by its own density and the densities of its milieux, for they threaten it constantly with loss of effectiveness. Moreover, this threat is not simply the residual possibility of failure, but is its inescapable presence, sometimes catastrophically. In a profound and inevitable sense, we live at the edge of an abyss, and cannot move our lives very far from its rim. The abyss, however, is not a region of sudden and remote transformations, but inhabits every practical activity and milieu. Our best activities sometimes have disastrous consequences; our greatest efforts to gain satisfaction sometimes result in catastrophe. That much of human life goes on, frequently modestly and successfully, in no way diminishes the ever-present fact of practical life that elsewhere human life is miserable, tormented, and that we cannot eliminate suffering and misery, for they are always densely and materially present in practical experience.

EXCHANGE AND EQUIVALENCE

One way to characterize the density and specificity inherent in human locales is in terms of mediateness joined with mediation. We are always in the midst of things, caught up in their influence, densely and specifically, faced with the inexhaustible consequences of our actions. Transcendence is always possible, but only locally, and there is no total mediation or reconciliation, in principle and in practice. There is no totality of beings or locales.

A particular form of mediation, fundamental in modern experience,[27] is given by a system of exchanges and equivalences, an economy of substitutions and replacements. Such a system is in conflict with the density and specificity of practices to the extent that every term, every condition, is dense and inexhaustible, excessive, irreducible to any equivalent. The density and materiality of practices are corollaries of locality, and are incompatible with any generic system of mediation, including one involving substitutive equivalences. There is no total mediation, only local influences and ramifications. It follows that there are no exact equivalences, for equivalence is also local, and every substitution is inexact. Density and specificity express this inexhaustible side of being in contrast with exchanges and substitutions.

Exchange relations in modern life are widely pervasive, even dominating and exclusive, though throughout are marginal strains that express the limitations of substitutive equivalences. Market theories of value, classical to contemporary, are based on such metrical equivalences. Currency is the great medium of exchange, mediating differences between goods in different sectors into equivalences. Similarly, an economic view of pleasure presupposes a system of equivalences in gratification, an exchange metric in which pleasures are measured and situated within an over-all quantitative system of values. Utilitarianism has struggled with this problem of the disparity between different forms and kinds of gratification only to reject a dense and specific view of differentiations among pleasures. Without a common measure—to the point where even Mill's distinction between higher and lower pleasures must be rejected as arbitrary—no systematic form of comparison, no rational means of evaluation, is possible. The premise that links exchange economies with comprehensive systems of mediation is that exchanges can be rational only if some universal medium of exchange provides the measure of relation—currency or pleasure. The alternative, in terms of locality, is that comparison is local, without universal and unrestricted application.

We may expand this economic model of exchange to other areas of human life and to other theories. We find that virtually no contemporary theory is taken seriously if it is not effectively an exchange theory based on a universal currency. Psychoanalysis, for example, is dominated by two systems of exchange. One is based on the pleasure principle: pleasure is the universal medium of desire. Given that assumption, we have two alternatives: either objects of desire are irreplaceable, promoting infinite longing and regression, or infinite substitutions are possible, substantiating the theory of sublimation. Sublimation is the second system of exchange.

In "The Relation of the Poet to Daydreaming," Freud establishes two relations: between children's play and daydreaming; and between daydreaming and art, emphasizing poetry.[28] If we assume that daydreaming is the result of an adult's efforts to return to the pleasures of children's play, and, more strikingly, that poetry is the equivalent of daydreaming, then art is effectively regressive, largely pathological and with infantile forms of gratification. Jung criticizes Freud's view of art as based on such an position.[29] However, Freud's argument is more subtle and more effective if we understand the relations between terms as exchange equivalences rather than item-specific. Cathexes are divertible from one object to another, largely indifferently: from children's play objects to daydreaming and then to art. Art succeeds to the extent that we are liberated from attachment to any particular objects, so that other objects may be, in the economy of pleasure, exchanged with them and substituted for them, liberally and almost indifferently.

Sublimation, then, where possible, presupposes a universal system of exchanges and equivalences, based on substitutions, in principle without end or limits. If we hold instead that any object of desire is densely specific, unique and singular or excessive, with relations and influences but not equivalences, then sublimation, in conjunction with the pleasure principle, will inevitably lead to despair. Significant developmental transformations from child to adult forms of gratification would in principle be impossible. Archaeology would totally dominate over teleology, both expressed in terms of the equivalences inherent in desire and power.[30]

A second generic form of substitutive equivalences can be found in language. Language enables us to speak of what is absent by substituting a present equivalent. Following Saussure, language (*langue*) is a system of differences, a model in which each linguistic element has value only in virtue of differential relations. Effectively, the system of linguistic differences is a system of exchanges and equivalences. Such a view of language largely neglects its density and specificity. These are visible only at the boundaries of different languages, exemplified in practice primarily in the difficulties of translation.

It is possible to discern a normative principle in the recognition that within any system of exchanges and substitutions there are densely specific entanglements. The primary form of alienation in Marxist theory is synonymous with the principle in capitalism that any laborer, like any instrument, is entirely equivalent with, substitutable for, any other that can perform the same tasks. Respect for humanity as opposed to instrumentality entails the principle that human beings are infinitely more than any instrument, that each is individual, transcendent inexhaustibly in relation to any particular roles assigned that individual. Similarly, a radical critique of technology may be expressed in the principle that there is no room in modern life for imponderable recesses of uniqueness and care, that every human, like every being, is manifested in terms of technical equivalences and functions.

The normative principle is that every human being is unique, and that exchange relations are inhumane, treating persons as means not as ends. There is a certain irony that in Kant's account of practical reason, every person is indistinguishable from every other insofar as they are generically members of a kingdom of ends. There is further irony that in practice everything is both means and end—in the language of practical judgment, exchangeable and mediatable—substitutable for other beings in certain respects, locally, as well as inexhaustibly transcendent of any equivalences. There is no avoiding the exclusions of power. I emphasize that it is not merely persons, but things that are densely and specifically transcendent over any system of substitutions and equivalences; moreover, that it is not individual things alone, but kinds whose heterogeneity is violated by equivalence and substitution. Whitehead defines value as "the intrinsic reality of an event."[31] This notion of value runs directly counter to the prevailing tendency in the Western tradition toward an economy of practice based on a generic measure of substitution and equivalence. It is rooted in a density and heterogeneity of events and things reflecting locality and inexhaustibility.

The ensuing discussion of practical judgment will be developed largely in terms of the tension between exchange equivalence and the density and heterogeneity inherent in inexhaustibility. It may, however, be worth noting that to emphasize heterogeneity, contrasting it with equivalence and substitution, plays havoc with a traditional understanding of human equality. If human beings are densely and specifically unique, individually and socially, in their circumstances and their prospects, and if density and specificity pertain to rocks and stones, plants and animals, then equality is neither determinate enough to be the basis of a human principle nor generic enough to define a comprehensive theory.

I respond by emphasizing locality. Exchange theories define a universal medium of equivalence as if it were generic and exhaustive rather than local. From this point of view, equality is not a universal measure but a local condition. There are no universal rights for humans as against animals, for some humans as opposed to others, for living beings as opposed to inorganic things. Differences and similarities, therefore singularities and equivalences, are always local, always densely and specifically situated within material conditions. One of the ramifications of locality here is that although there is no generic form of exchange equivalence, every practical judgment requires local substitutions. This tension is another manifestation of the fact that failure irresistibly haunts practice with no universal means of reconciliation. Density and specificity undermine universal principles and social and historical barriers, which reduce heterogeneity.

PLEASURE

The history of Western thought on the determinants of practice has largely revolved around the notion of value, which effectively imposes an exchange economy of equivalences in worth on a plenitude of inexhaustible and heterogeneous things. Evaluation here is incompatible with inexhaustibility and locality, is based on a universal system of equivalences in which the dense specificities of individual loci are transformed into generic reciprocal relations. Two things that have the same value may be exchanged, substituted for one another without loss. Logic and value merge here in a substitutive exchange that achieves mediation at the price of local determinations. Here an economic view of humanity and of being becomes predominant, almost without exception.

A subsidiary theme within such a history of valuation, at least as old and nearly as general, is the conviction that the only basis of value broad enough to match the pervasiveness of practice is that of pleasure. We value what gratifies us and devalue what displeases us. Pleasure and pain are the fundamental measures of practical judgments.

Such a position clearly flies in the face of the facts; for example, that human beings sometimes sacrifice their lives and their pleasures for others, for their country, even for animals and things, and that animals also do so. Why would agents do this? The answer is that they think it is the right or the best thing to do under the circumstances—that is, they undertake a determinative practical judgment. The facts indicate that pleasure is one of the relevant determinants, one of the factors to be weighed, but is not the sole or even the predominant determinant in practical judgment. The truth is stronger: pleasure and pain are, like value, less the origin or cause of practical judgments, and rather labels that express our assumption that all practical judgments are mediatable within a single system of exchanges. Pleasure is one of the pervasive metrics of practical valuation.

Yet the view that the sole basis of value is pleasure has been sustained not only in the face of the facts, but also in some of the most important positions found in the history of practical theory. Two examples may be mentioned. One is Mill's version of utilitarianism, in which a universal and common good is achieved by maximizing collective pleasure. The very notion of maximization is metrical, closely allied with the notion of a system of value in which all things and events are compared on a single system of equivalence. Although Mill is able, on such a presumption, to argue for the greatest latitude in individual differences, for heterogeneity—at least where human liberty is concerned—especially, that of freedom of speech and thought, and although such latitude and variation are clearly dominant values for him, they can be so in relation to pleasure only in a unidimensional way: that, on the whole, society and its individuals collectively benefit more from liberty and its concomitant eccentricities than from conformity and diminished variation. Variations and departures serve humanity in a mediatable way. There is no room in Mill's utilitarian theory for differences that are not comparable on the whole. On the other hand, he finds it necessary to introduce a distinction between higher and lower pleasures that manifests such incomparability.

The second example is Freud's pleasure principle, that all human actions are the result of a desire for pleasure, especially recessive, covert, and infantile pleasures. Adult life is the repetition of activities that have given pleasure, transformed by the unavoidable exchanges that enable energies to be diverted from one object to another. Freud's theory is one of equivalence and exchange. What makes it important is its powerful archaeology. The pleasure principle does not explain or capture our imaginations, particularly since there is a "beyond" the pleasure principle. What is explanatory in psychoanalytic theory is the history of exchanges and residues that cast their shadow throughout later practices. We act and live in the shadow of our former selves. This would be a powerful view of human life even where the sole determinant of practice were not pleasure.

The poverty of the pleasure principle is clear enough from the standpoint of its implied system of exchange equivalents, as if any and all human experiences and judgments were measurable on a single quantitative system of gratification. We do what pleases us and avoid what causes us pain. Those practical judgments that violate this principle are either vestigial expressions of an archaeological trace going back to earlier gratifications and pains or prospective deferrals of later gratifications. There is, in relation to the pleasure principle, little sense of practical determinants in which densely specific and incompatible concerns cohabit within a set of circumstances, in which practical judgment is unavoidable although the determinants conflict unresolvably. By contrast, Freud's understanding of language and archaeology is profoundly dense and specific.

The poverty of the pleasure principle is clearer if we add to our understanding of its implications three additional principles that describe the limits of pleasure as determinants of practice, which have been widely accepted in one or another modified form. These may be named by their most important progenitor.

(1) Some pleasures are destructive and must be avoided in all rational forms of practical judgment (Plato).

(2) There are higher and lower pleasures, and a greater quantity of lower pleasure does not outweigh a higher pleasure (Mill).

(3) The search for pleasure undergoes continual transformations and modifications, and allows for inexhaustible substitutions (Freud).

The first principle appears paradoxical, since what gives us pleasure must, by definition, be satisfying. Yet the evidence is that desire is not only frequently destructive, but may be unfulfillable. The recognition that pleasures differ qualitatively as well as quantitatively—most likely into more kinds and levels than two, stratified densely and infinitely—makes any system of exchanges and reciprocities incoherent. It follows that pleasure is not the answer to the question posed by practical judgment, but is one form of that question. Given what brings me pleasure, what gratifies me, what should I do? We repeat the question practical judgment imposes upon us, and there is no system of equivalences that can transform this question into calculation or deliberation. Practical judgments remain a dense and excessive form of practice no matter what is involved in their determination, whether deliberation accompanies them or not.

There is a relevant subsidiary principle that pertains to pleasure at a more subordinate level of analysis than that of the generic determinants of practical judgment. Human beings do—and should do—many things that cause them pain. Still, there are important reasons for not conforming thoughtlessly to principle and rule without consideration of one's own gratifications. "Do what you enjoy doing and nothing else." This formulation is too sweeping to be plausible or effective. "Try to maximize your pleasures in your undertakings if that is at all possible." Pleasures may not be maximizable and we may be called upon to sacrifice ourselves and our gratifications by the imperatives of our oppressive circumstances.

The subsidiary principle, however difficult it is to formulate acceptably, acknowledges that there is a potentially disastrous conflict between duty and pleasure, and, more important, that duty does not possess unqualified legitimacy and authority. Personal sacrifice is not the norm of practical judgment: the inexhaustible possibility of failure is the norm, but it is not incompatible with personal gratification; pursuit of duty at any personal cost is one of the prominent causes of practical failure. Overweening general principles are as dangerous as self-interest.

The three principles I have imagined to be derived from Plato, Mill, and Freud indicate that pleasure does not provide a metric of practical judgment, but poses endless questions to be answered through practical judgment and its results. There is no quantifiable metric of gratification; there are rather dense and heterogeneous pleasures and pains. And even if there were such a metric, it would not answer the question of what courses of action we should undertake, even if we knew the answer for all human beings for all time. Certain arguments against utilitarianism take the appropriate form: we should not punish an innocent person even if it would make everyone else more secure; we should not destroy a rich tropical habitat of many rare species of animals and plants even if it would benefit many people, not for that reason alone, for the habitat has its own integrity, its own worth, as do the creatures that inhabit it. There are other interests than human interests, even if human beings are the only rational or self-conscious creatures. There are other considerations than interests—local considerations pertinent to the inexhaustible plenitude that pertains to any environment. Pleasure and pain, benefits and deficits, only raise questions of practical judgment and do not answer them.

One argument against depleting the tropical rain forests is that most of the world's species of animals and plants live there, and we would deplete a large measure of the genetic stock of the earth by destroying their habitats.[32] The argument suggests that such a depletion would be harmful because human beings might need to draw upon that genetic stock in some indeterminate future. This argument is too limited, though it is worth noting that the notion of enriching our generic pool is only indirectly interpretable in terms of gratification and pleasure. It has to do far more with human necessities than gratification, with large-scale benefits rather than with pleasures and pains. More important, however, the plenitude of forms of life reflects the plenitude of nature, locality and inexhaustibility. By limiting ourselves to narrower, measurable conceptions of local goods and benefits, in the present, we curtail the richness of future possibilities. We rob Peter to pay Paul—a perfectly legitimate economic image, provided that we reject the principle that what is stolen and what is gained are commensurate. To the contrary, we deplete our future and nature's future in inexhaustible and often unimaginable ways in order to gain immediate benefit. The result is incalculable waste.

Every pleasure may be counterproductive and destructive, in inexhaustible ways. Every pleasure may be rejected as qualitatively deficient whatever its magnitude. Every pleasure may be exchanged for other pleasures. There are no absolutely mandatory pleasures, no unqualified gratifications, though some pleasures may be universal. Pleasure and pain are among the pervasive forms in which living bodies present themselves to practice, irresistibly. But this irresistible presence is not unqualified. There are other pleasures and pains than those that pertain to one's body. Moreover, the presence of a human body is not determinative for practice, but is one of the conditions implicated in practical judgment. We remain in the position we were before our hedonistic adventure; we face imponderable and inexhaustible decisions, having to take into account a plenitude of pleasures and pains along with an inexhaustible plenitude of other determinants. To this I add that these other determinants—histories, traditions, sedimentations, cultural factors—influence our exchanges and our practical judgments, and conversely. Desire is inseparable from judgment and practical determination.

DESIRE

We may approach the determinants of practice in a different way, not through the limits of pleasure but through the generic and excessive form of desire. Desire here is the form in which a material and practical creature relates to other beings through time and space in terms of influence. So generic a view requires detailed examination, for at the limits of its application, it loses some of its plausibility. There is no apparent room within it for triviality and irrelevance. I add locality and inexhaustibility. The former entails that there is no all-pervasive form of relevance. Desire is local in the sense that wherever there is relevance, there is influence and variation, belonging and departing. In particular, there is in-difference along with, inseparable from, desire. Desire contains within itself the complementarities of inexhaustibility, especially determinateness and indeterminateness. It includes the irrelevancies of locality.

In any situation or milieu, a creature acts and is acted upon, is relevant and influenced. These generic conditions of influence and relevance may, in relation to practice, be regarded as generalizations of desire. The moving principle of practice, in relation to acting and being acted upon, is desire, toward another thing to move or influence it. In so general a form, desire does not always involve a sense of lack, of incompleteness, as it has been traditionally understood, but rather, supposes a sense of alternative possibilities, what might be other, otherwise. The practical impulse inherent in alternatives is desire; equally, desire is the force in latitude that culminates in practical judgment. Desire and practice here are inseparable. We avoid the identification of desire with gratification or its absence, with possession or deficiency. In relation to practice, desire is the negative movement in the conditions of otherness that give rise to practical judgments: in particular, temporality and power.

Practical judgment involves time in multiple senses, not only that of past, present, and future judgments, the location of events in time, but including the temporality of the conditions and conse-

quences that mark the work of influence. Power and influence
belong to time in the generic sense that what we do always escapes
its present moment and exerts its influence on the future (though
the future exercises its own influences upon its determinations).
In relation to desire, this means that we may desire only what has
a prospective culmination, though we may dream nostalgically.
Even an imaginative desire to belong to a different time, that of
the Pharaohs, or a different world, refers to a practical future. In
imagination, temporality is doubled in relation to practice.

Similarly, any relation of a living creature to another, where
relevance is involved, is a temporal relation, culminating prospec-
tively, a relation of power. Power belongs to the conditions of
desire and practice, not simply as species of effectiveness and
domination, but generically, embodied in the principle that things
are constituted by their relations to others. Desire is the presence
of possibilities of influence from the side of an agent; power is the
presence of possibilities of influence from the side of a recipient
acted upon. In relation to desire and practice, constitutive relations
are power relations. In this way, practice, desire, and power are
inseparable. If we add that knowing and saying are always forms
of practice, then we have an inseparable quartet of knowledge,
practice, desire, and power. This entails that the inseparability
of knowledge and discourse from power is a contingency of the
pervasiveness of the different modes of judgment while the inseparability of power from desire is inherent in the temporality of
practical judgment.

I have noted the indifference in desire required by irrelevance:
we are situated among different creatures and things in local relations involving relevance and irrelevance. These are manifestations
of the complementarity of determinateness and indeterminateness.
In particular, this indeterminateness in practical relevance gives us
an important interpretation of the infiniteness of desire. The Western tradition has tended to associate the inexhaustibility of determinations of value with lack of fulfillment. Desires are regarded
as infinitely unsatisfiable. We understand Midas and Don Juan as
possessing desire to this degree. Yet not only does this mythology
presuppose that each desire is singly determinate—for there might
well be multiple desires that established limits for each other, limits
not of frustrated lack but of fulfillment—but the infinitenesses of

different desires are comparable on a single scale of frustrations and dissatisfactions.

To the contrary, inexhaustibility pertains not just to felt satisfactions and dissatisfactions—that is, to pleasures and pains—but also to the ramifications of relevance and irrelevance, the inexhaustible determinations and indeterminations of future events. What fulfillment of a given desire entails is as indeterminate in its future realizations as it is determinate, not only in the possibility that a present satisfied desire may be followed by dissatisfaction and similar subsequent desires, but also in the possibilities of very different, unimagined and unthought, desires and dissatisfactions. We can influence future consequences only marginally, yet practice responds to desires in terms of influence and power, which inevitably divide it. Our technological efforts to improve humanity's standard of living always result in depletion of our human and natural surroundings in profoundly disturbing ways.

Desire here is the form that heterogeneity takes in a locale involving possibilities of influence and power—that is, of practice. Such a formulation diminishes the emphasis on self-consciousness found in Hegel, and emphasizes practice instead. Yet even in Hegel, desire leads immediately to practice, to social and to political institutions. As interpreted here, desire pertains to the temporal, successive forms of relation that are conditions of power. In this sense, desire and power are inseparable from each other and inseparable together from practical judgment.

Equally inseparable from these, and inextricable from desire, are multiple and heterogeneous human bodies: all desires, like all emotions, pertain to bodies even when what is desired or reviled is intangible and immaterial—the meaning of life, the order of nature. This is to acknowledge the inescapable presence in practical judgments of material bodies, as determining conditions and bearing the brunt of future consequences. Thus, our bodies establish some of the most important and forceful conditions for our practices, but are also profoundly transformed by the practices we undertake. If we do not change the shape and size of our bodies very much through what we do, we greatly change their powers and desires. This presence of our bodies characterizes human practices in far-reaching ways; but reciprocally, practice profoundly and efficaciously characterizes human bodies, works repeatedly and pervasively on bodies.

That desires are always local, expressing indeterminateness and locality in relation to living, judging creatures and their practical concerns, repudiates desire's infinite movement and replaces it with inexhaustibility. Inexhaustibility here is a kind of infiniteness, neither Hegel's bad infinite of unending succession nor his good infinite of a circle; not even his infinite image of circles upon circles, but an inexhaustibility of entanglements, similarities and differences, overlappings and exclusions—relevance but not closure, restoration but not repetition. The inexhaustible openness of desire to other desires and to modes of judgment other than practice entails an inexhaustible reflexivity of desire upon desire— an unclosed movement that is nevertheless not circular—and an inexhaustible exteriority to desire in modes of judgment. Science never escapes desire, but it serves in its activities and validations as an external condition whereby desire may be interrogated and modified. Art, similarly, though deeply pervaded by desire, lifts us out of desire into an awareness that transcends possession, the fundamental form in which desire is encountered.

The image of desire controlling desire is recurrent in the Western tradition, from Plato's control of the appetites through reason and spirit to Freud's control of libidinal desires by the superego. Both of these images present us with practice as a form of domination, and convey a profound and inescapable truth. Yet both presuppose as well that the infiniteness of desire—in appetites and the id—is tempered by the possibility of transformations and inversions in desire itself—in Plato, love of the Good.

What is lacking in such views, given their emphasis on an external form of power over desire, is the capacity of desire to serve as its own other, analogous to the resistances in power. Something is thought to be required outside desire to bring it under control: reason or love of God. Desire is here infinite and infinitely powerful, controllable only by another infinite power. Yet the possibility of practical judgment rests on the capacity of desire to reflect upon itself inexhaustibly and provide its own limitations, even if in the form of excess. Such a reflexivity is not without violence and domination, but a domination that, through its own negation— but not universality—achieves a local completion or fulfillment. Fulfillment is as local as is desire.

I emphasize here the capacity of desires to undergo reflexive transformations, unendingly and inexhaustibly. Sexuality, for example, moves from a narrowly biological and reproductive activity in human experience to invade and pervade virtually every human activity.[33] Power moves from narrowly oppressive forms of control over subjects to invade and to pervade every human relation. Pain moves from a restricted opposition to pleasure to permeate human life with suffering.[34] In all these cases, desires expand in their significance through the reflexive influences of other desires and cultural practices. In the one direction, they become more pervasive and entangled; in the other, desires interact so profoundly that the excessive nature of any is transformed into limits in relation to others: infinite dissatisfaction is transformed into an inexhaustibility of manifestations and influences.

This inexhaustibility in relation to desire is its curse and its salvation. It is not unlike the complex situation of practical judgment, on the one hand, to be able to perform successful undertakings through the inexhaustible alternatives that are present in every situation, and, on the other to be haunted unendingly by prospects of failure. Failure does not replace success, but contaminates every success with inexhaustible alternatives; dissatisfaction does not belong to every desire, but inhabits the margins of multiple desires.

If desire is the generic form in which a practical, judging creature relates to others, to heterogeneity, then emotion is the generic form in which practical judgment relates to itself in relation to desire. Here emotion and desire are inseparable, though they bear profoundly different relations to practical judgment. Desire is the generic condition of practical judgment; emotion is the predominant form practical judgment takes in relation to desire.

In the Western tradition, two fundamental contrasts have defined emotion: emotion and thought; emotion and action. Emotions are conceived as both passive and irrational. Yet we find, in Spinoza and Whitehead, a more generic understanding of how emotion belongs to practical judgment, including its active and rational forms. Spinoza defines emotion as "the modifications of the body by which the power of acting of the body itself is increased, diminished, helped, or hindered, together with the ideas of these modifications."[35] When these ideas are adequate, the emotion is active and rational. Whitehead defines prehension or feeling as the vectorial relation that any external object bears to an experiencing subject. For both, emotion and feeling are as active as they are passive, depending on circumstances, and are inseparable from actuality and time—that is, from power and desire, from practice. Following Spinoza's lead joined with our generic understanding of desire, we may understand emotion as the form in which practical agents interrogate their practical capacities in relation to their surroundings: anger and fear where their capacities are threatened; love and joy where their powers are increased; grief where their powers are diminished by loss; exhilaration in the discovery of their powers. In all these cases, emotion belongs predominantly to practice and to thought insofar as it is practice.[36]

The interrogativeness of emotion makes it a form of practical judgment, the explicit interrogative form of desire. Desires are influenced by other desires and by external forces—for example, advertising, cultural formations, and forms of discourse. Inhabiting the spheres of influence are the interrogative presence of emotions, as self-directed forms of interrogative practice and as interrogative expressions of external influence. Practice here always has two sides, the two sides of practical judgment: violence and domination, on the one hand; limitation and transformation, on the other. Similarly, emotion and desire always have two sides, expressing external forces and dominations—the passive form of emotion in which it is the predominant expression of our limited powers—and interrogating our practical powers and capacities— the active form of emotion in which practical judgment judges itself. These interactions express the complexity of practical determinations: shaping the future while shaped by the past, contaminated ideologically, on the one hand; being the source of alternatives, on the other. Power and desire are inseparable, and it is in their interrelations that we may find the complex realities of practical judgment.

WILL

If desire is the generic form of relation involving a practical creature to other creatures and things, we appear to have no room for another relation in which practice associates itself with other things, no room for will beyond desire. Yet we think of having the desire but not the will to do good; we think as well that desire comes upon us out of our control, against our will: will frequently stands opposed to desire. It designates self-movement whereas desire frequently seems externally caused, though no sense of will is intelligible in the absence of external conditions and desire is a relation of self to other, in no sense entirely determined by the other. The question for us now is how to locate will in the context of my understanding of desire and power.

The relevant issues are found in Kant,[37] though he does not define will in sufficient detail for our purposes. Four characterizations of will may focus our attention: the will, free will, good will, and weak will. The question of *the* will is whether there is a singular faculty or form of practice distinct from the other conditions of practical judgment, distinct from power, emotion, and desire. In Kant, the distinctness of the will is as important as its autonomy. The will conforms to reason while desire conforms to inclination. In addition, the will is self-determining while desire is externally produced. Yet Kant cannot escape the determining force inherent in will—it is a kind of causality like desire—that requires not only a faculty of reason but a respect for its laws. Respect here defines will and is effectively a form of desire, for the good, determined by a universal rationality.

In terms of the understanding here, desire is local, no more universal than particular, no more external than internal. The locality of desire is incompatible with unqualified principles and with unqualified will. Nothing is good in itself without qualification, desired without qualification, only goods that result from complex and contingent practical judgments, successes mixed with failures. In this sense, there may even be no "goods" in the sense in which there are no "values": both notions presuppose an unqualified metric that pertains to objects regarded as practical ends. Without such a metric, however, without a quantitative rather than a qualitative interpretation of qualification, the determinants of practical judgments are always qualified by their mediateness and temporality. In Kant, will is inseparable from the efforts of reason to extricate practice from its contingencies and surroundings.

Thus, the notions of an unqualified will, the will, and practical reason are in Kant inseparable. The will, as a determinative faculty, conforms to its own laws. In this notion of self-legislation, we find autonomy, legitimacy, and the basis of the conflict between desire and will. If we reject the notion of the singularity of the will, deny that there is a faculty of will, we appear to sacrifice all the notions that define Kant's view of practical reason, leaving it with no sphere of determination.

I understand practical determination to be based not on a faculty or territory, but on ongoing judgment and validation. However, where Kant supposes that the fundamental moment in practical judgment is where the will opposes inclination, the fundamental condition for local practical judgment is mediateness: practical judgments transpire amid inexhaustible conflicts, desire with desire, reason with reason, contingency with contingency, mode of judgment with mode of judgment, all directed toward power and influence, pervaded by emotion. In this sense, conflict and heterogeneity are central to practical judgment, but are not explicable in terms of a conflict between will and desire.

The bearing of desire upon desire gives us a different sense of the conflict between desire and will: there is inherent in desire itself the power and the possibility of self-overcoming, based on a sense of force overpowering force—or, less violently, of force reconciling or neutralizing surplus power. Weakness of will, desire accompanied by a failure of will, is not a conflict of faculties, between desire and will, emotion and thought. Such a view misrepresents the heterogeneity of desire as much as the rationality of emotion and the singularity of will. Desires are plural, divided, and reflexive; they limit and enhance each other. Desire is force and power, and is as self-determining as externally determined. Only where taken to be fundamentally and intrinsically irrational, in that respect homogeneous, are desires in direct conflict with reason. Here reason is law alone. Here also desire is in permanent conflict with practical judgment, rather than one of its mediate components, and reason is an external determinant.

Practical judgment is the process of adjudicating courses of action among an inexhaustible welter of entangled considerations. In this sense, desire belongs to practical judgment in a variety of ways, as one of its moments, its moving force; as one of its determinants, in practical validation; as one of its means, in the reflexiveness of desire entwined with desire, realized in emotion. The same considerations apply to power, for power and desire are not distinct. Power is means and end, a moving force, and a determining factor for validation in practical judgment. Here, will is the nominal form of the possibility in practical judgment whereby we may deny that rational practice is in permanent conflict with desire. This possibility is the "causality" of which Kant speaks.

The will is therefore not an acceptable notion in relation to practical judgment: the definite article suggests too strongly the singularity and particularity of will. Similarly, the will is not free and autonomous, not because of the absence of freedom, but because freedom is not singular, and is pertinent to an individual agent more than to society and public activities. As far as freedom in general is concerned, practical judgment, individual or social, is unintelligible without the latitude of alternatives. Moreover, latitude is neither opposed to nor in conflict with external forms of determination such as causation or natural law, but belongs to every form of determination as possibility belongs to actuality, as polyphony is present within stillness, and conversely. Every determination is pervaded by alternatives; every practical situation bears alternatives within itself. Latitude is essential to practice and inherent in locality and inexhaustibility. In such latitude, pervading will itself, we find *akrasia*. Weakness of will belongs to will itself as its internal dividedness.

What is unlikely in thinking of the will as free is not only that there is no individual will, no faculty, but the suggestion that freedom belongs to individual agents more than to societies, institutions, and collectives. Freedom is not the private space within public determinants, even for Kant, for the laws of reason that define autonomy are public and anonymous, not private, personal, or subjective. Kant's model of will and autonomy is personal; his account of reason is public and universal. If we give up the personality of the will, on the one hand, and with it the personality of freedom, we may give up the universality of reason, on the other. We preserve its goodness by rejecting its universality. In this context, will is no freer than it is determined; freedom and determination are inseparably characteristic of mediateness. Every local situation—practical and generic—is located in the midst of things which are both determining and opening.

Will may be associated with the power inherent in desire that serves practical judgment. It is the force that practice requires in relation to the alterity manifested in desire, a relation of heterogeneity. It is required by the transcendence of practice in relation to desire, essential to its inexhaustibility. Will is self-determining, not in the sense that the determinants of practice reside wholly within

the agent or that agents can exercise unique control over themselves, but in the sense that every determinant is pervaded by
alternatives that can be implemented through practical judgments.
Will is an essential condition of practical judgment in manifesting
the possibility of effectiveness in practice.

Nothing can take the place in practical judgment of practical
judgments; that is, no external conditions and no methods of deliberation or emotional responses can take the place of having to
decide upon and pursue the best courses of action without rules
or criteria. There is no way to establish means for making practical
judgments that avoid the uncertainties of having to choose, no
methods of deliberation and valuation. This pervasive condition
of practical judgment may be described as the indispensability of
will in relation to power and desire as well as to deliberation and
understanding. Nothing we can know, nothing others can impose
on us, nothing in external conditions, nothing about the future,
can be substituted for an act of will. Will is the excessive reflexivity
within power and desire that is essential to practical judgment,
desire influencing desire, power influencing power, involving self-
control and self-direction. Equally, will is the condition that engenders the interrogative possibilities in emotion. Yet will in this
sense is always divided, always weak, incapable in itself of determining practice.

We come, then, to the good will, having rejected both a singular
faculty of will and a freedom in law unique to reason. Reason
belongs to practical judgment not in its form but in its activities—
the unending reflexive interrogation and reinterrogation of every
undertaking. There is no will, no unqualifiedly good will—for no
good is unqualified in the sense of rationality described here—
and no will that is more good than bad. Goodness and badness,
success and failure, are not properties of the will, as if in its purity
it might not be contaminated by its contingent locations. Will is
the division in power and desire that makes practical judgment
possible, that makes it possible to seek the good and avoid the
bad. Will is neither good nor bad, but practical judgments may be
successful or fail—almost always both—effective or destructive.

Another contrast involving will has not appeared so far in my
discussions of practical judgment. The contrast between desire
and will is implausible because desire includes within itself the
reflexivity and interrogation that will implies, and will includes

the dividedness within itself that characterizes desire. But there is the related contrast between willed goals and achieved results, between willed good and realized evil. This is not a contrast between faculties, but between effectiveness and impotence; this is a limitation in power, testimony to the limited causality of will and desire.

However, even this description is misleading: it suggests that within practical judgment there is a perfect inward possibility of goodness that is tempered by the imperfections of external circumstances. Goodness and evil both belong to external circumstances; they both belong as well to internal impulses, to desire and will. The goodness that is willed yet cannot be attained is not a perfection that reality fails to achieve, but a contingency in practical judgment that belongs to it intrinsically. Failures come not only from external oppositions but also from too great an inward purity. The inward purity proves to be impotent and a source of failure. Practical judgment has as one of its unending projects the overcoming of overly pure intentions that pretend to extreme goodness at the expense of relevant practical considerations.

In this sense, will belongs no more to reason than to unreason, to goodness no more than to evil, to success no more than to failure, to universality no more than to particularity, to deliberation no more than to emotion and practice. Will is the confluence of power and desire in the context first of practical judgment, where success and failure are determinate as forms of practical validation, then in the context of practical query, where interrogation and reinterrogation go on endlessly. Will is the moving spirit of unterminating practical judgment and semasis. It deserves a name, along with power and desire, as both determinant and impulse inherent in practice. But the simplicity of its name should not obscure the complexity of its entanglements, the locality of its functions, and the inexhaustibility of its relevances. Its name must not mislead us into thinking that there is a seat of practice or a site of goodness. To the contrary, entanglement and mediateness are inexorable principles of practice, of desire, power, and will.

TELEOLOGY

It would be helpful if we could interpret all practical judgments in terms of intentions and purposes—interests in Kantian terms.

Such an interpretation would entail that an action is a practical judgment only when purposeful, when designed rather than accidental. Yet the density and the specificity of human conditions make such an interpretation implausible. Events are frequently brought about by actions that are both teleological and non-intentional—that are designed and directed, but where no plan exists for their realization.[38] A similar view is expressed in Kant's understanding of art as purposeless purposiveness. These views express an important insight concerning practice that cannot be expressed without aporia.

The phenomenon to which Kant calls our attention is the design and order in works of art, and even in nature, that is the result of no definite purpose, that is directed toward the realization of no definite goal. Purpose is defined here in terms of goals while purposiveness is defined in terms of goal-less norms. Beautiful works conform to or establish standards and norms, even if, due to genius, they depart from any prior norms. The point is that works of art have no definite, practical goals inherent in their design, but require a different sense of order.

My concern here is not with art as much as with practice and power, especially those forms in which oppression and domination exert influences anonymously, rather than as expressions of the specific goals of particular persons or groups. Power here is dispersed and pervasive; it works through domination and resistance without focus on particular agents. Thus, anonymous, collective practice is teleological in its goals and directions as well as its results and works by means of or through practicing agents, but does not depend on their plans or purposes. The teleology belongs to the practices, perhaps to institutions, but not to particular persons or groups. Yet it is not independent of them.

We find here the confluence of two major conditions of practical judgment. One is that practice is directed toward results and the result of prior practices. Consequences in this sense belong to practical judgments as they do not belong to other modes of judgment, with the proviso that every judgment may be interpreted as a judgment in any mode. The second is that the consequences and results of practical judgments are densely specific and inexhaustible, and exceed any antecedent conditions including plans, purposes, and intentions. Practical judgments always accomplish, for good or for ill, far more (and far less) than is intended. The inexhaustibility—the density and specificity—of such judgments makes it necessary to regard them as teleological but as not always intended or planned.

To restrict our attention in practical undertakings to those overt consequences that we are in a position to anticipate is to repudiate all density and specificity, all inexhaustibility, in the practical affairs of human life. It is to transform the densely inexhaustible jungle of politics into the relatively spare landscape of philosophical morality, and to substitute rules and principles for inexhaustible contingencies. The terror in practical judgment, manifested repeatedly in political decisions, is that such judgment not only faces a largely unknown future, will produce far-reaching consequences that can only dimly be anticipated, but these consequences will profoundly influence human life. We are always on the edge of unforeseeable transformations, some catastrophic, and can act only on the basis of finitely understood alternatives. The natural consequence of such a situation is that we profoundly oversimplify our conditions and procedures, particularly by emphasizing rules and explicit plans. The inexhaustible contexts and consequences of practice then frequent the margins of human events without inclusion in explicit practical judgments.

The sense in which the results of practical judgments belong to them, and cannot be separated from them, requires a sense of teleology that is different from the plans and goals of agents, individual or collective, and of ends inherent in natural conditions that are not constituted by practical activities. We might say that an act is teleological in the sense that the agent who undertakes it has a prior realization of the goal toward which his action is directed, before that goal is reached. Teleology here is closely related to purpose, to means leading to ends, to plans, and to anticipations. There is, however, another sense of teleology, divorced from individual agents, that emphasizes that every practical judgment is directed toward consequences, toward the future and to specific events and occurrences, that are means to its validation. These two senses correspond to either the subjectively purposive teleology possessed by individual agents and the object or to event-centered teleology possessed by judgments. All judgments are teleological in the sense that they are semasic, subject to validation. But only practical judgments are teleological in the sense that they are directed toward the realization of particular states of affairs in the future.

A judgment is practical when its consequences matter to its validation. There is, in this sense, anticipated or not, foreseen and planned or not, teleology in the goals and the results that are inherent in any course of action. Courses of action, practical judgments, always have consequences, and it is the differentiations among such consequences that determine the validation, authority, and legitimacy of the relevant practical judgments.

We may say, then, that practical judgments are teleological in the sense that their consequences pertain to them, but that the consequences may not have been anticipated and can never be entirely foreseen. To suppose that foretelling the future, anticipating consequences, planning in advance are the central considerations of practical judgments is to trivialize their complexity, especially in their political forms. To the contrary, the unknown, unexpected consequences belong intimately and deeply to the actions that produced them and that profoundly haunt all human practices.

In this sense, we are always profoundly responsible for the consequences of our deeds, although we may not have anticipated them, although they could not reasonably have been foreseen, and although we made no plans concerning them.[39] They are determinants of our practical judgments. We are responsible in the sense that the consequences of our practical judgments belong to them inextricably. Practical judgments can neither be understood nor be undertaken rationally, cannot be cognitive, if they are severed from their consequences—any of their consequences. Yet there is always a profound tension among the consequences that are foreseen, the consequences that may be foreseen, and the consequences that are not foreseeable that defines the validation of any practical judgment.

It follows that practical judgments are always purposive and may be purposeful, in the sense that they have future objects and consequences that pertain to them as practical judgments, though none of these consequences may have been planned. Alternatively, practical judgments are always teleological—temporally and consequentially—though no agent could have intended some of the consequences that follow and every action has consequences that cannot have been intended. Teleology pertains intrinsically to practical judgments and query, not intrinsically to agents, though agents are responsible for the consequences of their actions, foreseen and intended or not.

What is involved is a thoroughgoing and far-reaching sense of the anonymity of certain judgments and events. Some judgments pertain specifically to human individuals as agents, others to groups and institutions. But some judgments pertain to human conditions anonymously, have objects and are directed toward consequences, though no nameable agency is involved. Not all practical judgments are performed by agents, though all practical judgments belong to human beings and their institutions.

All this follows from the defining impulse in practical judgment, to exercise influence. Practical influence always includes outcomes that are unanticipatable and unforeseeable from within any particular circumstances. Unexpected disasters are obstacles to influence even though unforeseen—especially if unforeseen. Consequences reflect back on their causes while the causes can only incompletely foretell their consequences. In this tension lies the imponderability of the future, the complex and divided relation to time that is inherent in practical judgment.

INFLUENCE

The entire discussion to this point may be summarized in the principle that practical judgment is directed toward exercising influence in human experience in relation to its natural surroundings and forms of life. Influence here is largely directed toward the future due to the temporal directedness of practice, though we should not overlook the influences we exercise over our past and over ourselves and our present circumstances. Nevertheless, though practice influences the past, and can be said to seek to influence it, such an influence requires a future and is realized through future consequences—a future that imposes differential conditions on its history.

The concept of influence here is closely related to Nietzsche's will to power and to the sense that power is everywhere. Yet in both cases it is important to relate power specifically to practice. In the sense in which every judgment is practical, experience is dominated by power and imposes domination over things. In the

same sense, truth and beauty are embedded in forms of practice
and instruments of power. Yet even here, whether instruments
and devices or not, truth and beauty are unintelligible as practical
norms, unintelligible as forms of power, insofar as they manifest
alternative modes of validation. What we may say instead is that
truth and beauty, even when they function as forms of validation,
are also instruments of power. We may add that they are such
instruments not as modes of validation but in the densely established discourses and disciplines that define them. Every established truth, every beautiful work, establishes a mode of influence
insofar as it enters practice. This is the sense that every epistemic
activity tends to become a discipline with practical exclusions that
manifest power.

One of the deepest concerns of practical life is whether there
are forms of power and influence that are not domination and
oppression. One answer is that influence is not always other-
directed, and, in being directed at agents themselves or included
within their practical judgments, imposes limits upon its forms of
domination by internal control and power. No theory of the superego can be intelligible without an understanding that its control
works in multiply reflexive ways. Similarly, though understanding
cannot escape from entanglements with power and control, there
are self-directed forms of understanding and power in which becoming aware of our own entanglements opens for us the possibility of new understandings. No form of practical reason can neglect
the powers inherent in self-control. Self-control here is that form
of practical judgment that addresses individual agents as fully as
their surroundings.

In the above cases, and in many others, the issue is not the
particular form of reflexive domination, whether a legitimate or
an illegitimate form of power, but the suggestion that influence is
only oppressive when it stands in an external relation, that there
is no oppression inherent in reflexive powers. Freud externalizes
the superego in relation to the id so that the image of domination
and violence returns. The question is whether all reflexive forms of
relevance are to be interpreted in terms of violence and oppression.

We have one reply to equating practical judgment with oppression, that when such judgment is self-directed (including group,
social, and institutional reflexivity as well as self-control), it may
not be oppressive or dominating and may make appropriate ad-

justments in relation to external forms of oppression. This reply requires extended discussion. Reflexive practices grounded in interrogation and criticism rather than in domination may exhibit nonviolent powers—or, alternatively, powers that reflexively overcome their own violences. But there is another way of posing the concern.

The question is whether influence is always *over* something, thereby imposing violence upon it. The proposed answer is that the sense of self-directed judgment does not require domination and oppression, though it is intimately joined with power and resistance. There are two ways of defending this answer. One, from the side of influence, asks us to consider our temporality, our past, present, and future, from the standpoint of practice. Practice is that form of judgment in which present judgments exercise influence, primarily over and by means of their consequences, but in other ways as well, over the past, in modes of thought and apprehension, through art and philosophy as well as through more physical forms of practice. Practice here is multiply embodied, in the actions undertaken and in their consequences; in its own undertakings and from the standpoint of other modes of judgment. The relations among these spheres of embodiment from the standpoint of practice may be described as influence without violence, though we must acknowledge that influence and power work reciprocally. Future consequences are the result of present practices, but present practical judgments are validated—determined and influenced—by their consequences.

A second way to understand a relevance that does not inherently involve oppression stems from an examination of what it might mean to "let things be."[40] For local beings are always mediate, in the midst of things, and their mediations, their locations, are determining. A being is located and locating, and is influenced and determined by its relations. It is nothing apart from such determining relations, and must be transformed by them. There is no non-mediate way to let things be, but, rather, we can let things be only by belonging to them and letting them belong to us, with the qualification that belonging is inseparable from departing, and departures in relation to practice manifest those forms of relevance that run the danger of violence and oppression. Still, the notions of violence and oppression may be inappropriate here.

More appropriate is the recognition that belonging is a constitutive form of influence and relation.

We are tormented by inexhaustibility and by our lack of control in practical judgment, not merely because of our finiteness and contingencies, as if we were weak before the forces of nature—which indeed we are, even where we devastate our immediate surroundings by our interventions—but because practical judgments inexhaustibly complicate further practical judgments with their dense and specific entanglements. The problem for any future involving humanity is always in part the human past in which human agents undertook practical judgments. This is the first principle of politics, that which makes it the paramount example of practical judgment: every effort at control produces lack of control, if only in some hidden spheres of human life. Every overt influence has its catastrophes, imposes sacrifices. Waste threatens all practical undertakings. The second principle is that political practices are of paramount importance to human life and further practices.

This first principle of practical judgment—the sacrifices required in every judgment—is at the center of the theory of practice developed here. The universality and generality of most moral and political ideals fade in comparison with the sacrifices they require to achieve their ends. In contrast with such ideality, we may consider a different standard of practice, one based on reason as query: an unending sensitivity and concern for the hidden consequences of every undertaking and for the hidden losses of control that are part of every practical design. Unreason haunts practical judgments, not so much in arbitrariness of impulse or specificity of whim, but in the uncontrollable failures that pertain to any course of action. Failure belongs to practice as its destiny.

NOTES

1. See, for example, Susanne Langer, *Feeling and Form* (New York: Scribner's, 1953). One of Langer's convictions, based on her view that the arts compose a field of forms of feeling, embodies a principle of assimilation, that one form of feeling must be subordinated to another in a multimedial work. This is a reductive principle in what is otherwise a strongly antireductive theory. The theme of domination and subordination runs through the Western tradition.

2. See Justus Buchler, *Metaphysics of Natural Complexes* (New York: Columbia University Press, 1966), pp. 119–22.

3. When Maurice Merleau-Ponty claims that "we cannot imagine how a *mind* could paint," he does not characterize fabricative judgment so much as its intermodality. Intermodality with emphasis on practice brings us to the central role of material bodies. ("Eye and Mind," *The Primacy of Perception*, trans. Carleton Dallery [Evanston: Northwestern University Press, 1964], p. 162).

4. G. W. F. Hegel, *Phenomenology of Mind*, trans. J. B. Baillie (London: Allen & Unwin, 1910), pp. 798–808.

5. Hegel, *Phenomenology of Mind*, esp. "Self-consciousness."

6. Immanuel Kant, *Critique of Pure Reason*, trans. Norman Kemp Smith (London: Macmillan, 1956), pp. 180–87. The schemata of reality, substance, possibility, necessity, and causality, each which makes reference to time, specifically or generally, are replaced here by multiple locality. Reality is being located; power is relevance in some and many locations; possibility is the polyphonic latitude opened up by multiple locatedness; actuality and necessity are closely related to stillness, joined by polyphony.

7. Kant, *Critique of Judgment*, pars. 2–4.

8. See my *Theory of Art*, esp. pp. 165–78.

9. Alfred North Whitehead, *Process and Reality*, Corr. ed., edd. D. R. Griffin and D. W. Sherburne (New York: Free Press, 1978), Parts III and IV. See my *Perspective in Whitehead's Metaphysics*, chap. 7.

10. *Science in the Modern World* (New York: Macmillan, 1925), pp. 69–70.

11. See John Dewey, *The Quest for Certainty* (New York: Minton, Balch, 1929).

12. See Rorty, *Philosophy and the Mirror of Nature*.

13. See Goodman, *Ways of Worldmaking*.

14. See Michael Polanyi, *Knowing and Being* (Chicago: The University of Chicago Press, 1969), p. 133: "To hold a natural law to be true is to believe that its presence may reveal itself in yet unknown and perhaps yet unthinkable consequences; it is to believe that natural laws are features of a reality which as such will continue to bear consequences inexhaustibly."

15. "We thus see (1) that genius is a *talent* for producing that for which no definite rule can be given; it is not a mere aptitude for what can be learned by a rule. Hence *originality* must be its first property. (2) But since it also can produce original nonsense, its products must be models, i.e., *exemplary*, and they consequently ought not to spring from imitation, but must serve as a standard or rule of judgment for others" (Kant, *Critique of Judgment*, par. 46, pp. 150–51).

16. "—Where there is power, there is resistance, and yet, or rather consequently, this resistance is never in a position of exteriority in relation to power. Should it be said that one is always 'inside' power, there is no 'escaping' it, there is no absolute outside where it is concerned, because one is subject to the law in any case? Or that, history being the ruse of reason, power is the ruse of history, always emerging the winner? This would be to misunderstand the strictly relational character of power relationships. Their existence depends on a multiplicity of points of resistance: these play the role of adversary, target, support, or handle in power relations" (Michel Foucault, *The History of Sexuality*. I. *Introduction*, trans. Robert Hurley [New York: Random House, 1980], p. 95).

17. "1. Ideology is not exclusive of scientificity. . . . 3. By correcting itself, by rectifying its errors, by clarifying its formulations, discourse does not necessarily undo its relations with ideology. The role of ideology does not diminish as rigour increases and error is dissipated" (Foucault, *Archaeology of Knowledge*, p. 186).

18. See the discussion of cosmology in my *Perspective in Whitehead's Metaphysics*.

19. "Where sex and pleasure are concerned, power can 'do' nothing but say no to them; what it produces, if anything, is absences and gaps; it overlooks elements, introduces discontinuities, separates what is joined, and marks off boundaries. Its effects take the general form of limit and lack. . . .

"[T]hou shalt not go near, thou shalt not touch, thou shalt not consume, thou shalt not experience pleasure, thou shalt not speak, though shalt not show thyself; ultimately thou shalt not exist, except in darkness and secrecy. To deal with sex, power employs nothing more than a law of prohibition" (Foucault, *History of Sexuality*, pp. 83–84).

Foucault emphasizes the constructive side of modern power, possible, I believe, only in virtue of exclusion.

20. See chap. 1, note 16. See also my *Limits of Language*, chap. 2.

21. Hans-Georg Gadamer points out that prejudice enables and circumscribes: what we understand belongs not to timeless universals but to local, determinate conditions (*Truth and Method* [New York: Seabury, 1975], esp. Part III). The reason is that determinateness is always a function of heterogeneity. Similarly, in Foucault, ideology is not debilitating. The reason again is that ideology makes judgment and understanding possible insofar as it restricts or delimits such understanding.

22. "Power is everywhere; not because it embraces everything, but because it comes from everywhere. And 'Power,' insofar as it is permanent, repetitious, inert, and self-reproducing, is simply the over-all effect that emerges from all these mobilities, the concatenation that rests on each of them and seeks in turn to arrest their movements.

"—Power is not something that is acquired, seized, or shared, something that one holds on to or allows to slip away; power is exercised from innumerable points, in the interplay of nonegalitarian and mobile relations" (Foucault, *History of Sexuality*, pp. 93–94).

Foucault distinguishes power from Power, the power that works everywhere, divided by resistances, from the Power that works through prohibition. Even so, Power belongs to power, expresses the dominating side of the exclusions power requires to do its work. See notes 16 and 19, above.

23. Charles Sanders Peirce, "How to Make Our Ideas Clear," *Philosophical Writings of Peirce*, ed. Justus Buchler (New York: Dover, 1955), pp. 21–41.

24. See my *Ring of Representation*, chap. 2.

25. Goodman describes this property as syntactic and semantic density and relative repleteness, adding multiple and complex reference. With the qualification that his analysis is restricted to referential symbols, he accommodates the importance of density and specificity to works of art (Goodman, *Languages of Art*).

26. See Dewey, *Theory of Valuation*, chap. 6; see also my *Learning and Discovery*.

27. See Foucault, *Order of Things*, esp. chap. 6, "Exchanging."

28. *Collected Papers*, trans. I. F. Grant Duff (New York: Basic Books, 1959), pp. 173–83; first published in *Neue Revue*, 1 (1908).

29. "Psychology and Literature," *Modern Man in Search of a Soul*, trans. W. S. Dell and C. F. Baynes (New York: Harcourt Brace Jovanovich, 1955).

30. For such a view, see Paul Ricoeur, *Freud and Philosophy* (New Haven: Yale University Press, 1970).

31. Alfred North Whitehead, *Science and the Modern World*, p. 131.

32. See Catherine Caulfield, *In the Rain Forest* (London: Heinemann, 1985).

33. See Foucault, *History of Sexuality*; see also my "The Limits of Sexuality," *Philosophy and Social Criticism*, 9, Nos. 3–4 (Spring 1984), 320–36.

34. See my *Inexhaustibility and Human Being*, chap. 4.

35. Benedict de Spinoza, *Ethics*, ed. James Gutmann (New York: Hafner, 1949), III, Def. III.

36. See my *Inexhaustibility and Human Being*, chap. 4.

37. "Nothing can possibly be conceived in the world, or even out of it, which can be called good, without qualification, except a Good Will. . . .

"The *will* is a kind of causality belonging to living beings in so far as they are rational, and *freedom* would be this property of such causality that it can be efficient, . . .

"The will is conceived as a faculty of determining itself to action *in accordance with the conception of certain laws*" (*Fundamental Principles of the Metaphysics of Morals*, from *Kant's* CRITIQUE OF PRACTICAL REASON *and Other Works on the Theory of Ethics*, trans. T. K. Abbott [New York: Longmans, Green, 1879], pp. 9, 65, 45).

38. Foucault expresses such a view in his understanding of power: "Power relations are both intentional and nonsubjective" (*History of Sexuality*, p. 94).

39. For a detailed development of this position, see my *The Nature of Moral Responsibility* (Detroit: Wayne State University Press, 1973), and *Injustice and Restitution* (Albany: State University of New York Press, 1993).

40. See Martin Heidegger, "The Origin of the Work of Art," *Poetry, Language, Thought*, trans. A. Hofstadter (New York: Harper & Row, 1971), p. 49: "What seems easier than to let a being be just the being that it is? Or does this turn out to be the most difficult of tasks? . . ."

3

VALOR

PRACTICE IS ONE OF MANY MODES of judgment and is capable of participation in many forms of query. It is rational not in virtue of its propositional structure or the deliberation that accompanies it, but as practice. It may be useful before proceeding further to distinguish such a view from some of the traditional approaches to practice that have dominated Western thought.

One such approach interprets practical judgments as judgments of preference: implicit in every practical decision, every practical undertaking, are alternative courses of action, different ends, among which we choose according to our desires. The assumption that practice presupposes alternatives is an expression of latitude: practical judgments are intelligible insofar as there are relevant alternative judgments. More problematic is the notion of preference.

There are several difficulties. One is that a preference may have no autonomous existence, may be entirely dependent on the practical judgments through which it is manifested. What we prefer is what we choose through practice. A second difficulty is that preferences may not be stable over different practical judgments. Studies in voter preferences show that preferential rankings vary with order of presentation.[1] This suggests that the notion of preference may be misleading as anything other than an expression of the latitude inherent in practical judgment. Third: the notion of preference with its congener, value, suggests that practical judgment is a form of pricing, a measure of the worth of an object or an undertaking in relation to other objects or events.

This notion of relative worth places us within an exchange economy of practice. A practical judgment is regarded as a form of valuation in which we determine the relative price or worth of diverse objects or events. Not only do we assume in such an interpretation that relative worth is stable enough to be determined, if only relatively and contextually, over a situation, but we presuppose two additional and far from self-evident features of practice: the effective currency of a value and a unidimensional metric for practical judgments based on a single measure of worth. These features are virtually identical. They amount to the stabilization of practice under the aegis of a single metric. Both the stabilization and the metric are indefensible in relation to practice.

A man runs into his burning house to attempt to rescue his children. Is it intelligible to think that the lives of his children are worth more than his own life to him? That he prefers them to himself? Those who restrain him do not suppose that his children are not worth it, but that he will fail to rescue them and be badly burned. The question of comparable worth does not arise, only the question of what he can and cannot do. We cannot even say that he chooses to enter the building rather than to stay outside and wait for others better equipped than he: he does not choose among an array of preferences, but does what he must. It is even less likely that he acts on the basis of gratification, that he seeks to avoid the pain that would result in the loss of his children, for it is a pain he has never experienced and cannot plausibly imagine. And all of this is true even as we know that some people would not risk themselves for their children.

The notion of worth or value taken as a property of an object or situation, even when understood to be the result of judgment and evaluation, presupposes either that there is a measure that allows all relevant objects and events to be compared—for example, the pleasure they bestow—or, more complexly, that the many factors and variables involved in practical judgment may all be mediated into a single system of evaluations. The notion of value here closely corresponds to the system of differences that constitutes a language. That is why we may think of both an economy of discourse and an economy of practice—both are systems of exchanges.

To postulate a single metric of evaluation is effectively to make the dense differences among objects and events vanish into their different worths: worth and value replace density and specificity. The locality and inexhaustibility of things are transformed into an arbitrary system of comparisons and replacements. The worth of the man's children, interpreted as the pleasure they give him or even as the pain their loss would cause him, can be overridden by anything else that can be compared to them in the same system of preferences. This will not do, not because the children have an infinite or overriding value, but because they have no value whatever. They constitute practical determinants of his life and experience. Once they exist and he loves them, they are not measurable on any scale whatever. They are precious insofar as they are incommensurate within his experience, insofar as they exceed any measure.

Moreover, it is not that children are human beings and are to be given unique respect as members of a kingdom of ends. Generic principles are as metrical as systems of preference. Human beings are frequently sacrificed to national purposes and are able to sacrifice themselves justifiably for other people and even for certain irreplaceable things. Certain things, like people, are irreplaceable and can justify great sacrifices—works of art, natural habitats. We have here one interpretation of the notion of "letting things be": things are substitutable for each other only in certain respects and there is a dense and inexhaustible excess to every being— its heterogeneity—that is neglected in a system of exchanges and substitutions, or brought under a universal rule. To this largely universal sense of exchange equivalences we may compare Whitehead's definition of value as the intrinsic reality of an event. I am interpreting this intrinsic reality as inexhaustibility and excess, as heterogeneity.

A system of preference is an exchange system that implicitly or explicitly legitimizes the substitution or exchange of any items of equivalent worth. It is all-inclusive and neglectful of the density and heterogeneity of individuals and kinds. A system of practical rules is similarly neglectful of density and heterogeneity; more important, it is based on arbitrary rather than calculated ends. Such views largely dominate the Western ethical tradition except for those activities and norms established in relation to God. Whitehead's definition of value participates in this tradition, as if only through God can the intrinsic nature of a person or thing somehow be realized, while in more ordinary human affairs, beings are metricized and systematized. Nevertheless, there is an absolute uniqueness and originality to every actual occasion in Whitehead: he calls it "value." It is equivalent with inexhaustibility. I call it "valor."

As it stands, this equivalence does not address the difficulty inherent in practical judgment of the need to act in densely specific situations. Here the specificity and density correspond to inexhaustibility with the qualification that there is no system of equivalences, that every being possesses an unmeasurable power, its inexhaustibility, that makes it valorous, not comparable with other equally inexhaustible beings. More accurately, every being is comparable to others in certain respects but not others, and there is no system of equivalences and comparisons. The closest we ordinarily come to recognizing this implication of locality and inexhaustibility lies in our sense, on the one hand, of the incomparability of persons in a kingdom of ends—never to be used, but always to be accorded the dignity appropriate to their freedom—and, on the other, of the incomparability of works of art—unique, sovereign, inexhaustible creations. In both cases, we restrict our sense of incomparability to humanity—in the case of art, through the notion of genius—effectively suggesting the subjection of all other natural things to a kingdom of domination.

I am concerned here with the inexhaustible valor of diverse things and kinds. Against this we may consider the assumption that without principles of calculation and equivalence, or without determinate rules for conduct, we will not be able intelligibly to undertake practical judgments. Yet the facts do not support such an assumption. To the contrary, rules and equivalences are made not found, made by practical judgments and their determinations where substitutions are the most effective of the alternatives available.

To think that practical equivalents antedate practical determinations is to deny the inexhaustible differences among heterogeneous things by treating them alike, as falling under an exchange system of value. We trade certain goods for others, effectively measuring them on a single scale of worth. Yet every such measure presupposes either the indifference of other people or a special privilege of some in relation to the things exchanged. Moreover, the idea of exchange is applicable only to pairs of human beings with things to buy and sell, or to barter, things they possess. Because I possess this piece of land, I may exchange it for something that you own. Ownership presupposes a principle of exchange equivalence, effectively distancing us from the heterogeneities of our surroundings. This truth is expressed today in slavery, in our profound repugnance at treating human beings as property, as if a human

being could be measured in an exchange relation without a surplus—on the auction block, for example. However, there is every
reason not to make humanity the distinguishing principle here,
for no being, human or otherwise, can be measured without
inexhaustible surplus. To the contrary, we are faced with the inexhaustible project in practical judgment of conferring value on
things when we act in relation to them, effectively measuring them
in relation to other objects and alternatives, though such valuation
diminishes their intrinsic reality and valor, reduces their
heterogeneity.

The notion of valor is incarnate: assignment to a system of
equivalences sacrifices material inexhaustibility save for those factors that constitute value. Consider the wear and tear on a dollar
bill, which serves its purpose so long as it is usable as currency.
Even beautiful places and the tools of a loving craftsman may be
cared for solely in terms that constitute their worth. Here a subur-
ban lawn may be compared with a meadow, a hotel beach with
an ocean preserve, a well-oiled machine with the prow of an ancient ship. Each may be regarded as too worthwhile to be neglected; each material thing may instead be regarded as beyond
price.

Practical judgment proceeds from human necessity: we are unable to avoid acting because not acting is still a practical judgment.
We are in this way bound to the consequences of our judgments.
But practical judgment presupposes a system of neither exchange
values nor normative principles. It presupposes no system at all,
though it may create a system: in some cases of exchange equivalences; in other cases of laws and powers. Rather, it presupposes
valor and responsibility. The rationality of practice does not depend on equivalences or rules, but on the interrogativeness and
inventiveness of practical query. And no rationality in practice can
eliminate the insecurities of the mediate and inexhaustible circumstances in which practical judgments transpire.

VALORIZATION

The traditional conception of value, explicitly beginning with
Hobbes but implicitly present before, regards practical judgments
as expressions of preference so that choosing among a number of

alternatives assigns them a differential value. The implication is that things differ in their value and can be exchanged for each other, substituted reciprocally, where their values are equivalent. This notion of value presupposes a system of equivalences.

Such a notion presupposes a universal measure of worth locating every feature of life and experience, including even priceless and invaluable things. It is to be contrasted with a very different sense of value, found in Whitehead's definition of value as intrinsic reality, as dense and specific difference. This notion may be interpreted to carry the meaning of exchange equivalence, for example, interpreting the intrinsic reality of a being in terms of the qualities in which it partakes, suggesting that two beings that partake of such qualities in the same measure are of equal value and may be exchanged. Such an interpretation presupposes that intrinsic reality is both external to and a measure of an event. Such a view is alien to Whitehead, for he regards actual occasions—the individual beings whose intrinsic reality is in question—as possessing actuality and creativity. What is implied here is that every real thing possesses a value that is a function of its reality, of its actuality and particularity, specifically and uniquely. Value here is not a measure of equivalence and exchange but an expression of uniqueness and heterogeneity. If we regard the former paradigm as moral, the latter is aesthetic. We are led to an understanding of ethics based on an aesthetic paradigm while we maintain the distinction between fabrication and practice.

The process in which equivalences are determined may be called "evaluation"; the process in which the unique and sovereign inexhaustibility of a being or kind is acknowledged may be called "valorization" to distinguish valor from value or worth. Valor is not measurable, nor are events and things equivalent in valor, but they are what they are, valorous in that respect (but not that degree). A valorous person is not equatable with any other valorous person or thing. Valor is much closer to the notion of virtue in Aristotle, but not to his view of hierarchy, pertaining to masters and slaves. It is not restricted to human beings, nor is it independent of what something does, independent of external influences, but is profoundly entangled in dense relations and consequences.

The notion of something valorous in itself suggests a traditional view of intrinsic value, as does Whitehead's notion of intrinsic reality. Yet valor is not an intrinsic or any other kind of value.

The notion of an end in itself suggests that it functions in a system of means and ends—that for which something else is done. Aristotle defines the good as that for which something is done, and the final end, happiness, as the end for which everything is done.[2] Yet nothing in his argument can sustain the view that there is but one end for human beings or for anything else: everything has its own end, its valor. We may choose to interpret this notion following Whitehead, in terms of an ideal that pertains uniquely to every individual.[3] Instead, we may choose to interpret it as neither ideal nor singular. Value traditionally suggests that things are measurable in relation to each other. Valor suggests the sacrifice that every course of action requires because there is no system of comparison. It includes relevances and consequences, but not the subordination of means in relation to the ends they produce, as if means were measurable in terms of their results. To the contrary, means are inexhaustible and determinable by consequences only in respect to practical judgment. In this sense, valor includes the inexhaustibility of things in relation to the specific determinants relevant to practical judgments.

Economists tell us that every gain involves a loss. This notion is the exchange equivalent of the sacrifice inherent in valor. From such a point of view, every loss is measurable on the scale of equivalences that is value, and we may ask whether what we lose justifies what we gain. To the contrary, however, many losses are neither evaluatable nor comparable, as in losses of human lives and works of art, deaths of tiny children and of the possibilities of life and experience that died with them. When someone we love dies, we lose something that has no price, that has no value, that is comparable to nothing else, that in this sense possesses valor. The inexpugnable sense of death, particularly vivid in relation to children, is the sacrifice of inexhaustible possibilities.

When valor is interpreted as an end in itself there is the suggestion that the loss is incomparable and ultimate, that something beyond price and measure requires an infinite movement for its comprehension. In this sense, a human life becomes absolute and absolutely revered, except that there is no place in human experience for such unqualified reverence. We grieve over our lost love, eventually resume our lives, better and worse for the experience, profoundly changed by it, never forgetting it. We are outraged over the murder of an innocent person and demand the death of the murderer, ignoring the fact that we intend to commit an absolute act in retaliation.

These responses show that whatever valor is, it is not an absolute metric in comparison with which all other values fall short. It is no metric at all, for it is not value. It is the condition of being important, inexhaustibly, and every being is important, for itself and for others. This sense of importance is related to the principle that to be is to be located, that an ingredient is important to its locale and, reciprocally, the locale is important to it. Importance may appear to be a normative, human notion, but it is generic, expressive of the relevances that obtain among shared locations and mutual powers. One of the outstanding features of Whitehead's cosmology is that he is able to interpret this notion of importance in pervasive terms, though he describes it as a form of value: the importance of something to the constitution and being of another. To be relevant is to be important in some ways; to be influential is to be important. Importance, or relevance, is multifarious and heterogeneous.

The generic conditions of valor are locality, inexhaustibility, and ergonality. No being is exhaustible in any particular locations, including locations in human experience, public or private, individual or social, transitory or enduring, in that sense promising inexhaustible but still local transcendences, promising inexhaustible possibilities of work. To be is to be inexhaustible, multiply located, transcending any particular locations, possessing inexhaustible resonances as well as unisons, inexhaustible alternatives and possibilities, working in inexhaustibly diverse ways, departing as well as belonging in any location. In this sense, valor pertains to the inexpugnability of being something, its inexhaustibility, the particularities of its locations and transcendences.

For there are two complementary sides to locality and inexhaustibility. One is the inexhaustible openness of any being in a location to other locations and relations. The other is the specificity and denseness of any particular location. Valorization is the practical meeting of these two dimensions of locality: the denseness and specificity of any locus that inhabits human experience and the inexhaustible openness of such a locus to new properties and conditions, to new locations. Any preferential decision in relation to any event or object neglects the inexhaustible possibilities of other properties, of other values, the inexhaustibility of any specific conditions and properties, their implication in multiple and heterogeneous relations, entangled throughout human events and conditions. Value imposes a metric that is doubly reductive, incompatible with locality and inexhaustibility.

There is a skeptical tradition in Western value theory that appears to recognize the incompatibilities inherent in locality and inexhaustibility in denying that there is any systematic and general basis for mediation and reconciliation where there are differences of value. This tradition acknowledges local incommensurateness, but in terms that violate mediateness. The value tradition assumes that events or objects can be compared on a single metric of worth. The skeptical response denies that events and objects can be compared where there are value differences. These are the two extreme positions, and neither is acceptable. Wherever there are differences there are possibilities of mediation, but there is no mediation or reconciliation of multiply heterogeneous differences together. What is to be rejected is not mediation but a universal form of mediation. Moreover, the mediateness of all practical judgments provides preconditions not only of differences but of mediations. Because we are human beings located in common milieux, we share many practical judgments. Nevertheless, there are conflicts, obstacles, and differences that can be overcome only proximately, contingently, under particular local conditions.

What valor encompasses that is absent from the dominant value tradition, except in such forms as Whitehead's view of intrinsic reality, is the locality and inexhaustibility of natural things, not simply our relations to such things and our judgments concerning them. Things are inexhaustible and local, so that our practical judgments are local in the double sense that we are local, in particular dense milieux, and that the things and events that concern us always exceed our relations with them, multiply, but are densely specific nevertheless.

Traces of such a view can be found in many Western writers, though frequently in a context that seems to demand an absolute foundation forbidden by locality. When Ivan Karamazov argues that no future paradise, even in heaven, can justify the suffering of one small child today, he touches on the principle that no child can be treated as but a means to any future benefit, however supreme. Such a view of the immorality of means is found in Kant's theory of the kingdom of ends and in other theories of the rights conferred on rational beings in virtue of their rationality. The terrible fact, however, is that whatever our theory of rights and ends, we will, implicitly or explicitly, utilize other people, rational or not, as means leading to future consequences. There is no escape from mediateness or from the inexorability of the future.

One theory without such absoluteness that expresses valor more than value is Dewey's view of the continuum of means and ends. While Dewey offers a theory of valuation that suggests problem solving, so that everything becomes a means to some future outcome, which itself becomes a means to further outcomes, he does not suggest a generic metric of value equivalences. He maintains instead the transformation of every being into means and of every means into further means, while every means is also an end. He speaks of temporal entanglements and material density and specificity.

In Dewey's principle of the continuum of means and ends, everything is both means and end: every means is an end and every end is a means. The principle entails that means and ends are dimensions of nature and experience, that every being and event mediately relates to its future but is also qualitatively unique. This qualitative uniqueness is valor, with the qualification that Dewey's theory of value does not emphasize incompatibilities and heterogeneities. He tends instead to emphasize the harmonization of means and ends in practice. He does not explore the possibility that intrinsic reality may forbid such satisfactory resolutions and harmonies, that incompatibility and heterogeneity are essential to practical judgments. He does not dwell upon catastrophes.

We may follow Dewey's view by emphasizing that valor is less an intrinsic condition in relation to things and more a feature bestowed on them through practical judgment, emphasizing valorization more than valor. Valorization is the process in human experience in which beings are judged to possess inexhaustible importance in their possibilities and relations. Things are important to us and to other human beings, are important in terms of what they lead to as means, but are important also to each other, in the conditions they establish. Inexhaustibility carries the weight of both of these notions, but valorization emphasizes as well the inescapability of practical judgment. Valorization is the expression of inexhaustibility and locality in practical judgment, expresses the work of things together in relation, mediately. It nevertheless points to more generic features of local beings.

Every locus inhabits multiple locations, is an ingredient in many different locales. In relation to every such location, an ingredient possesses a sphere of dominance that pertains uniquely to it, that is where it belongs. I call it "sovereignty" in relation to art.[4] This sovereignty is valor. It is found particularly evident in works of art, but cannot be restricted to them, for every locus is sovereign somewhere, belongs in some locations. I am referring here to where something belongs, and understand belonging to involve multiplicity and inexhaustibility. The notions of value and worth, insofar as they involve exchanges and equivalences, treat things as substitutable without regard for their sovereignty or for where they belong, without regard as well for their manifold possibilities and openness to variation. Rather, only a small subclass of possibilities and variations is relevant in evaluation, those directly implicit in the value metric.

The position to which we come, then, is that practical reason is not valuation or evaluation, not an expression of preferences or of a determinate scale of worth, but valorization, the judgment of practical relations that multiply locates events and things, responsive to their inexhaustibility. Valor is the sense of inexhaustibility borne by every locus, a sense of charity in every thing, joined with the sense of sacrifice imposed by the locality of practical judgment.

DEVALORIZATION

Among the recurrent themes in Heidegger's writings, along with his view of modern technology, is the notion of useful things ready-to-hand that are entirely "used up" in human activities.[5] I am speaking of consumable objects, things whose being and importance, relative to human experience, are as means only, entirely consumed in human practices. Primary examples are food and fuel, perhaps the only kinds of things that are entirely consumed. Even here, however, there is inevitably a remainder. In the case of fuel, consumption produces pollutants as well as enrichments; in the case of food, waste products are produced at such a rate as to threaten to inundate the life activities that give rise to them. Heidegger rejects this notion of things ready-to-hand as doing violence to the things themselves.

Similar themes echo elsewhere. An example can be found in Collingwood's distinction between craft and art.[6] In craft, according to Collingwood, materials are entirely subsumed under a particular practical end, directed to usefulness, are consumed without an irreducible remainder. In art, means and ends are not detachable, and there is no subsumption of the materials to an end but instead the transformation through imagination and expression of materials into a medium. In such a transformation, qualities of the materials and possibilities in the ends are so mutually implicated as to make the notion of use and consumption unintelligible.

In the context of locality and inexhaustibility, the notion of something entirely consumed, entirely subordinated to an external end or standard, is unintelligible. Instead, things work multifariously in their locales, milieux, expressions of their inexhaustible ergonality. No product can conform to any specifiable end, with no remainder or surplus. Every product, every thing, is inexhaustible, open to new possibilities, capable of new relations, surprising realizations, and embedded in inexhaustible milieux, open to new insights and determinations. The most routine products are capable of remarkable new properties and relations if they can survive into the future—as utilitarian vessels become glorious works of art, mediocre ornaments become works of camp, discarded objects become venerated antiques. More important, even when consumed, objects participate in the future through their consequences, in this sense never altogether consumed, for their consumption produces consequences, and these products have products. I am speaking of material products and results, of wastes, pollution, contamination, but also of building, manufacturing, and enriching. The fuel that is used up in production of a building not only produces new forms of potential energy, but new forms of life and practice.

No form of life and practice is susceptible to consumption without remainder; nothing can be entirely "used up." Being is inexhaustible, and consumption is local. However, there is a habit of thought and practice that consists in treating things as entirely consumable, a habit manifested strikingly in the production of mass-produced, effectively identical objects, any of which might be bought and used in the place of any of the others, involving exchange equivalence relations that have no room for surpluses or remainders. The notion of value, as a system of exchange relations, and the production of indistinguishable objects, pots and pans, pieces of papers, but also books, automobiles, refrigerators, tomatoes, and heads of lettuce, are intimately related as features of contemporary technological experience. In this respect, the modern technological world-view includes not only techniques and machines, but a way of thinking and living that is neither necessary nor defensible—transforming valorization into valuation, valor into value, inexhaustible beings into consumable implements.

The process in which products and natural things are regarded as entirely utilizable, to be ignored except as they may be consumed, subordinated entirely to particular human ends, may be called "devalorization." Valorization is the process in which the inexhaustibility of things and events is affirmed and they are recognized to exceed any particular locations. Devalorization is the process whereby things are subsumed under a given end or norm, merely a means. One of its prominent manifestations is the notion of technical perfectibility, as if an instrument might be evaluated entirely in terms of a single metric.

It is striking that in Heidegger, Whitehead, and Dewey the experience in which valor is prominent is not moral but aesthetic experience. In my view, art is the manifestation of inexhaustibility through intensity of contrast.[7] In art, then, the inexhaustibility of things, their sovereignty and valor, is revealed, and the impossibility of entirely possessing or using any such being is disclosed. In this sense, the alterity inherent in a sovereign work of art is inexpugnable. Even where a work is doctrinal, it manifests inexhaustibility. Art as art is valorization without failure. What may be added is that art is not art alone, but is also practice, and finds itself as practical judgment continually threatened by devalorization.

Devalorization belongs to practice as one of its pervasive forms of failure, forcefully emerging wherever power is in question. It is not, on this reading, a particular defect of contemporary life, of modern technology, but has through history accompanied practical judgment and query as conditions and consequences of power and influence. It is present wherever particular forms and methods of practice are taken to exhaust human life and experience, so that valor collapses into value and fulfillment is measured in terms of an all-inclusive system of values. It is a consequence of attempts at control surrounded by inexhaustible beings that escape every effort to control them.

There is little doubt that we must eat to live and that eating is a form of consumption in which equivalence substitutions are legitimate—one tomato for another—measurable largely in nutritive terms. Similarly, the production of refrigerators identical in all respects, including reliability and effectiveness, contributes greatly to the practical qualities of human life. Technology contains its own forms of quality control, and where diminished, diminishes the quality of life and experience. It is not repetition or consumption that is the danger. It is the way of life and thought that, due to devalorization, ignores the sacrifices involved in practice.[8]

The list of desecrations is unending. Land tilled under intense productive techniques becomes depleted; rain forests are cleared to make way for unproductive agricultural projects; chemical fertilizer factories contaminate their surroundings; energy-intensive techniques for producing fuel are required as more easily accessible fuels are depleted; species of life vanish forever. A value-oriented system measures each of these costs against the benefits involved as if there were a calculus within which all such beings might be scaled. Such a system is a prominent exemplification of devalorization.

There are some exceptions to this process. Human beings are regarded as rational ends in themselves when judged in ethical terms, not to be subsumed under external ends. Even here, however, human sacrifices are considered acceptable where social and collective benefits are great enough—in war and economic depressions, and including the punishment of criminals and enforced treatment of the insane. Other animals are sometimes included within the scope of ends in themselves, where we are to avoid unnecessary suffering inflicted on any living thing. Even rain forests and tundra are sometimes included where we recognize their fragility and irreplaceability.

The conclusion is that practical judgment and query can be rational only joined with valor. They do not define a superior norm over value—that would be unintelligible and destructive to practice—but remain joined with the sacrifices involved in practical judgments. Reason in practice is the process in which conflicts in valor are adjudicated, in which every being is respected for its precious and inexhaustible reality conjoined with the sacrifices that cannot be avoided. Such a practical reason ranges from forms of thought to action, from metaphysics to corporate management, from human beings to their natural surroundings, organic and inorganic. Mountains and oceans can be destroyed as thoroughly as species and habitats. Valorization and devalorization together inhabit the workings of power that constitute practice. No valorization can entirely eliminate devalorization in practice; only a continuing struggle to pursue practical query can obliterate it.

DOMINATION

Among the apparently inescapable features of practice is the domination, if not violence, that characterizes every form of practical judgment. Among the tragic aspects of practical judgment is that we frequently cannot wait for the future, when our powers will be more secure, but require control in the present when it is not available to us. Another tragic aspect is that we are always in some sense too late, inescapably entangled in a historical and practical past that we cannot influence, though we may judge it repeatedly. Temporality is both the curse and the blessing of practice: the one because even if we could gain control, it would only be effective later; the other because inclement circumstances present us with possibilities of future transformations. The result of this irresistible temporality is the imposition of practice upon events and conditions in the form of domination. I include here not only violent and oppressive acts, but rules and manipulations. Our efforts at influencing our surroundings, and their impediments, lead us to attempt to force things to conform to our will. Such forcefulness is domination, a paramount form of devalorization.

The importance of power in practical judgment suggests that every practice is domination. We must wrest from resisting nature the sustenance needed for survival and fulfillment; any other view is utopian. Contributing further to this view is the classical political tradition's emphasis upon opposing personal interests, closely related to the tradition's view of value. For the classical theory holds that individual human interests conflict, that domination and violence are both the result of such conflicts of interest and something that we may strive to overcome through reason. The irony of such an "overcoming" should not be neglected.

What is overlooked, on the one hand, is that human beings share so much in common, in so many diverse ways, that this view of conflicting interests is oversimplified, relegating all conflicts and differences to a single metric of interests and values, while, on the other hand, power and exclusion belong to practical judgment intrinsically. The issues of power and conflict are closely related. On the one hand, there are endless differences in understanding, loyalty, emotion, and point of view that are not reducible to conflicts of interests; on the other hand, human beings belong to heterogeneous collectives and share points of view as much as they differ, have harmonizing as well as conflicting interests. Power works wherever there is practice, whether there is conflict or commonality. Power belongs to practice, to valorization as much as to devalorization. To this I add that power turns back on itself, along with desire, and its self-imposed limitations entail neither violence nor domination.

The collective life of human beings, in large or small groups, entails that in some or many ways individual interests coincide, at least overlap, not because, coincidentally, they are the same, but because individuals influence each other's interests and emotions. The woman who runs into a burning house to rescue her children does so because they are important to her, because their lives coincide. And the coincidence is not accidental, but a feature of their common activities and judgments. Human beings who share their lives together may also conflict in bitter and petty ways, even catastrophically, but even so, their lives and interests are entangled profoundly. Even amid the pervasiveness and inescapability of conflict and heterogeneity, human life along with nature more generally is pervaded by deep relations and affinities. The depth of the issues of power and heterogeneity is a direct function of the complexity of the entanglements—affinities as well as diversities—that constitute the locales of practical judgment.

Interests may conflict, irreducibly, and may or may not be harmonizable under generic rules and practices. But they also may not conflict when a common collective life produces reciprocal valorization and understanding. The traditional view of interests and values has no room in it for collective judgments. Valor, however, pertains to any being, whatever its status, to individuals, collectives, and kinds, to persons and groups, to institutions and regions. The view of power that is derived from individual interests and a theory of value is inadequate to the scale of practical judgment, for it presupposes a relatively one-dimensional view of conflict. If interests could coincide, there would be no need for power. This is not an acceptable view. Valor and power are not opposed, though the former suggests that we should strive to avoid turning power into oppression. Power is situated through practice in inescapable contexts of valor. Nevertheless, that we should engage in practical judgment at all, required by the exigencies of inexhaustible valor, faces us with the terrifying condition that practical judgment always destroys something valorous, that sacrifice is inescapable, leading to domination. Practice in the context of valor entails the unavoidability of destruction.

Destruction is unavoidable in practice. We undertake practical judgments in surroundings that we despoil as well as enrich. We must eat to live, but may nevertheless admire the beauty of the creatures whose destruction is necessary to our survival. We cannot walk through the forest without crushing precious plants beneath our heels. All are valorous creatures and things. Yet valor is not restricted to living creatures. Every being and kind that surrounds us is precious and sovereign in inexhaustible ways. Similarly, we cannot live and engage in practical judgments without the exercise of power. However, I reject the conclusion that where we utilize power we cannot claim reason or valor. Power is pervasive and unavoidable for human beings, but it works in the light of valor. What is entailed is that no practical judgment can avoid failure and that no success can balances practical failures. There is no metric of equivalence.

A universal metric suggests that the density and specificity of practical determinations may be neglected in ascertaining what we may treat indifferently and what we may treat humanely, what we may treat with concern for suffering and what whose suffering we may ignore, that universal principles may replace the dark and inexpugnable side of practice with routine methods and calculations. To emphasize instead that power is everywhere[9] is to emphasize the pervasiveness of relations of influence and reciprocity—ontological considerations—and the pervasiveness in human experience of practical judgments directed toward influence—

practical considerations. To say that power is everywhere is to emphasize that every being is influential and is influenced, among the relations that compose locality. Such pervasive and dispersed influences coalesce into patterns of subjugation and domination. Agencies and individuals govern; rules and laws are enacted; institutions exercise overall effects; large-scale social and political institutions compose structures that take on lives of their own. The forms of practice that are instituted to oppose domination manifest it. The forms whereby we seek to avoid spoliation produce it.

Every normative principle that, on the one hand, constitutes a resistance to power—a principle of equality, for example—on the other, constitutes domination in a given milieu. Equality both resists privileges by inheritance and class and exercises power over disadvantaged, competing minorities. Every established freedom is a domination as well as a resistance—for example, freedom of the press is abusive in invasion of privacy; freedom of speech is abusive in relation to pornography and to public lies about public figures. In every one of these cases, the freedom legitimates abuses of power, is in effect an instrument of domination, has produced immense harm. No implemented principle can avoid such dominations and oppressions.

Some extreme examples do not so much make the point as dramatize its excesses. Opponents of abortion argue that it is murder and that life is sacred, but some who argue this way commit murder to support their stand. A similar point might be made about capital punishment, but a better example is that of war, particularly a just and moral war (if any can be that). The justice and morality of such a war are based on an overarching universal principle or norm against which the individual lives lost or won have no significance, nor do the lands and properties crushed by the battling armies. Such losses in relation to absolute norms share in the tradition's evaluative calculations: what fails to measure up is insufficient.

There are less dramatic examples. The point is that principles of goodness and justice both define norms of practical judgment and are themselves forms of practice, implements of power. There are no universal ethical norms or principles that do not exercise domination over some persons or objects. The most visible instance of this truth lies in the principle of property that treats things, if not persons, as entirely owned, so to speak, through and through, to the point where what is owned has no being other than as property. Property rights are devalorizing. At the margins, we recognize that even property belongs not only to its owner, but to everyone and to no one, and it is possible to betray something's valor by abusing it even when entirely owned and where no one else can exercise a competing claim. Works of art, significant inventions, profound secrets of life, every natural thing, once existent and known, are capable of being abused, a notion intelligible only where those who possess them have responsibilities that surpass rights of possession.

It follows that every rule or law is a ruling and a domination, not in the liberal tradition's sense of caution before the excesses of established institutions, but in the more generic sense that what exists exercises influence, and every such influence in practice influences the future and, as a result of failure, dominates over some people or things. While power is pervasive, dispersed, located in no particular apparatus, and while resistance is equally dispersed and pervasive, the contingent practical effects of power are destructive dominations, sometimes catastrophic, over institutions and groups, patterns of life, most importantly, over reason itself. All reason, every principle, is subject to impediments of power and control, leading to domination and oppression.

Acknowledgment of the pervasiveness of power and its impediments, leading to devalorization and domination, is profoundly hostile to utopianism. But it is also hostile to the skeptical conclusion that all powers are equal, that because violence and domination are unavoidable, any result is as good as any other. Such a conclusion leaves out the irresistibility of practical judgment and the presence of validation. We must choose and decide, undertake practical measures, no matter what, and we must do so without the help of unchallengeable principles—practical or theoretical—that can overcome the vicissitudes of domination and power. The conclusion is that power and valor, in their complex and conflicting entanglements, constitute the pervasive conditions of practical judgment.

VIRTUE

If evaluation and conformity to principle are reductive forms of practical judgment, if, then, utilitarianism and a kingdom of ends are untenable as models of rational practice, we may appear to be without a positive model of practical reason. In general, I deny that practical query must conform to principle or calculation to be rational. However, there is an important model in the Western tradition that suffers from none of the major defects that have been mentioned. This is the Greek view of virtue. It suffers from very different shortcomings.

In contrast to traditional views based on value and principle, practical judgment and query presuppose no general metric of evaluation or universal norms, only capacities and circumstances that make effective influence feasible, in particular, valorization and practical judgment. The notion of evaluation presupposes a system of equivalences in which every event and thing in human life is measured, so that we may evaluate the preferential weights of alternative outcomes of any course of action. Utilitarianism is based on such a system of weights and measures. Any practical undertaking is measurable in terms of an overall balance of benefits and losses. Yet there is, in general, no such overall balance, no such generic measure, and no univocal determination of benefits and losses. Practical judgment is inextricably involved in consequences and outcomes, but outcomes are not comparable in a unambiguous and comprehensive way. Mill's distinction of pleasures as higher and lower is relatively clear, if oversimplified, testimony to the heterogeneity of different pleasures and valors. If we add that there is no measure of valor in general, that any two beings are always in some respects incomparable (as well as comparable in manifold other respects), the entire utilitarian theory breaks down.

The standard principle-based criticism of utilitarianism is that it cannot in principle avoid sacrificing persons and things with intrinsic worth to causes and collectives that on the whole contain greater worth. The complex overall balancing of benefits and losses cannot accommodate intrinsic rights or merit. Even a rule-utilitarian theory, which holds that it is not acts, particular practical judgments, but general rules that are to be evaluated in terms of benefits and losses, cannot avoid the possibility that a rule will be justifiable in terms of general results that are repugnant because of the sacrifices imposed on a small number of people or things. The major weakness of both forms of utilitarianism is that the sacrifices required to attain overall benefits, either by acts or rules, are regarded as inconsequential and insignificant. A calculative procedure is substituted for the inexhaustibly complex decisions required in practical judgments. The frustration and despair that cannot be avoided in practical judgment, the confrontation with incommensurate valors in heterogeneous things that inhabit an indeterminate future, are buried in a calculative system of exchanges and equivalences in the sacrifices required of minority rights to benefit the majority. In political terms, utilitarianism amounts to the privilege of the majority over the minority, not simply in relation to those practical determinations that are legitimately determinable in an electoral process, but in all cases of practical judgment. This is a prime example of the way in which a theoretical system of practice may serve entrenched political ends and groups.

However, an appeal to principles and rules does not avoid the fundamental defects of utilitarianism. In rule-utilitarianism, the rules justified by their consequences may ameliorate in practice some of the sacrifices imposed by too crude a model of calculation based on acts. But the defect lies in the calculation of benefits and losses, however complex and sophisticated we make the model. Valuation is too narrow a notion to replace valorization, however rich the calculations. Similarly, though the notion that human beings have intrinsic rights based on rationality and autonomy endows individuals with protection against actions based entirely on majority benefits, the principles defining these rights are too arbitrary to be workable except on the basis of political practices and too general to be adequately sensitive to important differences.

Western ethical theory now holds that moral principles apply without exception to all human beings, undifferentiated by race or wealth. Yet there remain significant exclusions that indicate that the principles do not establish the operative norms, but only summarize prevailing practices. I am referring to continuing sex-based differences that rest on unavoidable biological and reproductive differences but that translate in social life into arbitrary vocational, personal, and role differences. An even better case is that of children, who are typically treated as if only partly human and partly property. More important, however, race, birth, and wealth were once considered determining properties of human value, dividing human beings into classes and groups in which different principles and rules applied. The problem, on the one hand, is that these differences—of race, birth, wealth, and social background—are significant in important ways, testified to by the importance of cultural differences in relation to many practices such as telling the truth and paying officials for services. The problem, on the other hand, is that far too many of these differences promote injustice when institutionalized and constitute indefensible conditions of practical life.

If there is no general system of worth on the basis of which all things may be measured, there are no general principles applicable to all things independent of their differences and uniqueness. The most evident indication of the limits of a rights-based morality is that principles conflict in every situation calling for practical judgment. If we grant that agents have rights and duties to themselves, even differential duties to their families and friends, then, in every case, unavoidably, there will be unresolvable conflicts between benefits to oneself and considerations involving others. We may add to any system of rules and principles a hierarchical system of rankings and priorities. The question is why we may suppose that any such system is general over individuals and groups, over cultural and historical differences, and stable through time. To the contrary, I suggest that mediateness strongly applies to rules and principles, that all practical principles, but especially those that define rankings and priorities, are themselves situated in practical conditions, and are the results of past practices and determinants of future practices, thoroughly pervaded by power and desire. Every system of rules, including rules of rules, is an instrument of domination, privileging one group over another.

It does not follow from these criticisms that practical judgment and query do not involve calculations of benefits and losses or appeals to principles and priorities. It would be impossible to justify a practical undertaking publicly without such calculations and appeals. Yet justification of practice is practice itself, requiring further justification. The justification, and any course of action that follows it closely, belongs to practice, not to theory, and must be supplemented by deep sensitivity to the differential sacrifices every such course of action entails. One consequence is that calculations of benefits and losses and appeals to rules are always local, exemplifications of local practices. In virtue of mediateness, practical judgment belongs to practice and not to theory in the sense that conformity to rule is only a factor in practical judgment, that practice is validated by its consequences in inexhaustibly diverse and local ways. Another way of putting this is that deliberation is one of the forms of devalorization necessary in practical judgment, but it is local, situated within the general practice of valorization.

The alternative model of practice that traditionally has replaced the calculation of benefits and conformity to rule is that of virtue. There are two fundamental features of this model. One is that the notion of virtue here is inseparable from the undertakings of practical agents in the double sense that no external determinants of practical validation exist outside the decisions of such agents who possess inexhaustible capacities of practical judgment, and that agents respond to practical situations without formulas or rules. The second is that practical agents serve as models or paradigms of valid practice, and that no more general form or means lying outside such paradigms may be substituted for them. In effect, we employ virtuous agents and their undertakings as exemplars, and there is nothing beyond such examples that can improve them. This is a model model. It is implicit in both of the positions described above, utilitarian and rule-based, in the sense that we may argue for their legitimacy only in terms of established practical intuitions in relation to particular cases. Such intuitions are the equivalent of the assumption that we are able, ourselves, to make practical judgments independent of any calculations or rules; or, instead, that we can recognize, in the practical judgments of others, valid and invalid results, that we can tell in particular cases when practical judgments succeed and fail. Above all, we recognize in the lives and practices of other people, at different times and under different circumstances, examples of better and worse character, excellences and defects, that are neither calculating nor based on rules.

This notion of exemplification and paradigm is based on the assumption that we can recognize excellence or virtue in practice without having a rule or system of calculations in which to evaluate it. We can recognize virtuousness, as practical valorization, even where there are no general rules or principles. Virtue, like valor, may be inexhaustibly diverse, subsumable under no other general heading.

Two distinct senses of virtue—if not many—are pertinent here. Both are found in Aristotle. One, the most notorious, is based on the conviction that there is an overarching model of human excellence toward which all practices are directed. I have noted that nothing in Aristotle's account can sustain the view that we must presuppose a single model of human excellence and fulfillment for all persons under all circumstances, but only that we function practically in the light of some standard of excellence, be it single or plural, that defines the validation of that practice. Nevertheless, this notion of human excellence is unqualified by function, if it differs by circumstances, and suggests that we interpret practical judgments in terms of an overall paradigm of human life. The most satisfactory practical judgments are those that contribute to the fulfillments possible in a life of excellence. I add that as a consequence of inexhaustibility, there are multiple paradigms of such human fulfillments. Only such a multiplicity can avoid Aristotle's claim in relation to slavery that some by nature are superior and others inferior.[10]

The second is more restrictively practical and is based on the role of practical agents as exemplars of effective practices. Aristotle speaks of acquiring virtue by imitating a virtuous human being. While the notion of imitation may be misleading in diminishing the importance of invention to practical judgment, there is a profound difference between imitating a judgment and imitating a person who judges. The former has no significant room for sensitivity to differences and invention; the latter, if the imitation of a sensitive and inventive person, demands sensitivity and invention from the mime.

Nevertheless, imitation is too restricted a notion, suggesting repetition rather than novel judgment and query. The function of a rational paradigm is not to impose conformity but to establish conditions. This is clear where we are speaking of science, though there is an enormous difference between treating science or scientists as paradigms and treating any of the results of science as paradigmatic. When a theory becomes paradigmatic, it becomes dominant and oppressive. Where a person becomes paradigmatic, and that person displays inventiveness and integrity, then those who follow are called upon to manifest similar personal qualities. The reasons why imitation is misleading is that it suggests repetition rather than invention. Rather, paradigms in practice establish conditions for future practice however these conditions are carried through. Kant's account of genius is the most felicitous we have:

the breaking of rules conjoined with the establishment of other rules. Where paradigms are inseparable from the imperative that every rule be called into question, we have a practice that can be both ethical and rational.

Virtue in the first sense, that of human fulfillment, even where we emphasize that there are inexhaustibly diverse and even incompatible paradigms—based on honor, principle, work, or love— presupposes an overarching norm of human excellence, and is incompatible with locality and inexhaustibility. Virtue in the second sense has the advantage of emphasizing the diverse excellences pertinent to practical judgments and the locality of such excellences within practice and in relation to other modes of judgment. What is crucial is that we can have a notion of virtue or excellence that is not predominant over all other virtues and excellences, a plurality of virtues that includes differences and heterogeneities.

Notes

1. Paul A. Samuelson, *Functions of Economic Analysis* (Cambridge: Harvard University Press, 1947).

2. Aristotle, *Nicomachean Ethics*, I. All references to Aristotle except as indicated are from *The Basic Works of Aristotle*, ed. Richard McKeon (New York: Random House, 1941).

3. Whitehead, *Process and Reality*, p. 84.

4. See my *Theory of Art*, and "Sovereignty and Utility of the Work of Art."

5. See Heidegger, *Being and Time*, and "Origin of the Work of Art."

6. R. G. Collingwood, *The Principles of Art* (Oxford: Oxford University Press, 1938).

7. See my *Theory of Art*.

8. It may be called *floccinaucinihilipilification*.

9. See chap. 2, note 22.

10. "Hence we see that is the nature and office of a slave; he who is by nature not his own but another's man, is by nature a slave; and he may be said to be another's man who, being a human being, is also a possession" (*Politics*, 1254A).

"Where then there is such a difference as that between soul and body, or between men and animals . . . the lower sort are by nature slaves, and it is better for them as for all inferiors that they should be under the rule of a master" (*Politics*, 1254B).

4

CHARITY AND SACRIFICE

THE ESTABLISHED FORMS OF PRACTICAL JUDGMENT are ethics, politics, technology, and everyday experience—the latter tantamount to life itself. All may be rational or include rational forms, though each is as susceptible to irrationality and dogmatism as to reason. Any form of life and thought is recurrently susceptible to dogmatism and blindness, especially in relation to its own canons. Reason is not, then, subservience to rules, however plausible, but unremitting criticism of every rule and condition, especially including its own rules and conditions. I assume that criticisms bring forth alternative possibilities of thought and action, alternative possibilities in life and experience. I do not assume that criticism produces agreement. The only agreement possible in reason is to disagree endlessly. The disagreements promote new forms of practice.

Where skepticism fails is not in the criticisms it directs toward established epistemic practices, criticisms that cannot be too strenuous, but in failing to turn its critical arrows at itself, thereby failing to grasp the local efficacy of the practices it condemns. The answers to skepticism and the truth it bears are the same: knowledge and understanding, agreement and disagreement, with the efficacies of practice, are local. It is another form of dogmatism to suppose that such locality is intrinsically defective, as if we were bound to strive for understandings and truths with no boundaries. Without locality, there would be no knowledge and no effective practices. Rational practices do not produce universal agreement but local and mutual interrogations, sometimes profound disagreements. The agreements as well as disagreements required by practical judgments are the local conditions that foster interrogation and criticism. The result that may be expected is further local agreement and disagreement, entangling and interpenetrating.

By far the most difficult of the forms of practical judgment to regard as rational is life itself, everyday practices, but including applications and ramifications of the other forms of judgment, ethics, politics, and technology, and also science, art, and religion. All the forms of life belong to everyday practical judgments insofar as we may experience them daily and insofar as the modes of judgment and query interpenetrate in lived experience. In this sense, everyday practice is a hodgepodge of modalities of judgment, of mixtures of reason and dogmatism, of habit and interrogation. It is not, then, and could not be, query in any of its more systematic or established forms. Yet every form of query imposes itself upon lived experience, in all its untidiness, and every form of query subjects itself to lived experience.

The quest for a meaning to life, given its complexities and incompatibilities, is a demand for life in general, in its entanglements and confusions, to become a coherent form of rational practice. Such a demand is effectively a closure upon life and experience, but especially on other forms of query, subordinating them to one comprehensive vision of fulfillment. To the contrary, life is where the plurality and inexhaustibility of local forms of practice and reason display their locality and heterogeneity, their endless excesses. In this profound and important sense, life is in endless contrast with any established form of query, not because we cannot live life as query, but because in doing so, we do not make it a single form, but, rather, display the inexhaustibility and locality of any form of query through multifarious other forms. This point, in relation to practice, repeats the principle that there is no complex form of practical judgment, however rational, that is not faced continually with failures, actual and possible, a consequence of local and inexhaustible valors. Valor presupposes charity, but imposes the inescapability of sacrifice. These together compose the pervasive conditions of practical reason.

CHARITY

Charity and sacrifice are the work in practical judgment of inexhaustibility and locality, together composing valor: the valor inherent in every being in virtue of its inexhaustibility; the inexhaustible determinants of every practical situation and its inexhaustible futures; the inexhaustible conflicts among local beings and events that define the conditions for practical judgment; the inexhaustible promises inherent in every open future, including promises of practical query. Charity is the sense of inexhaustibility that surrounds practical judgment. Sacrifice is the corollary in practice of the locality of being and judgment, the possibility of practical work. What charity and sacrifice demand within practical query is endless sensitive responsiveness to the conditions of human life.

Practical query begins with profound charity toward the inexhaustibility of things supplemented by unremitting concern for practical interrogation. Practical query is that form of practical judgment that adjudicates unending conflicts of valor; there is no life, no being or practical judgment, without such conflicts. Practical judgment is differentiated into its rational forms not by rule or law, by calculation of preferences and values, or by universality and generality, but by the range and depth of its judgments of valor based on charity and sacrifice. Agreement is not the measure of reason, only one of the alternatives that a rational practice may pursue; disagreement is another and an important consequence of reason in practice. Ethics is not qualitatively distinct from other forms of practice, both because there is no particular state or condition, principle or method, that makes practice ethical and because all practical judgment is faced with the same demand: to work toward valor within human experience by exercising powers. Yet every power is oppressive, and every power must respond to changing conditions, including the consequences of its own activities. Practical query is reason in practice, marked not by any particular form or structure, method or truth, substantive or formal results, but by unending criticism and interrogation. For no structural or methodic condition of practice is immune to the terrible risks of practice, that whatever promotes success achieves it through sacrifice, that failure is unavoidable.

Practical query is unending interrogation and validation within practice in relation to endless conflicts. It therefore sometimes requires heroic and idiosyncratic stands against the multitude, sometimes needs compromise and adjustment, sometimes stems from shared, public valorous understandings, sometimes produces far-reaching and abiding communities, and sometimes demands greater individualization, privacy, and differentiation. Query always involves shared locales and judgments. What is in question is whether such sharing presupposes conflicts mediated only in part through practical judgment; or, instead, whether within every soul there is a communal as well as heterogeneous points of view— a shared rational perspective or harmony of interests, achieved by intuition or calculation. Conversely, what is in question is whether heterogeneity presupposes unmediatable differences, or whether mediation is not always present as a possibility in the most hetero-geneous conditions—a possibility that does not and cannot elimi-nate incommensurateness. What is essential is a profound sense that practical agents can be—must be—responsive to perspectives other than their own, to the point of view of other people and even to the valor found within other creatures and natural things, though the agents' perspectives nevertheless remain theirs, and other kinds remain heterogeneous.

The fundamental principle of value theory is one of conflict among different values, but a conflict that can be mediated through comparison and balance. The fundamental principle of con-tractarian theories is one of conflict of different and opposing interests, but an opposition that can be mediated by contractual commitments. The fundamental principle of practice by rule is that oppositions can be accommodated within an overarching law. In every case, difference and opposition are overcome within a generic form of mediation. In every case, the inexhaustibility of heterogeneous beings is subordinated to a general principle. All these views may be contrasted with a practice based on charity and sacrifice, one that accepts conflicts as expressive of the locality and inexhaustibility of the beings and agents among whom practical life transpires. Here difference is as much an aim of practice as its impetus, and mediation is both local and potentially confining. I add unending interrogation based on locality and inexhaustibility.

We may ask, on the one hand, why ethics requires overarching generality, if not of principle, then of concern. What if, in con-formity to the locality of being, practices were always local, but locality were understood not in terms of scale, but as limitation, including the limitation of limitation? Locality here designates the impossibility of overcoming all differences, for that would be to overcome limitation, but includes possibilities of overcoming any difference, since every difference is limited. Given the locality of practical judgments, there is present in every practical situation

intimacy and collectivity. Ethics, here, is local and intimate, restrictive in its ramifications and in the urgency of the conflicts that
beset it; politics, here, is local and public, collective, concerned
with ramifications of utmost importance to many people and
things. In neither case is unqualified generality intelligible, for
charity and valor are always local and individual. They give rise
to local mediation.

For we may ask, on the other hand, how, given an exquisite
consciousness of sacrifice and failure, we can make any choices,
adjudicate any practical considerations. The answer again is local:
the choices as well as the sacrifices are local, which does not mean
that they are not immensely important and intensely painful, only
that success and failure possess no absolute metric. They belong
to practice; they do not measure practice from without. In this
sense, practice emerges from conflicts of valor and there is no
practical rule or generality that does not harbor sacrifice and
failure.

When we question "everything" we question nothing, for there
are no questions that do not belong somewhere, that do not, in
that setting and moment, presume what is not available to be questioned. The questioning that reason demands therefore requires
time, and "everything" can be questioned only in the sense that
whatever at a given time is available for questioning may be questioned while other questions await a future to which they are relevant. The point, however, is that rational interrogation here faces
itself and its limitations openly rather than awaiting the emergence
of questions blindly. Reason is the exercise of interrogative judgment in relation to itself, thereby to other beings, inexhaustibly
and temporally.

This interrogation, in relation to practice, is rational when it
faces, on the one hand, the inescapability of failure and the inevitability of sacrifice, confronting valor everywhere, and on the other,
the inescapability of practical decision. Practical query is the inevitability of decision meeting the inevitability of catastrophe. The
outcome of such inevitabilities is the conjunction of sacrifice and
of fulfillment that marks rational practice. By way of contrast,
there are forms of practice that proceed without awareness of sacrifice or are alert to few of its forms. Everyday and even philosophical morality are typically restricted to concern for only some of
the things we find around us: other human beings and living crea-

tures, perhaps the living environment. Only through religion have human beings traditionally been able to justify a view of human practices in terms of pervasive charity and sacrifice. Yet religious sacrifice typically seeks propitiation, though charity forbids it, and would diminish the terror of uncontrolled sacrifices by imposing its own. Charity requires and abhors sacrifice. The ancient religions sacrificed charity to sacrifice.

How can practical query be local without losing its plausibility and authority? This is a question of reason in a local practice. One answer is found in Dewey's ethical theory, the locality of problem solving in practice. But Dewey, more by temperament than by theory, does not deeply acknowledge the wounds of sacrifice. Even worse, he does not relate them to heterogeneous valors and perspectives. Yet these shortcomings may not be decisive. For we may ask how different Dewey's theory would be if we introduced within it conflicts of valor and the inevitability of sacrifice.

In Dewey's view, we act responsibly as practical agents experimentally: we try out certain practices to ascertain their results, modifying them as necessary. Such a view of practical experimentation expresses the fact that inexhaustible conditions produce unexpected practical outcomes, and that methods, principles, and rules derived from prior practices have only hypothetical legitimacy. What is missing is the sense that the experimentation is sacrificial, that in practice it cannot avoid failure and destruction. The notion of experimentation prevents us from permanently establishing a particular mode of sacrifice, but it suggests that we may in practice avoid sacrifices altogether. Failure in practice is transmuted into error. Practice is transmuted into inquiry.

Missing here is a sense of catastrophe defined in terms of conflicts of valor, the consciousness that whatever we do, significant harm will be done and that harm is not practically or emotionally neutral, but destructive. When a murderer is put to death we may think of that action as simple retributive justice, but in such a view of retribution, there is no acknowledgment of the importance of the criminal's life and person and a limited sense of the victim's suffering. In an imperfect system of capital punishment, where innocent people are put to death in miscarriages of justice, we trivialize their lives and the crimes of the guilty when we treat such injustices as but a defect in an otherwise legitimate system, as if legitimacy took precedence over valor. When we slaughter a herd of cows because they have contracted an uncontrollable disease, we may think of them entirely in economic terms, so that the only sacrifice is the owner's, to be rectified by compensation. The principle that every action and every being has a value, and that we can accomplish one set of goals only at the expense of another—we must pay for what we accomplish—is a weak approximation to a practical point of view based on valor. What is missing from such a view is charity, a sense of the waste and destruction in every practice.

Dewey's view of practice has been characterized as based on unjustifiable hope.[1] What is misleading about such a characterization lies not in the notion of hope but in its characterization as unjustifiable, thereby opposed to an unjustifiable pessimism and despair. Practical query requires charity and sacrifice. The density and complexity of practical entanglements may plausibly give rise to despair and pessimism, except that such a reaction neglects the new things and works that practice fosters, the accomplishments that sacrifices promote. Achievement as well as destruction belong to every successful practical judgment. To cherish what has been achieved is as important as to cherish what has been lost.

Practical judgment inhabits this darkly entangled region of mediateness, where hope is inextricable from despair, sacrifice from achievement, waste from fulfillment, charity from sacrifice. Practice belongs to this middle ground, not simply by virtue of the mediateness of all human experience and judgment, not simply as judgment, but by virtue of its relation to power and desire, both situated mediately and both reflexively interrogative. Protagoras claims that humanity is the measure. The truth is that there is no measure of human experience and judgment. But practical judgments are required nevertheless. They are required in the form of hope although they cannot avoid failure and sacrifice and although they can be responsible and rational only through a charity that runs so wide and deep that sacrifice haunts human practical experience. The other side of this profound truth, however, is that achievement runs just as wide and deep, that there is an unknown and unsung future to which every practical judgment contributes, a future filled with things to be loved and hated, cherished because we find ourselves among them inexhaustibly.

It follows that there is no rational practice that does not follow Dewey's view of valuation closely in the double sense that, through intelligence, we concern ourselves with means that produce satisfactory ends, in a densely entangled continuum in which everything utilized as a means is also an end and in which every end is itself a means with inexhaustible consequences. The notion of means gives us relevance and power, the conditions of practice. The notion of end gives us valor. I add inexhaustibility and, with it, charity and sacrifice. We can live only if other, inexhaustible things must die. We can sustain ourselves only if other, precious things are destroyed. Our question—practical and ethical—is how we are to mediate among our own valor and the inexhaustible valors of other things. It is a question of how we are to manage the waste that inhabits every practice. Practical judgment becomes query when this question is repeatedly asked, when interrogation is extended to charity pervasively and to the very forms of practice reflexively.

An inescapable tension involving sacrifice exists in practical judgment and query that no practice may resolve. It can be found predominant in many contemporary practical decisions, a result, in part, of the technological instruments that have transformed hitherto vacant possibilities into situations of choice and decision. Virtually all the matters of life and death that are now within our technological means present us with decisions to which ideality is largely irrelevant. For example, should an infant with a defective liver and brain damage have that liver repaired, assuming the infant will never function normally? We may think of such a case as the sacrifice of the child to the welfare of the child's parents and society, but we may also think of it as two forms of charity, in irreconcilable conflict, one based on the fulfillment of natural capacities, the other based on the valor in life itself.

Another unresolvable and controversial issue is that of abortion. In the case of human infants, the inexhaustible valorousness of their personal being is unmistakable and unquestionable. It does not, however, prevent them from abuse. Similar issues arise in relation to older people, at the end of their lives, but frequently with much less force since there is so little we can do to extend their productive lives significantly. In the case of a human fetus, there is no avoiding the infinite gap between valorizing the fetus as potentially a productive and rational human being and the freedom a woman carrying the fetus must have as a practical agent over her own person and body. There is an unresolvable conflict of valors and powers. To say that whenever a fetus becomes a person it gains an absolute right to live, whether at conception or sometime later, substitutes a rule for a decision whose rationality is manifested in the fact that there is no such acceptable rule. There is no ideal resolution of such an issue, only manifold sacrificial judgments.

A fetus may or may not be a human being from conception, but it is a fetus with human potentialities. It is, then, to be cherished, along with human beings but also animals and our inorganic surroundings. To make humanness or rationality, in some of their multiple forms, the distinguishing characteristic of moral worth sacrifices other beings to our species, but even worse, enables us to ignore the claims of other things upon us, as if by being "mere" things, animals, or property they do not merit charity and do not involve us in sacrifice. To the contrary, it is only insofar as we acknowledge their claims upon us and the sacrifices that we impose on them that we can relate to such beings practically and ethically. Practical query is that form of practical judgment that replaces an exchange, a property relation to things, with charity, acknowledging the inevitability of sacrifice due to the inexhaustibility of valor in every being.

It follows that there can be no absolute principles or rules in practical query, for with such rules in the context of inexhaustible charity and sacrifice, we should be quite paralyzed. Principles and rules represent the codification and implementation of established forms of practical judgment in relation to charity and sacrifice, but replace the particularity of valor and respect with generalities. All generalities obscure the dense specificities of sacrifice and valor with a general system of values and rules. All generalities are empty unless permeated by the dense specificities of charity, sacrifice, and valor.

In the case of public practices, it follows that the transmutation of a practice involving personal relations and decisions into a general law or even a sanctioned rule is profoundly different from, and is to be evaluated quite differently from, an individual judgment. Rules and laws are practical judgments that must themselves be subjected to the stern and unremitting interrogation that we give to the practices they sanction, but with the further condition that they have far more sweeping and oppressive consequences. Abortion is a sacrifice of human life, be it actually or potentially human, independently viable or not. But the sacrifices involved in a public prohibition against abortion in terms of human life and fulfillment are in practice far greater and far less controlled. The issue is deeply controversial, and should not cease to be so, for the controversy is the mark of sacrifice, and belongs in the public, political arena. What must be avoided is the sense that the relevant ethical issues can be made clear and uncontroversial, ignoring the inevitability of sacrifice. What cannot be avoided, even in this context of sacrifice and failure, is the necessity of legislation and promulgated rules. We may avoid promulgating one or another rule, but we cannot live in a society without rules. Here, practical query in its public forms of politics and its more personal forms of morality stand in permanent tension.

It follows that in relation to the rules and laws that cannot be avoided in social, public contexts of practical judgment, the practices that are most suspect are those that presuppose consensus. Controversy is the public form of charity and the manifestation of our awareness of sacrifice. Where controversy vanishes, in politics and public morality, practical judgment ceases to be interrogative, and we are in danger of sacrificing reason to routine and custom. Practical query and practical reason always involve, among their concomitants, a terrifying sense of failure and an unending despair at the inadequacy of any practical undertakings. No practical reason can afford to blind itself to the sacrifices practice involves. On the other hand, the profound and exhilarating fact is that even among such sacrifices, practice is capable of goodness.

WASTE

Valor presupposes charity but works through sacrifice. As a consequence, wherever there is practical judgment, even practical query, failure is inescapable. From the standpoint of charity, the form that failure takes is sacrifice. From the standpoint of devalorization, the form that failure takes is waste.

The most prominent forms of waste in contemporary society are the debris that contaminate the landscape as fruits of modern technology. Here waste invades the plenitude of nature as the destructive consequences of human activities. It is to be distinguished, in such cases, from the unavoidable sacrifices required by technological achievements. That is, sacrifice and waste are the destruction that practice requires, the one building upon charity, the other denying it. It is the goal of practical query to avoid waste, organic and inorganic, to transform as much as possible, through charity, the wasteful despoliations and inhibitions of heterogeneous things into valor. It is a goal altogether incompatible with any notion of a higher good to which lesser things may be sacrificed, as if they thereby receive their justification. No metric exists whereby waste can be transformed into sacrifice, only ongoing and incessant practical query is possible, only local mediation and interrogation. The line between sacrifice and waste is thin, and can be drawn in human life only as the result of unceasing practical query.

We may speak, then, of waste not only as the overflow of human activities into sewer pipes and landfills, eventually replenishing and contaminating our natural surroundings, but as the destructiveness that human life through practice wreaks upon itself and its surroundings where reason ceases and devalorization triumphs. And devalorization is inescapable in complex human practices, the wastefulness inherent in rules and ends. Sacrifice cannot exist without failure, without waste, not only because we are not omniscient, all-powerful beings but because mediation is always local. Yet there is, conversely, no assurance that any particular destruction or despoliation is inescapable, certainly not within inexhaustibility and locality, for there are always unrealized alternatives that await disclosure or invention. More important, no meaning can be given in terms of locality and inexhaustibility to total mediation, to the resolution of all conflicts and incompatibilities. The result through practice of heterogeneous conflicts is failure. Where failure belongs to public and political practices, it passes into waste.

It is perhaps more natural to speak of waste in terms of objects and things, the overflow from daily human activities. Yet there is a far deeper and more sobering waste, that of human life itself and of the natural world: diseased and poor, oppressed and hungry, powerless and weak; the vanishing of natural kinds and species. Here some human beings are wasted to the advantage of others, some natural things to the advantage of some human beings. From this vantage point, we can see why the issue of abortion refuses

to be settled: it is an unresolvable issue of sacrifice and waste—
or rather, it is unresolvable by general principle and rule. We are
continually at the margins, of life, politics and morality, of publicness and privateness, of our own and others' bodies. Waste is
unavoidable in any legislation concerning abortion—the waste of
human life, frequently uselessly. All we can do is to seek to trans-
mute waste into valor. All we can do is to engage continually in
practical query, founded on charity and leading to sacrifice.

The question will arise, in the context of controversies involving
abortion and war, economic disparities, poverty and disease, care
for the aged, the destruction of rain forests for agriculture, how
we can tell waste from sacrifice. We cannot expect a resolution of
such difficult practical controversies by rule or law. Rather, rule
and law represent forms of practice that we undertake amid the
controversies. Sacrifice and waste are not distinguishable by principle and rule, or by calculation and measure, but by practical
query based on charity. Only query can with reason judge the
results of prior query. It is said that justice must be tempered by
mercy, though where justice is understood in relation to charity,
mercy stands in no external relation to it. No system of justice
can function automatically however much we would like it to;
every act of justice is a practical judgment, faced with the complexities of the past and the indeterminatenesses of the future. The
likelihood of waste in public practices faces acts of justice no less
than acts of crime. Practical query functions no better under unswerving principles and norms in public than in private undertakings. Generality and universality are determinants that define one
side of the publicness of practical judgments.

Surrounded by the failure that threatens every practical judgment, inexhaustibly, waste is the form in which charity fails to
culminate in sacrifice. But the judgment that waste has replaced
sacrifice has no rule or measure, and belongs to practical query in
its complexities and entanglements. Put another way, repeating
my earlier conclusions, practical query depends on valor and on
charity, and seeks to avoid waste and failure. But amid locality and
inexhaustibility, waste is intermixed inextricably with sacrifice.

Every human life produces waste; every human society wallows
in its wastefulness. To live is wasteful. All we can ask is that valor
and charity lead to so deep and profound an interrogativeness in
practical experience that waste is transformed into sacrifice. This

means that we engage in a practical query that refuses to accept any loss, any violence or destruction, as incidental and insignificant, that affirms the unending project of practical experience to lie in the affirmation and reaffirmation of inexhaustible valor. The inexhaustibility of being lies in practice in the interplay between waste and sacrifice.

PROPERTY

Valor pertains to every being in virtue of its inexhaustibility, the conjunction of charity and sacrifice. Charity and sacrifice, then, pertain to every being from the standpoint of practice. It follows that human beings are not uniquely valorous, though they may be unique in some ways as practical agents and judges, and possess no absolute privilege in relation to other beings. Not only are human beings material things in certain respects, not absolutely different from other things, but things are inexhaustible and valorous.

The question to which we come is whether there is any dominion of human beings over nature that justifies treating things as merely property, to be disposed of as we wish. Does the importance of human beings in relation to practical judgment bestow on us singular authority? Is there a relation of property that entitles the owner to neglect charity, that eliminates the distinction between sacrifice and waste?

The issue of property is predominantly political, as in the long run are most practical concerns, even those that appear to be ethical, since it is a question of how differential relations of power and implementation are to be established within collective milieux. Yet the political side of property, apparently an issue of power, has not traditionally been defined without ethical qualifications. In Locke's words: "though man in that state [of nature] have an uncontrollable liberty to dispose of his person or possessions, yet he has not liberty to destroy himself, or so much as any creature in his possession, but where some nobler use than its bare preservation calls for it."[2]

Several features of Locke's view of the relation of persons to things are worth noticing. The "uncontrollable liberty" is not absolute or unrestricted, but is restricted to conformity with a nobler use. Human beings have no absolute right over themselves or any other creatures, even any possession, no absolute or arbitrary right. Locke's view manifests, at least in this instance, a strong sense of charity and a rejection of the contemporary view, found in so much post-Kantian thought, that there is an absolute difference between persons and things. The error lies on both sides: human beings are like things in many ways, complexly entangled; on the other side, things are not "mere" things, to be treated arbitrarily or with contempt. No one has any absolute right to treat any thing with disrespect, arbitrarily. In such terms, we are repeating the principle of charity in relation to practical judgment. Every treatment of every creature or being is a practical judgment, subject to criticism and validation, and there is no relation of agents to their practices that is not subject to such criticism. Without charity, we cannot validate a practical judgment; without charity, we cannot engage in practical query; without charity heterogeneity produces waste. With charity, practical judgment always involves sacrifice.

The first question of property for Locke is "how men might come to have a property in several parts of that which God gave to mankind in common?"[3] for there appears to be no differential relation of human beings to things under a cosmic perspective. Locke accepts a holistic divine or cosmic perspective. The fact, however, is that human beings, individually and collectively, are related differentially and locally to other human beings and to their surroundings, not only by differences in labor, but by differences in history, proximity, and mutual influence. Locke begins with holism and commonality, and must then find differences. If we begin with mediateness, then the first principle of practice, in relation to surrounding things, is that practical agents are situated differentially as well as commonly within their milieux, some more individual, some more collective, but differentiated as well as joined by history, capacities, labor, law, principle, power, and desire. Human beings are born into heterogeneous milieux, and there is no locale in common, no world in which all play a communal role. Human beings possess heterogeneous powers, desires, and histories—though each of these is shared by some other human beings.

Inexhaustibility entails that there is valor inherent in every being, including those that we come upon in the wilds of nature, those that surround us in our everyday activities, and those that we claim as property. There is, concerning all these relations, testimony in common experience that manifests an acute awareness of charity and sacrifice. Such awareness is not universal, but universality does not pertain to any ethics, to any practical judgment. To the contrary, all these examples are controversial, marking their practical relevance.

Every society, if it can afford it, sets aside natural areas for protection, sometimes entirely undeveloped, sometimes made accessible to human participation: national parks, animal sanctuaries, beaches, and forests. The argument for such protection is sometimes based on the enrichment of human life that such protected areas provide. Yet even where the areas are kept unspoiled, there is a sense of rightness. There is a sense that natural beings have a "right" to their place in things, and that they may be despoiled only under a higher purpose. There is also the sense that natural things possess inexhaustible potentialities for enriching natural and human milieux, that despoliation is wasteful.

The former reason is Locke's, and it is based on the principle that all things are the property of God, therefore present under a divine purpose and not to be arbitrarily despoiled. If there is justice in the principle that ethics is founded on divine order, it is not that ethical principles are manifestations of a divine will or decree, but that divine immanence is a legitimation of inexhaustible valor. What the examples of protection show, whether of parks or animals, or areas in which both flourish, is that valor can be acknowledged in all things, that every being can be cherished, even without divine sanction.

The second reason is present in the conviction that we destroy natural species of animals and plants at our peril, not only because they may be useful to human beings in unexpected ways, but also because they contain rich potentialities of life that we neglect in their wanton destruction. We destroy species of plants and animals, also natural habitats, we level mountains and pollute lakes and rivers, not only to the detriment of future human generations, but also to the detriment of those beings themselves and their surroundings, disregarding their inexhaustible valor. The potential usefulness of natural beings, inorganic and organic, is an application of their far more generic inexhaustibility. The reason why we must not blindly destroy what surrounds us is that we make the world a meaner place. Yet practice cannot avoid despoliation and destruction; it can only replace blindness with charity and replace waste with an inexhaustible awareness of sacrifice.

Many people share a reverence and love for our natural surroundings, for natural environments and living creatures. Few extend this care to livestock animals. Fewer have taken up the banners for the routine products of our technological civilization—knickknacks and memorabilia, plastic containers and other detritus. Yet there are manifestations in even our industrial culture, not merely among an artistic elite, of the inexhaustible potentialities inherent in every created thing, however mediocre. The primary form this takes is economic: something that someone has paid good money for, someone else will also. Everything must have some pecuniary value, and, in garage sales and flea markets, we see the economic form of charity at work. Virtually every item of property is attractive to someone; to discard it is wasteful; nothing need be wasted; someone can find a use for anything.

A tension exists in an industrial society between the scavenging of every thing that might produce a profit, the preservation of items for sale that appear to offer no benefit to human life, but which are bought and preserved, sometimes later sold to someone else who will cherish and preserve them, and the scavenging of places and items of great immediate value that can be realized only through massive destruction. An industrial society recycles and destroys, sometimes demolishing the most important items— buildings and ways of life—while preserving the most trivial. There is waste in both practices. But the irrationality of the practices does not obscure that they contain a far-reaching and profound fascination if not reverence for virtually anything in our surroundings.

An example that seems to violate charity is that of entirely consumable items. Setting items of food aside, for the moment, since they involve the preservation of human life, we may consider plastic knives and forks, package wrappings. Are there not present in every society material items, produced in immense quantity in industrial societies, that exist to be destroyed? Are there not items that are not only consumed, but also reproduced so often that there is nothing within any that cannot be replaced by a substitute? Are there not, then, in an industrial society, items that inhabit a system of exchange equivalents with virtually no surplus?

One can of tomato soup is indistinguishable from another. Yet manufacturers of even the most trivial and repetitive items constantly tell us that they are "new and improved," not simply to tell us that they will be more useful—that would be unlikely in the case of soup and crackers—but that they are distinctive and important. Even from a practical point of view, the capacity of a product to be different marks a distinctiveness essential to its inexhaustibility. Put another way, certain industrial products are marked less by individual variations and more by variations in type. But while there is no sacredness to individuality among cans and forks any more than among the grains of sand on a beach, there are still immense variations among products and beaches. Heterogeneity does not come in pre-established containers.

Where we find the distinctiveness and inexhaustibility of even ordinary products displayed is less in our everyday practical activities and more in art. Twentieth-century art transmutes ordinary products into works upon which we gaze with attention and fascination. Art manifests inexhaustibility. It manifests its own but also the inexhaustibility of any being upon which it showers its attention. And it may bestow its attention upon anything whatever in human experience, upon the most ordinary utensils and products including cans of soup, frequently with minimal artistic modification. What such art shows is that even the most typical item has its own valor, that although we may not cherish it, we might, and that we must be conscious that there is a far-reaching sacrifice in even the disposition of the most disposable products.

It does not follow that because every being has valor, because we cherish it, we may not sacrifice it. What we should not do is waste it, harm or destroy it without charity. In the dense, specific entanglements of practice, we cannot avoid sacrifices, and to cherish a carrot cannot entail that we should not eat it or any food, for we would then sacrifice ourselves, and that is no more justifiable. The notion of cherishing a carrot sounds bizarre because we so typically reject any intimate relationship to what we must destroy: we cannot seem to tolerate an ethics of sacrifice. Those with the deepest reverence for other creatures and for nature are frequently those who would most avoid a sense of sacrifice, as if there were some level of being that we could despoil and could convert to our uses without such sacrifices.

But it is impossible to live and to act without sacrifice, without using other human beings and things. And it is impossible—incompatible with charity and inexhaustibility—to live with confident distinctions and rules as to which sacrifices are acceptable and which are not. Rather, and such an attitude can be found in many human cultures, charity requires that we appreciate and respect the things that we turn to our uses, requires that we do not trivialize them under rules that obscure their valors. Here, gardeners, certain farmers, some people who raise animals for food, do so not with indifference but with love. County fairs celebrate the remarkable creatures and works that can be contrived in rapport with nature—huge tomatoes and distinctive sows. These are frequently celebrated, not for their profitability, but for their uniqueness. Many people in non-industrial societies make sacrifices to their gods for the abundance of the harvest and the hunt, in which they express the sense of sacrifice that life entails. But it is not, in either case here, a sense of sacrifice that entails despair or misery.

Another point may need emphasizing. We may produce industrial and agricultural products that are indistinguishable from each other—at least in the respects we consider relevant. They are in this respect quite distinguishable from other products, natural or hand-made, for many industrial products are quite distinctive. Nevertheless, the sacrifice of one carrot to a human meal is quite different from the sacrifice of an entire species of carrot or of the tropical rain forest. The one is replaceable, not simply in human life, but because its differences have been diminished by cultivation. Irreplaceability can be enhanced but can also be diminished by human practices. Valor and charity require us to recognize and affirm the differences that involve distinctiveness and uniqueness. Where human cultivation produces greater differences, enhances singularity and uniqueness, these become as precious and valorous as are less contrived, natural differences: they move in the direction of art. What is involved is inexhaustibility, not naturalness. What is cherished is the inexhaustibility in any being, but charity is not incompatible with sacrifice and cannot preempt it. It is rather incompatible with waste, with despoliations blind to valor, blind to heterogeneity. What charity demands is a profound concern with the distinctiveness and importance of what we find around us, with the distinctiveness of certain kinds of beings even where the individual examples of that kind are largely indistinguishable.

I have noted signs of charity in our reverence for our natural surroundings and for ordinary, everyday objects that we pass on to others because we respect them even if we no longer need them. I have noted stronger and more generic signs of charity in art, for art manifests inexhaustibility in relation to everything around it. Other recurrent signs may assist us to establish images whereby we may understand the nature of sacrifice. One example is found in young children, but it may last for many years, in some cases into adulthood. I am speaking of what are referred to as "security objects": teddy bears, other stuffed animals, crib blankets. These are ordinary objects that take on remarkable personalities and characters, altogether magical powers. Magical powers in general are manifestations of charity at work, a sign of inexhaustibility in the things that possess them. Children recognize these magical powers, even in industrial societies; they recognize that the most ordinary objects possess an inexhaustible plenitude of potentialities. Adults frequently are able to recognize such magical powers only in the presence of young children.

We may prefer to think that the attachment of the child to its blanket is a displaced affect from a more suitable object of desire, be it bodily or sexual. We may prefer instead to think that the magical powers belong not to teddy bears and stuffed elephants but to the human imagination in play. But even these interpretations manifest the inexhaustibility and consequent charity that we sense in relation to every being to which we pay close enough attention. This charity becomes art when we realize that anything given this kind of attention turns into an aesthetic object. Such an object is inexhaustible in its complex affinities and disparities.

Winnie-the-Pooh is a stuffed bear with a magical personality. Suppose Pooh had a stuffed hippopotamus with its own magical personality. Suppose that hippopotamus lived in a lake in a dresser drawer, a magical lake that was home to hippopotamuses and elephants. In this fantasy we see charity at work in the imagination of play. What it signifies is the inexhaustibility of any being and the charity that recognizes that inexhaustibility. What we may now consider in the same context is the nature of sacrifice.

Children eventually outgrow their stuffed animals and blankets. They do so while still children, and their embarrassment at their excess of charity, their surplus attachments, outweighs recognition that when things matter inexhaustibly, they do matter. Shall Pooh be cast into the trash, shall he be given to another child, or shall he be given a special place for as long as possible? The trash is a common choice, but it is a denial of a genuine attachment. The bear is too bedraggled to be given to another child, who would not in any case love him as his owner did. The special place manifests charity and love, but it is embarrassing and nostalgic. It is the only form of preservation that celebrates the plenitude and charity that constitutes the practical situation. But it is not always the only or only right thing to do, for example, where one's life is badly cluttered.

So we make the sacrifice; but it will be acceptable in later life only if we know that it is a sacrifice, if Pooh is given a state funeral, if there is pomp and circumstance that accommodates grief—yes, grief at the demise of a beloved toy. Without grief, there is no sacrifice, merely wasteful destruction. With grief, we go on to live our lives with the fullness of cherished memories that we need not be ashamed of.

To such experiences, a morality of law or even of general welfare can bring very little, for neither contains an adequate sense of charity or sacrifice. Surrounded by starvation and misery, such experiences seem immoral. Yet we can be within a moral-practical situation only if things matter, not merely their measures. Without charity, there can be no understanding of practical judgment. With charity, we recognize the inexhaustible promise of every being and the inexhaustible sacrifices that life requires.

CHARITY TOWARD ANIMALS

If every being is inexhaustible and valorous, and merits charity, are we faced with the insurmountable difficulty of being unable to make the vital distinctions necessary to practical judgment? We do, after all, feed grain to livestock and utilize livestock for our sustenance? How can we justify doing so?[4] Animals are compelling examples of the terrible sacrifices people have imposed on each other and other creatures in their ordinary practices and in response to natural terrors before unknown dangers. What we are faced with is the importance of animals as means to human life joined with the imperative that they, along with every being, are to be cherished inexhaustibly.

What seems to be required is a general argument that establishes the rights of all living creatures to freedom from suffering and to as much life and enjoyment as can be provided.[5] Yet why should anyone believe that such an argument might be forthcoming? We may have reservations about the efficacy of ethical arguments in relation to practical judgments and that unanimity is an intelligible ideal in practice. Rather, in relation to such complex matters as the use of animals for experimentation and as food, controversy rather than agreement manifests reason. Furthermore, the issues may not be ethical but political in the sense that there is no ideal resolution possible of conflicts involving sacrifice, no precise distinctions and general principles, only tenuous and temporary reconciliations on a scale of unsurpassed importance.

We are not inclined to sacrifice "lesser" humans to "higher" humans, younger to older, less intelligent to more intelligent. To the contrary, a nurturing, caretaker relation is imposed in practice upon more powerful and privileged agents, frequently flouted in fact but relevant nevertheless throughout human practical experience. Human beings are not all the same. Yet it does not follow that they are not to be treated as equal in relation to law or general principle, that sacrifices may be imposed upon such unequals without extraordinary justifications.

Similarly, however, even major inequalities among human beings and between human beings and animals do not entail disparity of treatment with respect to life, enjoyment, and suffering.[6] Even this account is somewhat strained, since differential treatment is typical in human experience, involving other people, animals, and things. What is crucial are the kinds of inequalities and treatments. Infants require a nurturing relation in which they are treated with greater care and concern than adults. Here inequalities of circumstance and condition entail inequalities of treatment. Yet children are not less human, do not have less moral weight, both because of their open future and their vulnerabilities. Why may we not argue in the same terms that animals in our care require a more strenuous rather than a less committed charity in virtue of our power over them?

If the things we own are valorous, does it follow that we may not use them, that they may not be sacrificed? That would be wasteful of our own capacities for life and experience. What is essential is that charity entails sacrifice, that there is no practical judgment without it, but that sacrifice presupposes charity. Charity is the sensitivity that makes it possible to transform narrow practical judgments into query, waste into sacrifice. What charity entails is a deep and unending concern for the beings that surround us, a deep and abiding sensitivity to their inexhaustible natures and potentialities. Practical query always leads to principle and rule, but no path exists to such generality and validation is inexhaustibly tempered and enriched by charity.

Some animals are highly conscious, and to claim that they cannot experience pain and enjoyment is indefensible. The speciesism here is not simply moral self-justification, but is the self-aggrandizement of overweening arrogance, that all important experiential and valorous qualities belong to human beings. Reason, we say, is found in language; animals are not capable of linguistic reason. But they have distinctive personalities, are self-directed, endure and survive, respond emotionally and affectively, are sensitive and able to learn. People who live with pets have no doubt about differences in their personalities and characters, responsiveness and intelligence. An animal is not replaceable by another, not as a pet, without inexhaustible surplus. Animals are not rationally equivalent to each other, not in domesticity and not in the wild, no more than are human beings.

We are considering so-called higher animals, but the argument is not that because such animals resemble human beings they have moral rights absent in other animals. It is rather than we incur charitable concerns toward them in virtue of the special forms of valor they possess, their heterogeneities, and different concerns toward other creatures, organic and inorganic. Some creatures, like ants, are neither self-aware nor unique: their valor lies more in their collectivity than their individuality. Even so, wanton destruction of an ant, pulling wings off flies, is unethical because of its wantonness. Even ants and flies have a right to live, to the extent that such life can be lived without conflict with other powers. Even a rock has a right to preservation, protection against abuse, though it cannot experience its own destruction. If there must be sacrifice, it must be accompanied by charity; otherwise it is blind and heedless, empty waste.

In the ways many people treat their pets, naming them, caring for them, sharing life together, nurturing them and protecting them against pain and suffering, allowing them as much freedom and joy as possible, we may discern an important example of charity in an established form of life. Yet there is no rule-governed, principled, and compelling argument to justify such a treatment or sharp distinction between creatures that merit such treatments and those that may be used if not abused. No argument is needed or possible beyond that based on inexhaustible valor. Every being, every creature, merits charity. But there is no avoiding sacrifice. Rather, what we strive for in practical query, ethically but especially politically, is to diminish the catastrophic nature of such sacrifices. We can do so in our homes, among our pets, but not always in our forests and parks, and not for all animals, especially in the wild. We cannot avoid catastrophic sacrifices of human beings in war, in prisons, even in city streets. We cannot avoid considering our limitations as practical agents, what is and is not in our power, when we undertake practical judgment and query. We cannot avoid questions of power as well as of desire.

It is inevitable that we should come to questions of vegetarianism, since they inhabit the important middle ground between our cherished pets and our affinities with nature, the ground on which we exercise our powers and impose dominations because our lives are at stake. Other important questions concern the use of animals for human betterment, as beasts of burden but also in experimentation—medical, biological, and psychological. How far may our charity toward other creatures take us, to what extent may we reduce the arbitrariness of our sacrifices of them?

Human beings need to eat to live, but they may be able to live well without eating meat, and eating meat may cause them harm. Certainly without eating plants and their fruits, humans could not survive for very long. Is vegetarianism the only ethical position that follows from charity toward animals? What of a similar charity toward plants and their fruits? Moreover, though it is by no means a compelling consideration, animals are frequently not as scrupulous about the valor of other animals, and prey upon them. We may reply that it does not follow that we should be bound by such natural depredations, that we are not forced to imitate the less charitable side of nature, but there is certainly an affinity between our charity toward natural things and our admiration for their workings. One answer is that although animals engage in practical judgments, they are not capable of profound or far-reaching practical query. They do not interrogate their own practices inexhaustibly, though they are themselves inexhaustible. Another response is that certain predators are essential to maintaining the ecological diversity of a habitat, which would otherwise be overrun by a small number of species.

So far as we know, plants are not conscious of their destruction, many would die in any case with the onset of inclement weather, and they apparently do not suffer. But if they did suffer, and if they were conscious of their impending destruction—made all the worse by their lack of mobility, waiting impotently for their doom—then we would have to treat them differently. Their uniqueness and irreplaceability are relevant also, and their capacities for life. We might have to sacrifice them, for sacrifice is unavoidable, but charity demands that we pay close attention to their natures. Charity requires that we pay close and unstinting attention to the things that surround us.

Yet we frequently do the opposite. We arrange for the slaughter of animals for food, hidden from public gaze, perhaps because we cannot tolerate the enormities of what is required to satisfy our hunger. This practice is not very different from the execution of criminals behind closed bars, largely in secret, though there have been, in other times, great crowds who enjoyed the spectacle of a public execution. Even so, however, in the latter case, there was the celebration of the criminal and of the criminal act, that they should be publicized with such fanfare and excitement. These too are forms of charity and sacrifice.

Human beings cannot live without sacrificing some of their natural surroundings to their own survival. What is required by charity is open affirmation of the nature of sacrifice and, consequently, diminution of sacrifice where possible, and judgment of it somehow, but always as much as possible avoidance of waste. Here it becomes necessary to recognize genuine costs and conditions. It takes twenty to thirty pounds of grain to produce a pound of beef, but the latter is not that many times as nourishing, and may be destructive to our health. We could eat meat that was not as costly in grain; we could eat leaner meats that would be better for us. We could eat as little meat as possible. We might avoid meat altogether.

Some forms of meat and fish are not produced by cultivation

but by hunting and fishing. Some people are more tolerant of the human use of cultivated creatures than of creatures in the wild—the former are thought to have no other destiny, are cultivated as fodder. But such cultivation obscures the fact that it is living creatures, with sensibilities and awareness, that are so cultivated, as if they were unfeeling forms of nourishment. Emphasis on natural foods and life tends to obscure the fact that what must be destroyed in natural things—although that destruction may be better for us—are creatures that have lives and fulfillments of their own. Yet how relevant is it that some animals are cultivated by human beings for food while others live in the wild? How reprehensible is it that wild creatures are hunted by human beings, sometimes merely for sport, while domestic animals are raised for food and slaughtered routinely?

Vegetarianism is the analogue of pacifism, an ideal ethical practice that we may hope would be effective in an ideal world, a kingdom of ends, but which, in a world of conflict and injustice, cannot always be sustained. In the latter case, we may be attacked by an imperial power or may be called to battle to defend our friends who are being treated harshly and unjustly. In the former case, we might find that vegetable protein is not entirely satisfactory, especially for children, that to live well we must supplement a vegetarian diet with small amounts of meat in addition to milk and eggs. Alternatively, we may be able to develop biological techniques that would make the slaughter of animals unnecessary. Pacifism and vegetarianism interrogate the norms of everyday activities and judgments in far-reaching ways, to the point where we may be led to reconsider our entire relation to politics on the one hand, to living creatures on the other.

A role exists for ideals that human life and practice cannot do without, a role that preserves their ideality not so much in opposition to reality and practicality, as if ideals were luxuries we might relinquish, but one essential to practical judgment. These ideals are not a touchstone against which practical judgments are measured, always falling short, but are a form of interrogation to which practical judgments are submitted. The mistake lies in thinking that such ideals are superfluous in relation to practical judgment when in fact they are one of the most powerful forms of interrogation. These ideals, so long as they do not become entrenched rules, express a profound awareness of valor.

Practical query depends on the presence of such ideals because they embody forms of interrogation and charity that cannot otherwise be expressed—for example, that we might be able to treat all living creatures, all natural things, with compassion, that we might be able to establish an enduring and positive peace. That we cannot does not mean that we should not—or, rather, we should not regard failing to realize such ideals as a necessary form of failure to the point where we abandon the charity embodied in the ideals. A powerful example is the ideal of life that governs discussions of capital punishment, pro and con. A "realistic" politics is frequently no politics at all, or political query, since it refuses to entertain the ideals that define the possibility of practical reason.

What strenuous vegetarianism makes us consider, where we have not already considered it, is that we frequently mistreat animals and other living creatures unnecessarily, wastefully, that we ignore their sensitivities and sufferings, their lives and joys, and treat them as if they were insensible things. Moreover, inorganic things are sometimes treated with greater sensitivity than are animals raised for food. By a strenuous vegetarianism I mean one that is loud and strident, one that has as little chance of becoming a norm as world-wide abolition of capital punishment. What abolitionism makes us aware of is that there is no practice without sacrifice of something valorous, but even more, that life is one of the prominent forms of valor, one we share because we are alive.

I have emphasized the question of the use of animals for food. A more complex question is the use of animals in medical experimentation. Let us assume—it is far from settled conclusively—that many human lives are saved through experimentation on animals. The question is whether any magnitude whatever of animal suffering and abuse may be justified by the saving of a single human life—or two or three—or simply to detect potential allergic reactions. At what point may we say, as thousands of dogs and cats, rabbits and mice, are made to suffer, that tests for allergy, for minor toxic reactions to cosmetics, are unjustified? I do not know the answer to such a question or even how to determine a principled answer. I do know that the question is important from the standpoint of charity. Animals, like all things, partake of an inexhaustible plenitude of possibilities of fulfillment and valor. To ignore such a plenitude is outright lack of charity. To accept it, however, is not to abolish all experimentation, but to seek to reconcile the conflicting claims of the different creatures involved, just as we seek to reconcile the claims of different human beings where similar differences are involved. Such a reconciliation cannot be defined by either unswerving principles or unchallengeable distinctions, but must remain open unceasingly to further interrogation—to far-reaching and potentially radical interrogations.

Another factor may be considered, marked by the difference between a rational practice and moral legislation. To enact a law, to promulgate a principle, is quite different from a particular practical judgment, even practical query, to the extent that it imposes a form of domination over other human beings who may differ. I am concerned here with areas of overlap between political and ethical determinations. Great moral conviction does not automatically justify moral legislation, in part because conviction frequently masks dogmatism and lack of charity, in part because legislation imposes domination on others' practices, frequently wastefully and uncharitably. Human beings are, however imperfect, in charge of their own destinies as practical agents. Charity toward them entails permitting, even encouraging, them to make their own practical decisions. Transition from childhood to adulthood is marked profoundly by the realization that we can stand in a caretaker, nurturing relation to other practical agents only so far, and that they must make their own decisions even where we disagree with them. Charity requires us, in recognition of the capacities and powers of other human beings in relation to our own, to temper a strong caretaker relation with a more respectful and cherishing concern.

With respect to children and animals, however, and many of the ordinary things that surround us, we are unavoidably in a caretaker relation, one that, moreover, constantly becomes more acute with increases in technological powers. These creatures and things cannot take full responsibility for themselves where we have dominion over them; we must therefore treat them even more charitably. We come to one of the very few practical principles that seem to me inescapable: that where power over other beings is most explicit, charity entails that we as much as possible avoid sacrificing them to our own interests and values. Such a sacrifice is blind to the valor of other beings and devoid of charity. There is no way around the qualification "as much as possible"; nor does it follow that we may not slaughter animals for food or use them in experiments. What follows is that we accept the obligation to respect the combination of vulnerability and valor that marks their relation to us. We undertake greater responsibilities in relation to beings under our dominion than in relation to beings who are our equals in power and authority. Charity can, in relation to other human beings and to animals in the wild, entail respect for their way of life. Charity in relation to vulnerable beings in our care forbids us to abuse them.

What pertains to practical query, then, is not so much the decisions and judgments to which we come, the arguments we accept and the principles we impose, but the interrogative processes in which desire, power, valor, and charity work together in practical judgment. Here, because desires vary, and conditions of power are unstable, because there are incommensurate differences in being and locality, there will be frequent disagreement. But disagreement does not manifest failure in practical query: it may rather express the presence of query itself. There would be no need for practical query in relation to animals if our relation to them were not divided into conflicting and even antagonistic orientations.

Our humanity, practical and even theoretical, is defined by our relations to animals, practical and theoretical, as well as by our other relations. How we understand ourselves is a function of how we understand our affinities and differences with other creatures. How we relate to ourselves practically is a function of how we treat other creatures. We find here a practical query that accepts the inexhaustible range of interrogations inherent in charity and the unavoidability of sacrifice.

CHARITY AND HUMAN BEING

The fundamental questions of practical judgment are: What kinds of beings are we involved with in practice, including ourselves? What powers are deployed in this relation? How is this relation characterized by desire? What are the relevant circumstances and conditions of this relation? What shall we do? The pervasive condition in all these questions is that of mediateness. We undertake practical judgments within established relations involving other beings; practice engenders other such relations. The identities and qualities of the beings involved, including ourselves, are frequently deeply influenced by our practices, including influences we can neither intend nor foretell.

In the case of inorganic beings and perhaps less self-conscious forms of life, our relations are characterized by power and desire with little judgmental reciprocity. Whatever reflexive interrogativeness is involved in our practical determinations toward lawns and beetles is probably embodied in our own charitableness and sense of sacrifice. Even in relation to animals like dogs and cats, apes and porpoises, where understanding and feeling are unmistakable, where caring and reciprocity are strong, and where our practical judgments are responded to with practical judgments in return, and conversely, the capacity of such animals to respond to practical query by practical query is constrained by language and culture. A double negation follows of that aspect of practical query relative to which our judgments are tempered by the judgments of others because we can be confident that, though they differ profoundly with us, they have engaged in as complex and self-critical interrogations as we have ourselves. Against most of the Western tradition, charity entails that in such cases we take on a greater obligation to fulfill the double role of agent and critic. Nevertheless, many relations with other forms of life have traditionally been founded predominantly on power and desire—on our own desires and powers insofar as we can interrogate and influence them; on the powers and desires of other beings insofar as they invade our lives and territories, and resist our own powers and desires. At best, we may share the desires and powers of other creatures through imaginative affinities.

In the case of other human beings, however, we are faced not only with power and influence in relation to desire and charity, but also with practical agents who share and oppose our powers, but whose explicit viewpoints, understandings, and practices are unmistakably different from our own. Charity, in relation to other human beings, takes on quite different qualities and characteristics to the extent that we no longer simply observe other people or are present to them, but are challenged, opposed, or supported by them. Amid the many supportive and communal activities in human social experience there is the continuing experience of disagreement concerning the ideals and activities that are relevant to rational practice—not merely over preferences and strategies, and not merely by those we regard with loathing and contempt, but by people we have to respect as much as we respect ourselves, though we may not love them. There is, here, in relation to human liberation, a form of interrogation and charity that is not altogether distinct from the sensitive responses of animals to us and the resistances of things to our powers.[7] Heterogeneity pervades human life and judgment.

In the case of practical judgment, specifically in relation to other practical agents, there are multifarious forms of resistance inherent in plenitude and inexhaustibility, but there is a special resistance as a consequence of the fact that the other beings engage themselves in practical judgments. Not only are we subject to other agents' activities and powers, but our powers and judgments are subject to further interrogation and judgment. Our judgments and interrogations are deeply affected by the judgments of other people. This is particularly significant where these other people are objects of our desires and powers, where we seek to act among them and upon them.

It follows that practical judgment and query, where other human beings are involved, include very different forms of interrogation from practical judgments where we act upon other beings and creatures who, though they may be very powerful as well as resistant in certain contexts, are not as reflexively critical as other people, at least not explicitly and unmistakably so. Involved is a transformation of the nature and depth of query, the interposition of new and more profound forms of interrogation and validation. This is true even where the forms of power and resistance are asymmetric, for in the judgmental responses of other people there lie irresistible forms of interrogation and validation. Practice depends on the judgments of other people, as objects and as judges themselves. Practice also depends on our responses to their responses, and conversely. In this sense, practice is deeply semasic, judgment turning back endlessly on judgment. Practically speaking, this means that other people make judgments for themselves even as those judgments deeply affect us.

It follows that practical judgment is subject, in its consequences and activities, to the judgments of others, not merely as outcomes, but as reflexive interrogations. What others do and what their judgments mean and involve become ingredients of practical interrogation. In practical query, other people play roles different from the those played by other beings, even other living creatures.

Though it would be an exaggeration to overlook the practical judgments of animals in relation to human beings—the fact, for example, that pets provide peace of mind and are an antidote to stress for many people—animals do not seem to engage in practical query in relation to our own practical query. Yet they may be responsive to our subtle and hidden needs and emotions as no human beings can be, even we ourselves, and may care for us deeply, even sacrificing their lives for us.

It follows that practical query in relation to animals and other natural beings is, for human beings at least, in a predominantly caretaker relation. The greater the powers of humans over their environments, the stronger is the claim of the valorous beings in those environments upon our charity. The weaker the powers of human beings, of course, the weaker are these claims, though they cannot be negligible. Wild animals in their own habitats, if remote from human activities, exercise their powers without human concerns or invasions. Nevertheless, we must be alert to how far-reaching contemporary industry and technology make human invasions, how indirectly or inadvertently most habitats and creatures are vulnerable to influence by human practices. It follows that we abuse our caretaker relation if we suppose that we can know with assurance what is good for other creatures.

Even if we are in a caretaker relation with other human beings, as with children, however, such relations are overshadowed by the far more important semasic relations of judgment to judgment, query to query, potential or actual. Other human beings make our own rationality apparent by interrogating it rationally; in this sense they fulfill and challenge our judgments with their own. This reflexive relation of practice to practice, desire to desire, that can be found primarily among human beings is the most important feature of practical reason.

Charity in relation to oppressed living creatures entails a rich sensitivity to valor and to sacrifice. Charity in relation to oppressed human beings also entails the interrogation of practical reason itself, of practical reason's oppressiveness. We are not the measures of our own deeds; nor is there any absolute measure. It follows that what others think and do in relation to our practical judgments is as important a practical response as any we can make and is important reflexively to our own practical judgments.

One implication of the pervasiveness of judgment and power

is that practical query is situated in contexts of oppression and liberation. The exercise of power, however dispersed, is always oppressive, and resistance to power is always a challenge to any form of practical query. Practical query, especially those forms that we think of as ethical and political, always transpires within unbalanced contexts of power and desire. Liberation is the resistance present within overt practical query.

Many of these matters have been discussed in prominent ways in recent feminist literature that addresses questions of liberation in domestic as well as public terms. The overriding concern for feminists is whether the majority of human beings—female adults and children of both sexes—have been systematically excluded from centers of power as agents and systematically included as primary objects of desire—frequently sexual but also economic and domestic. Knowledge, power, and desire are inseparably joined in modern society in relation to sexuality.[8] From a strongly feminist point of view, the oppression of women takes precedence over all practical concerns other than, and inseparable from, the future of humanity. Women are virtually universally oppressed without exception, in large and small ways. The oppressions range from being underpaid for equivalent work, being objects of sexual manipulation and abuse, and possessing incomplete rights to money and property in industrial societies, to being unable to receive equivalent educations and make personal decisions in poorer countries, to having much shorter life spans as a consequence of inadequate health care in relation to their productive and child-bearing roles in still poorer countries. These largely political oppressions—in the sense of scale and importance—have domestic counterparts. Women and children are frequently regarded as property, without the qualifications charity and valor impose on the abuse of property.

But women and children are not property; they are practical agents, incipient or actual, with negligible or significant authority over their own decisions. Query entails that no social or cultural forms of relation and status be taken as adequate of themselves, nor permanently valid, but that they be subjected continuously to strenuous criticism, interrogation, and re-validation. Here feminism plays an essential practical role of resistance to forms of sexual domination that calls established forms of practice, public and private, to account. If we add that the oppression of women is not separate from other forms of oppression and subjugation, that the institutional powers that manufacture desire do so in ways that produce conformity and ensure their own perpetuation, not least by capturing the wills and emotions of human beings, then a discourse of sexual liberation is a discourse of human and natural liberation.

Many men respond to feminist criticisms by claiming that men are also oppressed. Some women respond to feminist criticisms by claiming to prefer the advantages that accompany the subjugation of women in affluent democratic societies, for example, that women may not be required to compete in the public world or to go to war. Both responses are important, though they lack the sensibility that they demand from their opponents: a sensitivity to subjugated voices. When we speak for others in a caretaker relation we subjugate them just as effectively as and sometimes even more deeply than when we force them into acts against their will. That practical query always works in terms of liberation reflects the inescapable condition that practice begins and ends within mediate practical conditions, including the implications and ramifications of prior workings of desire and power. We must heed subjugated voices because subjugation as well as resistance belong to every context of practice and power.

The golden rule is that we should act toward others as we would have them act toward us. Missing is the asymmetry of established powers and practices, that in situations of power and desire are patterns of domination and oppression. Thus, not everyone and not everything can reciprocate equivalently, for they may be both vulnerable and ineffective. Part of what is involved is the asymmetry and lack of reciprocity in a caretaker relation. But there is the more important point that what we would have others do presupposes that we may anticipate it imaginatively and emotionally. We presuppose that differences among practical agents are not so extreme and profound that we cannot anticipate their judgments. It follows that we must differentiate our practices toward other people in two important ways: one in relation to our charitability; the other in relation to their heterogeneous powers and voices. Where we can, we must let others speak for themselves, in their own voices, and struggle to understand them. And they must, and will, demand that right for themselves. Reason as well as charity demand it. Where we cannot, or where their voices are dim, we must care for them charitably. But in both cases, the forms of charity are local, for individual voices and vulnerabilities are not commonly shared, and the assumption that there is such sharing and commonality tends to blind us to relevant differences.

Charity requires that we heed the judgments of other people, but power and resistance will make us do so in any case. Practical judgments are validated by their consequences, but these consequences include the practical judgments of others. In this way, practical query includes within its purview not only what happens to others as a result of its practices, but others' subsequent practical judgments. Practical judgments possess no intrinsic privacy or uniqueness, no intrinsic authority owned by individuals over the validation of their practices. Even where others are very different from us, their judgments are included within the future that validates our present practices.

It follows that the voices in which people express their sense of oppression are among the most important voices to be listened to in the context of practical query. Many people consider such a continuing sense of criticism to be divisive and antagonistic, and would prefer a more communal sense of tradition and solidarity. They overlook that this tradition and community that they admire imposes its own forms of oppression, that within consensus there is domination and the subjugation of different voices and different positions. Even more important, in the emphasis on consensus there can be found an inherent dogmatism that refuses to call itself into question.

What must be added to the need to listen to other people speak in their own voices of their oppressions is emphasis upon this discourse as a moment in an unending process of practical interrogation. There is a form of community that achieves consensus by prohibiting differences and obscuring conflicts. There is a discourse of antagonism and conflict that restores our sense of heterogeneities without mediation. There is in addition to both a practical reason in which we preserve the relevance of other, heterogeneous voices and their oppressions as part of our own practical undertakings. Only this merits being called a rational practice. It may achieve those forms of community that rely on charity and the unstinting interrogations of practical query, but it will not impose community where differences are more relevant. It will strive to avoid imposing rules where charity forbids.

Inherent in the conjunction of power and desire in relation to charity is a tension that characterizes practice—ethical and political practices—in relation to other people and to other creatures: between a caretaker relation defined by power and encouraging resistances to such powers. Charity cannot help us choose between these alternatives; it can only promulgate the sensitivities that enable us to act responsibly. Where we are in positions of authority and power with respect to other people, charity requires that we care for them in terms of what we understand their virtues and qualities to be. Where we confront our equals in authority and power, charity requires us to heed their voices as definitive of their virtues and qualities. I add that when we protect children from harm by care and concern, we must consider the consequences of overprotection upon their practical capacities and voices. Similar considerations apply to social programs that bring human beings under their care, presuming to speak for and to represent them. In a caretaker relation charity is present largely in a self-blinding form leading to oppression and demanding liberation. As feminist writings testify, women have subjugated themselves to men, by custom and by rule. Blindness to the oppressiveness of such relations can be overcome only by strenuous efforts at sensitivity to others where they cannot speak for themselves, by equally strenuous efforts to listen when they are able to speak for themselves, and by a deep awareness that speaking for oneself is a cultural product.

Two questions may intrude at this time. One is how we are to resolve disagreements over public and domestic policy. In the case of children, for example, we find very different opinions on just how much voice they are entitled to, whether they have rights comparable to those of adults. Some disagreements are cultural, based, for example, on differences in established public voices. In a society in which most adults have little control over their public lives, children can be expected to be controlled even more, in the name, perhaps, of their own good. But even in a society dedicated to adult liberation, a caretaker principle may be advocated as appropriate to children and vulnerable adults, a principle that amounts in many cases to treating children as parental property. A second question is how in the context of charity and concern we are to deal with abusive and destructive human beings. The most forceful examples again are in relation to children, when they are abused by their parents and other adults. If we care for other people, what do we do with those who abuse their powers and seek at any cost to others to gratify their desires?

The first question repeats the fundamental question of practical query, for it is not only our differences with others that characterize our practical interrogations, but also differences within ourselves. There is not, and cannot be, in relation to practical judgments, complete agreement over courses of action, certainly of a general, political nature, but also in relation to intimate and domestic milieux. Human beings have multifarious affinities and share many milieux, but important and heterogeneous differences remain amid the commonalities. We find ourselves in different circumstances and different times in our lives, and do not always agree with our former judgments. In effect, we invalidate them. More important, practical judgment changes conditions, and we find ourselves changed by our own and others' practices, so that we must somehow anticipate the consequences of our actions upon others and ourselves.

Heterogeneity is the central concern of politics, but it is inherent in practical query. Were agents to remain unchanged by their practices so that they did not call their prior judgments into question, or were other agents to agree routinely with our judgments, then practical query would only involve beneficent consequences. But there is no universal measure of beneficence or valor, and there is no practical judgment that is immune to the criticism that it is arbitrary in certain respects. On the other side, however, differences transpire within collective, shared milieux.

It follows that disagreement on practical questions be understood to belong to practice fundamentally, that while we may seek agreement, it is not because that agreement is required within practical query, but because fostering agreement is sometimes one of the achievements of practical success (and sometimes a form of failure). Disagreement is where practice as query finds its interrogations, and without continual interrogative challenge practice cannot be query, cannot be rational. This, I believe, is Mill's deepest insight. We always have more to gain from disagreement and controversy than from consensus. Every practical question of any depth and importance leads away from everyday and moral decisions to politics, for that is where we recognize the importance of the issues and the inevitability of deep disagreements.

The second question is also one of disagreement, but is less one concerning disagreements over practice in the context of charity and valor and more one concerning how we are to treat those who exploit and abuse others, in the case before us, those who mistreat children. This is a complex political question on the one hand of punishment and social reform, a complex question of evil on the other, particularly as to how we are to distinguish differences that belong to practical query as part of its rationality from differences that define the need for punitive practices. I will discuss these two issues later. But a simple reply may be noted here that returns us to the pervasiveness of practical judgments. We may begin by again rejecting the view that punishment is somehow external to practice, as if the ideal in practical query were either consensus and agreement or free and open controversy. Such a view denies the reality of material powers and oppressive forces.

Some views of relativity in practical judgment suggest that we cannot justify judgments of universal scope where others disagree. Given that there are always disagreements, especially given the position that disagreement defines the rationality of practical query, it may appear to follow that we cannot justify any particular courses of action, especially those directed toward other people who disagree, no matter how destructive their actions. Practical judgments of a punitive nature can only be regarded as dispersions of power and arbitrary desire.

If such a view requires that there be an absolute foundation of practical judgments, then such a foundation is incompatible with locality and inexhaustibility. If such a view requires that there be the possibility of universal agreement as a measure of individual differences, such universality is incompatible with the nature of query. But query also contains within itself interrogation of both arbitrariness and paralyzing relativity, for they too are forms of practice, and can be judged to have failed even among strenuous disagreements. No way can be found around the fact that the judgments of others serve as important tests of the success and failure of practical judgments; conversely, however, we must, as practical agents, respond to the practices of others with criticism and disapprobation, in certain cases with censure and punishment. Only in the context of such disapprobations can certain practical judgments be validated. But validation entails invalidation; disapprobation, in the context of disagreement, entails reconciliation and compromise. More important, there remains an immense difference between individual disagreement and institutional enforcement, between practice and law. That practice requires sacrifice, of others and ourselvesm cannot be avoided, but we must work in the context of charity. It follows that we should not hesitate to punish those who abuse children as severely as we can, along with all people who abuse vulnerable creatures in their power. The political implications of such a conclusion remain to be considered.

IMPLEMENTATION

Despite the conflicts between general rules and principles and the sensitivity and charity required for practical query, there is no way to implement practices stably without promulgating rules and establishing laws. On the one hand, there is no way in which practices can be implemented publicly without codification and promulgation; on the other, implemented practices coalesce into implicit rules. Reasons exist for this: some analogous to the reasons that define the role of general principles in inquiry and discourse; some specific to practical judgment. No form of thought, public or private, and especially no communicable discourse can be intelligible in individual instances alone, but coalesces into kinds; every public practice achieves some commonality; all practical effectiveness is stable over a range of implementations; we cannot think of or relate to events and circumstances in practice without affinities and differences. However, it is not that universality is one side of reason, as in Hegel, an irresistible rational principle, but, rather, it is a consequence of the inexhaustibility of nature that it teems with things and kinds. The complexity and heterogeneity of things gives rise to classifications by similarities and differences.

In relation to practice, principles and rules are practical judgments, instruments whereby we are able to relate effectively to people, things, and events that would otherwise overwhelm us with their complexity and inaccessibility. Within this instrumentality, there is the need to share our practices with other people and to be able to repeat them reliably if those practices are to be successful. Laws and rules provide a public and explicit commonality that practice requires to be stable and repetitive. They are

requisites of publicness and commonality and expressions of publicly effective practical judgments.

Similarly, language and thought require stable conditions and
express established forms of commonality. Moreover, language
and thought are indispensable to practice and understanding
though simplifications as well as distortions of what they address,
due to inexhaustibility. The distortions here are not the result of
defects of language or representation but of the inexhaustibility
that transcends any knowledge or expression.

It is important in this context to emphasize the two sides of
inexhaustibility in relation to language and representation. Not
only are things inexhaustible, so that whatever we may think and
understand about them, whatever powers we may establish over
them, they transcend such relations inexhaustibly, but also all the
forms of human being—including language, discourse, power, desire, and valor—are themselves inexhaustible. Inexhaustibility entails that every being transcends any of its relations, specifically or
generically, including any of the forms of knowledge and practice.
Thus, language has its own structural forms and constraints—
syntactic and semantic—that characterize its specificity and inexhaustibility in relation to whatever may be said in language;[9] discourse inexhaustibly transcends the forms of language and syntax
in historical and cultural conditions; power and desire belong to
language and discourse, but transcend them as well as each other
inexhaustibly. Similarly, the forms of generality and structure that
inhabit our codes and rules are the result of our inquiries and
practices and influence them greatly, and do so as a consequence of
their own characteristics and excesses. Beings inexhaustibly exceed
what we can know and say about them as well as our influence
upon them, but, reciprocally, our practical judgments inexhaustibly transcend their conditions, human and natural.

It follows that we find ourselves within public, large-scale, political milieux as well as private, intimate milieux, that we undertake practical judgments together with other people and explain
and justify those judgments to them, but also undertake practical
judgments that differ from others', even in opposition, without
being able to explain and justify them, and that the locales we
inhabit are influenced by our public practices and codes as well as
their determinants. We act in relation to circumstances and in relation to other people who are affected by our actions. Practice

always has a public as well as a private side: privateness and publicness are complementary. Rules and laws are public forms of practice in which the inescapability of failure, especially its demand for
effectiveness, constantly war with charity and valor. All general
principles of practice, however just, are deeply wasteful.

To implement a practice publicly—say, a prohibition against
official lying—it is essential to promulgate a rule. We may hope
that such a rule will constrain the defectiveness of finite, incomplete judgments, forestall the abuses inherent in arbitrary power
and uncontrolled desire. But every such rule is a strategy of power
as well as an expression of desire. Every such rule, no matter how
pervaded by charity, is devalorizing. Thus, within a society that
prohibits individuals from lying to each other, and especially from
lying to public officials, there are frequently covert rules that justify lying in the name of national security, and people are punished
for truthfulness while others are misinformed by sanctioned
misrepresentations. Every society that prohibits lying in some
circumstances or by some individuals requires lying in other circumstances. That some people may consider the prohibition
against lying to allow no ordinary exceptions in ordinary circumstances—everyday or domestic circumstances, among private individuals—only reinforces the conviction that lying is a "moral"
issue within a system of political codes and practices. Morality can
suggest universality only within a context in which universality
without exception is unintelligible.

Kant suggests that we may think of lying as an activity that
would be impossible to carry on universally, that it is parasitic on
telling the truth, and that we might imagine universal truth-telling
but not universal lying.[10] He ignores the inevitable conflicts in
practice between telling the truth and causing (or not preventing)
harm. But there is a deeper difficulty, that to draw so sharp a
distinction between truth and falsity expressed in universal, practical terms presupposes an unequivocal distinction between them
which, if a regulative ideal acceptable in contexts of inquiry and
science, is inappropriate in relation to practice. Kant assumes that
there is a (practical) truth that might be implementable universally
against which lying is measured. But if we take any specific examples from practical contexts, we find that we cannot so easily
distinguish truth from falsity. They are distinguishable unequivo-

cally, without surplus, only where practice establishes the terms of such distinctions by conventional rules.

When a person asks how his new hairstyle looks, is it true and is it desirable to say that it is true that it is somewhat unattractive? When a child shows you her drawing of a pig, and you think that it looks more like a cockroach, is it right to say so, is it even true to say so, or would a cockroach in fact look more like a pig? When a country is at war, and a strenuous battle is fought, is it right and true to concede that the battle was not won when it was not lost?

What is overlooked in such cases, especially by Kant, is that the characterization of a claim as true or false in a practical context is itself a practical judgment, one that is to be judged by its consequences in addition to its other modalities. Truth and falsity are not independent properties, factual determinations, except in relation to propositional query, whose methods presuppose and are designed to support the presumption of such independence. Only where we may presuppose unbiased factual determinations, independent of power and desire, or where we may establish methods that define such independence, can we accept so unequivocal a distinction between truth and falsity. Relative to any practice, however, there is no escape from bias, no independence from power and desire. Both propositional judgment and scientific query are practical judgments due to the multimodality of judgment.

Lying belongs to practice in the double sense that it is itself a form of practice and that it is validated by means of practice more than by assertion or inquiry. The implementation of a practice in a rule or principle is itself a practice that imposes strategies of power and regulation upon subsequent practices. I have noted this important difference between law and practice: in particular, the question of undertaking an act or approving of one is quite different from whether there should be a law prohibiting it. The promulgation of a law has its own consequences far beyond the consequences of individual practices. Such a distinction is in part one between ethics and politics, one of scale and relevance. But there is a corresponding distinction between a practical judgment involving an individual undertaking and one involving public implementation and codification, particularly where sanctions are involved. Law is where practice achieves its most explicit representations and vividly manifests oppression through neglect of charity.

Principles and rules are unavoidable in the implementation of practical judgments, even of practical query, for there is no understanding, even in practical terms, that is not in some respects general, thereby overly simplified. But rules and laws can be validated in query only in relation to unceasing charity and valor, which provide the necessary tests in terms of consequences and applications. Implementation of a form of practice, then, is first codification and then charity, where codification itself is based on charity. A profound conflict exists between the valorization of charity and the devalorization of rules.

In its more reflexive interrogative forms, query requires us to understand that every practice, and especially every rule and law, functions covertly as well as overtly. Rules and principles frequently come into conflict. But the ways in which established rules oppress are to be found, not so much in the rules that oppose them, but in the destruction they work in individual lives. Valor and charity, realized in sacrifice, pertain to every codified rule and principle. The central conditions of practical query are charity and valor, not the rules that codify the results of query in public practices.

An important consequence is that there is an enormous difference in practical query between practices judged to be wrong and those judged to call for punitive sanctions. There is, moreover, an important difference in practical judgment and query between practice and its implementation. We undertake practical judgments of one kind when we speak out against a certain practice, when we refrain from such a practice ourselves, when we seek to sway public opinion in favor of our position, and judgments of another kind when we promulgate and enforce a law. In the movement from an individual judgment to a law, we move from a sensitivity to valor that does not require codification to a generality that is meaningless without rules. For example, when a woman asks us to tell her what we think of her new shoes, we may tell her they are lovely without worrying about rules, and we may disapprove of someone else who bluntly tells her they are vulgar. But we are functioning here at an individual level of sensitivity and care, and we may be reluctant to generalize that, in other such cases, one should be more supportive than honest. When we seek to sway public opinion, general categories and rules become unavoidable. Even where we are able to avoid the promulgation of explicit laws, our practical judgments establish precedents and define rules. There is no escape in practice from influence and power.

We are, in any practice, caught in the midst of complex forms and levels of practical judgments: some at a more individual level where the specific consequences of an individual action are important; some at a more public level where common understandings and shared convictions are important; others at a public, political level where general rules and laws are essential. Implementation in relation to many but not all levels requires general rules and codes; the validation of any rule and code, any implementation, even any practical judgment, requires inexhaustible sensitivity and charity.

A number of important distinctions follow in levels and degrees of practical implementation. For example, there will be, in any society, certain practices that must be punished effectively, sometimes harshly—for example, murder, rape, theft, and fraud. There will be, in any society, certain practices that will be generally disapproved of, but that cannot justifiably be prohibited—for example, certain forms of psychological abuse, certain forms of profit-making, failing to help those in need. There will also be certain ways that people act that we may find abhorrent with no tendency to promulgate a rule or even a customary prohibition—for example, tactlessly or insensitively ignoring the feelings of others. The distinctions among these levels are extremely important, but they are anything but clear, and most controversies in practical judgment and query follow from confusions among the levels and the practices related to them. The point is that it is only by establishing these levels and distinctions that practical query can raise its level of interrogative reflexiveness to higher levels—that is, by questioning the distinctions themselves, in general and in particular practices. In all these cases, sensitivity to valor and sacrifice and consequent charity are the only basis we have for pursuing practical query.

It follows that codification and implementation in practice are always in conflict with charity, each supplementing the other as its form of interrogation and validation. In this sense, devalorization is not so much opposed to charity as a moment in its public realization, provided that devalorization does not become paramount. General codes and rules require charity to blunt their oppressive powers and their subjection to desire. Charity that is too individualized, however admirable, is not an implementable form of practice—not a "form" at all. In this dialectic, we find the most important questions of practical determination.

NOTES

1. Richard Rorty, "Method, Social Science, and Social Hope," *Consequences of Pragmatism* (Minneapolis: University of Minnesota Press, 1982).

2. John Locke, *An Essay Concerning the True Original, Extent and End of Civil Government*, in *The English Philosophers from Bacon to Mill*, ed. E. A. Burtt (New York: Modern Library, 1939), p. 405.

3. Ibid., p. 413.

4. And, indeed, perhaps we cannot justify doing so. See Peter Singer, *Animal Liberation: A New Ethics for Our Treatment of Animals* (New York: Avon, 1975).

5. Ibid.

6. Ibid.

7. For this understanding of resistance, see Foucault, *History of Sexuality*, pp. 95–96: "—Where there is power, there is resistance, and yet, or rather consequently, this resistance is never in a position of exteriority in relation to power. . . . These points of resistance are present everywhere in the power network. Hence there is no single locus of great Refusal, no soul of revolt, source of all rebellions, or pure law of the revolutionary. Instead there is a plurality of resistances, each of them a special case: resistances that are possible, necessary, improbable; others that are spontaneous, savage, solitary, concerted, rampant, or violent; still others that are quick to compromise, interested, or sacrificial; by definition, they can only exist in the strategic field of power relations. But this does not mean that they are only a reaction or rebound forming with respect to the basic domination an underside that is in the end always passive, doomed to perpetual defeat. . . . They are the odd term in relations of power; they are inscribed in the latter as an irreducible opposite."

Power is everywhere in the sense that that is how practice works and that patterns of subjugation and rebellion are results of complex coordinations directed by no person or group. Power, here, along with desire, is one of the great forms of mediateness while resistance is the negativity that is always present within power. Power and resistance, along with desire, are the pervasive practical forms of locality that are otherwise expressed in terms of charity and valor. These are all inseparable, for the valor and inexhaustibility of a being sustain its powers and enable it to resist others powers, expressed on the one hand in terms of power and desire, on the other in terms of charity and valor. Charity is acknowledgment of the inexhaustible plenitude of other beings. Among the practical ramifications of this plenitude are power and resistance.

8. "[T]he essential thing is . . . the existence in our era of a discourse in which sex, the revelation of truth, the overturning of global laws, the proclamation of a new day to come, and the promise of a certain felicity are linked together" (ibid., p. 7).

9. See my *Limits of Language*.

10. Kant, *Fundamental Principles of the Metaphysics of Morals*.

5

POLITICS

PRACTICAL QUERY IS DIVIDED into many forms: the ceaseless interrogation of possibilities of influence and work, the interrogation
of ways in which desire may be mated with power. Practical query,
through endless interrogation and validation based on charity
and sacrifice, adjudicates the conflicts of valor that compose lived
experience. These conflicts are a consequence of locality and inexhaustibility in the context of the work of practical judgment. They
express the condition that there is no intrinsic global fulfillment—
retrospective or prospective—inherent in the inexhaustible plurality of things, for in this plurality there are obstructive differences
as well as supportive affinities, and there is no overarching common measure. Every judgment, every work, is faced with
sacrifice.

In another sense, the many forms of practice—including ethics,
politics, technology, discourse, and religion—testify to important
practical differences, not least because practice belongs to practical
query in order to adjudicate such differences in lived experience.
One of these major differences is based on the functions of principles and rules. Morality is frequently associated with ideal principles; politics, with coercion and regulation; ethics, more with
intimate and personal relations; politics, with public institutions
and implementations. The distinctions between these, their overlapping and inseparability, are central to any understanding of
practical query. Every such distinction exists to be transcended.

I have argued against the claim, in any sphere of practice, of
unswerving principles and rules, however ideal. Principles and
rules conflict in all important spheres of application and practice,
a consequence of inexhaustible valor, and manifest coercive forms
of power. In this respect, the universal forms that express traditional Western morality are forms of practical influence. In this
sense also, all practice is fundamentally political; ethics and moral-

ity are intimate, local forms of practice permitted within and encouraged by established systems of power.

It follows from the side of practice that ethics belongs to politics as its intimate other, the relevance of private spheres of practice within any public system of control. Publicness and privateness are complementary, dimensions of being and human being. Manifested in practice, they take the forms of politics and ethics. Politics is concerned with public and far-reaching practical issues of great moment for many people or over many different locales; ethics and morality are concerned with circumscribed practical issues of importance in relatively few locales. There are more or less coercive, authoritarian, permissive, and individualistic forms of politics, but there could be no political practice that did not define relatively private spheres of activities regulated less by public sanctions and law, and more by custom and rule, activities inhabited by proximity and care. One reason is that power works more effectively when hidden, but the deeper reason is that there can be no overarching, total power, no complete totalitarianism, however overwhelming political power may be. No overarching system of domination can control every locale within it. There are always local milieux with restricted influences. Within any system of entrenched powers, there are resistances everywhere. Private spheres of practice are among the locales where power works coercively while covertly conjoined with multiple resistances.

It follows that spheres of privateness within public systems of social relations and political practices are locales of resistance and sites where political forces are oppressive. This doubling defines the ambiguous role of ethics within politics: enforcing the dominations and oppressions that pertain to any established system of power while situating important resistances to them. A similar doubling can be seen in the role of ideality in ethics: ideal principles promote oppressions, are forms through which power is exercised, and are predominant forms taken by resistance.

There can be no ethics or politics without ideals, and every practical ideal is ethical. In this sense, there is no conflict between politics and ethics; nor could there be, for ethics is a major voice in which politics criticizes its sacrifices. It is, however, not the only such voice, and when it becomes too demanding, when it stridently demands sovereignty over all conflicting alternatives, it

forces us in reaction to give precedence to politics. Because morality and ethics, with the principles and ideals that define them,
belong to politics as one side of the conflicts that politics must
adjudicate, such precedence is unintelligible. There can be no politics without practical ideals, and all such ideals are ethical. But
ethics and politics may nevertheless be distinguished, within their
reciprocity, in terms of the scope of the practical judgments they
involve.

Practical query includes ethics and politics, inseparably, the latter the form of practical judgment in which far-reaching and important human concerns are at stake: life and death, the future of
humanity and the earth, the oppression of women and minorities,
ethnic identities, national sovereignty, control over the environment, trade and the economy, war and peace. Compared
with such considerations, ethical questions tend to have diminished importance except where they have political relevance. Thus,
whether we should lie to a woman with a terminal disease about
her condition pales by comparison with whether our country
should go to war. On the other side, whether physicians should
lie to their patients for what they take to be their benefit, whether
public officials should lie in the interest of national security, are
political questions, practices affecting the lives of many people,
and are adjudicated in political terms, by governmental and institutional regulation. It is the large-scale importance of technology
that makes it predominantly political practice.

When we add to the relative lack of importance of ethical questions the dominance and authority of political practices, we must
conclude that ethical ideals prevail by sufferance, are permitted and
even encouraged by political forces to represent private spheres of
ideality within the conflicting public spheres that compose political
judgments. In this sense, in modern life, politics holds authority
over ethical ideals. Ideality and intimacy are unavoidable in politics; what politics seeks is hegemony over them, typically relegating them to minor roles, with minor consequences, while utilizing
them as instruments of domination. To this we must add that just
as power is everywhere, resistance is everywhere, and to allow
private spheres of practice is inevitably to promote resistances
within them.

In order for practice to be query, it must be unceasingly interrogative, typically realized in established forms. The doubling of

politics and ethics in relation to each other represents one of these recurrent forms of interrogation. Thus, ethics is one of the repetitive forms in which politics interrogates itself. But ethics, interpreted in terms of universal principles, is one of the forms through which political oppression works, and includes only certain forms of interrogation. Both of these moments are traditionally included within the sphere of ethics: the one, the role of ideals in relation to political efficacy, justice as compared with expediency; the other, a concern for individuals and specific cases in contrast with regulation by law. Here ethics, as ideality and charity, interrogates the limits of political practices. Yet these interrogations are forms in which politics interrogates itself and is practical query. Ethics is one of the forms through which politics makes itself query.

Politics is the adjudication of conflicts of valor in the context of issues of great scale and importance, involving consequences for many people, over large territories, and through time. Ethics is defined within politics as composing the intimate spheres in which conflicts of valor can be adjudicated face-to-face, in intimate and ideal terms. Such spheres of ideality are possible only where there are conflicts of valor with relatively modest consequences and importance. These are the locales of private practice, with the qualification that such a distinction can be neither theoretically defensible nor clear. Nevertheless, it is impossible to treat every practical decision as momentous, to trace the consequences of every practical judgment in detail. And every decision works face-to-face in some practical spheres. Principles and rules then serve two distinct purposes: as instruments of political practices, established in law and its enforcement; as constituting the spheres of morality, where they define the ideal side of practical interrogation. A political regime that has no sphere of ideality, or does not equate such spheres with privacy and ethics, cannot profoundly interrogate itself and cannot be rational, cannot even accomplish its work. No such régime could exist except briefly, in extraordinarily constricted forms. It does not follow that either ideality or morality can replace the complexity of political practices.

POWER

The principal dimensions of practical judgment are power, desire, and knowledge. These, in their interworkings, compose the forms in which conflicts of valor appear, demanding unending practical judgment. I have defined the difference between ethics and politics in terms of scale, regarding the former as a pole of differentiation within the latter. I could have moved in the opposite direction, from ethics to politics, with the implication that the only valid form of practical query is politics, not ethics, in virtue of the limitations imposed by principles and ideals upon practical reason. In other words, to the extent that practice is query, every principle and ideal, every practical relation, must be questionable, must be criticized. But such interrogation cannot take place within a practice in which outcomes are calculated in terms of overall benefits, where the formulas of calculation and the nature of benefits are not repeatedly and profoundly called into question, or where principles are not criticized as oppressive. Politics is a form in which ethics and morality interrogate themselves, just as, reciprocally, they are forms in which politics interrogates itself. Nevertheless, in virtue of the dominance of entrenched contemporary political forces, politics exercises practical authority over its own ideals.

The issues here concern ideology and liberation. Once we grant the premises that all practices effectively belong to practical judgment, in this case to politics, that every norm and principle is constituted by prior practices, and that politics exercises dominance over its subpractices, then it follows that every ideal is ideological, every notion of liberation is constituted by and within political practices. There is no escape, and there is no non-ideological solution. All theoretical solutions to this difficulty are foundational and indefensible.[1] A truer or more scientific discourse is no less practical, no less historically situated, no less ideological or influenced by desire and power, than a false one. Truth and falsity belong to human life and the practices that define them. The role of understanding is not to authenticate or legitimate except as understanding belongs to a discourse or to some discursive practice, for knowledge is unavoidably situated.

Every discursive practice includes within itself divisions between what is acceptable and unacceptable, true and false, legitimate and illegitimate, just as every form of power includes within it forms of resistance. Yet that some forms of discourse are unacceptable does not entail that they lie outside discourse. Similarly, that some resistances oppose and inhibit the workings of power does not entail that resistances are not power. To the contrary, in both cases there is a polarity that belongs to the domain of judgment, and it is within this opposition that criticism and validation belong. No discursive practice can exclude a practice from its purview, as if it were not relevant to its validity, except in local and situated terms.

We may leave discourse aside for later discussion. The issue in relation to power is not only that power is everywhere, dispersed, but that resistances are also everywhere, similarly dispersed.[2] Power is not a force wielded by some over others, but is inherent in practice itself. That some people control others is an expression of power but also of the specificity and density of practice and of its material consequences. I add that practices obstruct each other, just as events and creatures do, a consequence of inexhaustible plurality. Therefore, wherever there is practice, there are resistances within. In this sense, power and resistance are less complementary than repetitions of each other, representing the obstructions and excesses within being and experience.

Juxtaposed with this generic view of power and resistance are many traditional issues of politics: that some wield control over, coerce, others, that governments arrogate all coercive powers to themselves, that people who live under an unjust government have a right and a duty to rebel. A generic view of power entails that there are no "levers" and the state cannot be regarded as the sole wielder of power, cannot intelligibly arrogate all powers to itself, only certain highly visible forms of coercion, and these rest on hidden and subtle interplays of power, but also of resistance, that pervade the social structures through which the state is effective. There are cumulative effects of coercion and prohibition that constitute the dominance of one group or class over another. But these are results, not causes, and include resistances. The pervasiveness and unavoidability of practical judgment, within the context of inexhaustible differences and obstructions, give us the unavoidability of power and resistance. Power and resistance are effectively the same: practice itself, divided by differences. We cannot escape from power or resistance, though we may hope to diminish domination and oppression.

Power and resistance manifest the polarities of inexhaustible differences in human life and practice. To this we may add inexhaustible differences in scale and the reciprocities of public and private locales. Power belongs to practice at any level of scale, public or private. But where power has non-egalitarian effects, especially of an enduring and structural nature, there politics is present in its public forms. One of the fundamental differences between public and private practices is that private practices concern relatively transitory and marginal effects whereas public practices are public and political in virtue of enduring practical developments. In this sense, feminist theory has made a permanent contribution to our understanding of politics by showing how private spheres bear within themselves enduring public structures of domination.

If every practical relation involves power, nevertheless there are relations in which power and resistance appear mutual. Over time, in a private relation, there may be no enduring dominance, but reciprocation, give and take. Such a relation—of love or friendship—is no less one of power and resistance, is no less practical, and involves no less a concern with influence, but the relevant activities join power and resistance mutually rather than enforcing the dominance of one party over the other, as in the authority of employer over employee, government official over citizen, parent over child. Wherever we have established forms of control and power, we encounter publicly determined disparities in authority and dominance. The form of power here is political in virtue of the consequences and implications of such imbalances. We may define friendship as the mutual and private interrelation of practical agents in the absence of enduring, one-sided forms of dominance. We must conclude that friendship is rare in human life, pervaded as it typically is by differences in authority. More important, the friendship that has typically been celebrated in the West as a model of ethics has been exclusively between men, who in this situation exclude women from mutuality and reciprocity.[3]

While many writers have found it reasonable to imagine that large-scale structures of dominance and control may be deeply influenced by intimate relations, that how people live their private lives might profoundly and irresistibly influence effective forms of political power, experience testifies to the immense coerciveness of public forms of influence. In part, this is more to acknowledge the greater influence of public political forces upon domestic life than the reverse. But it is also an implication of the importance and force of political practices, which are defined by the scale and gravity of their consequences. Experience testifies to the effective-ness and coerciveness of governments and institutions, far more than of individuals and families, over the lives of their members. There would be no governments or institutions if they were impo-tent. And when they become impotent, they give rise to crises.

It follows that the notion of a powerless state or institution is incoherent. Instead, we may prefer one kind of power to another, covert to overt forms, more persuasive to coercive forms, more centered to dispersed forms. Moreover, the powers of a state or institution are not "owned" by them, not in the sense that they may simply impose them. Rather, the coercive powers of a state express the overall accumulation of powers dispersed throughout human life, within a particular society and in relation to other societies and states.

How, in this context, may we resist the coercive powers of an unjust and tyrannical government? This appears to bring us back to the legitimation of any form of power. But I have rejected the notion of an unsituated set of norms of legitimation and with them the idea of legitimizing power. Power is everywhere; therefore, there can be no question of its legitimacy not reflecting the work-ings of power. Rather, the relevant questions are those raised by local government practices within our local practices. Questions of resistance are not theoretical, but practical questions.

There is no escaping power, for power is effectiveness in prac-tice. What can be opposed instead are the forms power takes in any particular situation, manifested by what and who are ex-cluded, and the system of dominance established as the result of large-scale practices. I am speaking here of resistance in relation to a dominant structure of power, where the resistance itself is a form of power, though perhaps one without dominant institu-tional structures. Here we come to questions of efficacy, of the validation of certain forms of opposition and resistance. The issue is whether we should oppose dominant forces by developing equally large and dominant structures, effectively repeating more of the same, or whether other forms of resistance do not commit us to the oppressive structures of what we oppose.

We may consider the following:

(a) Power cannot be avoided, for it is inherent in the nature of things and their relations. Practice is the relevant mode of judgment.

(b) Systems of dominance may be resisted, but not without tensions between coercive forms of opposition that exercise their own forms of domination and less coercive forms that lack effectiveness.

(c) Wherever there is power, there is resistance, but unchanneled resistances may dilute established structures of power without constituting new forms of power and without establishing satisfactory and enduring consequences.

(d) Moreover, resistances do not stand in an external relation to power, but belong to it in the double sense that they may reinforce established structures and that every system of power contains its own forms of opposition. Every system and tradition is divided within itself.

(e) Nevertheless, entrenched forms of opposition exercise their own forms of power, especially over prohibited or unacceptable forms of opposition.

(f) It follows that no line can be drawn between opposing an entrenched system of domination and being subordinated within it. There is only the unceasing interrogation of political query. The responsibilities we bear in political judgment are endless, and endlessly ramified.

Issues of ideology and the legitimation of power have no overarching theoretical solution, only local, practical resolutions that cannot avoid threats of failure. In the context of political query, these failures may be catastrophic. For politics confronts the most urgent and far-reaching problems of human life. In this sense, opposition, liberation, the demand for justice, and legitimation are all concerns established by political judgment itself.

POLITICAL QUERY

Practical judgment has two goals. One is inherent in judgment itself, that it may give rise to further judgment and to query, for query is the ongoing fulfillment of the interrogativeness inherent in selection and validation. It is a fulfillment realized not in completions, but in incessant activities. The second belongs to practical judgment uniquely, that it may achieve satisfactory work in relation to life and experience. Both goals are temporal, directed toward the future from within human history, individual and collective. It follows that when we speak of practical validation, we confront two purposive forms, not just one, with conflicting realizations. For although query may be satisfied by ongoing interrogation and validation, practice demands satisfaction in particular outcomes. It is the practical side of practical query to which failure and despair are attached, not to query, for from the standpoint of query itself, failure opens up new possibilities of future interrogations.

This prospect in practical query of new forms of life and experience characterizes the inexhaustibility of human being from one side. I have characterized it as hope. There is a hope inherent in judgment and query that we may think of as a promise for the future, not so much a belief in progress—though hope has frequently taken that form—as in the capacities demanded for invention and insight. Science profoundly manifests the plausibility of such a hope, for we have always been able, no matter what the difficulty, to develop new forms of scientific understanding, new instruments and means, to expand our understanding deeper into nature. The dangers brought by the fruits of science, in technological implementation, do not diminish the hope of further scientific discovery. Art, philosophy, and politics manifest an analogous hope, that human life will never lack resources to produce new works of imagination and power. It seems fair to say that query cannot exist without this sense of hope, and it should not be thought unfounded. For the founding and abandoning of hope, if rational, themselves belong to query and are enacted by it.

What is missing here is the other side of practical query, that it is practice. The hope described pertains generically to query and specifically to science and to art more than practice. When we ask instead whether science will improve human life, help us resolve political and ethical difficulties, whether art can make us better human beings, we regard each of them as practical. This hope is far less plausible. In practice we confront the poignancy of sacrifice and the unavoidability of failure. In practice hope is inextricably mixed with despair.

The omnipresence of failure pertains to all practical query. But where accompanied by desperate and far-reaching sacrifices, practice is political. Political query is the form of practical query that addresses consequences and issues of gravest importance in human life. The ethical claim that the death of one person is as important as the deaths of many is unintelligible from the perspective of a public practice. The earthquake that kills 10,000 rather than 10, the epidemic that strikes 500 rather than 5, the bomb that kills 350,000 rather than 35, all are far worse in this respect than the alternatives. Numbers are not the issue, merely the manifestation. The forest fire that devastates 100,000 acres rather than 10, the oil slick that pollutes 100 miles of beach rather than 1, the bankruptcy of a corporation with business in 100 cities rather than 1, all are of far greater import than their alternatives, due to scale. One of the features of traditional ethics is that it works with principles and ideals that suggest that issues of scale are not relevant. This can be true only where practice reflexively permits the restriction of certain spheres of practice to private spheres in which ideality and principle are not in impossible conflict.

Such restriction is fundamentally political. In this latter sense, ethics belongs to politics as the sphere of ideality that would be predominant were we able, in practice, to ignore the catastrophic sacrifices that are the result of conflicts of scale. Ethics belongs to politics, that is, at a lower level of interrogativeness, and manifests a less demanding form of reflexive criticism than required by political query.

Ethics belongs to politics as composing the spheres of ideality which are possible, virtually as enclaves of privateness, within the public practices that confront the catastrophes of human failures. Yet politics always contains privateness and ideality; human collective life contains spheres of intimacy and universality; practical determinations are filled with ideals. One of the determinants of the success of political query is the extent to which private spheres of human life are able to function ideally, in relations of proximity, within public practical life without constantly confronting unresolvable conflicts, able to function ethically without extreme political undertakings such as war and state violence. Similarly, it is a determinant of the success of political query to establish responsive and supportive communities in which differences are mutually adjudicated rather than divided by enmity and violence.

The logic of this view of politics is that political query is a form of reason that conforms to no agreed upon principles, rules, or ideals, especially to none derived from other, less political spheres of practice. In this respect, politics may be the most prominent paradigm of practical reason, possibly the most prominent paradigm of reason altogether. Two kinds of arguments are needed to make this case: the first that politics may be understood, in its practices and not its theory, as a form of reason; the second that all forms of reason follow the paradigm of politics more than other paradigms that have been dominant throughout the Western philosophical tradition. We may add that the complex and sophisticated paradigm of politics, without its name, deeply inhabits the Western literary tradition.

That reason does not conform to rules can be established by appeal to art and philosophy, for neither, in its large-scale traditions, conforms to rules, methodological or substantive, but questions every rule and norm, in the one case primarily by example, in the other propositionally. That the Western tradition has not associated art and philosophy in their full inventiveness and interrogativeness with reason betrays one of the weaknesses of that tradition. We may think of art, philosophy, science, and politics as composing a multiplicity of modes of query.

The theoretical argument is that reason cannot close off interrogation without closing off itself, that the presence of irrationality is marked, not by irregularities but by dogmatism, by adherence to unquestionable principles. Query is unterminating interrogation and validation, not just in the sense that further questions may always be raised, however marginal and inconsequential, but in the profound sense that the authority of every discipline is always in question. This tension cannot be avoided, in any form of understanding or reason, between the inescapability of established norms that define a particular form of judgment and the imperative in reason that no established norms be beyond question. The tension is present at the boundaries of every discipline, where on the one side the effectiveness of judgment requires the determinants of established conditions while on the other side each discipline requires interrogation from other disciplinary points of view than its own. These interrogations transform the disciplines that give them impetus.

Based on the long-term history of art and philosophy, each is a form of query for which nothing is taken for granted. To every established form of art we may bring different forms, based on different premises. To every established philosophic principle we may bring opposing principles, for it is in their tension and interplay that philosophic reason resides, in the interrogations more than in the regulations. But it is in connection with practice that unceasing interrogation brings unceasing sacrifices and failures. Only in relation to practical judgment can there be failure. Only in practical judgment is failure the result of reason.

We may understand the fundamental difference between ethics and politics to lie in the scale of issues that politics addresses: issues that pose such far-reaching threats to human life and its surroundings that failure and despair are not to be avoided. Morality and ethics inhabit the margins of practical query in the sense that so few lives and so small a part of our surroundings are affected. The question of whether we should terminate the life-support system of a comatose patient, posed to his family, is an ethical one, no less tragic or compelling, no less sad and valorous, no easier to determine. But the question posed to the associated physicians is an institutional question, affecting in principle many other patients, setting a rule, establishing a policy. A question of professional ethics is, in terms of the view of politics developed here, a political question in virtue of the institutional scale of the relevant practices. The most provocative as well as the most important contemporary moral questions are political in this sense, pertaining to institutional resolutions. Political query is in this sense typically a function of institutional practices.[4]

It follows that only where moral questions possess demarcated limits in scale and importance can they be distinguished from their political and institutional forms, and the latter are a more complex form of interrogation and query than the former, which are effectively circumscribed. We may refuse to honor this distinction between morality and politics, with two important consequences. One is that ethics and morality lose their ideal supremacy in comparison with the untidiness of political query, and confront us repeatedly with normative principles and overall benefits in tension with variances and departures in individual cases. For query in politics is not so much defined by scale as by ramifications of scale. Where issues are of political importance, we cannot rest content with any established procedures or norms. Politics confronts us with questions of such grave importance in human life, leading so deeply into an open and undecided future, that no question may remain unasked, no criticism unvoiced. Politics is where we recognize that every rule and regulation must have exceptions, that practice transcends any general procedures and principles yet cannot function without them, and that we cannot escape from the insecurities of practical judgments by denying their importance, for the issues in political query are the most important that face our world.

The second consequence of rejecting the distinction between morality and politics is that the tensions between them pass into each of them, thereby diminishing their force. When this happens, practical query loses the impetus that defines it, loses the sense of urgency that characterizes failure. The tensions are between ideality and finiteness, universality and valor, publicness and privateness, to mention just a few. To take the first, political query depends on ideals: they represent the norms in relation to which every individual case is determined, with the qualification that such individual determinations, inherent in the inexhaustibility of individual beings, are the test of the ideals. The meaning of failure as well as of sacrifice depends on this tension between charity and ideality. Where morality and politics coexist, typically in the form of private spheres of practice within public spheres of practical determination, then each expresses something exterior essential to the rationality of the other. Were there but a single complex sphere of practical query, politics or ethics, there would be the danger of blunting the conflicts that practical reason requires to be rational. The result would be analogous to identifying all forms of reason with science, expanding the dominion of the latter but opening its inexhaustible complexity to include philosophy and art. Such an expansion would offer the possibility that science is to be understood to be more complex than is usually expressed in traditional practices, that it includes other modes of judgment within its practices. But there is also the danger that certain questions about the nature of science would no longer be intelligible, because they depend on external perspectives for their intelligibility. Similarly, a politics without ideals lacks the heterogeneities that enable us to understand what is of practical importance. Put another way, the tension between expediency and ideality belongs to political query, is part of its interrogativeness. Where this tension diminishes, politics is in danger of losing its rationality.

The point may be clearer with respect to the tension between private and public spheres of practice. For while all practical roads lead to public issues and have public consequences, the recognition that not all consequences are of equally grave public importance, that there is irrelevance as well as pervasive relevance, is essential to locality and inexhaustibility. Politics is divided within itself, along with all forms of tradition and practice, into distinctive forms of practice, public and private. Families and friendships inhabit spheres of private life that, though deeply influenced by public practices, and reciprocally influential themselves, take on lives of their own. All practical judgments, ethical or political, take place face-to-face, in spheres of proximity. To inflate politics to include all forms of practice runs the danger of making it monolithic. Practically speaking, it is to make it totalitarian.

This inexhaustible dividedness of politics makes it the paradigm of practical query. By comparison, narrower spheres and methods of practice are simplified by scale or principle. Politics works within the terror of an open and indeterminate future that it will contribute to profoundly, changing itself in its practice. The fundamental truths in politics are that we can never anticipate the novelty of the future and that our practices contribute to that future and are transformed by it.

Practical judgment can be understood as interrogative only by emphasizing its temporality, as future practical judgments criticize the norms and conditions established by past practices. Such interrogation may be manifest without being expressed propositionally. For example, in science, there is explicit controversy over the interpretation of evidence, but there is also criticism that consists in setting aside established conclusions and beginning investigation again, based on different assumptions. In art, there is the explicit validation of criticism, but there is also the interrogativeness expressed in the ways works of art are influenced by other works, how they reflect that influence, make use of the contributions of their predecessors, define their own original contributions. In philosophy, there is explicit challenge to the premises and assumptions of established schools, but there is the challenge of taking a very different approach to philosophical issues, of understanding these issues in different ways. In all these cases, historical mediation is required for subsequent judgments to reflect upon their antecedents. In the same way, practice interrogates and validates former practices in the conformities and departures that manifest its relations through time. Practical judgment belongs to history and to traditions, and these, in their temporality, manifest far-reaching criticisms of their predecessors. The most obvious of these manifestations lie in the tradition itself, for every tradition is divided within itself by subtraditions that reflexively interrogate each other. Nothing can replace the condition that it is the future that defines practical judgment, a future that bears practical relation to its past.

We come to the question of how we are to tell the difference between a succession or oscillation in practice, a sequence of political judgments, and a political query that produces valid judgments through time. If political judgment is interrogated and validated by other political judgments, without universal ideals, how do we avoid the conclusion that there is, in history, merely a succession of judgments, the triumph of the victors?

One answer is that every history of practical judgments is normative, that it is inherent in practice to define norms that influence the future. Thus, there cannot be "mere history," for history is regulative if it is to be influenced by practical judgments and influential over the future. Norms belong to history in the double sense that they cannot escape from history and that no history and no discourse can function without them. This answer is important, but it appears to ignore the major issue. How can we establish political norms that legitimately take precedence over others, where all we can do is to follow one set of norms or another? Far worse, practical norms always impose coercion on those excluded from power, the victors triumphing over their victims.

An analogous question may be raised in relation to science. If we understand inquiry to be situated historically, utilizing norms and methods established historically, then how can we avoid the conclusion that inquiry is a succession of activities with self-imposed authority? The point is that epistemic authority emerges from within query. I add that it is not from itself alone that inquiry gains authority, but from the other modes of query as well. The intermodality and multimodality of query are essential to the legitimacy of any judgment.

There is another answer. Rational authority can be established only from within query itself, and is intelligible only insofar as it is based on query. We cannot raise the question of the epistemic authority of either a mode of query or any of its judgments except in terms of methods that define and validate that authority. The danger here is not of arbitrariness, for that is something we cannot avoid, but of dogmatism, coercion, and blindness, that we should accept judgments and methods uncritically and uninterrogatively. Query, here, in its multiple modalities and reflexivities, is the only means we have for criticism and interrogation. We must recognize the inevitability and unavoidability of such query, including its historicity and temporality, its coerciveness and violence, but also the imperative within it to expand its means and interrogativeness, multimodally and intermodally.

Practical query, in its more intimate and private spheres, tends to appear less interrogative and more arbitrary to the extent that traditional teachings—rules and principles—are taken as sacrosanct. Here different traditions produce different practices. Where future consequences are recognized to impose far-reaching interrogations, where traditional teachings have only proximate value, where charity and sacrifice are foremost in our practices, we find ourselves engaged in political query, whose validation lies in future query, reflecting the terrible dangers of political query. The immediate relevance to any practical judgments of charity and sacrifice, in their interrogativeness, marks the presence of practical query.

LOCAL JUSTICE

A traditional view of justice is expressed in Plato's *Republic* where, although surrounded on all sides by injustices and imperfections, we may presume to seek knowledge of the Form of the Good, including justice, on which the well-being of both the state and individuals rests. If there is injustice, there must be a form or ideal of justice against which it is measured. An unsituated, ahistorical norm of justice is required as the basis of our ethical and political judgments.[5] A more contemporary view asks us to imagine, when faced with issues of justice and injustice, that we are in an "original position" in which we do not know if we are rich or poor, privileged or destitute, among the majority or minority, and so forth. Justice here is based on judgments independent of particular circumstances.[6] The assumptions are that reason is independent of history and that fairness is blind. Both of these assumptions are incompatible with locality.

My view of local practice entails that practical judgment is always situated in the midst of things and that charity, sacrifice, and valor are locally rather than universally determined.[7] It follows that ideology pertains intrinsically but not destructively to practice. Ideology is not incompatible with truth and science but, rather, belongs intrinsically to them without destroying them. What it destroys is their universality. My question here is what idea of justice follows from such a view of practice and ideology.[8] My answer is that there is no legitimate bird's-eye view of justice, only a worm's view, from within. Justice is a form of practice and cannot be extricated from its risks and sacrifices.

Power and ideology are so pervasive, situated at so many points, that they describe and influence truth and falsity, justice and oppression. Justice in this sense is not separable from ideology and power, but a site at which they work. What is required is to separate them from central forms of domination; similarly, what is required is a theory of justice that is not a theory of (total, absolute, unqualified, or perfect) Justice.

Such a view has been criticized as nihilistic.[9] We cannot function in human social and political terms without norms of justice, norms that enable us to function and that constrain our activities and evaluations.[10] The question here is whether, in their traditional roles, such norms are unintelligible and instruments of domination. Principles of justice can at best be rules of thumb implicit in and responsive to injustice. Crudely put, in local terms, we cannot imagine or conceive of ideal justice, only recognize injustices where we encounter them. Such a recognition manifests charity. Injustice, here, is local where justice is totalizing and ideal: wherever we find injustice we must oppose it, in the ways that are available to us, given that every such way is incomplete and promotes other injustices as well as resistances.

In social and political affairs, where justice and injustice are involved, there is no unconditioned ideal, no intelligible sense of perfection, and each of us is biased and narrow in certain ways. Despite this, we can oppose injustices and give reasons for doing so, reasons and practices that others may applaud or oppose. The point is that only by participating in such activities—conversational and practical—can we be said to function under norms and ideals. Reason here is embedded in ongoing practices and criticism. As long as we engage in practical activities, efficaciously, and are able to formulate criticisms that engage those activities, we are participants in a form of reason, and there is no other form of reason where justice is involved. It is a rationality that contains the terrifying realization that we will always fail in destructive ways to understand and to attain justice—even worse, that in political practices ideality is oppressive and sacrificial.[11]

The first principle of politics, understood to involve opposition and power, conflict and control, is not that anything goes, but making do: producing agreement where there are clashes of values, achieving reconciliation amid enmity, squaring the circle we might say; but also promoting differences amid conformity. That we are inevitably surrounded by injustice does not entail that there is a clear ideal of justice that everyone can understand though led astray by special interests and biases. Rather, there are issues we do not and cannot be expected to agree on; moreover, agreement is itself a form of violence. Included here are not only disagreements of principle and opinion, but disparities of circumstance, experience, community, and history.

There is no perfect ideal of justice, only continuing and difficult, frequently confused struggles against injustice. There cannot be adjudication of every difference both because we do not belong to sufficiently widely shared communities and may not accept the struggle to establish one, and because it is in the struggle to achieve justice and to oppose injustice that such communities are formed and rejected.

Rather than assuming that there are or could be ideals whose establishment would define justice for all against which we may measure daily injustices, we may through charity acknowledge only the presence of recurrent injustices. Struggles against them may, under certain conditions of peace and community (but not under others) produce relatively pervasive norms that we may generally share. What can be shared under such circumstances is always greatly limited. Similarly, rather than assuming that we live in communities involving such mutual respect and affection that we can adjudicate any differences, we must recognize that some differences are too polarized and opposing, that only by reconciling them somehow, even by force, can a community be attained in which adjudication is possible. Moreover, even where community has been attained, it cannot eliminate differences forever, and must function amid the continuing possibility of covert violence and injustice. I add that even community has but a local, limited purview, and that it constantly threatens individuals and groups with oppression.

Generally speaking, what is required in the pursuit of justice is not conformity to rule but profound sensitivity to differences of circumstance and identity, especially to differences involving injustices, past, present, and future, differences based on valor. What is required are charity and sacrifice as determinants of political query. Impartiality is plausible only where certain kinds of lawful communities have been developed, which ironically, being unseeing, are constantly threatened by new forms of injustice arising behind and within the laws and procedures that govern them. It follows that impartiality is always misguided as a norm. Instead, what is required is exquisite sensitivity to every form of injustice— a sensitivity that takes for granted that its greatest successes mask within themselves new injustices and that blindness and insensitivity are inevitable. Such a sensitivity to injustice is an expression of charity.

We can recognize injustice where we encounter it, but such an encounter is always local and always grounded in local circumstances. On this basis, justice is not blind but profoundly involved in tangible conditions. The image of blindness is not based on a veil of ignorance that we may suppose that just individuals draw over what they know of themselves and others—a preposterous suggestion—but is specific testimony to an agreement that we have hammered out through political actions not to consider certain differential circumstances relevant to large-scale practices. Such an agreement presupposes that these circumstances and differences are relevant at more local levels of practice. If ethnic differences are irrelevant in courts of law, they are of utmost relevance in religious practices, and it is unjust to seek to control them. Similarly, it is unjust to subject children of different races and languages to common standards of language and social practices without consideration of their different cultural backgrounds.

Justice is war." "Might makes right." How do we avoid the position that justice is simply the result of power? Without secure ideals, how can justice be anything but relative to opinion, at least to social practices? The general answer is that justice is and can be but a local outcome of practical query and that query irresistibly belongs to history and its future. In this sense, it is the responsibility of political query to determine justice as the valid outcome of complex practices aimed at opposing injustice. It is an endless, inexhaustible responsibility.

Four more specific answers can be given. One is that while there is no supreme ideal of justice, and no formula for achieving it, there may be constant awareness of and struggle against injustice. Here injustices are local, and resistances, equally local, take the forms available in the circumstances. The point is that we do know injustices—manifestations of charity—where we find them although we do not always know either how to oppose them or how to realize alternatives that do not produce other injustices. Such knowledge is local, from our particular points of view as ethical and political agents. I add that the regulative principles that have traditionally defined ideals of justice—disinterestedness, balance, harmony—continue to function in local terms. We appeal to such principles and the ideals associated with them—that define "fairness," for example—within our struggles against injustices. But every such ideal and principle must be balanced against historically oppressive conditions and the prospect that it may contribute to further injustices. Disinterestedness may foster greater imbalances; where conflicts are entrenched, the demand for harmony may be oppressive. No regulative principles can escape from the reality that they will be employed to rationalize established forms of domination. The only ethical response is so unrelenting a struggle against injustice that even the most privileged principles and norms are opposed where they contribute to injustice, with recognition that the struggle will foster further injustices.

The second reply is that no ideals or rational principles can avoid the tests of history. The contemporary opposition of utilitarianism and rights theory is not simply a theoretical, but a political opposition. Its resolution will come by practical and political developments, not by philosophy alone. It will depend on political confrontations over social strategies directed toward conformity and individual deviations. Here the nature of the relevant society and the demands of its members for protection and tolerance are important. General ideals of justice are either vacuous or rules of thumb honed through particular confrontations and struggles. Struggle against injustices, clamor to be treated fairly, provide the only milieux in which justice can be attained, by political not just discursive means. I add that this political process is not where reason fails, but is itself a form of reason, one that forcibly manifests its own limitations.

The third and fourth answers are most important theoretically. The third is that the principle that might makes right is invalid because might frequently makes wrong. Violence produces injustice. Political activities inhabit locales filled with justices and injustices. That historical and social practices are essential to determinations of justice and injustice does not entail that they produce justice blindly. Rather, every such determination is tested in the arena of oppression and injustice. Here we can understand the argument that modern forms of justice are forms of domination against members of minority groups. If so, then we will find injustices in the very fabric of "justice." We presuppose that we can recognize injustices and that we are capable of criticizing every political institution that would establish justice. We struggle to oppose injustice, in all the ways we can, for that endless struggle is our justice.

This is the fourth reply. We must pursue and speak of justice in many ways, not just one, from many different points of view, none of which is satisfactory by itself. As agents, we speak of justice as victims and oppressors, recognize injustices and oppose them. In doing so, we work within history and its circumstances, appealing to established norms and procedures and seeking to improve them. Here ideals and adjudicative processes play an essential role. But there is another voice, that of a reflexive criticism that acknowledges not only that all such norms are fallible, but that they serve entrenched interests of domination and violence. We judge and criticize from within, because there is no completely external point of view, but every internal point of view is inexhaustibly divided. The claim that justice is merely opinion, historical sedimentation, speaks only in one undivided voice and fails to express its own limitations. The claim that we presuppose an ideal of justice in our practices also speaks in an undivided voice. Each voice demands the other.

Justice is not simply a sedimentation out of history because it sediments with injustice. Might contributes to the determination of justice—and also injustice. In taking circumstances into account, in recognizing that we belong to history, we do not abolish our capacity to recognize injustices, but include our circumstances and our ideals in such recognitions. To take an example, in a peaceful community under law, problems of justice may be resolved by appeal to common norms and ideals. In a functioning community, differences may be resolved by adjudication. But in an oppressive, authoritarian regime, injustice may demand violence. In these cases, disputes over the kind of society we inhabit must be tested by unceasing struggles in the light of our ethical ideals. But we cannot establish justice without covert injustices. We cannot confront established power without challenging our own legitimacy. We cannot eliminate the terrible risks at the heart of political practice.

Several rules of thumb may guide us in our opposition to injustices. One, by far the most important, is that justice is never for the dominant and powerful, but always for the weak and powerless. The majority rules by dominance and power, custom and law. The injustices to be fought most strenuously are against the powerless. And the most seductive of these injustices are perpetrated in the name of justice for the majority.

Second, it follows that the problem of legitimacy can never be resolved. Every institution that is delegated authority to administer justice takes on greater power than can be right. Every form of power coalesces into illegitimate patterns of domination.

Third, there is an important distinction between public and private morality, legal norms and general principles, total and local justice. Among the frequent causes of injustice are efforts to transform a local norm into a general rule. All norms and rules are local, some of wider scope than others, but always pregnant with conflicts and oppositions. Every understanding of justice is divided into many conflicting voices and requires such a multiplicity if it is to be effective.

Fourth, ideals of community and fairness, dialogue and adjudication, are finite, local regulative norms. As regulative, they supply the measures of just practices; as finite, they are neither attainable nor would they be ideal if attained.

Fifth, there is no positive peace or positive justice. There can at best be avoidance of the most destructive forms of violence. A positive peace suggests that we may overcome all but trivial differences. From the standpoint of locality, major differences cannot and should not be overcome.

These rules of thumb give us a working definition and positive view of justice. Power here includes all forms of influence and control over human beings, individually and collectively. And power, though everywhere, coalesces into patterns of effective domination and oppression. We may associate justice with the ongoing, endless dissipation of such patterns of injustice, with the pursuit of structures of power that are not patterns of oppression, with the qualifications that no such state is attainable and every struggle hides from itself that it is a form of oppression. It would be wrong, however, to think of such a view as pessimistic. Optimism and pessimism cannot be based on norms that lie outside local struggles against which they are measured, but lie within, in possibilities of adjustment and reconciliation. Practically speaking, we win many battles against injustice. Theoretically, there are always possibilities of new measures to resolve imbalances of power.

Among the lessons we have learned from history are that the struggle against injustice is never completed, frequently painful, often confusing, and sometimes destructive, but most important of all, that those who oppose local injustices most strenuously are frequently led into other injustices by their zeal, and that injustices are covert as well as overt. There is then the further lesson that injustice is fought best by those who are zealous but restrained by powerful prohibitions. Here there is a prominent role for established principles of justice, conjoined with unrelenting self-criticism. What is needed, more than rules, is a capacity to listen to people speak in their own voices rather than being spoken for, a capacity for attempting to understand their point of view—with the qualification that we will never hear or see enough, not only because points of view may conflict unresolvably, but also because every voice requires the future for its determination.

LIBERATION

If power is everywhere, inherent in practical judgment, and if power sediments everywhere into patterns of domination and oppression, then the first concern of political practices is liberation. This is true even where the political realm is fragmented into violently opposing armies, for each does its work by domination. In such cases, liberation may require dispersed rather than restricted forces. Further, if power is joined with desire, knowledge, and discourse, so that rules, regulations, principles, and utterances all serve entrenched powers and exercise domination, then it follows again that the first concern of political practices is liberation. Liberation is the manifestation of charity in relation to dominating power. That there is also resistance everywhere does not alleviate the need for liberation, but demands it as the outcome of political practices. Liberation is the condensation among dispersed resistances produced by effective political practices. We may add that the mediateness of practice located in situations already typified by discourses and rules entails that liberation and resistance are always constituted by established forms of power and domination. Even more strongly, there is no liberation from power, only liberating strategies of power. Liberation is both political practice itself and a manifestation of political powers.

Every practice works by means of power, and wherever there is power there arise issues of domination and liberation. To this I add that just as forms of power become more effective as they are institutionalized and regulated by rule, forms of liberation themselves require institutionalization and regulation to be effective. Liberation, here, is not antagonistic to power and politics, but one of the forms of political practice. We must add in addition that even the most liberating institutional forms and rules establish their own forms of domination and oppression, and engender liberating reactions.

My hypothesis is that power works by imposing collective strategies of control typifying the power of one class or group over another, though the power may not be wielded by any group or class or within their intentional control. Power imposes effective strategies of domination. That is, even dispersed, power is political in its ramifications and characterized by far-reaching and large-scale implications and consequences, whether or not it is liberating. Even liberation is political, wields power and is characterized by dominating and oppressive institutionalization.

We may wonder whether such collective forms of domination and oppression are inevitable, whether—thinking ideally—it would be possible to have every dominant power offset by equivalent resistances, whether there could be a future human life in which oppression and abuse were replaced by forms of beneficent and harmonious authority. Since wherever there is power there is resistance, perhaps we may evade the practical concerns of liberation by emphasizing the negativities within power itself, that power divides itself into domination and resistance. Several considerations are relevant. One is that we have never known a form of power that was not oppressive—which is to say that effective power, however dispersed, works by control and domination. A second is that the form of the ideal here depends on a notion I have rejected, that of equivalence and exchange. For there may be no metric of power, no system of equivalences; worse, the notion of equivalence is hostile to valor and charity. There is no balance or harmony of powers, as if they might be exercised without sacrifice. Rather, the dark side of power is that it is always oppressive, always has covert consequences, always involves the imposition of controls on others. Thus, third, political power always incurs disastrous risks, a consequence of the mediateness of human experience and practices, a peril that we trivialize when we propose a balance of forces. Fourth, then, power works asymmetrically. Even reciprocity, as in international trade, must accommodate cyclical imbalances and the decline of certain national powers as others emerge.

Liberation is primarily a political concern though there are important domestic, private oppressions. Among the latter may be included the abuse of children by parents, of women by men, of animals by their owners, of property by its possessors, and of the environment by developers. In each of these cases, there are private, domestic forms of abuse that primarily affect particular individuals and their immediate surroundings, though in the aggregate, collectively, they constitute large-scale patterns of domination and oppression. In each of these cases, moreover, there are resistances wherever there is oppression, and the oppressed exercise reciprocal powers. Thus, grown children sometimes abuse their parents and younger children are sometimes capable of certain forms of tyranny over relatively impotent parents; women are sometimes capable of terrorizing individual husbands and lovers, not to mention their sons; animals sometimes turn on their owners—though here, the disparity in powers becomes predominant; things frustrate our purposes and cause us suffering; the natural environment may resist our plunders, and may retaliate with violent catastrophes.

All these cases share the common structure of practical query divided under powerful tensions into public or political and private or moral forms. Liberation under charity and valor shares the predominant feature of practice with generic measures, that, however effective publicly and politically, both typically neglect personal influences and consequences. Institutional forms of liberation frequently fail to transform domestic life and individual practices. One reason lies in the inadequacies of general norms and principles; another lies in the isolation of private spheres within public practices. For it is one of the predominant features of public practical judgments that certain private spheres of domestic practice be maintained as sites of refuge and domesticity within the far-reaching ramifications of public practices. The irony is that these private spheres of liberation exercise their own forms of domination within the strategies of institutional norms. Even in a society in which public abuse of women and children is forbidden, there are domestic forms of torment and oppression. Moreover, these domestic forms may be pervasive, representing social configurations of domination that overrule publicly promulgated norms.

The primary forms of liberation are political even in relation to the domestic and private examples above both because the autonomy of private practical spheres is instituted politically, a function of political powers, and because in most cases the only effective measures available to remedy oppression and abuse are political. We may interfere directly in the abuse of children by their parents or wives by their husbands, but where public forms of control systematically subordinate either of these to the other, not only may we be ineffective, we may be forestalled and even prevented from acting effectively. If children are not protected under law, then they are subordinated to their parents' powers against well-wishing observers even where there are overt forms of oppression and abuse. If women's rights are not protected under law, by institutional alternatives, then they may be effectively subordinated as legal persons to their husbands' authority. Far more important, even where certain specific forms of abuse are prohibited, coercive powers may covertly exercise domination and oppression. A husband who is prevented by law from beating his wife may be encouraged to refuse her the right to control her own property or to decide if and when she wants to have children. Political forms of practice so permeate our personal judgments that we cannot relate personally to other people except within the practical spaces defined by political measures. The most important and far-reaching forms of liberation function at this juncture of private and public determinations.

I have suggested that questions of liberation pertain to every consideration of politics and justice, that there is no positive justice but only continuing and strenuous opposition to injustice. Liberation is this continuing and strenuous opposition to the oppressions and dominations of power. Every practice imposes such oppressions and dominations; every practical agent is subject to such oppressions. Liberation is the ongoing voice of resistance that makes charity compelling. It is resistance transformed by query.

LEGITIMATION

Wherever there is power, that is, wherever there is practice, collective or private, there is domination and oppression, inherent in the requirements of practical judgment. Wherever there is such domination, there is resistance, and the form that resistance takes is that of liberation. Such a general account does not immediately raise questions of legitimation. Yet such questions are frequently taken to predominate over all others where political practices and ideology are involved.[12] How, in the midst of things, do we legitimate the voice of freedom?

A prior question is why liberation requires legitimation, and what forms of legitimation (and liberation) are acceptable that are not themselves forms of domination? If the answer to these questions is based on mediateness, then legitimation is a practical matter, not theoretical. Legitimation is one of the forms practice takes, as is liberation, whereby power is exercised. It follows that there are no forms of legitimation and liberation that are not themselves forms of domination, that struggles for justice and freedom are never-ending, not in the sense that they elude our grasp, but in the sense that justice and liberation are moments of refuge from the continuing burden of injustice and oppression. Similarly, query is never-ending, not in the sense that knowledge and truth escape our grasp, but in the sense that knowledge and truth belong to query as the unceasing interrogation of every alternative, every possibility of error. Error is the soul of propositional query, constituting it as unceasing; injustice and oppression are the heart of practical reason, constituting it as unceasing. In both cases, the inevitability of error and injustice do not belie the possibility of truth and liberation.

What follows is that it is doubly mistaken to seek to define ideal norms of liberation, mistaken both in overdetermining the relevant norms and principles and in the suggestion that without being able to define justice we cannot resist injustice, without being able to define freedom we cannot resist oppression. To the contrary, these are defined by their resistances. The point inherent in ideology is not that we must somehow be able to escape it, but that because we will never escape to a condition free from ideology, practical truth lies in the activities of resistance from within—that is, in unceasing practical query. In this context, legitimation is not an answer, not something that can be achieved through practice, but is a continuing question in every political practice, analogous to the inescapability of liberation and resistance in every application of power.

Two important qualifications may be noted. One is that every public and far-reaching form of practice must be regulated by rule, however proximately. Formulated norms of liberation and justice therefore play an essential role in practical query, as the only effective means for the promulgation of practical measures. The only way in which practices can be politically effective is by the promulgation of rules. I add the formation of large-scale institutions that impose and apply such rules. No practices can be widely effective, as politics demands, without rules and the institutions that apply them. What follows is that ideology can be fought only with the institutions that regulate it, with the qualification that these are not any less ideological or oppressive for being the only instruments available. Such principles and rules can only be interrogated and fought by diligent attention to charity and valor.

The second point is that ideology, like all forms of practical judgment, seeks to be effective, in this case by controlling the forms and practices of liberation. A demand for legitimation suggests either a permanent basis for social practices or a dividedness within every ideology. For corresponding to the inseparability of power from resistance, ideology is inseparable from its critique. Instead of thinking of legitimating politically liberating practices somehow on assured theoretical grounds, we may regard questions of legitimation as defining political query analogous to the way in which questions of truth define propositional query. In this sense, propositional validation is associated with truth—or, more accurately, with the authority of truth: for example, with the legitimacy and importance of science. Practical validation is associated with influence and authority—more specifically, in the case of politics, with the authority of practical measures of influence.

Given the pervasiveness and inescapability of power, practical query always imposes questions of liberation, of freeing human beings and their surroundings from forms of power that oppress them. Such questions concern charity in the double sense that only by charity can agents who wield power be brought to modify it and that charity is the audible expression of the submerged voices of those who are exploited by established forms of power. Included here we may find the oppression of individuals and groups, classes of human beings, but also the abuse of animals and natural conditions. The question, raised by charity, is how to free any of these from the domination and control of oppressive powers. The answer is the practice of political query itself.

POLITICAL LIBERATION

One of Hobbes's striking claims is that no human or natural power can be so great that it cannot be threatened. Such a claim suggests the principle that wherever there is power there is resistance, with the qualification that Hobbes personalizes power, and neglects its pervasiveness and dispersion. It follows from such personification that a personified sovereign power is required to ameliorate the terror of the state of nature. If we regard power as dispersed, then sovereignty neither is a plausible alternative to anarchy nor is it plausible that it could wield whatever power is required. Rather, what are required are social and institutional forces that harness power and diminish its violences.

It follows that liberation can never be instituted by social and institutional formations and forces, but only within them. This truth is an expression of resistances in relation to power. They are not external to power but belong to it; liberation is not external to oppressive political forces but works through them. Hobbes's state of nature is terrible because power exists there without control, in the absence of political reason. Yet the institution of reason and control neither eliminates power nor achieves liberation. To the contrary, once we begin to interrogate strategies of power and liberation from the standpoint of practice, then even they, as rational achievements, must be called into question as oppressive and coercive. Every form of reason is questionable, for questioning is reason itself. Likewise, every form of power is opposed by other forms of power and liberation, for power is always external to itself in resistances and oppositions.

What makes liberation political is not its relation to power, for power is everywhere, at every level, including its resistances. Rather, political liberation pertains to the larger formations of power with far-reaching ramifications and consequences. In a crude sense, political liberation is always in crisis as compared with everyday, ethical liberation. The intimidation and indoctrination of children by their parents, if not their abuse, is frequently considered acceptable, almost inescapable; the intimidation and indoctrination of many children by a teacher is not, and calls forth collective or institutional countermeasures.

Although power is everywhere, and although wherever there is power there is resistance, power and resistance, along with oppression and liberation, are not identical. Resistance belongs to power; liberation is always in relation to oppression. I assume that power coalesces into strategies with large-scale political and institutional implications.[13] I further assume that these large-scale forms give rise to dispersed oppositions that constitute resistance and liberation.

How can we argue that power must be exercised in large-scale institutional formations, that practical strategies will inevitably coalesce into political predominance and oppression?[14] We may follow Hobbes in recognizing that power is not absent in the state of nature, but rather political resistance is absent. Such a resistance is not simply opposing, balancing power, but a response to coalesced, dominating power. Thus, we have the two answers previously noted as to why political power coalesces into larger formations. One is that the scale of political practice is immense, that political practice is concerned with far-reaching issues and concerns, and that these require institutional formations and generic regulations. The second is that without such formations and codes, there could be no resistances.

If we try to imagine a sphere of practice without resistances, we tend to imagine a form of domestic activity—a community or family. We presuppose that all relations among people involving power are either direct and face-to-face or mediated by community voices. We effectively deny the political and collective nature of such practices and activities, that the scale of practice overpowers the capacities of private, communal relations to deal with conflicts and divisions. We presuppose that not all power relations are dominating and oppressive, requiring resistances. For resistance and liberation pertain specifically to imbalances of power and control. To the contrary, politics is testimony to the inexhaustibility and locality of practices and powers, requiring sweeping resistances and movements of liberation.

If we accept the conclusion that power, though everywhere and always accompanied by resistances, nevertheless establishes strategies of dominance and oppression, then we may identify resistance and liberation with opposing voices. I add to such voices continuing confrontation with the possibility that their forms of opposition establish new forms of domination. I include such examples as a revolutionary group gaining power while relations within the group—among men and women, adults and children, racial and class differences, and so on—remain oppressive; a minority group gaining power only to establish oppressive classifications within it that divide privileged and disadvantaged, strong and weak. Power works everywhere by stratification and domination, including strategies of domination that develop in opposing forces. Liberating movements develop inner forms of domination.

The role of liberation in political query is analogous to the role of charity in relation to practice in general. It is the manifestation of inexhaustibility in relation to the sacrifices of practical judgment. It is only as we repeatedly raise questions of liberation in the context of every political situation and practice that we can express our understanding of charity. And it is only as we recognize that power always works by domination and oppression, everywhere, that we can confront the pervasiveness of questions of liberation. Charity in political terms takes the form of liberation.

HUMAN LIBERATION

The forms of oppression and domination are legion—all the forms of human life. There are oppressions at more private, intimate levels of human practices as well as at more public, political levels. There are oppressions of individuals and oppressions of groups, oppressions by direct relations, face-to-face, and by indirect relations. In all the major forms of oppression, there are implicit forms of domination that support the predominant explicit strategies of power: the oppression of racial minorities, women, children, the poor and homeless, but also the abuse and exploitation of animals and the environment. The pervasiveness of oppression suggests that it be identified with the workings of power. The pervasiveness of the need for liberation then suggests that it be identified with the resistances within such workings of power. We must add the qualification that power and resistance, oppression and liberation, cannot be separated formally or by rule, but only by unceasing political query.

Such identifications entail that there is no "liberated" form of human life and practice, especially at the scale of political practices. No matter how liberating, responsive, charitable, and ideal, political query takes place together with the inevitability of sacrifice and the ubiquitousness of power. That is, it works by exercising power, and the exercise of power can be effective only by imposition and domination. Traditional and contemporary forms of anarchism possess at least this much truth: every government wields oppressive powers. However, it is also true that governments do not wield powers as much as situate them and that wherever there are human practices there are asymmetric powers and dominations, in every human institution, particularly those of massive scale. Corporations wield predominant powers and exercise important influences, sometimes of greater impact than national states. Governments and national states are not always more oppressive or abusive than other entrenched political structures and agencies, but are far more visible.

There is no liberated form of human life and practice, but there are liberating practices. Liberation belongs not to consequences but to practice itself. It is not a state achieved, which is why questions of legitimation cannot be answered, but a continuing concern within practice as to whether a particular system of political domination is acceptable despite its sacrifices and oppressions. Questions of liberation and legitimation, then, are identical, and together belong to ongoing political practice.

What most forms of anarchism proclaim is the pervasiveness

and oppressiveness of power and the superiority of voluntary associations and practices. Voluntarism is the corrective to oppression. Yet it remains a form of collective power. If power is everywhere, it must include voluntary practices in the double sense that what people voluntarily accept is the result of entrenched, covert powers and that what people voluntarily do exercises power, however covertly. That people agree voluntarily to buy advertised goods does not eliminate the fact that the manipulation of desire is an important exercise of power. That people agree voluntarily to go to war does not eliminate the fact that unknown causes and unanticipatable consequences of such decisions will deeply influence their lives and those of their descendants. Voluntary associations and practices are not alternatives to power and oppression but one of their explicit forms.

Questions of human liberation, then, are none other than the unavoidable questions of political query in the context of entrenched powers. Yet we tend to identify questions of liberation with much more visible forms of domination and oppression: of one country by another, one minority by another, even of a majority by a minority, of women by men and even by other women. In doing so, we acknowledge the significance of the stratifications of power into groups and structures. But we overlook the fact that most forms of power work covertly and pervasively. Even more important, we neglect the fact that most liberating practices covertly impose their own forms of domination even on those they would liberate. An important example is found in language, for to tolerate minority languages is not to eliminate the consequences of linguistic differentiation—in particular, that most societies are structured in terms of dominant linguistic structures, politically but also economically and vocationally. Privilege possesses discursive forms.

Charity entails a caretaker relation toward those who are powerless or less able. Yet charity also entails that those who have voices must be listened to. For speaking for others is itself a form of power and domination. It follows that charity in its caretaker forms is required and oppressive. Liberation is frequently dominating and confining. It is impossible to expect a structural resolution of this antinomy, as if there were a certain formal role that we might assign to others' voices and to our capacity to listen. There is no rule in query for distinguishing what is legitimate from what is not. To the contrary, charity entails that every form of power be known to be dominating, including its own manifestations, that power is asymmetric, intrinsically oppressive. To be effective, practical judgment must exercise power and exert influence. To recognize this is to recognize the importance of sacrifice.

The conclusion is that human liberation is inseparable, virtually indistinguishable, from political query, that such query recurrently confronts the two poles of practice: the effectiveness it requires and the dominations and oppressions that effectiveness produces. Liberation is the voice of charity in the context of inescapable political judgment, the voice that makes politics query.

VIOLENCE

The modern state arrogates all violence to itself, at least that violence under its control, among its means of domination. Here we must include not only violence directed toward its own citizens, through its police overtly and through the implicit or explicit encouragement of violent crime, but violence directed toward other states, through its military forces and the oppressions imposed during any war. Here punishment and intimidation, however framed by moral principles and however supported by the majority of citizens, are overt and covert forms of domination.

If violence belongs to the state as one of its means of oppression, then liberation cannot avoid relations to violence, either as instrument of resistance or as means whereby power is to be avoided. From the standpoint of ideality, violence appears an abhorrent form of practice to be avoided wherever possible, its only justification that of means necessary to its own overcoming. Yet I have rejected ideality as inadequate to practical query, especially political query. How then are we to understand the relation between political query and such explicit forms of violence as revolution and war? These remain unresolved issues in the modern state, including the issue of punishment, a prominent form of state violence. In this case, the violence is acknowledged by everyone to be unavoidable, required by the exigencies of practice, one of the prominent and inescapable forms of sacrifice. All that we can do in response is to engage in ceaseless practical query, based on charity, and to avoid the injustices of unexamined principles of punishment. All we can do, in other words, is to recognize the inseparability within political query of every form of violence from the unending demand for liberation.

This conclusion may be extended to war. In the context of locality and inexhaustibility, there is no positive peace, no ideal state of human life freed from the insecurities and failures of political practices. There is unavoidable conflict and evil, and consequently, a continuing need for political violence. In practical terms, it is not that we must always be preparing for war or engaging in it, even in a world threatened by nuclear destruction, but that where there is no ideal and positive peace, where states rule by violence and domination, where there is oppression and suffering, war is not always the worst alternative. Indeed, "better" and "worse" are misleading, for they presuppose a metric for determining where violence and destruction are justified. To the contrary, violence and war are among the prominent forms of political practice; both face the indeterminatenesses inherent in every practice. Both remain alternatives within political practices, whether or not actually implemented, inherent in the scale of importance and the conflicts that characterize political query. It follows that both belong as much to liberation as to oppression.

Questions of political practice are questions of liberation. There are inevitably entrenched powers against which any practical undertaking involving charity must align itself. Are violent measures always or ever justified? Even more extremely, are practices that delimit no specific foreseeable results, but that involve violent and destructive means, ever justified in response to oppression? Can a practice that repudiates all norms of judgment be justified as a liberating form of practice?

The first question concerns justification. If what we mean by justification is that a revolution is justified only if the balance of violence and destruction caused by the revolution is less than the violence and destruction it would remedy, then there probably can be no justified revolution. But the justification here is not relevant to practice, for it presupposes a metrical equivalent in violence and destruction. It presupposes that we may compare the dead—in numbers or in their agony—though we recognize that there is no metric for such comparison.

From the standpoint of revolutionary practice, no such presupposition can be sustained. At the extreme, where a régime is sufficiently oppressive, any revolutionary practices may be thought justified if necessary to overthrow it. And we may go further, to claim that if moral principles stand in the way, forcing us to compare destruction and suffering before and after the revolution, then that morality is part of the system of oppression. Rules cannot be applied without exceptions. Moreover, however ideal, rules participate in systems of domination and oppression. What such a position overlooks is that the revolution itself belongs to and defines another system of domination.

There is no metrical system for evaluating the pain and suffering under an oppressive régime in comparison with the pain and suffering caused by a revolution, and, even if there were, it would not settle the issue. Some revolutions would be necessary even if they caused more destruction than they prevented, if the oppressions of the régime they opposed were too arbitrary and capricious. On the other hand, not every opposition to a system of domination is justified in leading to violence. What we would like is a formula, a set of distinctions, that would tell us when a revolution was valid and when it was not. What we would like is for something outside of practice to determine it so that we might escape its indeterminatenesses.

For this is precisely the point: in practical judgment, even as query, there is no escape from catastrophe, no escape from the terrible nature of terrible deeds, from pain and suffering, destruction and misery. We can try to minimize destruction and suffering, but there is no quantitative measure of relative suffering. Even worse, every such measure plays a repressive role in a system of domination. On the other side, however, we cannot make any liberating political judgments without appeal to principles and ideals, for example, of justice and injustice.

There is no stable, ideal form of justice, and every ideal and principle exercises domination and oppression over those who conform to it. Nevertheless, it is possible to oppose and to triumph over injustices. Even so, such a triumph can never be ideal, is always local, and the opposition is unending. The struggle against injustice is equivalent with the struggle for liberation. And it is essential that every such struggle keep the alternative open of extremity in practice if that becomes necessary. There can be no question of ceding all power to established systems of domination, to the national state for example, not where our most pressing concerns are struggles against oppression and injustice. It is also essential that every such struggle combat its own dominations.

The answers to how it is possible to struggle against injustices without possessing a stable norm of justice, how it is possible to struggle against oppression without possessing a stable norm of liberation, are that every such struggle is local, against local oppressions and capable of achieving only local liberations; that we can understand and evaluate such oppressions and liberations only because they are local; that every such struggle belongs to history and must be qualified by particular circumstances and conditions—judgment is local; that power, which is present in any conflict or struggle, is divided within itself by resistances and always works by domination and oppression; and finally, that liberation is a many-voiced and many-headed struggle.

The first principle here is that of locality. It entails that liberation and opposition be understood to be local, qualified by conditions and divided into many voices. Because understanding and liberation are local, they can be effective only in local terms. It follows that there is no absolute measure of the justification of a practice, but there are the local justifications and measures that there are. More important, every local situation involving human life and experience involves practical judgment. When practice involves a certain scale, it becomes political, and political judgment always involves continuing struggles against injustice and oppression. These are the practical result of political practices carried on as best we can. It follows that revolution does not require extraordinary justifications, but is a major and important form of political practice. All political practices are potentially extreme. It follows further that revolutionary activities share in the insecurities of all political practices, and political query cannot avoid questions of whether it will make things worse than before and of the forms of oppression it will engender.

A second principle emphasizes the unavoidable historicality of practice, that it begins in established conditions and confronts an open future, but even more, that it begins as the result of past practices and is judged in terms of its future consequences. Judgment in practice, especially in political query, not only belongs to time along with all judgments and interrogations, but utilizes time as its measure. There is truly a sense in practice, especially political query, in which we must wait for the future to determine the outcome and justification of any course of action. This is as true for revolutionary activities as of any other major form of practice.

A third principle entails recognition that every political régime and institution is divided within itself by resistances and oppositions and exercises domination and oppression. This is as true of established régimes as of those to be established through practical undertakings. It follows that there is no régime that is so dominant that there are no resistances and oppositions within it and no ideal régime that can avoid oppression. But it follows also that revolutions and other violent forms of resistance are not so much alternatives to entrenched powers as the forms of resistance within them.

I add a fourth principle, that liberation speaks in many voices, that to any discourse and practice of liberation we must bring different voices and practices, from within and without. Thus, the movement of liberation itself becomes a régime, dominant and oppressive, at least over its members, frequently over a wider range of human relations. In this context, the threat of revolutionary practice is not that it would violently resist an entrenched system of power and domination but that it typically blinds itself to its own oppressions.

The conclusion is that violent revolution is an important alternative within every established system of power, a form of liberation necessary to the presence of forceful resistances. Every government is situated in a context of political alternatives where, if its coerciveness becomes too overt or too repressive, equally overt resistances, including violent means and coercive responses, must and will emerge. What must be added is that power and resistance function whether practice is interrogative or blind, and that the question of revolution must be one that belongs to query. The issue of revolution is not that it sacrifices lives and property to a new order, for there is no political practice without sacrifices, but that it does so blindly, neither deeply interrogatively nor based on charity. Here the interrogativeness is not simply in words or deliberation, but belongs to practice. The difficulty of revolution is that its typical means are forms of compulsion and oppression to which it must itself be blind to be effective.

Along with war and revolution and every other form of violence, there can be no absolute prohibition of violence of any kind. What takes its place is the continuing opposition and conflict of ideal principles with political exigencies, the unending promise of failure and despair. All that we can do within this situation, not so much as a remedy but simply as a fulfillment of the promises and demands of practice, is to make practice query, to interrogate and validate it as profoundly and as deeply as we can, with a continuing openness to new forms of understanding, criticism, and practice. Interrogation here belongs to every mode of judgment, though since we are concerned here with practice the forms of practice must be developed that are interrogative of other forms.

Here we may interpret terrorism in two ways. One, the simplest to evaluate out of context, consists of forms of violence directed at innocent people and at property—violence and destruction, largely at random—and is a form of resistance without purpose. Its predominant quality is cruelty, injustice. Its classical theoretical name is nihilism, the position that no norms, local or total, have legitimacy. Its blindness consists in failing to acknowledge that like every form of practice, it exercises dominations and oppressions, that it functions for those it harms more as a system of coercion than of liberation. Terrorism in this sense fails as query. It opposes and destroys without reflecting on its own oppressions. It is a relatively rare and aberrant form of the violence that composes organized resistance, and a small part of what is called terrorism by established powers as part of their political legitimation. It is sufficiently rare that few if any forms of practice correspond to it without qualification. Rather, established political forces utilize a rhetoric critical of such terrorism to mobilize their political forces against quite different forms of opposition and violence.

The second interpretation is of terrorism as an extreme form of resistance against local injustices. Like every form of practice, it is subject to the tests of the future, but one that is willing to accept the risks of its present excesses to rid the world of an abhorrent system of oppression. The view that opposition to injustice is always local has the consequence that there is no absolute standard against which terrorism may be measured. It is necessary to reject even the highest ethical ideals when engaged in acts of liberation—or, more accurately, to reject any ideal principles and to replace them with unswerving charity. What is unfortunate is that organized violence is typically devoid of charity.

The latter view of political violence appears to situate it within query. The question for query, however, is how we are to recognize that a given form of practice has failed, what such failure entails, and what remedy remains given such failure. An analogous case is that of capital punishment. Once a person has been wrongfully executed, or even rightfully executed in a form blind to charity, then no remedy remains, no restoration of life is possible. In the context of political exigencies, surrounded by failure, practices based on valor will seek to avoid catastrophe, where that is possible, out of charity and cognizant of sacrifice. The point involved in sacrifice is that what is destroyed is precious. Blind violence is first of all blind, and cannot belong to query. But we are describing not violence but its context and implementation. And I add that our condemnations and reprisals against blind forms of political violence are practical judgments, employ power, utilize their own forms of violence. The condemnation of violent acts as "terrorist," "nihilist," or "blind" is never innocent, never free from practical, political determinations, and typically employs established powers of the national state against the enemy it has identified and reviled. No categorical labels, moral or political, however ideal, can escape the indeterminatenesses of practice—power, desire, violence, and destruction. No form of practice can escape its dangers.

It follows that violence belongs to political query intrinsically and unavoidably, if not as an implemented means of domination then as a possibility in liberation. All that we can do is to confront the issues it raises recurrently and unendingly, that is, to engage in political query given the omnipresence of violence and of failure. Violence and destruction are in this sense, given valor and charity, intrinsic marks of failure yet unavoidable in political practices. This ineradicable tension marks the deepest truth of political query.[15]

THE HUMAN ENVIRONMENT AND ITS FUTURE

Human life and experience are always situated among natural and social surroundings, directed from the past to the future. All human life and experience are practical in this sense, particularly to the extent that judgments are directed toward the future. For practice is that mode of judgment which is not only situated in its environment and propelled from its past into its future, but which is validated in and by its future. In this sense, the future belongs to practice uniquely.

Political query is that form of rational practice in which issues of great moment and scale are judged and resolved. These involve other people and the requisites of human life, however they may be understood and implemented—relations between national states, the distribution of wealth and food, the mobilization of armies, but also care for the environment and explicit concern for the future.

All practical judgment shares this explicit concern for the future, but sometimes a more personal or intimate future than that implicated in political practices. For politics, in its determinants of scale, faces the unknown and effectively uncontrolled future of humanity, even of the world and the accessible universe. There cannot be a practice that does not look to its future for its validation, but there are many deeds that have no wider purview than that of one's person or family, possibly one's community. Yet there will inevitably be a human future, inevitably a natural future. Because we cannot escape the questions that are brought before us by that future, we must engage to answer them, in political query.

Humanity will have a future but each human being will die. Human life will someday come to an end, but nature will continue. Death and extinction are inevitable and universal, but never total: something always continues. Life and death, endurance and extinction, are always local. It is the province of politics to confront the locality of such relations—that is, to seek to relate to the terms of death, given its inevitability, and to define our relations to what will continue.

The future to which our practical judgments are directed is inexhaustible, as is the environment in which we are engaged, not least because the future and our environment includes us and our practices, so that we contribute inexhaustibly to their determination. There can be no possibility of completely controlling the future or our surroundings, not because we lack the power—though every power is divided by resistances—not even because power is everywhere and owned by no one, but because control belongs to an inexhaustible future by divisions and oppositions. Every present undertaking enters the future not only facing unknown dangers, but constituting new and unanticipatable dangers. Every political practice constitutes the milieux in which subsequent practices transpire and the conflicts and oppositions that such practices seek to resolve. Similarly, every local practice belongs to multifarious other locales that together constitute the environment, but only locally. Inexhaustibility here is locality, and every political undertaking is local but of indeterminate ramifications.

Do we have an obligation to the future? We face the future inevitably in the consequences of our undertakings. Do we have an obligation to preserve the environment for future generations? We are part of our environment in any case, and our actions will constitute locales for future undertakings. Insofar as we are agents engaged in practical judgments, the future and our present and future surroundings pertain both by necessity and importance, for they are determinants of our present judgments.

The inexhaustibility of the future and of our surroundings entails that we will be faced with never-ending conflicts and inadequacies, that catastrophic failure threatens all practical judgment, especially at the scale of politics, an ingredient of any human future. Failure haunts all practices, especially those with political ramifications, but such failure is not incompatible with success.

The basis of practical judgment is valor, inexhaustible charity and sacrifice. The question of our relation to the future and our environment is the question of political practice in the context of charity. Every action affects the environment and the future, but some actions do so more perniciously than others, some do so with more sweeping consequences than others, some may be performed less thoughtfully and interrogatively than others. Inexhaustibility threatens all practical undertakings with inexhaustible prospects of failure. We may tend to forget that it also promises inexhaustible prospects of fulfillment—especially within the inventiveness possible through query.

Query is unterminating interrogation and validation. Inherent in such a form of judgment is invention: the promise inherent in query. In relation to practice and to politics, query promises possibilities of new forms of human relations, new forms of activity and judgment, realized in new institutions and social structures. That political query cannot avoid failure does not entail that it lacks success, for the prospects of failure and success are inexhaustible. Rather, political query inventively transforms our institutional practices and relations to our own practices and rules and to our surroundings, at the expense of unavoidable sacrifices.

This continuing relation in practical judgments to their future and their environments—practical judgment, immersed without escape in conditions determined by the past, in possibilities of invention, open to the future and to external influences—is political query itself, based on charity and defined by sacrifice. Political query, more than any other form of practice and judgment, faces us with immense powers of interrogation and control as well as our inadequacies and limitations—our finiteness and locality—as well as with the resistances in power, the indeterminatenesses in determination. Political query is possible only because we are faced with issues of great moment, of great scale, implying that we are able to function and to engage ourselves with such issues of great scale and importance. It is in political query that we find and test the limits of our limits and our possibilities of transcendence at a level of generality and inclusiveness in which even human nature is implicated.

It follows that there is no escape from political query and no alternative to its rationality—no alternative to understanding that it is rational. It is rational because it is interrogative, validative, and inventive. It is rational also because it is the only means we have, the only form of judgment, that embodies practical undertakings of a scale of importance in which human being and natural being are in question. Such questions arise in philosophy as well as politics, but only the latter addresses such questions in and through the future, through what human being and its surroundings are and will become.

Notes

1. For a quite different view, see Jürgen Habermas, *Communication and the Evolution of Society*, trans. Thomas McCarthy (Boston: Beacon, 1979), p. 70: "Speaker and hearer can reciprocally motivate one another to recognize validity claims because the content of the speaker's engagement is determined by a specific reference to a thematically stressed validity claim, whereby the speaker, in a cognitively testable way, assumes with a truth claim, obligations to provide grounds, with a righteous

claim, obligations to provide justification, and with a truthfulness claim, obligations to prove trustworthy."

From my point of view, Habermas overlooks that theory belongs to practice as much as practice belongs to practice (though not only to practice), while assumptions concerning truth and communication are not independent of the practical judgments they define, but arise within and are constituted by them. Grounds, justifications, and trustworthiness are as practical determinants as they are theoretical, and cannot be determined independent of mediate, situated practices. I add several qualifications. One is that while theory belongs to practice, it does not belong to practice alone. Theory and practice can neither be entirely separated nor entirely conjoined, but are deeply interrelated while inhabiting spheres of their own as part of their inexhaustibility. Locality and inexhaustibility entail relatedness and excess. Thus, one answer to the problem of ideology is that it is situated among means for establishing truth, even though such means are no less situated in forms of life and practice, in history, than ideology.

See, by way of contrast, Foucault, *Archaeology of Knowledge*, p. 186: "1. Ideology is not exclusive of scientificity. . . . 3. By correcting itself, by rectifying its errors, by clarifying its formulations, discourse does not necessarily undo its relations with ideology. The role of ideology does not diminish as rigour increases and error is dissipated. 4. To tackle the ideological functioning of a science in order to reveal and to modify it is not to uncover the philosophical presuppositions that may lie within it; nor is it to return to the foundations that made it possible, and that legitimated it: it is to question it as a discursive formation. . . ."

Here, ideology is to be understood, along with science, to belong to discourses and to practices, and to have no autonomous legitimacy, no non-discursive foundations. I add that since ideology and science—that is, falsehood and truth—are inexhaustible, they transcend any particular discursive formations, belong to inexhaustibly multifarious discourses. The sources of critique lie within this plenitude of locations.

2. See chap. 2, note 22.

3. See Jacques Derrida, "The Politics of Friendship," trans. Gabriel Motzkin, *Journal of Philosophy*, 85, No. 11 (November 1988), 632–48.

4. See here Michel Foucault, *The Birth of the Clinic: An Archaeology of Medical Perception*, trans. A. M. Sheridan-Smith (New York: Random House, 1973).

5. See note 1, above, for a contemporary view of such norms.

6. "One feature of justice as fairness is to think of the parties in the initial situation as rational and mutually disinterested" (John Rawls, *A Theory of Justice* [Cambridge: Harvard University Press, 1971], p. 13).

7. See Benjamin R. Barber, "Deconstituting Politics: Robert Nozick

and Philosophical Reductionism," in *The Frontiers of Political Theory*, edd. Michael Freeman and David Robertson (Brighton, Sussex: Harvester, 1980), pp. 23–46, for a similar criticism of Nozick (Robert Nozick, *Anarchy, State, Utopia* [New York: Basic Books, 1974]) as beginning with a non-public, non-conflicting sphere of norms and power relationships. Barber criticizes Nozick for a non-political theory of politics. The first facts of politics are situatedness, conflict, and distortion.

8. For one reply, see Michel Foucault, *Power/Knowledge*, ed. Colin Gordon (New York: Pantheon, 1980), pp. 27–28: "In my view one shouldn't start with the court as a particular form, and then go on to ask how and on what conditions there could be a people's court; . . . my hypothesis is not so much that the court is the natural expression of popular justice but rather that its historical function is to ensnare it, to control it and to strangle it, by reinscribing it within institutions which are typical of a state apparatus.

"There are two forms which must not under any circumstances be adopted by this revolutionary apparatus: bureaucracy and judicial apparatus. Just as there must be no bureaucracy in it, so there must be no court in it. The court is the bureaucracy of the law. If you bureaucratise popular justice then you give it the form of a court."

[". . . Then how is it to be regularised?]

"I'll reply to that by what is, of course, an evasion: it remains to be discovered."

9. See Michael Walzer, "The Politics of Michael Foucault," *Dissent*, 4 (Fall 1983), 490: "[O]ne can't even be downcast, angry, grim, indignant, sullen, or embittered *with reason* unless one inhabits some social setting and adopts, however tentatively and critically, its codes and categories. Or unless, and this is much harder, one constructs a new setting and proposes new codes and categories." Everything depends on how one understands the tentativeness of such codes and rules. One of the foremost truths of political query is that the promulgation of rules far exceeds their justification, frequently catastrophically.

10. Nancy Fraser, "Foucault on Modern Power: Empirical Insights and Normative Confusions," *Praxis International*, 1, No. 3 (October 1981), 286: "[O]ne cannot object to a form of life simply on the ground that it is power-laden. Power is productive, ineliminable, and, therefore, normatively neutral. . . . [such norms] are what *enable* us to speak, at the same time and insofar as they *constrain* us."

11. Other paradigms of practical reason have been proposed, see, for example, Hilary Putnam, "How Not to Solve Ethical Problems," *The Lindley Lecture* (Lawrence: University of Kansas, 1983), pp. 4–5: "The way *not* to solve an ethical problem is to find a nice sweeping principle that 'proves too much,' and to accuse those who refuse to 'buy' one's

absolute principle of immorality. The very words 'solution' and 'problem' may be leading us astray—ethical 'problems' are not like scientific problems, and they do not often have 'solutions' in the sense that scientific problems do. . . .

"I suggest that our thought might be better guided by a different metaphor—a metaphor from the law, instead of a metaphor from science—the metaphor of *adjudication*."

The legal metaphor of adjudication presupposes community. "To successfully adjudicate ethical problems, as opposed to 'solving' them, it is necessary that the members of the society have a sense of community" (ibid., p. 8). Similarly, see Richard J. Bernstein, *Beyond Objectivism and Relativism: Science, Hermeneutics, and Praxis* (Philadelphia: University of Pennsylvania Press, 1983), p. 231: "[I]t is not sufficient to try to come up with some new variations of arguments that will show, once and for all, what is wrong with objectivism and relativism, or even to open up a way of thinking that can move us beyond objectivism and relativism; such a movement gains 'reality and power' only if we dedicate ourselves to the practical task of furthering the type of solidarity, participation, and mutual recognition that is founded in dialogical communities."

Such an appeal to community is a covert appeal to another species of ideality. Even worse, it overlooks the deepest truth of any system of justice, that it is a system of control, of domination and power. The community in dialogue and adjudication presupposes shared experiences and outcomes. What makes injustice so pervasive is that amid community and shared experiences there are deep-seated oppositions and clashes. To emphasize community is to demand it although there may be differences that cannot be overcome, points of view that should not be shared. Differences in point of view and experience are sources of important human achievements. Adjudication and dialogue determine their own forms of tyranny.

12. See Jürgen Habermas, *The Legitimation Crisis*, trans. Thomas McCarthy (Boston: Beacon, 1975).

13. Some of this is clear in Ivan Illich's writings, for amid his extreme aversion to industrial society with its institutions and codes there is tacit recognition that institutional oppression can only be fought with alternative institutions and codes, of equivalent political scale. See, for example, *Tools for Conviviality* (New York: Harper & Row, 1973).

14. Even Foucault does not go this far, and rather suggests that such predominance and oppression, such manifest strategies of power, are a consequence of modern strategies, of Enlightenment thought and practice. See *Order of Things*.

15. See Sergio Cotta, *Why Violence? A Philosophical Interpretation*, trans. Giovanni Gullace (Gainesville: University of Florida Press, 1985),

pp. 138, 140: "What concerns us is to see that violence be revealed by reflection not as the *only*, but simply as *one* human possibility: that which realizes itself in an immediate and passional reaction to varied encounters without reciprocal understanding between empirical events and sensibilities; and that which remains unresponsive to the call for relationship coming from the ontological structures—the possibility that is always a latent snare but not an unavoidable fatality.

"Charity has its own roots in the most intimate regions of being, where not only the structural rationality manifests itself but so also does the vital need (inseparable from it) that such a relation be willed and, therefore, confirmed and promoted in actuality in the varied experience of life. . . . The genuinely radical answer to the excessiveness of violence, which seizes everything for the benefit of the egocentric subject, is that of the superabundance of charity."

6

TECHNOLOGY

TECHNOLOGY IS A FORM OF PRACTICE, perhaps the most important modern form, virtually identical with material practice itself, if we understand practice as instrumentality. It is, however, more than an instrument, both because practice itself is more than instrumental and because technology itself is inexhaustible. Like every form of practice, technology transcends its boundaries, transforms human experience in unanticipated ways, beneficently and maleficently. There is no large-scale form of practice to which we owe so much for its human benefits and toward which we feel such repugnance for its destructiveness and inhumanity.

We may begin our discussion with a distinction between pure and applied science, distinguishing both from technology.[1] We may think of applied science as the application of science to practice, technology as practice itself. Yet the rise of modern science and the industrial revolution make such a distinction difficult to maintain.[2] Before the rise of modern science, technology had to depend on the methods available to it. With the growth of modern science, technology could employ science among its means to practical ends, giving rise to modern technology. Yet science uses technology no less, if for different ends—the discovery of truths about the natural world. The pervasiveness of the different modes of judgment, their multimodality and intermodality, is especially striking in relation to modern technology.

What is important is the invasion of certain forms of practice into other forms of judgment, derived in part from intermodality and multimodality, in part from the pervasiveness and the force of practical judgment. Technology has become the dominating form of practice that virtually defines modern life. In this sense it is indistinguishable from contemporary political practices, under dispersed rather than centralized control. Moreover, it is less an overpowering form of dominance than the form in which contemporary dominations are expressed. This invasiveness belongs to practical judgment intrinsically, with industrial technology the contemporary form of such domination. Query utilizes means drawn from all the domains of judgment, seeks maximal inter-modal interrogation and validation. Practical query functions under an imperative to strive for maximal intermodality. Further-more, practice always functions by means of power, transforming intermodality of means into invasiveness of results, domination and oppression, unless pervaded by other intermodal forms of interrogation and invention.

I have noted the reciprocal relation between modern technology and science. I add the close relation between technology and art. Both produce artifacts, yet technology is not predominantly fabri-cative judgment or art. We recall the distinction between *technē* and *poiēsis*, technique and art, defining *technē* as production ac-cording to antecedently determinable ends, a notion largely inap-plicable to art.[3] It is closely related to a view of practice as dependent on ideal norms of perfection.[4]

Yet technology is incompatible with perfectibility in two im-portant respects. One is that the incessant changes inherent within it make any stable perfection impossible. Second, more important, technology, like politics and art, produces and subverts norms through its own activities. All practical judgment, and especially practical query, depends on an open and undetermined future. In this sense, all norms, derived from past experience, can only be hypothetical for the future. In this sense as well, there can be no technological perfectibility, because the norms of validation applicable in that future will not conform to the norms inherent in the practices that produced that future.

What we find in technology, along with all political practices and every form of practical query, is the presence of norms and principles that emerge from the practices themselves, bearing the uncertainties, vicissitudes, and imperfections of time. The devel-opment of such norms from within is not a failure of instrumental-ity, as if there might be a truth of being or human being that could define their fulfillment. To the contrary, practice always belongs to practice (though not only to practice), and there is no escape for practical judgment and query from the entanglements of other practical judgments and queries. What there are instead are the critical and interrogative perspectives possible because practice is not the only form of judgment and query and because practice is divided within itself by manifold subpractices, institutions, and conditions.

Modern technology produces artifacts, seemingly an endless supply of them, ranging from useful objects like automobiles and refrigerators through ornamental accessories like door handles and hubcaps to largely useless and even ugly souvenir and tourist items. We may ask whether these fabricated objects typically meet specific needs, whether their ends are specifiable in advance, or whether like all objects, practical and otherwise, they originate in certain needs and specifications but thoroughly transcend them. We may also ask whether it is the production of artifacts that distinguishes technology or the practical purposes that it fulfills.

One view regards instrumental objects entirely in terms of antecedently specifiable purposes and consequences. It is the classic view of *technē*. Collingwood makes it the center of his distinction between art and craft. In craft, means and ends are distinct and the end is preconceived.[5] In comparison, art is expressive, realizing its purposes only in its production, surmounting any antecedent intentions. Such a view of art is persuasive, for it emphasizes the possibilities of novelty and insight that surround the production of works of art. Yet it is doubtful whether any objects meet Collingwood's definition of craft, and far more doubtful whether technology is less open and transformative than art. This view of craft and technique as based on antecedent ends dominates our view of technology, but the view is implausible in most respects, particularly in relation to any large-scale forms of practice. Within the repetitiveness of technical activities, there is a staggering plenitude of possibilities and forms.

Does technology produce objects for the sake of those objects, whether or not in terms of antecedent norms, or for the sake of the consequences in human life to which those objects contribute? It seems that, unlike art, where the aim of the activity may be thought to produce sovereign works, technology produces artifacts for practical ends. And although our technology is one of fabrication and contrivance, we may imagine a psychological or spiritual technology whose means are not fabricated material objects but techniques of thought and meditation. And there have been such technologies, real and proposed, in monasteries and utopias, perhaps the most striking example in B. F. Skinner's *Wal-*

den Two.[6] A behavioral technology would not produce material things but behavior, acting through the controlled environment. What is essential to its technology is the organization of its forms of practice. Technology may be associated more with practice, modern technology with organized practices, than with the objects produced. Even so, it produces a plethora of objects.

We may consider some examples. A representative list of technological artifacts might include refrigerators, automobiles, computers, skyscrapers, and medications. This list is composed entirely of material objects, but not objects as such, for each is important not for what it is but for what it does. In the sense in which objects include blades of grass, stones and rocks, technological products are not objects but implements. In this sense, a computer, and especially a computer program, is not an object at all, and is not produced to be an object, but is a implement for the production of certain results.

Yet while certain of these implements may be thought to be produced to antecedently determinable specifications, many are not. Refrigerators may meet antecedently specifiable ends but computers and medications may not. Computers especially, though they conform to definite specifications, accomplish tasks that no one could imagine of them through their specifications. The same is true for most architectural works, including skyscrapers, and for all generic technologies—that is, technologies designed to produce technologies. Some technological instruments are designed to enable more sophisticated technological designs and developments. These are specifiable only so far. And the same is true of all practical and technological implements: what they can do and produce far exceeds their antecedently determinable specifications. I am speaking of the inexhaustibility of technology and its implementations.

Modern technology produces material artifacts in immense quantity, and some of these are ornamental rather than useful. We may include here souvenirs, knickknacks, and gewgaws like porcelain cats and plastic reproductions of the Parthenon, but also recordings of musical and dramatic performances. Yet the production of artifacts takes place in many societies, technological and otherwise; modern technology provides an immense transformation of scale (and conversely: large-scale institutions employ a correspondingly large-scale technology). Bad taste, whatever we take it to be, reaches a new scale through technological means. Nevertheless, some of the artifacts that technology makes available—books and phonograph records, for example—have made the greatest works of human experience far more widely accessible. Technology also engenders new forms of art, which have deeply transformed our aesthetic sensibilities, an example of its invasiveness.[7]

This invasiveness of technology is a manifestation of its powers, of the materiality of all effective practices. Effectiveness and domination cannot be separated. Technology shares its divided nature with all major forms of human life and practice. Yet neutrality has been frequently claimed for it.[8] Nevertheless, there is no practice that does not inhabit human life densely and specifically, which is to say that it follows specifically from prior practices and produces specific consequences for the future, dangerous, divided, and fulfilling consequences.

Are there forms of reason that do not divide against themselves? Locality forbids it. Rather, there are forms of reason whose contradictions and internal divisions do not have disastrous human consequences, as perhaps in science and art, may even contribute to further achievements. And there are forms of reason whose internal oppositions have devastating human consequences—all the forms of political practice. In this sense, technology is a major and predominant form of political practice, along with the maintenance and implementation of bureaucratic systems of imprisonment, taxation, warfare, and social welfare. Each of these is heavily technologized, but would be wasteful and destructive even without modern technology. What such technology does is to present us with practical powers at an altogether different scale, so that there is no escape from the prospect of devastating consequences, but also remarkably far-ranging beneficial consequences, as in the development of higher-yielding hybrid crops. What modern technology does is to transform manifold local spheres of practice into far-reaching political forms.

The urgent question of technology is whether it can so dominate and oppress subjugated voices, so overcome the divisions inherent in practices and human being, that no other voices and no other perspectives can have materiality. In principle, due to locality, this is impossible; in practice, power works through genuine forces and dominations. The oppressiveness of technology, like that of other modern political institutions and practices, belongs to it in virtue of scale and effectiveness, belongs to it as practice. What is at stake is whether there can be practices that have large-scale and far-reaching ramifications, but that can escape the destructive powers and influences that they exercise. For this to be possible would be for their powers to be immaterial.

Such sweeping and destructive forms of practice are deeply human. I cannot accept a humanism that presupposes that, apart from practice and from technology, there is a being that is human. Rather, technology, in its dividedness, is one of the forms whereby human being is itself, divided as in all human forms of practice. It is one of the most self-conscious, interrogative forms, though with immense and frequently devastating limitations. There is a tragic heroism that occupies the practical realm, related to sacrifice. Technology interrogates and reveals this tragic side of human being and its surroundings in ways that no other form of judgment and query can, revealing astonishing and novel—but not always beneficent—possibilities. One conclusion to be drawn is the dividedness of all far-reaching query, especially in practice: the dark side of human practical life.[9] The central question technology poses is fundamental to human being, whether there is a profoundly different way in which we may be human, and different ways in which we may relate to nature.[10]

THE TECHNOLOGICAL ORDER

1. Technique has become the new and specific milieu in which man is required to exist, one which has supplanted the old milieu, namely, that of nature.
2. This new technical milieu has the following characteristics:

a. It is artificial.
b. It is autonomous with respect to values, ideas, and the state.
c. It is self-determining in a closed circle. Like nature, it is a closed organization which permits it to be self-determinative independently of all human intervention.
d. It grows according to a process which is causal but not directed to ends;
e. It is formed by an accumulation of means which have established primacy over ends;
f. All its parts are mutually implicated to such a degree that it is

impossible to separate them or to settle any technical problem in isolation.[11]

These observations compose a part of Jacques Ellul's complex understanding of technology. It is worth commenting on his points in order to clarify the relation between technology and practical judgment.

1. It is in a sense true that contemporary human life transpires largely within technological surroundings whereas it once transpired more within nature. But to say this and no more entails that technology is not natural and that our entanglements within technological orders are different from other human relations. Yet we are also entangled within social and political milieux, surrounded and influenced by massive and powerful institutions and bureaucracies. And we cannot think historically without confronting modern history; we cannot think scientifically without understanding modern developments in science, or philosophically without traversing its recent forms. It is not a trivial question whether technology is the unique material and dense form of contemporary human life, even in industrial societies, or but one of many such forms, which cohere and conflict in many ways, some insidious and implicit, others obtrusive and overwhelming.

2a. Technological milieux are artificial; but so must any human locale be artificial after centuries of effective practices. Practices exercise their influence upon the future; every future is therefore artificial and likely to be technical. If we were to retreat from technology (ignoring whether it is feasible to do so), we would find our newly "natural" surroundings would be quite as artificial, the result of practical judgments, if not perhaps as technical. Human societies are artificial if they are practical. Nature and artifice are, then, less opposing than complementary. Artifice is no less "natural" than nature, and certainly no less inexhaustible. Nature is never innocent, but absorbs all technical implementations into itself, within its plenitude.

2b. Technological milieux are autonomous, at least in certain important respects. But this cannot mean that they are not influenced by what lies outside them. Rather, it means that a technological milieu takes on a life of its own and exercises its powers upon its surroundings. It does so as a form of political practice, and political practices possess not so much independence as power, exercise domination over other orders, and thus coerce them. It is not that technology cannot be influenced by the state, but that once established in institutions and practices, it wields power over the state as well.

2c. Questions of how closed and how small are the circles of power exercised by any practical institution are profound and difficult. On the one hand, practical milieux are complexly entangled with desire and power, and compose overarching locales with densely material influences. On the other hand, each institution takes on a life of its own, and transcends any of its entanglements. This is a generic local condition, related to inexhaustibility. The powers that technology exercises manifest its inexhaustibility. I add that it could not achieve the hegemony claimed by its critics without overcoming all inexhaustibility, including its own.

2d. To say that technology grows according to causality but not teleology is to deny that it is a form of practice. Yet there is no practice that is not validated by its consequences, and there is no practical query that is not purposive, implicitly if not explicitly the anticipation of ends. In addition, however, every practical judgment gives rise to unanticipated consequences, which it influences causally but may not intend.

2e. Closely related to this last point is the alleged primacy of means over ends in technological societies. From the standpoint of the entanglements of means and ends it is unintelligible that means could attain unqualified primacy. There could be no practice without ends in the double sense that every practice has ends, if only proximate ones, succeeded indefinitely by others, and that the validation of practical judgment is in terms of outcomes, in that sense ends. Perhaps the question is whether there are determining ends of validation for technological practices. Here technology teaches us the lesson inherent in all complex practices: that the subjection of practice to antecedently determinable ends is indefensible, for practice transforms ends and means. However, it is equally indefensible to engage in practices without ends, at least in view. To the extent that technological societies pursue activities without deeply questioning their consequences and results, they are irrational. To the extent that technology is insufficiently interrogative, it is irrational—like every other such form of judgment.

2f. The interpenetration of technological ingredients, so that no technical problem can be settled in isolation, is a pervasive condition of nature in general and of practice in particular. I am speaking here of conditions that define the entanglements of complex beings and practices. Once again, technology presents us with a vivid form of far more pervasive and important conditions.

In the evolution of Technique, contradictory elements are always indissolubly connected. . . .

1. All technical progress exacts a price;

2. Technique raises more problems than it solves;

3. Pernicious effects are inseparable from favorable effects; and

4. Every technique implies unforeseeable effects.[12]

Nothing here is unique to modern technology, not even to contemporary life; everything here is important for practical judgment generally, especially in its political forms. Every practice imposes sacrifices; every practice institutes new difficulties while it attempts to resolve those that called it forth; these difficulties are not only inseparable from, but are virtually indistinguishable from achievements and resolutions; every practical judgment enters an unforeseeable future that it will transform in far-reaching ways.

A consequence is the unintelligibility of any notion of progress in general. Such a progress is incompatible with sacrifice and charity, and depends upon a universal metric. Progress pertains to some subdomains of judgment, and only in certain respects. There has been progress in medicine to the extent that we can defeat some of the major diseases that have wasted humanity, to the extent that we can remedy many physical defects by surgery, to the extent that life expectancy has increased. There has not been corresponding progress in human security, in the elimination of poverty, in the avoidance of war, in freedom from oppression. Even in medicine, deaths are produced by new diseases such as AIDS and by medicine itself, by mistreatment, incompetent physicians, and technological implementations, so that progress is always mixed. Locality requires us to reject the entire notion of Progress, reserving it at best to certain improvements in human life, some important but local. Technological improvements have freed many human beings from certain kinds of drudgery, but presented them with other drudgeries, problems, and insecurities. The natural sciences, similarly, in their advances, confront us with dangerous, life-threatening powers. The same case can be made for large-scale political and social organizations, some of which offer important improvements over the past, but always confront us with immense and unanticipated difficulties. It is not technology that possesses these properties uniquely, but practice in general, with technology one of its most important and influential forms.

Technology is neither uniquely threatening and dehumanizing nor uniquely beneficial and empowering, but is practice itself in its large-scale contemporary and political forms. It contains the panoply of practical entanglements, the dense and specific materialities, that characterize practical judgment, especially in those far-reaching political forms that are most autonomous, with lives of their own. The issue of technology, then, is the generic issue of practical query—not one problem, but inexhaustibly many, the question of how we are to be able to work toward the future, given that our forms of practice determine and transform that future, enrich and despoil it. It is a question of whether practice is possible where control is impossible.

The aporia here belongs to practice intrinsically, but especially to political practices insofar as their consequences are of utmost importance. What may seem unpersuasive is the identification of practice with control, especially in political contexts where control is impossible. More important, control suggests but one side of practice, doing rather than undergoing, domination and oppression. "What, then, is the real problem posed to men by the development of the technological society? It comprises two parts: 1) Is man able to remain master in a world of means? 2) Can a new civilization appear inclusive of Technique?"[13] Given the urgency and oppressiveness of modern political institutions and practices, there appears to be no escape from questions of mastery and control: whether we can control our own products and institutions; whether humanity will remain master of its own destiny. Against such an irresistible question there is the suggestion that the notion of mastery itself is the issue, a technical notion that obscures any non-technical alternatives. The idea that humanity should be master of technology may be the difficulty more than technology itself, suggesting the domination of nature and technique rather than a shared cohabitation.[14]

Ellul asks whether a new civilization can appear that includes technology. Such a civilization already exists, for our civilization includes technology and influences it and is influenced by it. This reciprocity pertains to all complex material practices, to politics and science as well as technology, though each of the former is complicated by the latter. The question appears to be whether a civilization can appear that enjoys only the benefits of technology without its defects, that avoids the materialities, entanglements, and dividedness that pertain to all its manifestations. This question appears to require a civilization without practical judgment, at least in its political forms, a form of practical query that can escape politics, a system of humanistic norms that are independent of material and technological practices. The question is hostile to the divided nature of practice itself.

> a. . . . the technical society is not, and cannot be, a genuinely humanist society since it puts in first place not man but material things. . . . Human excellence, on the contrary, is of the domain of the qualitative and aims at what is not measurable. . . .
> b. Technical growth leads to a growth of power in the sense of technical means incomparably more effective than anything before invented, power which has as its object only power, in the widest sense of the word. . . . When man is able to accomplish anything at all, there is no value which can be proposed to him; when the means of action are absolute, no goal of action is imaginable. . . . Again, where Technique has place, there is the implication of the impossibility of the evolution of civilization.[15]

(a) I have established that perfectibility is incompatible with practical judgment and therefore with technology, that practical judgment confronts us poignantly and compellingly with imperfection. The deeper point is that technology along with other forms of practice, especially practical query, in their dividedness, are intrinsic human excellences. However, no human excellence is undivided against itself. The materiality of practice belongs to it as its pervasive means and condition and as an inescapable consequence.

(b) The pervasiveness of power within technology is an expression of the dispersion of power throughout human life and practices. But again, it pertains to practice itself, in its larger forms, not specifically to technology. Ellul's view of technological power pertains to power in general, with the qualification that power belongs to practice, not simply to technological practice. And it is dispersed throughout practice to the point where no person or group exercises it. Technology is the particular modern form that most forcibly expresses the dispersions of power. I must add is that technology's capacity to transform human life and nature is so great that it functions almost entirely at the political scale of practice, where the dispersions of power and the potentialities for failure in practice are immense.

Practice exercises power over human beings, and largely succeeds in its goals by threatening freedom, dignity, and responsibility. These belong to practice intrinsically yet are most threatened by effective practices. This is the poignant contradiction inherent in practice, from which we cannot escape. It is manifested in the nearly irresistible language of mastery and power over technology that we bring forth to describe the powers of technology and other political practices over us. We must gain mastery over the practices that would control us although the pursuit of mastery increases the powers arrayed against us.

We must seek to influence the future of human life and practice, and can do so only through practice, by exercising power in terms of desire. But we can distinguish between forms of practice that are effective through restricted forms of interrogation, without being query, and forms of practice that accept the unending demands of rational interrogation. Here we may say that modern technology, while one of the most far-reaching forms of practical query, capable of interrogating any form of human desire and responding to it through every form of human power, explicitly and implicitly, overtly and covertly, is, of itself, restricted and defective. The questions inherent in technology cannot remain within technology, cannot be provided in technological terms alone; but likewise, they cannot be deprived of whatever technological resources might be available. Like every far-reaching form of political practice, technology forces us to confront the inexhaustibility of practice and its inextricability from every form of query.

To be avoided are certain views of technology: (a) technology is less rather than more human—it is one of the greatest of human realizations; (b) technology must be made more humane—it is an unmistakable side of humanity and of reason; (c) there might be more beneficial, non-technological forms of practice—technology is practice itself, in its divided complexity, including beneficent and maleficent products and activities. Rather, technology must be made more interrogative and more charitable—more practical query—including a far-reaching sensitivity to the violence it imposes on the things that surround it. Like all major forms of practice, technology must make sacrifices to its accomplishments. Like all other major contemporary forms of practice, it is insensitive to its own forms of violence and domination, insufficiently interrogative of its wastefulness. Yet of itself, through more technology, it cannot be so sensitive and interrogative. Only through multiple and profoundly entangled forms of query can such interrogations and sensitivities be realized. That is, technological practices must be supplemented by unending queries, in multifarious forms, practical and otherwise.

THE QUESTION OF TECHNOLOGY

I have refused to accept the simplicity and transparency of the question of technology. Yet we may hesitate at endorsing Heidegger's understanding that the modern world is defined by technology or his claim that the essence of technology does not belong to technology itself.[16] The entanglements and materialities of practice disperse the essences of any human activity, any mode of judgment and query, among the modes of judgment, including practice and beyond. The essence of technology lies within technology as much as anywhere else, but not within technology alone. Practice reveals the temporality and situatedness of every work and condition. One of the important realizations of technological understanding and practice is in further technological practice. Nevertheless, technology cannot to be understood or articulated through technological means alone, or through practice alone. No form of judgment or query, no form of interrogation, can capture its own or any other essence, including those of art and philosophy. Locality and inexhaustibility are incompatible with any univocal sense of being and essence.

We may consider two major themes in Heidegger's view of technology. One is that technology challenges—or violates— nature in the form of the standing-reserve, making whatever it touches ready-to-hand, transforming it into available means.[17] Yet technological implements are not less objects than means, nor is technology more instrumental than it is revealing.[18] More important, technology is a far-reaching transformation of human and natural being, one of the major forms of practice. However, and this is the second theme, technology can challenge and reveal, can make things available for human uses, only by virtue of a more original unconcealing essential to human being that is not technology, that lies within the relation of humanity and Being.[19]

The view that in order for technology to be effective, there must be an already-established, more fundamental relation, may be understood in terms of mediateness. Technology, like every form of judgment, originates within established conditions and contributes to the establishment of other conditions for future judgments. The question of primacy is unintelligible from the standpoint of political practice, for it is its fate to be caught up within proximate but urgent and far-reaching projects with nothing more primary than itself.

Mediateness entails, along with its rejection of anything more fundamental and primary, that practice, including technology, is inexhaustible, from within and from without. From within, technology and practice are capable of transcending any limits, of any kind—only to encounter other limits. From without, technology and practice include only some of the forms of judgment and provide only some of the forms of knowledge and validation. Technology is query, but like most forms of query, can interrogate its own forms of interrogation only limitedly from within. Indeed, technology is a thoroughly intermodal form of query, combining propositional, practical, and fabricative judgments into new constellations. This intermodality is the source of its power. What technology cannot be is the sole acceptable intermodal form of query. What technology can do is to wield the greatest practical powers that humanity has at its disposal.

Nevertheless, in Heidegger, the disclosure of a more originary form of belonging and revealing than technology reveals itself to be "no mere human doing."[20] It follows that what makes technology possible is something not entirely within human mastery, not something technological. I understand this incompleteness of technology in terms of mediateness, locality and inexhaustibility. The conditions of practical judgment always transcend possibilities established by any practice, including practical query. This transcendence is backward and forward, in relation to prior conditions and in relation to an unknown future. We cannot forget the inexhaustibility of things, even within technology, because we are constantly confronted by the shadow of inexhaustibility in the future technology brings to pass. This shadow, following Heidegger's language, shows itself as concealment in unconcealment.[21]

The fundamental contrast, for Heidegger, is between technology as standing-reserve and *poiēsis* as bringing-forth.[22] He appears at times to suggest that only through confronting the forgetfulness of Being through art can the dangers of technology be overcome.[23] Yet the possibility of this kind of questioning through art does not lie outside technology, but within it. Technology shares with every form of practical query the greatest dangers and greatest achievements in human experience.

> Thus the coming to presence of technology harbors in itself what we least suspect, the possible upsurgence of the saving power.
> . . . How can this happen? Above all through our catching sight of what comes to presence in technology, instead of merely gaping at the technological. . . .
> The essence of technology is in a lofty sense ambiguous. Such ambiguity points to the mystery of all revealing, i.e., of truth.[24]

I respond that the mystery is inexhaustibility, that the questioning inherent in the human spirit is query, in its many forms, including practical query and technology.[25] The mystery is heterogeneity.

TECHNOLOGY AS QUERY

There is a view of science, not identical with the sciences themselves—it may be called "scientolatry"—that adulates science far beyond its enormous interrogative and validative potentialities, frequently to the point where science is regarded as the only acceptable form of reason, in certain cases to the point where science is regarded as the only proper guide to human life and practice. Where science is then predominantly propositional query, and intermodal in the service of propositional truth, scientolatry is a form of practice that installs science as the predominant foundation of permissible practices. It is, then, foundational and oppressive, diminishing every other form of practice that is not grounded in science and that opposes itself. Without going into the historical origins of such a standpoint, that a particular form of discourse should be given hegemony over all others reveals the exercise of power as it dominates our understanding of rationality and query.

There is a view of technology, not identical with technology itself—it may be called "technolatry"—that exaggerates its productive capacities and flexibility far beyond its interrogative and practical efficacy, frequently to the point where it is regarded as the only acceptable form of human practice, whether or not guided by science. In the case of scientolatry, the disparity between the modes of propositional and practical judgment testifies to the inadequacy of establishing science—predominantly propositional query—as the foundation of human practices. In the case of technolatry, the plurality and dividedness of forms of practice testifies to the inadequacy of establishing technology as the sole or primary form of practical reason. Similarly, the supposition that the foundation of practice lies in philosophy is similarly inadequate, neglecting the plurality of modes of judgment and query as well as the dividedness within practical judgment itself.

In the case of scientolatry and technolatry we find not merely the recurrent tendency toward the hegemony of some form of judgment and practice, some form of query, as a reaction against a plurality of legitimate forms of validation, against mediateness and inexhaustibility: we find as well the dominance of one form of practice over all others—an authority that constitutes oppression. The primary motivation may be an aversion to indeterminateness and insecurity, but the result, from the standpoint of practice, is the exercise of power, of one mode of thought over others, one mode of discourse over others, one mode of practice, however complex, over heterogeneous others. In our time, the propositional form of such hegemony has been expressed as a question of science: whether science is the primary voice in which reason speaks, in which truth can be said, and in which practice can be legitimized. Here, what is not science is denied legitimacy. The practical form of such hegemony has been expressed as a question of mastery: whether human beings will be masters through practice; in particular, whether human beings will be masters over technology or oppressed by it. Here what is not mastery is denied legitimacy. When we add to these questions the dense materiality of human practices, especially through technology, the powers that technological implementations work upon human life, we face our contemporary predicament in its most imposing forms.

The notion of mastery is a practical, even a technical notion. Science does not provide mastery over nature through the discovery of truth but through the application of discoveries in technological projects. Similarly, neither art nor philosophy provides mastery over our human surroundings nor even over ourselves, but rather, serves as a voice in which reason interrogates itself. Mastery belongs to technical practice, and it is tempting to identify it with practice itself. Even in the present context, emphasizing charity and sacrifice, I have been unable to define practice except in terms of influence—in all apparent respects indistinguishable from mastery over the future. What is required is to distinguish influence from mastery, practice from one of practice's most pervasive forms.

Let us suppose, provisionally, that practice is defined by mastery, over our surroundings and ourselves. Let us provisionally identify this idea with *techne*, especially with the suggestion that the solution to technical problems will always be technical. If what we mean is that practical problems will always have practical solutions, that practical judgment is the form in which we resolve our practical difficulties, then the conclusion is indisputable. I add that practical judgment, when it becomes query, also becomes intermodal, and that *techne* is not identical with practice itself, not even technological practice, but one of its forms.

I have provisionally adopted Collingwood's view of *techne* in contrast with art. In craft, means and ends are distinct, entailing a distinction between planning and execution, raw materials and finished products, form and matter, as well as a hierarchy among techniques.[26] There is clearly something to this view of craft, this view of certain kinds of practices, in the sense that we sometimes produce artifacts whose purposes and structures can be anticipated reliably in advance, based on antecedent norms, while in the production of works of art the expressive nature of the production may transform any antecedent aims into very different realizations.

However, this "reliability" inherent in the anticipation of the ends of certain techniques is a technical notion quite inappropriate to either science or art, to philosophy, and even to most forms of technology. To be reliable, something must be related to time in terms of a known and controlled future, while the different forms of query are as adventurous and transformative as they are controlling. In its interrogative and inventive activities, query challenges reliability and security, introduces openness into any practices, brings any relation of reason to the future. The word "challenging" in Heidegger's reading suggests violence. In my understanding, query challenges the future and allows itself to be challenged by it. The challenge here is an adventure toward the future and a sense of awe before its dangers. The violence is inherent in finiteness; the violences must be transformed into sacrifices.

What makes modern technology so urgent an issue for contemporary life is that it is the major form in which contemporary political and institutional practices demonstrate their lack of political neutrality. A consequence of modern technology is that there is virtually no escape by private citizens from the surveillance of the state, a consequence that nuclear destruction and pollution threaten not only human life but the lives of most other natural creatures. However, technology is not so much the cause of the greater oppression possible in contemporary life by state powers as its manifestation. Technology is rather the way in which entrenched contemporary forces exercise their powers, the way in which politics achieves its goals, which are to resolve at as large a scale as possible what cannot be resolved in principle or at any other scale. It follows from such a view that technology is political practice first and foremost. It is, however, not political practice itself, in its richness and complexity, because it constitutes a fundamental and pervasive division within such practice. Just as reason is divided into diverse forms that compose interrogative standpoints for each other, practical reason is divided into multiple interrogative forms and standpoints. In this sense, contemporary political practices are deeply and pervasively technological, but not technological alone, insofar as such practices are intrinsically divided and to the extent that technology does not define all interrogative standpoints.

Fundamental to practical judgment is that every undertaking, the exercise of every means, institutes unknowable and unanticipatable consequences. This is a result of inexhaustibility generically and of the density, specificity, and materiality of practices in particular. It is the predominant and irresistible condition of practice to be confronted with uncontrollable events, an open and indeterminate future, not least in virtue of the fact that every effort at control transforms that future in uncontrolled ways. Collingwood supposes that there is a notion of mastery inherent in craft and realizable through it, and he neglects the fact that every means engenders unmastered consequences. The idea of craft itself is implausible, going back to Aristotle's view of *technē*. We might say that modern industries require and impose such a notion of technique as part of their apparatus. Yet even in such industries, however large and dominant, every product and every means opens up inexhaustible prospects of novelty, however disturbing. Among these prospects are novel interrogative standpoints and perspectives. It follows that no practical means can impose mastery without effectively undermining themselves, and that practical control is the end of practice and unrealizable except through unending further practical judgments.

Collingwood appears to believe that in a craft like woodworking or pottery, the ends are determinate in advance, controlling the utilization of means, while in art, expression joins means and ends inseparably. I would argue, following Dewey's principle of the continuum of means and ends, that means and ends are always inseparable. But the issue goes further. Rather, there is in practice an internally divided, opposing tendency to reduce practical query, with its unavoidable prospects of failure, to reliable patterns of activity. When this happens, we substitute technique for practical query in quite similar ways to substituting method for propositional query.

A useful analogy is with the notions of "normal" science and "normal" discourse: both appear to be confronted now and again with prospects of abnormality.[27] Yet it is a sociological and an historical more than a theoretical condition of science that it restricts abnormal science to relatively rare moments, generating scientific revolutions; and it is implausible that normal and abnormal discourse are distinct. Rather, every discourse is both normal and abnormal throughout. Every rule is made to be broken, if not now then later, and every breaking of a rule establishes new rules. We may avoid breaking rules for two important practical reasons, to gain reliability and security, and so that our practices may be defined densely and materially. But, then, this is the point, that we are always within practices defined by rules and that exercise their powers and effectiveness through those rules, but the rules can function effectively only because they may be disregarded at any time and to the extent that they include such departures within themselves.

Let us then distinguish technology as practical judgment and query from both technique and technolatry as we distinguish science from scientific method and scientolatry. As a form of query, science may employ repeated and determinate methods, but these serve its validative aims as propositional query and have no greater authority. As query, science achieves propositional validation through the most inventive and interrogative activities developed. It by no means follows, even from our utmost respect for the accomplishments of science, that it engages a repeatable method beyond any proximate considerations, but rather, employs whatever methods it can devise to its interrogative ends. In this sense, science is a rich and complex form of propositional query that employs determinate methods and discourses to the extent that they are effective, and abandons them where query requires it to do so. Invention belongs to science intrinsically, insofar as it is query.

Techne is that form of practice that we may identify with antecedently determinable ends that determine the relevance of means, in that sense displaying and imposing mastery. Techniques are the structural methods and devices that serve *techne*. But in general, technological practice is neither *techne* nor technique, and is certainly not dominated by either of them as suggested by technolatry. Practice is a form of query that may utilize techniques, may even follow the constraints of *techne*, may define rules and structures that determine acceptable norms, but, as query, must pursue its own interrogations and inventions, and must abandon any norms, any rules, where its own demands require.

Several considerations establish this conclusion. One is based on the unavoidability of error in relation to truth. No form of knowledge can attain more than a contingent freedom from error, which circumscribes all reason and interrogation. As a consequence, the process of interrogative validation is unending. In practical judgment, as a consequence, there are no rules or norms that can serve more than proximately and locally.

A second consideration is based on the mediateness and entanglements of practice. Every rule, every norm, is a practical judgment, established by past practices and subject to future practices.

In these ongoing practices, norms can have only a proximate, local validation.

Third, "normality" and "abnormality" cannot be sharply distinguished in discourse and practice. We are always situated in normal conditions but on the edge of departure and variation. To make ourselves understood in any discourse, we may find that we must employ devices that no one has ever employed before. To achieve the ends of any practice, we may find that we must depart from the ends of past practices in ways that would have been unintelligible before. The importance of invention to query, even inventions of forms of query, is inescapable.

Fourth, every form of judgment, including practice, is deeply and pervasively divided within itself and among the other modes of judgment. In this dividedness—between practical judgments in general and technological judgments particularly, between political practices in general and technological implementations—no rules can be more than locally valid. Technology is inseparable from political practices and not to be identified with them. In this difference lie the interrogations that constitute technological and political practices as query.

We come to the question of how technology can be query. The generic answer is that practice can be query as much as can any other mode of judgment—through unending interrogation and validation—and that *techne* and technology are situated within practice and practical query. Yet they may not themselves be query, or may be severely truncated forms. For example, the conditions that define *techne* traditionally make it impossible for it to be query, for query cannot accept any antecedent norms as more than locally and proximately relevant. Collingwood's view of craft is a technical notion deficient in relation to any established craft. In such a craft, such as shipbuilding or gardening, antecedent norms and raw materials exercise constraints but open an unknown future to alternative possibilities. Even repetition in craft plays its role in changing the future. Nevertheless, repetition as such is not query.

How may we tell the difference between empty, undirected variations and the interrogativeness and inventiveness of query? Modern technology more than any other form of practice faces us with the poignancy of this question, since it hovers continuously between the twin specters of monolithic and imposed utilitarian reason and mindless and uncontrolled variation. Yet if query is unterminating invention and interrogation, technology is query in some of its most imposing forms. Technology, along with but surpassing many other major forms of contemporary practice, interrogates the far-reaching practical possibilities in any human practical conditions from the standpoint of what may be done about them, promoting endless novel possibilities of life and practice.

Among the most important forms of invention are those that introduce novel possibilities into life and query. Technology, here, in virtually all its manifestations, from the most unobtrusive to the most powerful, changes the shape of human life and nature, and introduces novel possibilities of future life and practice. Contrary to Collingwood, most of these influential possibilities are neither anticipatable within technological practices nor controlled—or, more accurately, are controlled without being anticipated. It is the fate of political practices to transform the future, even to the point of changing the shape of human being and its surroundings, through its own activities, to some extent in anticipatable ways, but typically in ways that go beyond any anticipations. This is the sense in which practice requires its future for validation: bringing about a future that will define the worth of present practices without our being able to foretell that future. Practical validation always escapes the determinants of practice.

I add that the future that escapes our anticipations, the uncontrolled novelties and abnormalities of discourse and life, are frequently profoundly disturbing. Political query not only seeks to establish control within a context that is beyond control, which it renders out of control, but locates us within the transformation of the very norms that it requires to be intelligible. We are, then, faced continuously in political practice with the sense that we do not know what we are doing, though we may in fact be doing all we can. The capacity to live with such violence and disturbance may be developed within query collectively—as in abnormal science—but we have not acquired the ability to enjoy such capacities in our practical lives. Thus, technology situates the greatest disturbances of modern life, where we enjoy the greatest plenitude of benefits and the most overpowering forces of destruction. The most obtrusive face of this internal opposition is waste. We have never, in human history, controlled so much through practice and wasted so much at the same time, wasted human lives as well as other living things and the natural things surrounding us. This waste is what practice imposes in a political context that is impervious to valor.

The tendency of technology to produce more and more technology may be interpreted as closure and entrapment, but it may also be interpreted as the capacity of technological practices to build upon past achievements, to remedy errors and to attain more powerful results. We must avoid the suggestion that technology offers the only legitimate perspective on itself. We must avoid technolatry. What testifies to technology's rationality is the capacity of query, including subsequent technology itself, to call its past results into question, in all the ways that is possible, including subsequent practical judgments. Here the materiality of technology, its capacity to change the future, works against its own inertia, and constantly challenges its past determinations. Such interrogations, from within technology, require intermodality to be query.

It appears of unique importance to many writers that technology tends to produce more and more technology, though this may be no more remarkable than that nature produces more and more nature, that trees produce trees, mammals produce mammals, that human experience produces further experience. Moreover, these natural productions are no more controlled and controllable, no more foreseeable, than are the consequences of technology, and perhaps conversely. Technology is a major and powerful form of query but not the only form and not able to overcome its own limitations. But then, no form of query can entirely overcome its own nature, but every form requires transformations from without as well as from within. Again, query requires intermodality.

Nevertheless, technology, along with other forms of political practices, is a form that challenges every other form of query—the test, we may say, in contemporary terms, of science and philosophy, the site at which their capacity to be effective in human life is at risk. We may define technology as query in terms of two conditions. Technology is situated, and must remain situated, within wider and more comprehensive fields of practical judgment and query, the practicalities that define its validation from within. In addition, technology requires every other form of judgment in relation to which its nature can be judged through invention and interrogation. Given these conditions, technology is profoundly query in relation to the other forms of query, one of the most powerful forms of invention and interrogation. It is query where it is interrogative of the other forms of query and deeply and profoundly interrogated from the standpoint of these other forms. It is only one of the major forms of query.

Technology is query in its inventiveness and interrogativeness, but especially in how it defines the sites at which interrogation in human life is most influential. It cannot, however, be in charge of its own rationality, any more than any other form of reason can be in sole control of its own nature. It follows that we must bring to technology all the other modes of query that are relevant to it: philosophy and science, art and other forms of practice, including religion and ethics.

There is no overarching form of query that preempts the relation of any form to the others. What this means in particular is that there is no form of practice that, followed closely, overcomes the disparities and disjointedness of the other forms. Rather, each is a resistance within the sphere of power of any form of practical query; and even practical query exercises power and must be resisted. Thus, we may add that technology is the most striking form of resistance located in contemporary forms of practice, with the proviso that we may find resistance, itself a form of power, quite as oppressive as any other established form of practice. Technology is the contemporary site at which the major powers that oppress human life work and the greatest resistances make their mark.

With this understanding in mind, we may return to the question concerning technology to distinguish technolatry as the view that technology is self-enclosed and self-governing from the view that technology is, if not the predominant form of reason in our time, a major site where the forms of query intersect. Here we note the powers of technology and its capacity to transform the conditions of query itself. Technology transforms human life and query, changing the everyday conditions of thought and spirit, and producing a different world enriched by technological contributions. This doubling is not unique to modern technology, but pertains to all technique and practice. It shows that, at a large enough scale, human activities and practices transform the conditions of human life and reason, not least in creating new spheres of production, fabrication, and practice. We live in a different world today—

with the qualifications that there are no absolute differences, only inexhaustible differences among inexhaustible similarities, and that like every world, this technologically produced world incessantly imposes problems upon us even while we engage in practices to control it.[28]

Technology is the contemporary site at which we encounter the two sides of inexhaustibility most forcefully, where practice encounters the promise and oppressiveness of invention and interrogation. Because technology so profoundly amplifies the conditions of human life and experience, it is the form of reason, along with politics, that most powerfully shows us the limits inherent in reason and human being.[29]

POLITICS AND TECHNOLOGY

Modern technology and politics belong together, inseparably. While each has different local concerns, their scales are so similar, and they are connected so deeply, that they are effectively indistinguishable in and as practice. I am again addressing the density and materiality of practices.[30]

What technology and politics reveal in practice is their inseparability and, more generally, the inseparability of human and natural locales. What we learn about the natural world and its potentialities defines the human world, practically speaking. Our forms of social organization define the means available for understanding natural events. In relation to judgment, this phenomenon produces multimodality and intermodality. In relation to practice, however, technology and politics both function under the imperative to utilize whatever means are available to accomplish their ends. Technology and politics are thus the forms practical query takes at its most pervasive scale while they jointly compose important forms of differentiation defining political query. In this sense, politics is the generic practice that includes technology as its primary contemporary means—including behavioral and social technologies— while conversely, political practices are required by technology as its primary contemporary forms of control. One of the important forms of contemporary political practices is the shaping of desires and expectations by technological means. In return, technology shapes the forms of political practices. Technology and politics are inseparable without being identical.[31]

There is a fundamental reason, lying in the nature of practice itself, for the pervasiveness of this union of political, economic, and technological forces. The mediateness of practical judgment and its impetus toward control make every larger form of practice an agent that utilizes other forms of practice and places it at their service. The result, however, is not wholeness and harmony, but practice surrounded by dividedness, divisions as much sources of inspiration for new practices as of past and present difficulties.

This widening of technology into politics and human life in general is not, then, a uniquely perverse feature of technological development, not one of its idiosyncrasies. To the contrary, practice itself demands technology, not in the sense that practice can be realized only through technical instruments, but in the sense that where technological means are available, practice must employ them and beware of them; where technological means are not available, practice must invent them. In this sense, technology is as much part of practice as understanding, intuition, intensity of experience, and charity and sacrifice. It follows that humanity is profoundly technological.[32] Similarly, technology is profoundly technological; one technology produces another as practice leads to practice.[33]

These are ramifications of mediateness. There is no knowing and no judgment, certainly no practical judgment, that does not begin and end in the midst of other judgments and established conditions. The plausibility of the idea that technology presupposes technology rests on our inability to separate technology from practice in general—not a relation of identity or equivalence, but entanglement and inextricability. In this sense again, technology is an irresistible ingredient of practical judgment and query, and one of the forms that practice must take to realize its imperatives. It is most of all political.[34]

Technology has profoundly influenced politics because it is politics, at least among its irresistible and compelling forms, and politics influences the future of politics. Modern technology renders political life and practice more political in the double sense that the decisions required are more urgent and penetrating while their scope of influence widens inexorably. In this sense, then, technology is the form in which contemporary human life is political and a form to which political judgments are irresistibly drawn, since to be political where technological powers exist requires that such powers be employed and controlled.

That technology is politics, if only one of its manifestations, has important implications. To think that we can "use" technology rather than live within it, that we can somehow control it by means that are not technological, supposes either that it has no density and materiality or that there are other forms of practice that are equally and materially dense. But the presence and irresistibility of technology are due to its influence and powers. We must hazard the suggestion that technology is the major form that power takes in our time, that its irresistibility is due to the fact that there is no other form of practice that is equally tangible and material.

We find, then, that technology is irresistible generally, in contemporary life, and irresistible from the standpoint of political practices, whether overt and a function of state regulations or covert and a function of social institutions. This irresistibility is not a function of its oppressiveness and our captivity, but of the ways in which technology inhabits practice in general. Crudely put, there can be no effective non-technological form of political query. However, there can be no effective form of political query that is captive to, entirely overcome by, technological methods and interrogations. Political query leads to the other forms of query, including science, art, and philosophy, and employs them wherever they can help to influence the future. However, it is the fate of political query to confront the far-reaching incongruities inherent in human practices, throughout query, including the heterogeneities of every form of query from the standpoint of the others. There can be no harmony of all practical spheres in the context of locality and inexhaustibility. There are, however, whatever forms of reason are achievable within the context of local and inexhaustible forms of practice.

NATURE, TECHNOLOGY, AND HOPE

Among the contrasts that define the established critique of technology is that between artifice and nature, between human and natural production. Aristotle distinguishes natural production, whose principle of movement lies within itself, from production by artifice, *technē*, whose cause of movement lies outside what is moved.[35] It is a contrast to be resisted strongly, on a variety of grounds: artifice belongs to nature because human being is a natural being; technological production enriches and expands what is naturally available; it is indefensible to glorify blindness in nature in contrast with directed production and fabrication. The most misleading of the suggestions inherent in the contrast is that technology is not one of the intrinsic characteristics of human being: it is as intrinsic a human quality as is the practice that defines its modality. Without such an understanding, we will never be able to affirm the importance and vitality of works of art, which may be technologically proficient and artificial but also sublime and enriching. Art belongs to artifice as much as technology belongs to artifice; art does not, however, belong any the less to nature and is no less enriching for its artificiality or technicality.

Yet there is an important insight within this distinction between nature and artifice, a sense that in comparison with nature, technique and artifice are deficient. If we affirm that these are no less part of nature for being artificial and technical, then the insight must be reformulated in terms of the deficiencies of our understanding of *technē*. We are addressing the material effectiveness of technology in contrast with a wealth of unknown and possibly forgotten possibilities.

What is most disturbing about technology is that it invades the other modes of judgment—invades and oppresses them. In a sense, this invasion and oppressiveness are a manifestation of the materiality and specificity of practical judgments. The issue is one of power: practice requires the employment of powers and imposes subjection to powers, from which, within practice, there is no escape. But we may dream of escaping, at least in the context of alternative possibilities and other modalities of judgment. Where we confuse the dream with practicality, we replace the blindness of oppressive technology with the blindness of empty illusions. Even more disturbing, the illusions are typically not effective resistances to the forces of technology and oppression, but moments in their influences.

The lesson is not to abandon illusions as a play of ineffective alternatives but that illusions may not be empty, that the play of alternatives is not always ineffective, that dreams and alternatives belong to other modes of judgment and densely and materially to practice. Query, in any of its modes and forms, must be effective if it is to be query. This is again to affirm that whatever modality query may have, it also is a mode of practice.

To criticize technology for its destructive as well as its benefi- cent side is to affirm its effectiveness as a form of practice. Practice always confronts the future with entanglements of power and the difficulties they produce. To criticize technology for its oppres- siveness is to affirm that it is one of the most powerful of political forces; yet political query is confronted constantly by the oppres- siveness of material powers. To criticize technology for its artifi- ciality is to bifurcate nature, denying that its powers and possibilities include both technology and art. This last criticism is extraordinary in that we criticize technology for being limited, for being forgetful of inexhaustibility, but do so by forgetting the inexhaustibility of nature and technology.

To emphasize that technology belongs to human being on the one hand but to nature on the other, just as human beings belong to nature, is to affirm that humanity is one of the most illuminating and far-reaching expressions of locality and inexhaustibility. With the triangle of locality, inexhaustibility, and ergonality, however, we may reformulate the criticism of technology. It either: (1) blinds us to inexhaustibility, and thereby imposes a monolithic form of human being upon all other forms and closes off available possibilities; or (2) is a determinate form of practice, of human and natural work, possessing immense material powers, which we employ in order to influence our surroundings and experiences, but find is one of the most destructive forces within our experi- ence. The latter deficiency is not unique to modern technology, but pervades modern practice, especially political practices, how- ever rational they may be.

The deficiencies described in (2) pertain to contemporary prac- tice itself, its mediateness and materiality. The question is whether there is not some truth to the deficiencies describe in (1): a particu- lar blindness, a more far-reaching closure upon alternative forms of experience and thought. To what, however, are we comparing the forgetfulness and powers of technology? To the yearnings in everyday life for stability and reliability? To the dogmatism of many authoritarian religions? To scientolatry more than technola- try? The deficiencies in all these cases are parallel: abandoning query and, at least theoretically if not practically, denying inexhaustibility. Human experience testifies to the recurrent and explicit denial of locality and inexhaustibility joined in practice with unending and inexhaustible variation and division.

A consequence of inexhaustibility is that every form of practice, however imposing and oppressive, is pervaded by divisions complementary with its powers. It follows that even within the most technological of epochs, the rule of technology will be opposed and resisted by other forms of life and experience, but even within technology itself. But more must be said, for the powers and the resistances are not different, even in the sense of different modalities and available alternatives. Every form of being, including human being and all forms of experience and practice, is divided within itself by oppositions that constitute the inexhaustible workings of time—but not time alone. Present undertakings always influence the future in specific and unforeseeable ways.

It follows that the powers of technology have their greatest influence upon the future in the most unpredictable ways. Even further, technology is the source of the most destabilizing of occurrences as frequently as it imposes uniformity and conformity. The material powers of technology make it oppressive and confining and destabilizing and liberating.

The most prominent consequence of oppressive power and influence in practice is the production of waste, in human lives and throughout our natural surroundings. Waste here is despoliation, sacrifice without charity. It is prominent in every society, but especially manifest in war. The urgent practical question of technology, here, becomes a question of avoiding waste, though sacrifice cannot be avoided. It becomes a question of sensitivity to charity and to its profound connections with sacrifice. It is, then, a repetition of the generic questions of practice. Technology is material practice at a political scale for which oppressiveness and waste are most apparent and least avoidable. The question is how we can maintain technology in conjunction with charity, a question subsidiary to how in contemporary life, given the scale of human lives and institutions, we can carry on political practices, including the activities of governments and social institutions, but also the employment of technological instruments—with hope as well as charity.

One answer is that we have no choice but to engage in political practices by means of query because otherwise we will engage in political practices without it. There is no avoiding practice in human life, no avoiding the future. We can only engage in practice rationally or irrationally, thoughtfully or blindly. And if we choose reason, then we are committed to unending interrogation, and to interrogation of interrogation, with charity the basis of all practical judgment and validation. This answer is true and sufficient, but it neglects hope.

Can we be hopeful in the context of contemporary human experience with its enormous waste and destruction? There have been immense advances in medicine and human comfort, if by no means universally. There is a hope that is grounded in a dream of progress, a hope utopian at the extreme in its illusion of harmoniousness and stability. This hope is incompatible with locality and inexhaustibility and is nullified by technology. There is no progress, not because there could be although we live in an imperfect world, but because the notion of progress is unintelligible. Every advance requires sacrifice.

There is a different hope, one inseparable from practical query itself and its inexhaustibility. This is the hope that engages us in practical query rather than in dogmatic forms of practical judgment. We cannot avoid practical judgment, we cannot avoid political practices. The future, with its uncertainties, faces us inevitably. But we may ignore our role in this future by living it without interrogating it. Here interrogation in the sense of query is temporally and functionally unending. Yet to carry on such interrogation, implicit or explicit, is to live in a certain light of hope—not a hope in progress or harmony, in practice without sacrifice, not a utopian hope, not a blind hope that all will be well whatever we do, not a dream of a cosmic drama in which we are participants, but the hope that what we do has material influence, will make a difference, and that what we do can be judged good, however locally.

Political query faces the most oppressive, difficult incompatibilities and oppositions inherent in human and natural being from the standpoint of practice. What can and what should we do given that we are faced with difficulties with no principled solutions and that our actions will produce further difficulties unendingly? What should we do, given inexhaustible charity, where practice entails catastrophe? The answer, given in practice, embodies a certain hope: not the hope that sacrifices can be avoided, but the hope that our practices will be good, in the future, in its terms if not our terms today, a goodness that is not just the triumph of victors. A hope belongs to query that is inseparable from the intelligibility of practical judgment. This hope pertains to the most terrifying of political practices, to the most oppressive and wasteful of technical environments, just where that hope is most hidden. It is the hope inherent in inexhaustibility, its openness to the future. It is a hope inseparable from the most terrifying fears for the future. It is a hope that is most prominent in and hidden by contemporary forms of politics and technology. It is a hope that will be embodied within and deeply threatened by future technological developments. For technology, like every other form of practical judgment but especially at a political scale, is divided within itself by the heterogeneities that haunt finite practices.

Notes

1. See James K. Feibleman, "Pure Science, Applied Science, and Technology: An Attempt at Definitions," in *Philosophy and Technology*, edd. Carl Mitcham and Robert Mackey (New York: Free Press, 1972), p. 36; reprinted from James K. Feibleman, *The Two-Story World*, ed. Huntington Cairns (New York: Holt, Rinehart and Winston, 1966): "The applied scientist as such is concerned with the task of discovering applications for pure theory. The technologist has a problem which lies a little nearer to practice. Both applied scientist and technologist employ experiment; but in the former case guided by hypotheses deduced from theory; while in the latter case employing trial and error or skilled approaches derived from concrete experience. . . .

"The applied scientist fits a case under a class; the technologist takes it from there and works it out, so to speak, *in situ.*"

2. "There is now only the smallest distinction between applied science, the application of the principles of pure science, and technology. The methods peculiar to technology: trial and error, invention aided by intuition, have simply merged with those of applied science: adopting the findings of pure science to the purposes of obtaining desirable practical consequences" (Feibleman, "Pure Science," p. 38).

3. This view of *technē* runs through Aristotle and Plato. For a more contemporary version, see Collingwood, *Principles of Art*, chap. 2. See note 5, below. Even so, ends emerge from the activities of query, and cannot be separated from those activities.

4. See Friedrich Georg Jünger: *The Failure of Technology* (Chicago: Regnery, 1956), p. 33. "By what sign can we distinguish most clearly the striving for perfection, that leitmotiv of technology? By what phenomena can we best measure technological progress as it has developed from crude and uncertain beginnings?"

5. See Collingwood, *Principles of Art*, pp. 15–17: "(1) Craft always involves a distinction between means and end, each clearly conceived as something distinct from the other but related to it. . . . (2) It involves a distinction between planning and execution. The result to be obtained is preconceived or thought out before being arrived at. . . . (3) Means and end are related in one way in the process of planning; in the opposite way in the process of execution. In planning the end is prior to the means. The end is thought out first, and afterwards the means are thought out. In execution the means come first, and the end is reached through them. (4) There is a distinction between raw material and finished product or artifact. . . . (5) There is a hierarchical relation between various crafts, one supplying what another needs, one using what another provides . . ." (Collingwood, *Principles of Art*, pp. 15–17).

He distinguishes craft from fine art, from expression, *technē* from *poiēsis*. Intermodality and multimodality make it impossible to sustain a sharp distinction between *poiēsis* and *technē*.

6. B. F. Skinner, *Walden Two* (New York: Macmillan, 1962).

7. See Walter Benjamin, "The Work of Art in the Age of Mechanical Reproduction," in *Illuminations* (New York: Schocken, 1968).

8. For example, see Emmanuel G. Mesthene, "Technology and Wisdom," in *Philosophy and Technology*, Edd. Carl Mitcham and Robert Mackey (New York: Free Press, 1972), p. 111, adapted from *Technology and Social Change*, ed. Emmanuel G. Mesthene (Indianapolis: Bobbs-Merrill, 1967): "[T]echnology might be deemed an evil, because evil is unquestionably potential within it. We can explore the heavens with it, or destroy the world. We can cure disease, or poison entire populations. We can free enslaved millions, or enslave millions more. Technology spells only possibility, and is in that respect neutral. Its massive power can lead to massive error so efficiently perpetrated as to be well-nigh irreversible. Technology is clearly not synonymous with the good. It *can* lead to evil."

9. See Don Ihde, *Technics and Praxis* (Boston: Reidel, 1979), p. 140: "1) Could it be that technology itself *is* an expression of the essence of humanity, not merely in a distorted sense, but in all the ambiguity found in man? 2) And, if so, what is the phenomenon of technology such that it so clearly *amplifies* the very possibilities of that humanity such that man may become a threat to himself?"

10. To ask this question is to be led to Heidegger's recurrent thought

of modern technology as posing a surpassing threat to humanity and the possibility of other ways of being human. See Martin Heidegger, *Discourse on Thinking*, trans. J. A. Anderson and E. Hans Freund (New York: Harper & Row, 1966), p. 55: "Releasement toward things and openness to the mystery belong together. They grant us the possibility of dwelling in the world in a totally different way. They promise us a new ground and foundation upon which we can stand and endure in the world of technology without being impeded by it." I add that it is not humanity alone that is in question.

11. Jacques Ellul, "The Technological Order," in *Philosophy and Technology*, Edd. Carl Mitcham and Robert Mackey (New York: Free Press, 1972), p. 86; from *The Technological Order*, ed. Carl F. Stover (Detroit: Wayne State University Press, 1963). See also Jacques Ellul, *The Technological Society*, trans. John Wilkinson (New York: Knopf, 1964).

12. Ellul, "Technological Order," pp. 97–98.

13. Ibid., p. 88.

14. "Man, who exploits the ensemble of means, *is* the master of them. Unfortunately, this manner of viewing matters is purely theoretical and superficial. We must remember the autonomous character of Technique. We must likewise not lose sight of the fact that the human individual himself is to an ever greater degree the *object* of certain techniques and their procedures" (ibid.).

15. Ibid., pp. 90–91.

16. "[T]he essence of technology is by no means anything technological; . . . Technology is not equivalent to the essence of technology. . . . Thus we shall never experience our relationship to the essence of technology so long as we merely conceive and push forward the technological, put up with it, or evade it" ("The Question Concerning Technology," in *Basic Writings*, ed. D. F. Krell [New York: Harper & Row, 1977], p. 287).

17. "Everywhere everything is ordered to stand by, to be immediately on hand, indeed to stand there just so that it may be on call for a further ordering. We call it the standing-reserve. . . . The word 'standing-reserve' assumes the rank of an inclusive rubric. It designates nothing less than the way in which everything presences that is wrought upon by the revealing that challenges. Whatever stands by in the sense of standing-reserve no longer stands over against us as object" (ibid., p. 298).

18. "And yet, the revealing that holds sway throughout modern technology does not unfold into a bringing-forth in the sense of *poiēsis*. The revealing that rules in modern technology is a challenging, which puts to nature the unreasonable demand that it supply energy which can be extracted and stored as such" (ibid, p. 296). "Technology is therefore no

mere means. Technology is a way of revealing. If we give heed to this, then another whole realm for the essence of technology will open itself up to us. It is the realm of revealing, i.e., of truth" (ibid., p. 294).

19. "One essential way in which truth establishes itself in the beings it has opened up is truth setting itself into work. Another way in which truth occurs is the act that founds a political state. Still another way in which truth comes to shine forth is the nearness of that which is not simply a being, but the being that is most of all. Still another way in which truth grounds itself is the essential sacrifice. Still another way in which truth becomes is the thinker's questioning, which, as the thinking of Being, names Being in its question-worthiness. By contrast, science is not an original happening of truth, but always the cultivation of a domain of truth already opened, specifically by apprehending and confirming that which shows itself to be possibly and necessarily correct within that field. When and insofar as a science passes beyond correctness and goes on to a truth, which means that it arrives at the essential disclosure of what is as such, it is philosophy" (Heidegger, "Origin of the Work of Art," p. 62).

Technē is not included here, but it is included in Heidegger's "Question Concerning Technology."

20. "Precisely because man is challenged more originally than are the energies of nature, i.e., into the process of ordering, he never is transformed into mere standing reserve. Since man drives technology forward, he takes part in ordering as a way of revealing. But the unconcealment itself, within which ordering unfolds, is never a human handiwork, any more than is the realm man traverses every time he as a subject relates to an object" (ibid., p. 300).

21. "All coming to presence, not only modern technology, keeps itself everywhere concealed to the last. Nevertheless, it remains, with respect to its holding sway, that which precedes all: the earliest" (ibid., p. 303).

22. "*In truth, however, precisely nowhere does man today any longer encounter himself, i.e., his essence.* Man stands so decisively in attendance on the challenging-forth of enframing that he does not grasp enframing as a claim, that he fails to see himself as the one spoken to, and hence also fails in every way to hear in what respect he ek-sists, from out of his essence, in the realm of an exhortation or address, so that he *can never* encounter himself" (ibid., pp. 308–309).

"Enframing, as a challenging-forth into ordering, sends into a way of revealing. Enframing is an ordaining of destining, as is every way of revealing. Bringing forth, *poiēsis*, is also a destining in this sense" (ibid., p. 306).

23. "Because the essence of technology is nothing technological, essential reflection upon technology and decisive confrontation with it

must happen in a realm that is, on the one hand, akin to the essence of technology and, on the other, fundamentally different from it.

"Such a realm is art" (ibid., p. 317).

24. Ibid., p. 314.

25. "The closer we come to the danger, the more brightly do the ways into the saving power begin to shine and the more questioning we become. For questioning is the piety of thought" (ibid., p. 317).

26. Collingwood, *Principles of Art*, pp. 16–17. See note 5, above.

27. See Thomas S. Kuhn, *The Structure of Scientific Revolutions* (Chicago: The University of Chicago Press, 1962); Rorty, *Philosophy and the Mirror of Nature*.

28. See Friedrich Dessauer, "Technology in its Proper Sphere," in *Philosophy and Technology*, Edd. Carl Mitcham and Robert Mackey (New York: Free Press, 1972), p. 334; from Friedrich Dessauer, *Philosophie der Technik: Das Problem der Realisierung* (Bonn: Cohen, 1927): "Technology is the school where mankind learns by illustration how a reality of a different sort, without disturbing the laws of nature, powerfully takes possession of the world of research, augmenting it, exalting it."

29. "Alongside the world of natural conditions, there enters in our time, on an overwhelming scale, a metacosmos resonant with power—the technological world. Beside the trees of the forest stand the houses of men. The air is cleft by mechanical birds; vehicles rapidly glide over land and sea; and the human voice no longer knows any limitations of space. . . . And this world *has the exactness of the other world* of natural science. Its conditions of being-such exhibit the same certainty as the laws of nature. But this world is a much more fertile foundation for philosophy. For it contains far more than the character of natural law.

". . . we see that from this process there emerges not perhaps a sum or combination of materials or material characteristics, but something which completely transcends that, a completely new essence; *we experience in this object something of the secret of being*" (ibid., p. 324).

30. For a different view, see Nathan Rotenstreich, "Technology and Politics," in *Philosophy and Technology*, Edd. Carl Mitcham and Robert Mackey (New York: Free Press, 1972), p. 151; from *International Philosophical Quarterly*, 7, No. 2 (June 1967), 197–212: "*Politics* represents the set of means by which man puts to use the forces inherent in his social organization. In this sense, politics also denotes man's struggle for his share of social power. *Technology*, on the other hand, represents the set of means by which man puts the forces and laws of nature to use, in view of improving his lot or modifying it as may be agreeable to him. Politics, then, is a purely human domain, while technology lies between man and nature."

The distinction here corresponds too closely to a distinction between what is human and what is natural. From the standpoint of locality, humanity is as natural as anything else. From the standpoint of practice, what is natural is as much part of practical judgment, therefore as human and social, as anything else. In addition, we cannot defend a distinction between politics and technology where technological representations dominate political practices, or, from the other side, where technological developments are political, with far-reaching and pervasive ramifications.

31. "In the very same way that technology influences the course of politics, the course and logic of politics influence technology: they transplant it from the realm of relations between man and nature—to which our abstract definition ascribed it—to the internal human realm. Thus technology influences politics in two manners: (1) it reorganizes the political forces, while (2) it becomes a political asset. On the one hand, its influence is causal, while on the other its influence is that of a much sought-for agent of power" (ibid., p. 151).

32. "The very relation between human existence and technology is rooted in a fundamental aspect of human reality: man must rely upon utensils to satisfy the requirements of his subsistence" (ibid., pp. 151–52).

33. "Technology was not created by man with his bare hands and capacity: it is one technology that produces another" (ibid., p. 152). André Malraux says the same thing about art; and we might say it about science. (*The Voices of Silence*, trans. Stuart Gilbert [Princeton: Princeton University Press], 1953, pp. 14–15).

34. "Technology's indirect influence on politics is double: (1) it has widened the scope of politics, by increasing the number of participants in a sphere destined to improve man's existence; (2) it has narrowed its scope, by concentrating man's interest on the demand to improve his life and by giving him a yardstick according to which everything is to be evaluated by technological criteria" (Rotenstreich, "Technology and Politics," p. 153).

35. Aristotle, *Physics*, 192B6–35.

7

PRACTICAL QUERY

I HAVE CONSIDERED, to this point, practice as judgment and query, particularly the relations between the locality and inexhaustibility of practical judgment and the situatedness and interrogativeness of practical query. What we may consider now are forms of query insofar as they are forms of practice. I have said that every judgment may possess any modality—an awkward locution mediating between the modality that a judgment possesses in particular contexts of utterance and interpretation and the interrogative potentialities of intermodality. It follows that every judgment is, or may be, a practical judgment, that every mode of query may be questioned from the standpoint of practical query and as practical judgment itself. This intermodal practicality is revealed by every biography, portraying the material historical presence of a person or group, the practical side of their judgments, which possess importance because of their judgments in other modes. It is also revealed by and characteristic of the multimodality of everyday, lived experience, where the modes of judgment and query meet and where they exercise their practical influences. Multimodality entails that every judgment may possess any modality.

Every judgment has consequences. There is no escape from such consequences or from their temporality. There are, however, properties of judgments to which such temporality and consequentiality are of no direct relevance, including properties that pertain to them as judgments—that is, in terms of selection and validation. Beauty in art and truth in science, embodied in material representations, have consequences and are validated through time into the future, but they are not validated in terms of their consequences as are technology and politics. Nevertheless, the relations of judgments to their future implicate every judgment in the modality of practice, that form of judgment concerned with influence and directed toward the future.

Every judgment has consequences and a future; every judgment may be validated as a practical judgment. But the truth of a propositional judgment—that George Washington was the first President of the United States—is not a form of influence over the future, though the fact it describes and the truth of the judgment have consequences, and their utterance exercises influence. Similarly, the beauty of a musical work—Beethoven's last string quartet, for example—does not rest in its control over the future though its influence upon other composers and audiences has been immense. On the one hand, the validation of such propositional and fabricative judgments would be unchanged even if their consequences were disastrous; on the other, they might exercise influence and power even if false in the one case and trite in the other. There is no escape from the possibility that certain scientific discoveries may prove harmful to humanity or that certain artistic works may have harmful ethical or psychological consequences. The locality of diverse modes of judgment entails that their different forms of validation are also local and diverse, incommensurate relative to the others.

Nevertheless, though not every mode of query is practical, and does not therefore relate in that mode to its future in terms of control, every form of query requires its future for validation and articulation, requires a semasic future, judgment upon judgment. Time belongs to query in general no less than it does to practical query in particular, in different if overlapping ways. There is no beauty or truth that belongs to judgment independent of the mediate conditions of human life, independent of what human beings do, of their practices. Query demands its future for invention and interrogation as well as for validation. There is no point at which query can cease to be interrogative and inventive without ceasing to be query and without abolishing judgmental validation. Query requires a judgmental future, but it does not as query require influence over that future. To the contrary, the importance of invention to query and of query's relation to the indeterminateness in inexhaustibility entail that influence is not in general relevant to query, only to practical query in particular. This doubling of temporality is what makes the practicality of judgment and query so important.

Among the implications of this doubled temporality is a continuing tension between the temporality of judgment in relation to the other modes and the temporality of practical judgment. The ways in which judgments, especially within a form of query, relate to the future, as well as to the past, are heterogeneous from the standpoint of other modes of validation compared with the influences involved in practice. Reason here is not only divided, but in internal conflict. Yet this conflict is not a lapse from a potential perfection, but is inspiration to interrogation and invention, to new forms of reason.

This topic defines the focus of the discussions in this chapter with the qualification that I will consider other modes of judgment and query only to the extent that they define this tension with practical judgment constituting our predominant relation to temporality: the tension between our semasic future in judgment and query and our practical future with its material consequences. An additional qualification may be noted; my concern here is with promises that emerge from Western forms of query more than with non-Western forms of discourse. Even so, the multifariousness and heterogeneity of query as we understand it works against any view that Western reason might be self-sufficient.

DISCOURSE

To interrogate query as practice leads to language and discourse, for these have been the predominant forms in which the Western tradition has understood reason propositionally. Yet neither language nor discourse, as it stands, is always query. We sometimes babble, speak without thinking, say whatever crosses our mind. Moreover, discourse is as practical as it is propositional. Language and discourse belong to all the modes of judgment, including practical judgment, as, reciprocally, the modes of judgment belong to them. Nevertheless, we may distinguish language from discourse by defining the latter as the practical form taken by the former. I am addressing the ways in which discursive utterances work, exercise control, are validated in terms of their consequences.[1]

It would seem uncontroversial that discourse—speech and writing, indeed, all forms of utterance, linguistic and otherwise—should be practical judgment. Utterances have consequences and are themselves consequences of other judgments. Yet the dangerousness of discourse—its "ponderous, awesome materiality"[2]—is incompatible with many traditional views of language. Such views emphasize the "airy immateriality" and "transparency" of language as requisites of its rationality. What is at stake is the rationality of propositional truth and science, even the rationality of the Western epistemological tradition, as these have commonly been understood. It is an issue, in part, of the practicality of truth.

A traditional way in which this issue has been interpreted is in terms of the opposition of theory and practice. That linguistic utterances are practical appears to make them less theoretical. Yet in the local theory of judgment developed here, every judgment is interpretable with any modality, propositional, practical, and fabricative. Although the mode of validation appropriate to each mode of judgment is incommensurate in certain respects from the standpoint of any other mode, there is no contradiction involved in a judgment possessing both propositional and practical validation. To the contrary, every judgment possesses multiple modalities, is sometimes valid in many modes, sometimes valid in some and not in others, depending on its locations. There is furthermore no perfection involved in seeking validation in many modes at once, for other modes of validation are engendered through the inventions of query. Moreover, conflicting locations do not vanish, or become irrelevant, with new modes of validation. The inexhaustibility of query is manifested as thoroughly in the heterogeneity of judgments as in their congruence.

It follows that while not every judgment is explicitly propositional or practical, every judgment may be interpreted as propositional, and every judgment may be interpreted as practical, although there is no generic synthesis of these modalities. Heterogeneous perspectives can be brought to bear on every utterance. Practice is one of the generic perspectives inherent in judgment and language; linguistic utterances are practical insofar as they have consequences and are consequences of other practices. I am calling the practice of language "discourse." It follows that linguistic utterances are always discursive, may always be understood as practical, whatever other functions they may serve and whatever other modes of judgment pertain to them.

Another way, according to Western tradition, in which the relation of language to discourse has been formulated is in terms of ideology. Insofar as discourse is entangled practice, it cannot recognize truth and liberation autonomously, can only do so within theory.[3] Theory here acquires privilege in relation to practice because practice is blind. Yet such a privilege assigned to theory makes it immune to criticism and effectively closes it to practical query. Neither truth and liberation nor theory can be autonomous relative to practice. Rather, discourse is not only practice, but may function within any mode of query, opening it to interrogation and criticism from within and without. Practice is one of the important ways in which propositional judgment may be intermodal query.

In this century, the issue of whether language is discourse has been interpreted in terms of a view of language as an abstract, detachable object. Saussure takes language to have three primary forms: *langage*, *langue*, and *parole*.[4] The last term evokes a further distinction, between speech and writing, but we may set that aside. From the standpoint of discourse, writing is as practical and effective as is speech, and there is no privilege that may be given to speech over writing.[5] Far more important are the privilege and autonomy accorded *langue*: it is a "self-contained whole and a principle of classification."[6] This self-contained whole is the synchronic network of differences that constitutes the system of linguistic signs.[7] Such a synchronic view of language is incompatible with the practicality of language as discourse and the complex, reflexive temporality that defines judgment.

Several issues are involved. One, in relation to linguistics, is the premise that grounds Saussure's approach to language, that a science of language is possible only if language comprises a distinct principle of classification, if language is autonomous and unique. Here *langue* is the condition of a science of language, for otherwise, language would be implicated within the entire range of conditions of human experience, since any may be given linguistic expression. A second issue, less explicit in Saussure, concerns the epistemic functions of language.[8] At stake is the autonomy (at least detachability) of the referential functions of language relative to discourse. Even in speech-act theory, what is required is that reference and predication be detachable from the notion of a complete speech act so that propositional acts can be well defined.[9]

To hold such a position is to defend a notion of the autonomy of *langue* against the possibility that there can be no object of thought that is language for the reason that language is inseparable from thought or judgment in any of its forms (though not every thought or judgment is expressed in language). Corresponding to the closure on query that *a priori* theoretical principles impose, the principles or rules that define the autonomy and detachability of language from practice and discourse close it, in at least those respects, to interrogation and modification from the standpoint of discourse.[10] Closely related is the mediateness of linguistic utterances within material conditions, the semasic relevance of the future. Utterances may be rational, may belong to query, only in terms of their judgmental future, and thereby may possess consequences and influence the future. To regard language as autonomous is to disentangle the general temporality of judgment and query from the particular temporalities of practical judgment.

The view that language is always discourse is to be distinguished from the view that language is always practice. That language is practice, for example composed of speech acts, does not entail the entanglements of language in practical judgments—discourse—to the point that even propositional expressions are defined by what they accomplish rather than what they mean (what they refer to and what they predicate). To the contrary, it is possible to emphasize the practicality of language, that utterances are acts, without relinquishing the view that there is a system of signs and rules (*langue*) embedded in language that is the basis for its expressiveness. What is involved is the autonomous nature of either language or some structural component of language relative to the complex entanglements of discourse in practical judgments.

Essential to understanding language as discourse is the view that the defining functions of language are expressibility and understanding, and that, in practice, language is modified wherever necessary to attain such understanding, including lexical and syntactic modifications.[11] In this sense, language is "motivated" by the functions imposed upon it in discursive practices while transcending every function inexhaustibly—"motivated" while still "arbitrary," expressing the complementarity of determinateness and indeterminateness in relation to language. It follows that no part of language may be considered immune to modification, even if innate, including its syntactical part. These functions, insofar as linguistic utterances are effective, entail that they are practical judgments and belong to discourse as well as to theory and to languages. What they do not entail is that language is discourse through and through—that is, practical judgment alone. The autonomy of lan-

guage is inseparable from the autonomy of propositional judgment
and validation. We cannot replace such a view of linguistic autonomy with an equally strong view of the hegemony of practice.

Suppose it were true that some subsystem of *langage* composed
an autonomous system of syntactical or structural relations. Suppose further that such a *langue* were not acquired, but innate.[12]
In what way would this impede the claim that language is practice,
and further, that language belongs to discourse? We are considering the claim that there is a competence in language, corresponding
to such structural relations, to be distinguished from performance.
The crucial notions in a structuralist view such as transformational
generative grammar are of an "ideal speaker-listener in a completely homogeneous speech-community, who knows its language
perfectly."[13] The notion of an ideal language is inescapable where
we are speaking of linguistic autonomy, and it is unintelligible.
Similar notions are found in speech-act theory.[14]

The question is whether language is perfectible, and is analogous to the questions of whether thought, understanding, and
knowledge (as well as being) are perfectible. In all these cases,
only one form of what is to be perfected is taken as paradigmatic,
perfection in a particular kind. Thus, it would be unintelligible to
suppose that musical thought might be perfected, but perhaps
more intelligible to imagine that propositional thought might be;
and it would be unintelligible to suppose that knowledge could
be perfected if we included a dense and particular knowledge of
individuals, and only intelligible, perhaps, if we emphasized
knowledge of the fundamental laws and constants of the universe.
Similarly, if language includes whatever is uttered in linguistic
form, everything that linguistic utterances do—that is, performances—then perfectibility is both impossible and unintelligible.
No standards can define whatever language might do, any more
than standards that define whatever thought, reason, or being
might do. New forms of reason and thought emerge that overthrow any given standards and norms. Similarly, the inventiveness
of language is not restricted to sentences never encountered before,
but includes the capacity to make language express what could
not have been expressed before. We may call this the principle of
expressibility—"that whatever can be meant can be said"[15]—but
cannot then restrict it to language. Rather, we can express anything
worth expressing in linguistic form—but also in visible, audible,

or structural form. However, to do so we may have to transform language or any other medium of expression in ways that cannot be anticipated in advance and that may be shocking to those encountering these modifications for the first time.

The place where such inventions are encountered most commonly is in art; this fact promotes Kant's view of genius.[16] Kant restricts the sphere of genius to art, though others have extended it to include science and every form of knowledge, claiming that they are equally the breaking of rules conjoined with the production of norms—originality conjoined with normativity.[17] To the extent that language expresses whatever we want to express, including originality and inventiveness, language must itself be original and capable of new and unanticipatable inventions. Invention in query, therefore in language as well, cannot be restricted to antecedent norms and canons.

The autonomy of language is closely related to its perfectibility. With abandonment of such perfectibility, particularly in relation to the epistemic functions of linguistic utterances on the one hand and their ontological conditions on the other—their locality, inexhaustibility, and ergonality—language becomes inextricably entangled among the diverse functions and features of human life and its surroundings, entangled among their practicalities as well as their generic conditions. In addition, we approach an interpretation of the "ponderous, awesome materiality" of discourse and of language. What is involved is the widespread importance of language in human life and practice: the densely specific condition that so much of human experience and its practices transpire within and by, and are thoroughly entangled with, language. Here it is not that linguistic utterances are practice—discourse—but that judgments are discourse—but not discourse alone. These conclusions are the reciprocal determinants of the materiality of discourse.

That language should be thought perfectible, in any respect, suggests that it cannot be practice, for practice is not perfectible. However, it is not as practice alone that language is imperfectible, for neither propositional knowledge nor art is perfectible either. One way to characterize the imperfectibility of discourse is through the principle of expressibility. There is no perfect or unique way to express any thought or meaning, but some way, somehow, to express what we mean. Discourse is a major site at which expression is accomplished. Another way to characterize the imperfectibility of discourse is by emphasizing the contextuality of utterances, that every utterance belongs to locales that define and delimit it. There is no ideal linguistic expression because there is no ideal human locale. We understand what people say and write, what they express, in terms of relevant contexts, theirs and ours. But none of these milieux or locales remains stable, and the instability is imperfection. Contextuality does not undermine expression but facilitates it. Perfection in language, understood to entail an ideal linguistic form for any thought or meaning, would prohibit communication, since we could never explain what we mean. The presence of surpluses—near synonyms and alternatives—is required for the acquisition of novel meanings.

Still another way to characterize the imperfectibility of discourse is in terms of the indeterminateness of the future. As practice, discourse belongs to the uncertainty of consequences over which we have only limited control. Utterances enter a public world in which others interpret and judge what they find, and there is no way that the author can maintain control over others' interpretations. All the uncertainties and risks of practice pertain to linguistic utterances and to discourse.

There remain the ramifications of the materiality of discourse, the relations of power and desire that characterize it. For only through such relations can we understand its practicality. Yet to speak of the "materiality" of discourse is, in the Western tradition, including most recent writings, to speak figuratively—to speak, that is, without density and materiality or specificity and precision. Language—including speech and writing—inhabits the airy regions of thought and understanding. In the view developed here, there can be no unconditioned play of signs, any more than there can be an unconditioned play of productive relations, of atoms or factories, because they have weight and materiality. What is effective must possess weight and materiality, the entanglements of practice.

From the standpoint of discourse as practice, density, weight, and materiality—that is, relations involving power—belong to discourse as they belong to every practice. Practices matter, they determine the future and are determined by the past. That such determinations retain the presence and relevance of alternatives and possibilities wherever judgment is involved does not contradict the complementary truth that discourse belongs to human life and experience by influence and weight, that it expresses the consequences of relations of power and contributes to future power relations. Alternatives do not arise from immateriality, but within effective, local relations.

The materiality of discourse is its situatedness, temporally and historically, within relations involving power and desire. It follows that discourse is practice, flowing from the past and directed toward the future. The notion of an autonomous and unconditioned play of thoughts and ideas is rejected, and, with it, the notion of an untrammeled truth. Truth is weighed down by and entangled within the materiality of the past and its consequences for the future. Also rejected is the notion of a language that, ethereally, can be freed from the material presence of events that control it. Language and discourse inhabit spheres of power. My concern is with the differences in human life and experience that language makes, perhaps the most profound question of language.

A related question is how there can be truth within such materialities of discourse. Several difficulties appear. One is that the materiality and density of discourse, the location of discourse within spheres of power, situate it as a form of practice concerned with antecedents and consequents, not with truth. A second is that to recognize the density and materiality of discourse entails that power and desire work upon every utterance and within every human locale. It follows that no truth can free itself from the entanglements of materiality—its ideology. A third difficulty is that truth, like justice and morality, is both controlled and a form taken by power and control. Here truth to a lesser extent sets us free than it is always spoken in a voice of domination and manipulation. Nevertheless, to deny the materiality of discourse denies it influence, makes it epiphenomenal.[18] My concern is to affirm the density and materiality of discourse without rejecting the possibilities of truth and science.[19]

Two aspects of the density and materiality of discourse may then be emphasized. One is that discourse is practical though it is also scientific, artistic, and philosophical—propositional, fabricative, and syndetic. Unless we recognize the practicality of discourse, we cannot regard it as humanly effective. Without understanding the materiality of discourse to involve power and desire, we cannot expect anything we say or think to influence the future. The point of having ideas, of uttering words, of engaging in discourse, is to make a difference. And the differences are consequential, pertain to the future and belong to discourse as practical judgment. Moreover, if discourse is practice, it follows that it belongs to other practices, that practice follows from and leads to other practices. It involves relations of power and desire.

I have posed the question of truth in relation to discourse as how the density and materiality of discursive practices can be kept from suffocating truth under their weight. One answer is that truth is airy and immaterial, though it can be overcome by materiality. The answer is contradictory. If truth can be suffocated, then it must be material. The suggestion is that to the extent that propositional query is practice—and every judgment is a practical judgment—truth is either impossible or obstructed. To the contrary, truthfulness is inseparable from practical judgment. It is only because judgments are practical and have a past and a future that truth is possible. It does not follow that propositional and practical validation are indistinguishable, that they do not conflict, that modes of validation are not incommensurate. This confluence of support and heterogeneity is one of the important determinants of judgment in general and practice in particular.

To the question of whether truth can be suffocated by the materiality of discourse, I have responded that truth could not be realized without such materiality. Somewhat less generally, we may ask what we could mean by truth in the absence of materiality—that is, without past and future determinants. The truth we are speaking of, and the knowledge with which it is associated, are located in query, for they can be located nowhere else. Moreover, the question of the suffocation of truth by materiality and ideology, along with all other skeptical and critical questions concerning knowledge and truth, also belongs to query if it is to be intelligible.

Truth is not suffocated by the materiality of human events and the density of human discourses because without that materiality, without dense and specific practical judgments with specific and weighty consequences, truth would be unintelligible, not merely impracticable and ineffective. There is no airy and immaterial truth, no gossamer realm of ideas, because the presence and effectiveness of query requires the density of its materials, especially of the discourses that situate it.

Another way of putting this is that knowledge and truth are constituted by judgment and query, and depend for their invention, interrogation, and validation upon densely specific discourses with rules and prohibitions, discourses that exclude from legitimacy and authority and prohibit by rule. This can be seen in science as well as in other established forms of discourse: a scientific public is required with an entrenched discourse that defines what is authoritative and what is acceptable.

A stronger conclusion is that truth is located within discourse and query, and has no meaning apart from them. Truth cannot be suffocated by discourse because truth belongs to multiple discourses. Truth pertains to discourses and to practices, which suffocate and enclose it but also release its potentialities and make its achievements possible. There is no truth independent of any discourse; but there is no entrenched truth that belongs to only one discourse.

We return to the generic question that defines the focus of this discussion. What difference, practically speaking, does discourse make? One answer is that discourse is practice, among its other modes, and results in all the differences in human life that practice can make. A second answer is that truth and beauty can matter only because propositional judgment is also practice. Discourse is dangerous and terrifying but also capable of truth and beauty only because it is dense and material, practical as well as theoretical. The specificity of discourse lies in its relation to language, given that there is virtually nothing that we do and think that we could not do without language, but that we always do through language. This conjunction of latitude and necessity is the dangerousness of discourse.

I conclude that query does not depend on discourse nor does discourse entirely depend on query, but that each cohabits pervasively and uneasily with the other in the multiple modes of judgment that compose human life and reason. That discourse is practice follows from the fact that judgment and query are multimodally practice. The consequence is, practically speaking, a repetition of mediateness. We are always within discourse and utterance, as we are within judgment, but we are never "trapped" within any mode, for to be within judgment, discourse, and query is always to be open to new and varied manifestations, inexhaustibly but also locally.

To answer questions of the difference discourse makes, we require a multiplicity of rational standpoints, a multiplicity of forms of query, whereby we may interrogate each from the standpoints of the others. Here the alleged transparency and detachability of language, whether structural or based on rules, would prevent us from interrogating its materiality and weightiness. Language must be discourse, must be practical judgment, in order to be interrogated and articulated. But it must also belong to multiple modes of judgment and query, as they belong to it, in order for it to be interrogated. Questioning the differences that language makes, its practicality as discourse, entails that discourse is inexhaustibly open to further judgment from the standpoints of a multiplicity of modes. We have returned to the principle of expressibility to add that just as language is a representational form in which any meaning may be expressed, and must be adaptable to such variations of expression, it cannot be the only form in which meanings are expressed, for it would then be closed to interrogation. It follows, further, that for language to be expressive, it must be discourse, must be practical judgment if it is to belong to any mode of judgment, is to be effective. The difference language makes is the difference query makes, with the qualification that query is divided into multiple forms. Consequently, discourse and language are similarly divided.

Science

The temporality that belongs to query in general and practical query in particular pertains to every form of query, including science. Science is practice in at least the double sense that it is a practice and is practical judgment. It is, moreover, practical judgment in at least two ways: belonging to spheres of practical judgment and query and influencing the future. Query is inevitably and inescapably a practice, but only in certain respects—interpreted in certain ways—is it to be understood as practical judgment, emerging from its past and validated by its future.

The sense in which science is a practice is the sense in which it is query, understood in terms of the mediate, situated judgments that compose its activities. Science is historical, expressed in diverse stories of its development, and its practical validation is inseparable from such stories, past and future. Science is a practice in several respects, one of which is that it could not function without other practices with their influences and consequences. I include experimental and observational practices, in laboratories and in the field, but also theoretical and mathematical practices. I also include Wittgenstein's sense of these as "forms of life," having histories and materially determining the local conditions or rules of discourse, and include their interrelations and reciprocations.[20] Science is a practice in being a discourse and in belonging to other discourses, intermodally, where discourse is the practice of linguistic utterance. I add the insistent sociality of scientific discourse, the importance of common understandings (and heretical departures) that define a public scientific community that shares experimental activities and general conclusions. Even the language of science belongs to human history. The voice of science is a human voice, where humanity is understood mediately and contingently as forever part of histories that make a profound difference to whatever falls within them. Here query is understood to be material and determinate in its influences and in what influences it.

We approach a view of science as practice in the sense of practical judgment and query, and may make another distinction. We may distinguish between science insofar as it contributes to practical judgments and query and science insofar as it is practice, as it influences and controls the human future as science. In the former sense, we are speaking of the role science plays in the practical spheres of technology and politics, including communication and war. In the latter sense we are concerned with what science implies for the future insofar as it is a voice of propositional reason. We are concerned with the practical consequences of propositional query manifested in specific and tangible discourses and events.

The former role of science in practice is as a primary and, in some cases, irresistible component of other forms of practice. Technology is the major form that embodies the practical work of science, but since technology is the predominant form in which a sophisticated practice transpires, science through technology invades every modern form of practice. All have been dominated by technological developments. This dominance is especially striking in leisure activities, which bring human beings into nature, where we see the marked effects of technology and science. The most inaccessible of terrains are invaded by snowmobiles and helicopters. The most inhospitable of natural surroundings are made more accessible by technologically sophisticated forms of food storage, lightweight materials for clothing and supplies, etc. In this remarkable way, technology simultaneously brings us closer to nature and places us at an unbridgeable distance from it. I am acknowledging the presence of technology within nature in the divided way that characterizes local and inexhaustible beings and practices.

Technology is the predominant form of contemporary political practice, therefore the predominant form in which science is practice, in which it is subsumed under other forms of practice. There are forms of practice—political and technological—that strive for mastery and control through the use of all available human resources, including the resources provided by modes of query other than practice—science and art, even philosophy. Science therefore has a role to play—intermodally and multimodally—within other forms of practice, to the point where its own rational concerns may be subsumed under those other forms. Like every form of query, science may be subordinated—even "bent"—to the constraints of other forms of query, intermodally.

This sense of the practicality of science must be contrasted with the third and most interesting sense: the practical consequences of science itself, subsumed under no external judgmental constraints. In starkest terms, the question concerns the impact of science upon human life, setting aside the practical influences that involve other modes of judgment and query. It is the question of what the presence of a particular form of reason entails for the future. It is a question that addresses the density and materiality of practice at a fundamental level.

In a profound and important sense, this question addresses issues that transcend intelligibility, though intelligibility is inescapable from the standpoint of query. The question is what difference science makes, as if experience might be different without science, as if we could imagine human experience without science and propositional reason. But science is not open to that kind of difference, particularly where it is the predominant form of propositional judgment and query. There are other forms of propositional judgment—everyday experience, mythology, folklore among others—and even of propositional query—in courts of law. In these other cases, however, propositional validation is

subsumed under the auspices of other modes of judgment: only
in science is it predominant. In this sense, science is propositional
query itself, taking specific forms emerging from its own imperatives, to attain propositionally valid judgments. It is driven by the
interrogations and inventions that constitute propositional query,
leading to technical rigor, sophisticated instruments, controlled
practices, even theoretical languages where demanded by its interrogations. For all that, it is entangled within the other modes
of query.

If science is the explicit form of propositional query, then the
question of the difference science makes becomes the question of
the differences involved in propositional judgment and query, even
a question of the difference reason makes—as if we might live
without reason. This is not an intelligible question, not only because it is asked from within reason, but also because it would
not be asked except for the demands of reason, in this case from
within philosophic query. The question is unintelligible because
it is human being and experience we are interrogating as if they
might lack judgment and query in general, propositional judgment
and science in particular. The question is as unintelligible as that
of the difference made by truth. There could not be human being
without truth; there could not be being without truths that might
be told of it, whether or not human beings could tell them. There
cannot be human being without reason and truth, but there might
be other forms of reason and truth.

There could be nothing human that did not involve judgment
in general and propositional judgment in particular: judgment and
its modes are defining characteristics of being human, of relating as
human beings to the world. There might, however, be a universe
without human beings, without interrogation, without consciousness, and without life. Thus, one part of the answer to our question of the practical relevance of science and propositional query
is that we are speaking of the differences made by reason to human
beings and by human beings to their surroundings. But the question then cannot be whether there might be human beings without
science or propositional judgment, but rather whether there might
be a very different kind of science and propositional judgment.
Alternatively, it is a question that seeks to understand the practical
consequences of science and propositional query even where they
are acknowledged to be inevitable. Here the question is one of the

difference that resides among the different modes of reason from the standpoint of any mode in particular.

This is the complex and subtle context in which the analogous and pervasive, but deeply constricted question of science is typically asked: whether a particular discipline or method is scientific—for example, whether metaphysics is a science, whether psychology, psychoanalysis, certain forms of social and human understanding, are sciences. Such questions are typically legitimating and excluding: whether a particular discourse constitutes a legitimate use of power; whether it composes acceptable authority. Such a question addresses reason itself, in terms of the voices that constitute authoritative rationality, and of the exclusions that judgment and query impose on human experience. Within the context of propositional query, and of manifold other forms of query, the question whether a given practice or field of judgment is science is prejudicial,[21] not simply in the sense of mediateness and entanglement, but in the sense that it excludes other forms of query, including propositional query, as illegitimate. To what extent are the achievements of any form of reason—propositional query in particular—the result of a sacrifice of other rational forms and achievements?

What difference does it make to human experience and its surroundings that science exists as one of the fundamental and pervasive forms of truth? One answer is that this difference is unintelligible since there could not be a human experience without propositional judgment and query, and these are science. Similarly, questions of the difference that is truth are unintelligible, since there could not be a human experience without truth, could not be being in general without its truths. Truth and reason belong to ergonality, to nature's work. What difference does it make that science as we know it, as it has developed historically and materially, speaks in the authoritative voice of truth? What difference does it make that science has taken the specific forms it has? In part, these are historical questions, difficult as they may be to answer, that look to contrasts among alternative epistemic forms.[22] Questions of difference here, of the differences made by science, can be answered only by understanding the difference that science is or was, historical questions that fulfill themselves only by projections into the future, where science and other forms of reason take us.

In further part, questions of the differences made by science are questions that science does not and cannot ask itself. They are questions that require forms of query external to science, external to any particular form. Every discourse is materially and historically constituted, therefore limited, and among these limitations are questions it cannot ask, frequently about itself, that must be asked from the standpoint of other modes of query. This is the reason for the impossibility and unintelligibility of a supreme, synthetic form of reason: it would inevitably be blind to some of its own limitations and exclusions.

In his *Introduction to Metaphysics*, Heidegger confronts Leibniz's question of the existence of the universe: why is there something rather than nothing?[23] This question is analogous in certain ways to the question of why there is science rather than something else—thought or poetry (though these are not possibilities in place of science, but forms of query together with science). To Leibniz, the question of the existence of the world is necessary and answerable—in terms of God. From the standpoint of locality and inexhaustibility, the question is unintelligible and has no answer. Any answer would violate locality. However, even within this context of unintelligibility, asking the question is essential, for only by asking it can we confront possibilities that make a difference but do not accommodate alternatives.

The questions we are asking here do not have the breadth of the question of the existence of the world, partly because they address science rather than the world, but also because they address the difference science makes only from the standpoint of practice, for the future, in and for human life and experience. Nevertheless, even in this form these are unintelligible questions within and for human being and concerning human being in the context of its natural surroundings.

The unintelligibility of questions of the existence of the world and of the differences made by propositional query and by truth does not foreclose their importance and relevance, but transforms our understanding of them. We ask such questions in order to bring under interrogation aspects of being and judgment that cannot be interrogated from within any established form. We are, that is, concerned with the limits of reason and of inexhaustibility—always from within, local limits essential to query. In connection with science, the question is whether it can be resisted and what that might mean. My answer is that it is resisted both by other modes of query and by the possibility that any of its particular forms is arbitrary relative to propositional query. One of the most important of these resistances, then, lies in the interrogations that can be brought to science from the spheres of practical query. Other resistances derive from the interrogations to be brought to science from other modes of query, including those that remain to be invented in an undetermined future. In connection with truth, the question is whether truth itself can be interrogated. The answer is that it is interrogated by the other modes of query and their modes of validation, by the incommensuratenesses that define the interrelations of multiple modes of query.

The generic question of the difference science makes addresses the nature of truth and reason in terms of their heterogeneity. Such a question is unintelligible, but expresses the dividedness in reason and truth, therefore in science, that expresses their locality and inexhaustibility. I conclude, at this generic level of analysis, that query in general, and science in particular, manifest along with truth the generic conditions of being: in particular, its heterogeneities. Truth is the final authority in propositional query, but is irresistibly divided by heterogeneous truths and other forms of validation that bring it under interrogation.

We may briefly return from this generic level of interrogation to several distinct and important questions of science as practice. The question whether there might be human being without science is equivalent, first, with whether there might be human being without reason (at least propositional reason), and is unintelligible. However, there might not be reason as it has densely and materially developed, especially in the form of modern experimental science, and in the form of authoritative truth. There might be very different forms of social and human sciences, represented in the contrast between psychoanalytic and behavioral psychologies. The question, then, second, is whether science must take the form it does, analogous to the question of whether modern thought must take the form it does, divided into specific disciplines. There are diverse sciences—physics, chemistry, mathematics, biology; distinctions between certain sciences—natural and human, social and behavioral, physical and cultural; and distinctions between the sciences and other human practices. The question here is not whether there could be human being without propositional query, but whether there could be human being without the disciplinary distinctions that define contemporary human thought, including the dense materiality of scientific practices. Might there not be other forms that science as propositional query might take without sacrificing propositional validation?

The question here is one of necessity in human being, of its *a priori* conditions construed as broadly as possible. What query suggests, what locality and inexhaustibility suggest, is that there can be no such *a priori* conditions, for they would be unconditioned. Questions of the difference science makes, along with similar questions concerning any of the modes of query and query itself, address the inexhaustibility and locality of query. As a consequence of locality, every form of query might be different, would be different, a function of the material local conditions of human practices. Construed broadly, as a consequence of inexhaustibility, query is the activity of reason, and is divided into heterogeneous forms. The tension here between science as propositional query generically, employing whatever activities are required to attain propositional validation, and science in any of its particular forms, expresses the joint relevance of locality and inexhaustibility.

Here the recurrent question of science—whether a given practice is science—is to be understood not only as one of legitimacy and power but to address implicitly the multifariousness of science if it is to be a voice of propositional query. The question of whether psychoanalysis, for example, is a science is not whether it is predominantly propositional query, for it could be that and much more. It is a question of authority that masks the implicit assumption that there are definite conditions that propositional query must meet to be science, rather than that propositional query may take any form required to attain validation. In other words, the exclusionary question of science's legitimacy is incompatible with science as query and especially incompatible with multiple and heterogeneous forms of query.

The third question of the difference science makes is a question of power and authority. Which practice shall have authority, even hegemony, over the discursive voices of propositional query? A naïve answer is that no such voice should hold hegemony over query, over reason and interrogation. For without some forms of authority invested in the establishment of norms, there cannot be

interrogations of a certain kind. Without assuming certain conditions inherent in relativistic physics and quantum mechanics, we
cannot begin to raise questions about the age and beginning of the
present astronomical universe, nor of its future. Yet equally, from
the standpoint of query, every rule and norm, every limit, raises
the possibility of abrogation, raises new possibilities of interrogations from within and from without concerning the acceptability
of such restrictions.

Questions of science's authority concern whether other discourses and propositional voices can participate in the ongoing
practice of propositional query, can make their different contributions, as they influence and inspire inventions and departures.
That any form of propositional practice might be altogether excluded because it is not science betrays an impoverished view of
propositional query and of query in general. It is one of the forms
in which contemporary scientolatry exerts its particular violences
upon human life and practice. Here we see, in the guise more of
scientolatry than science, the difference that a particular scientific
practice can make, in a violence done to human being and reason.

The overarching principle of query is that no particular form
or mode of judgment can be given predominance over the others,
even over other forms within a particular mode, except proximately and in relation to particular judgments and practices. What
is valid or not is not a question of generic or *a priori* legitimacy,
but belongs to query. Neither as propositional nor even as practical query can science take precedence over other forms without
imposing closure upon rationality. Here science may be understood to be a pervasive form of propositional query, but scientolatry is the practical discourse in which science is given illegitimate
hegemony over other discourses and practices. Here, the difference that science makes is nothing other than query's transformation of human being. The difference that scientolatry makes is one
of violence and oppression. It is a political and practical, not a
propositional form of practice.

Are there differences that science makes that violate natural
things and impose themselves oppressively on human experience?
If the answer to this question is affirmative, it is because of the
density and materiality of any practices, including the practices of
propositional query. Query makes a difference, not only in its
inventiveness and openness to the future, bringing new possi-

bilities into existence, transforming established conditions, but it inevitably delimits only certain possibilities as relevant, and establishes new material conditions. Query is no less material and tangible in its practices than any other form of practice.

Are there differences that science makes that constitute the mark of its progress—to expose to us the errors in belief and understanding that constitute everyday experience and past scientific convictions? What is required in response is sensitivity to the material ways in which a form of query works through power and exclusion, denying privilege to unorthodox voices. To be a material, effective discourse, a form of query must exclude; but such exclusions always go far beyond the requirements of validation.

Questions of science's authority hover unresolvably between two alternatives: we can interrogate our activities and our surroundings only locally, from within such activities and surroundings; without such interrogations, carried as far as possible, in multifarious forms and modalities, we cannot claim reason or validation. Questions of science as practice confront us with the inevitability that what we do to understand things is situated mediately among those things and heterogeneous others, is influenced by them densely and materially and influences the future. Science, along with every form of query, is a creature of power and desire. It is, however, no less query, no less inventive and interrogative, no less validative for its specific temporality.

Questions of science as practical judgment, then, are questions that belong to query itself in its intermodality. They are not answerable in their most generic forms, but in the local forms in which query exercises power and is determined by desire through exclusion and prohibition. Nevertheless, that such questions can be asked generically is one of the most important conditions of intermodal query, philosophically and more generally. We have here one of the generic conditions of rational judgment: that it may be query only to the extent that it is suspended between unending interrogation and the dense material influences that constitute any definite practice, between inexhaustibility and locality. In practical terms, science, like every form of query, threatens us with oppression and authority at the same time that it is one of the most powerful ways in which oppression and authority are resisted. Science is practically—especially through scientolatry—one of the most intolerant forms of practice at the same time that it is one of the most powerful manifestations of inexhaustibility and charity. In these respects, science is a primary manifestation of the dividedness of rationality, truth, and being.

ART

Questions of what difference science as practical judgment makes for human life have proved to be questions touching on the limits of intelligibility, on locality and inexhaustibility, in ways not accessible from within science itself or any of the established modes of query. They address the junctures between modes of query, pointing to differences in general—locality and inexhaustibility—and differences in and for human being and judgment. We find ourselves addressing the pervasiveness and irresistibility of practice at a point where its own limitations are evident. It is the point where technology—the political practice in which science is deeply implicated—is deeply and irresistibly influential yet limited and incomplete.

Similar questions asked about art—the difference art makes from the standpoint of practice—may be given many of the same answers given in my discussion of science, but others may be added. For art, especially including poetry, has been understood by many philosophers to concern itself overtly with heterogeneity, to be inexhaustible, in ways masked in our experience by science and technology.[24]

The question is what difference art makes as practical judgment. Our first concern, then, is with understanding the practicality of art, though art is not merely practice, is not practical judgment alone or primarily. I begin, then, with another difference, between practical and fabricative judgment. It is a difference that has traditionally been difficult to define, between aesthetic and practical values. The reason is due to the pervasiveness of the modes of judgment as well as the differences between them. Works of art have consequences, influence the future, portray human beings in practical settings, delineate ethical and political circumstances. Practical objects, used in domestic and technical activities, are designed according to formal as well as functional considerations, not to mention where function defines form as a principle of design. A striking feature of art is that it inhabits the region between these different considerations, between fabrication to influence the future—practical judgment—and the production of artifacts for display—fabricative judgment.

I call this region between, "contrast": the inexhaustible interplay of similarities and differences. It is reflexive and self-referential; contrasts can be built upon contrasts inexhaustibly. This contrasting interplay of similarities and differences is inexhaustible and manifests inexhaustibility. And since the interplay of similarities and differences is the revelation as well as amplification of inexhaustibility, art is the manifestation of inexhaustibility through intensity of contrast.[25] The interplay of the modes of judgment and query permits us to distinguish fabricative from propositional and practical judgment without requiring that it be independent of them, indeed, acknowledging that wherever there is judgment, there are its different modalities. To judge is always to produce something—fabrication—that will influence the future—practice. Nevertheless, within this generic practicality of every mode of judgment art possesses a mimetic capacity to display itself as practice, included within its complex contrasts.

Like science, art is practice in several senses, some of which are more important for our purposes here than others. Art is a practice as well as practice. In the former sense, like science, art inhabits the spheres of human life and being, historically and materially. It is something human beings practice, engage in, to be understood in historical and contextual terms. Art here is local practice. There is no heavenly beauty, no realm of Forms, apart from the activities by which human beings realize them—though these activities, through inexhaustibility, transcend any of their conditions in the sense that they involve novel alternative possibilities.

Art is a practice, along with science, philosophy, and technology. But it is also practical judgment, influencing the future and influenced by the past, manifesting desires, exercising powers. It is, again like science, practical judgment in two senses: subordinate to other modes of judgment and query, ornamental and ancillary; and itself practical judgment, making a difference in human experience. It is also practice in a third sense, inseparable from the others but to be distinguished from them, inherent in its contrasting capacities: art incorporates explicit practical judgments as components of some of its most intense contrasts, confronting moral issues, portraying human characters in profound practical difficulties, expressing the inexhaustible complexity of practical entanglements.

The first sense, of subordination and ornamentation, pervades human historical experience. Art is found wherever human beings are found, and is present in all human activities: religious ceremonies, mythic depictions of an unknown human past, dance and music celebrative of important historical and cultural events. Here art is within the other activities of query, sometimes not predominant in its time and place, but with the remarkable capacity to endure long after the other activities have passed from the scene. Art here is among the most important of ceremonial and celebrative forms in which human experience is commemorative, among the most important of forms in which the passage of time is held fast, in which important events lose their transitoriness and belong to time enduringly.

If we expand the notion of art to include technological design in public works, governmental buildings and urban structures, then there can be no judgment that is not fabricative production. Every building, however utilitarian, inhabits a landscape that it controls, not simply in relation to its consequences, but structurally. A public work defines the space and movement surrounding it as well as the qualities of sound and vision that define its environment. This salient practicality makes public art more controversial than any of its private forms. Art is utilitarian but also far more, is practical through the unique structures in which it participates. In this sense, fabricative judgment serves practice—politics, religion, technology, everyday experience—in applied forms analogous to the applications of science. In this sense, there is no form of practice that does not embody fabricative judgment, frequently fabricative query, to the extent that every practice builds and contrives.

This view of practice is the most apparent, but it is also in important ways the least profound. A dramatic way to enforce the difference between art that serves practical judgment, that plays a role in other practical activities, and the ways in which art is practice as art, is by raising questions of public support for the arts, typically a question that requires practical justifications.[26] The analogous question did not arise in connection with science because the utility of science is so obvious that the question appears to have no practical importance. Even in connection with science, however, many scientific activities and practices are concerned with understanding the nature of our physical surroundings at a scale that may have no practical usefulness whatever in any sphere other than that of science—for example, questions of the beginning of the universe, involving remote and largely invisible galaxies. Is astrophysics useful, and should it be supported by public funds? The question arises, but can largely be neglected, since so many of the activities of science have enormous public implications.

The approach to the practicality of science, construed in such narrow terms, neglects the most important way in which science is practical, not in serving utilitarian ends, in relation to other modes of judgment, but as query, as a voice of reason and of truth, but especially as a primary form of human and natural being. This is the generic form of practicality that pertains to science as propositional query, the difference that science makes that cannot be intelligibly delineated, though it can be interrogated, because it expresses one of the primary forms of query. It includes the presence of query itself as an expression of humanity and the practicality that is the influence of query upon subsequent query, one of the most important of practical implications inherent in reason. Reason contributes to its own future, thereby practical judgment and, if interrogative of how it does so, also practical query.

Questions of the public support of propositional query are questions concerning whether it is justifiable publicly to support activities that human life cannot and will not get along without. There will always be science, with or without public financial support, or, if not modern science then other important forms of propositional query. What public support accommodates is propositional query at a certain scale—one that blurs the distinction between propositional and political query. Thus, it belongs to politics to concern itself with the question of the ceremonial, symbolic, and significant ways in which science may be encouraged to continue and to be effective.

Similarly, the question of public support for the arts is not simply a question of the practical consequences of support for museums and orchestras, even for individual artists, for this question typically treats art as in the service of other modes of judgment and query—citizenship, redistribution of resources, public education, and so forth. For example, museums and orchestra performances are typically attended by relatively economically privileged members of an industrial society, so that in economic terms alone, public support for such activities is a transfer of resources from poorer to richer citizens. This is a powerful argument against the practicality of art in the service of human life and experience, in terms of who is affected and how. I add that affluent people may be expected to support the activities that they consider important, and that art will not wither, will always be with us as one of the voices in which the human spirit sings. Public support of art, even more than science, cannot be necessary to the continuance of art, however helpful it may be to people who find it difficult either to survive as artists or to people who find it difficult to support their interests in art. Moreover, where there has been public support, there are fundamental practical questions of control and power over the works produced and how they are to be displayed.

What has been left out is that art is a primary human voice and that it is inevitably practical judgment, as art, apart from any of the other modes to which it contributes—especially apart from education, instruction, public activities, or technical design. Art makes an unavoidable difference in human experience to such an extent that it is unintelligible to imagine human life without it, including historical masterpieces preserved in some form for the future and, far more irresistibly, the continuing production and display of future works of art.

Public support of art, then, is the political expression of a symbolic and ceremonial truth: that human experience is artistic experience, that human and natural being is inseparable from the being of art. We may emphasize public works and displays in the arts we support, so that we effectively glorify and celebrate nationalistic and regional qualities as we celebrate the powers and qualities of art. Or, we may prefer to celebrate artistic activities more widely and less publicly, still, however, manifesting the inseparability of human life and the works of art that inhabit it. Here art is one of the primary and most important expressions of human and natural possibilities, including the practical consequences of its presence and our support of it. Here art itself is practice. We may include other contrasts, born by works of great popularity or social relevance, as in non-Western ceremonial arts.

The sovereignty of an individual work of art resides in its inexhaustible capacity to define itself in relation to other beings and works in its unique and special ways. It does so in terms of indissoluble bipolar relations: one side reflexively returns to the work of art—its uniqueness of style and form—the other side may have any reference whatever. These are the components of the contrasts that define artistic value. Thus, the inexhaustible interplay of contrasts that is a singular work of art manifests the inexhaustibility of that work and of whatever falls within its sphere of relevance. In the former capacity, the manifestation of the inexhaustibility of the work gives us the unmistakable sense of its sovereignty. We must not subordinate a work of art to anything that lies outside it, for that would diminish its sovereignty and presence. To this must be added that such sovereignty may, in the contrasting interplay that defines works of art, include anything found in human experience, including new imaginative contrivances that will influence the human future.

In art, then, especially Western art, we find that the unique and singular presence of individual works carries within it an inexhaustible promise of novelty and originality conjoined with mimetic and representational relations inhabiting every corner of human experience. Each individual, singular work is inexhaustible and manifests inexhaustibility in its contrasts. This interplay of singularity and contrasting multiplicity provides the intensity that is our experience of artistic value. And it includes practical as well as propositional relevance, part of the profound intermodality of great works of art. This is the third sense in which art, in the most salient and obtrusive way, is practical and moral: mimicking practical judgments and query in its contrasting developments.

To recapitulate: art is practice in the following senses: (a) it is a practice, historically and mediately situated in human experience; (b) it is practical judgment situated within and among other modes of practice, serving them and subordinate to their modes of validation; (c) it is practical judgment in a contrasting, mimetic form, portraying practical concerns involving power and desire in human experience from the standpoint of intensity of contrast, manifesting inexhaustibility, here imposing the modes of validation inherent in fabricative query upon practical components derived from other modes of judgment; (d) it is practical judgment and query as art in its revelation of inexhaustibility.

Art has frequently played the role of political and moral opponent within entrenched forms of power and practice—and equally has spoken for established practices. Art has frequently been shocking in its departures from established modes of thought and imagination—and has as frequently supported established forms. These conditions are consequences of the importance of invention in art and of its manifestation of inexhaustibility. What art discloses, in its most repetitive forms, are the transgressable limits inherent in any practice. The reason for this is that art as practice is the manifestation of inexhaustibility and valor, including within itself an irresistible sense of charity. In the context of art, no work and no being inherent in a work is substitutable for, equivalent with, any other work or being, but is incomparable in its inexhaustibility and glory.

PHILOSOPHY

Philosophy is practice in the ways shared by science and art, but it is practical judgment in a more reflexive way than either of them. Not always, perhaps not in the majority of its works, philosophy nevertheless has been regarded by many Western philosophers—Plato and Spinoza, for example, as well as Hegel—as the form in which human life is lived to the fullest, the highest form of practical reason. It is the philosopher-king who lives in the light of the Good, philosophers who realize in themselves the self-consciousness of Absolute Spirit, and a philosophical understanding that defines our relation to God. Not only is philosophy here the form and activity that is the highest form of practice; it is practically influential over the temptations that stand in the way of human fulfillment. I am speaking of the intimate connection between philosophy and wisdom, with wisdom understood as the practical fulfillment of the possibilities of human life and being. In this form, such an understanding is deeply overstated, for wisdom is practical query, not philosophy. However, practical query can include any practice within its scope, in that way including philosophy as well as the other modes of query, science and art.

Both science and art are reflexively responsive to the presence of practical judgment within them, to their own relevance to the future, the former overtly in the human sciences, the latter in explicitly doctrinal works. Moreover, science and art have been repeatedly proposed as the supreme realization of human spirit, the highest life that human beings can live. Yet to the extent that one might live a life of science, such a life does not include within itself an explicit knowledge as science that such a life is the highest practical achievement; to the extent that an artist lives the highest life of inspiration and genius, such a life does not explicitly include as art the affirmation that practice is served best by art.

Only in relation to philosophy does it appear that this circle closes. From the standpoint of query, such an appearance cannot be correct, for philosophy, like every other mode of query, demands interrogation from without as well as from within. Nevertheless, an important realization is present here in relation to philosophy and query: while we may engage in query without affirming its rationality, either propositionally or practically, philosophy offers us a different relation to reason, for it is included within reason and includes it within its own interrogative practices. Philosophy includes itself as practice in a unique way, among its most remarkable characteristics. Its reflexivity is one of the most important implementations of Socrates' maxim of self-knowledge: not knowledge of oneself, but philosophy's reflexive interrogation of itself. This questioning of itself is quite different from the view that philosophy provides its own legitimation. It is an endless critical pursuit.

Before considering this practice in greater detail, I will review the forms of practical query that pertain to philosophy analogous to those discussed in relation to science and art. Philosophy is *a* practice in the multiple senses that it is situated historically and temporally, socially and culturally in dense and material human events, influenced by them and influencing them. It is a creature of power and desire. There is no escape from this temporality and mediateness; nor should there be. Yet this mediateness and practicality of philosophy—its historicality—goes against most of its major Western traditions even in their contemporary forms.[27]

The entanglements of philosophy among contexts of power and desire pertain to all the forms of judgment and query. My concern here is with the tension that prevails between the apparent timelessness of philosophical discourse and the temporality this discourse betrays. It is this tension that engenders the recurrent revolt against metaphysics, as if philosophy were somehow more unified in its atemporality than science or art. Rather, philosophy unceasingly interrogates its own standpoints, including those that make certain of these interrogations intelligible. But it does so collectively and generically rather than in any particular works. And it does so in even its most dogmatic forms, and confirms the sense that resistance, found everywhere intertwined with power, can take any form.

A more explicit affirmation of the historicality and mediateness of philosophy, emphasizing its practicality in the double sense that it belongs to human life and experience and influences the future, is found in the view, closely allied with the classical American tradition, that philosophy has no unique and privileged relation to human experience, certainly none that stands apart from practical judgment. Rather, philosophy is one of many critical voices in which human query manifests itself.[28] This image is particularly important to the extent that it denies philosophy hegemony over other forms of reason and emphasizes the activities of philosophy generically and collectively rather than the conclusions of any philosophic work or system. The image is deficient to the extent that the practices of philosophy serve to reinforce established powers. Philosophy may fail to fulfill its critical promise as practical query.

Even this view of philosophy as critical discourse fails to express the sweep of the practicality of philosophy. Philosophy is practice in the sense of a form of life—a form in which certain critical as well as substantive voices find expression. It belongs to history and influences the future. What is left out is the double movement that pertains particularly to philosophy, in which it is a practice that is stringently critical of every voice, theoretical and practical, including its own. Certainly such stringent self-criticism is not true of all philosophy, implicitly or explicitly. But it is true of many of the most influential Western works; and it is frequently true implicitly more than explicitly.

Some of this understanding is captured eloquently in Santayana's view of the "heretical" side of philosophy, manifested in the singular and powerful works that pervade the Western philosophic tradition.[29] Such philosophical writing is heretical even where it appears most dogmatic, for in the spectacular extraordinariness of its vision and the remarkable uniqueness of its perspective, a powerful philosophic work challenges and transforms an entire cultural understanding. Philosophy is heretical in such works even where they explicitly reaffirm a cultural worldview, in its style and in its synthesis of heterogeneous viewpoints. In this profound and important sense, the Western metaphysical tradition cannot be rejected altogether, but is rather a tradition highly critical of itself in nearly every work, metaphysical or anti-metaphysical.

Philosophy is a form of practice that is critical of practices. Not every practice is as critical, not at least as explicitly. Not every practice is as heretical, iconoclastic. It follows that philosophy is practical query in its reflexive relation to other practices, though that does not exhaust its nature. In this role it is intermodal and multimodal, even where its intermodality and multimodality are remote and hidden: it is so as a collectivity more than in its individual works. Nevertheless, following Santayana, we may say that it is through its individual authors and works that philosophy heretically transforms our sense of the particularities of practical judgments that mark our sense of philosophical achievement.

That philosophy is practice in this second sense of practical judgment, in relation to other practices, is an important aspect of its intermodality. Philosophy interrogates the other forms of practice from within its own practices. It does not follow that philosophy makes very much difference to them or that its interrogations should predominate over them. Indeed, there is a recurrent sense within other disciplines that philosophy intrudes upon them to their detriment, not simply in a distractive, but often in a destructive role. Philosophy cannot tell artists how to paint or audiences how to respond. It cannot dictate conditions to the sciences. It raises critical points from its own perspective as query, always relevant to its own pursuit of syndetic validation, and is only sometimes relevant to the practices in other forms of query, through intermodality and multimodality.

There have been moments in the history of philosophy where its contributions have deeply influenced other forms of query. Such examples as Aristotle's view of biology and physics throughout much of medieval thought, Locke's view of government throughout much of the English-speaking world, and Kant's view of the autonomy of aesthetic judgment throughout much of Romanticism indicate moments where philosophy constituted the norms of certain practices and forms of query. In virtually every one of these cases, the question remains as to whether the role of philosophy was helpful or detrimental, liberating or oppressive. It is a question that requires answer from within these other modes of query and from within philosophy itself.

Philosophy is practice critical of practice; and to the extent— it may not be entirely explicit or dominant—that philosophy's strictures influence practice, it is practical judgment and query. Philosophy is practice in its intermodal relations to other modes of judgment, and influences them and the future—for example, where it is able to promote theoretical departures in physics based on logical and philosophical considerations, or where it criticizes the entire modern view of science as based on technological rationality. Here it is philosophy's critical relation to other forms of query that defines its practicality.

But there is the more pervasive and more interesting case of the practicality of philosophy itself, as philosophy, the difference that the presence of philosophy makes in human life and experience. The existence of philosophy makes a difference to the future, a difference, once again, that cannot be absent if philosophy is understood to be profoundly human, but that must be interrogated though it cannot quite be answered. Philosophy makes this difference—or rather "is" the difference—whether or not it is effective or influential, whether or not it is culturally biased, Western or non-Western, for the future will inevitably include it in some form, however different from the present. The crucial point in relation to the sense of the practicality of philosophy with which we began is that the interrogation of the difference that philosophy or science make in human life, where these are understood as forms of query, propositionally or syndetically, belongs to philosophy itself—though not to philosophy alone.

We may name the interrogation of the difference that query makes whatever we choose, and may interrogate that difference in any way we choose, from the standpoint of any mode of query. But traditionally, in the West, such an interrogation has been regarded as philosophical. When we ask from within physics what practical difference physics makes, we are given an answer in terms of natural laws and material conditions, an answer without practical relevance. When we ask from within science more generally what practical difference science makes, we are given answers in terms of a multiplicity of sciences: psychological, historical, and sociological. Such answers are important, and may tell us something of what we seek to understand of science as a practice and as practical judgment in relation to other practical judgments. What science can reveal of the practicality of philosophy typically concerns its effectiveness and influence: whether or not philosophical activities affect the future. What science does not give us is an answer to the question of the difference in human life and the world that is science as query—the form of the question that belongs specifically to philosophy. For us here, the question defines a generic perspective based on locality and inexhaustibility.

The difference made by art is interrogated in certain respects more profoundly by art itself than by any other mode of query. Much of twentieth-century art has consisted in precisely this interrogation—the challenge to any established norms or standards, even to the nature of art itself, manifested in works that refuse to be works, that find a way to reject any interpretive standards. The question of what it is to be art has virtually no answer after most of this century has raised it—or rather, anything can be art, anything may be given aesthetic value, any activity may be transmuted into art, almost without change, by the work of artists. Again, although such manifestations reveal insights into the nature of art that no other form of query could provide, there are insights into the nature of art that cannot come from within, that must come from science and philosophy as well as from politics and everyday practices. The particular interrogations and insights that constitute the contributions of philosophy to understanding the difference that is art again fall within a generic perspective, a far-reaching vision of human life and nature.

The practical difference that is philosophy can be judged from the standpoint of any mode of query, including practical query itself, ethically and politically, but also economically and technically. The contributions of the human sciences are especially relevant, because philosophy is included within the spheres of human practices and activities. Thus, there are important questions about the role of philosophic and other rational activities in all cultural forms, the enrichment of human life by philosophic interrogation and criticism, the role of philosophic discourse as critical of other discourses, as contributing to reason and understanding but also to a sense of fulfillment and enrichment. It is possible that we may reject certain forms of philosophic discourse as destructive to fulfillment, as culturally biased, or we may regard philosophy as essential to a fulfilled life. Far more likely, if we are not philosophers we will regard it as a surface phenomenon, making little practical difference in the ways in which most human beings live. These determinations may come from within propositional, practical, or fabricative query, may arise in any mode of query.

Yet the traditional form of this question is philosophical: philosophy addressing itself reflexively. The question of the difference that is any mode of query, regarded practically, is a question not only of the effectiveness of the practice but of the work done by the practice. While philosophy may in its particular works have influenced only a small proportion of human beings, it has certainly influenced some deeply and pervasively. Nevertheless, its density and tangibility are not manifested entirely through the effects of its works, but are manifested also in its presence, in the existence of a form of reason other than those of science, art, and practice, a form that judges them critically.

The difference that is most important here is of the presence of multiple and heterogeneous modes of query in syndetic relation. There is no one form of truth or authority, no single voice in which human reason expresses itself, no complete and unified story of humanity. Here art and technology are as important differences in relation to science as is philosophy. In addition, however, philosophy is a promise of new interrogations, new perspectives and insights, a promise that exhibits locality and inexhaustibility. It is a promise that it makes to itself, reflexively, as part of its critical work; it is a more reflexive promise than can be found in the other modes of query.

Every mode of query expresses locality and inexhaustibility. Every mode of query interrogates every other and itself reflexively. Every mode of query is practical query in the sense that it makes a difference, tangibly and materially, and interrogates such differences wherever they are found. What philosophy uniquely has to offer has three components. First, philosophic query emphasizes a particular mode of judgment, syndetic judgment, and produces interrogations that repeatedly struggle with heterogeneity. In virtue of locality and inexhaustibility, there can be no entirely general, comprehensive perspective on the world, on being in general or human being. But there can be comprehensive and pervasive perspectives that permeate human life and judgment. Philosophy presents us with inexhaustibly diverse and comprehensive perspectives in its particular forms of reason. Second, in virtue of its emphasis on syndetic query, philosophy interrogates the other modes of query as to how they belong together. In this sense, philosophy shares with political query the generality of scale, but not the urgency and practical importance, that requires the most far-reaching interrogations and judgments. Third, philosophy brings itself under its own interrogations, reflexively and explicitly, in a way that no other form of reason provides. Practical judgment may be as reflexive, but it cannot be as explicit. Here, the cultural biases of philosophy are addressed within its own self-criticisms.

The difference that is philosophy, that defines it as practice, the difference it makes in human experience, is interrogable from within every mode of query: propositional, practical, fabricative, and syndetic. Every such difference is expressible from within every mode of judgment and by every mode of query. The practical difference that philosophy makes is a conjunction of its emphasis on generality and on the heretical and transformative powers that belong to its interrogations. These transformative powers are shared by every mode of query. What philosophy offers is a realization of the reflexive powers inherent in syndesis: the promise that the most diverse, local, and inexhaustible experiences and beings can be synthesized—locally and inexhaustibly—into a comprehensive if local point of view. The heretical side of the greatest works of philosophy is testimony to the sacrifices required to attain synthetic vision.

Art manifests inexhaustibility through intensity of contrast upon contrast. Philosophy realizes inexhaustibility through its own multiple presence, critical and systematic, through multifarious works and perspectives, each a local manifestation of a synthetic expression of diversity and plurality. Art and philosophy, along with the other forms of query, represent the mysterious and even miraculous sense that reason is forever open to the most remarkable transformations. The most unifying of systems is open to further diversity; the most heterogeneous systems are comprehensible synthetically, where synthesis is always local. Such an understanding moves us from philosophy to religion.

RELIGION

"Religion," Whitehead tells us, "is what the individual does with his own solitariness."[30] From such a point of view, the practical side of religion is temporary and expedient, while religion has a more transcendent function.[31] Yet wherever religion appears in human experience, it expresses practicality together with other modalities of judgment.[32] Ritual and faith are certainly practical, though not practical judgment alone. For religion includes all the modes of judgment, explicitly and implicitly, and frequently dogmatically. Belief and rationalization, for example, constitute a side of religion that frequently conflicts with other modes of query, particularly science and philosophy. Religions are typically, at least in part, doctrinal and dogmatic, based on beliefs that admit no interrogation and replacement; but they are also joined with inexhaustible variations in interpretations and applications, with unending adjustments of doctrine to the changing faces of human experience. Here the rational side of religion is important, if restricted to but a late phase in human history, a coherent ordering of life.[33] Such an ordering of life is preeminently practical, in its concern with the direction of conduct, however much it may be concerned with generality of thought. It is syndesis conjoined with practice.

The rationality of religion, as Whitehead conceives it, is not the subsumption of religion under philosophy but the transformation of doctrinal and dogmatic religious judgments into query.[34] Here, religion is the practical side of philosophy, implementing its general ideas into the particularities of experience and practice, including the craving for universality that inhabits the particularities of human practices. Reciprocally, philosophy is the conceptual and theoretical side of religion where that is understood to be the synthetic realization of practical life. Neglected in such an interpretation are the holiness and uncanniness that compose so much of religious experience: the former closely related to charity; the latter, to sacrifice.

I have discussed the practicality of philosophy without reference to religion: philosophy is practical in the four senses that it is a practice, situated in material history, with determinate influences; it serves other modes of judgment in a practical form; it has dense and material consequences for the human future; and it constitutes a practical manifestation of the continuing openness of judgment to query, to unending interrogations and inventions. Where does religion fit into this view of philosophy as practical judgment? If we begin with the last of these practical characteristics, the inexhaustible openness of philosophy to reflexive criticism and

interrogation, constantly beginning anew and constantly confined
by its mediate historical and practical conditions, then religion has
traditionally constituted a practical constraint on the interrogations of philosophy, a dimming of its light by the insistent presence
of dogmatic absolutes. If we begin, however, with the third of
these practical characteristics, the material form in which philosophy influences the future in terms of its ideas and works, then
religion is one of the major forms in which philosophy attains its
practical particularities.

This relation between philosophy and religion, together with
the relation between religion and science, constitutes an implementation of the question whether religion, with its doctrines, can be
query, or whether it is at best the dogmatic side of other forms of
judgment and, correspondingly, whether they are what religion
would become if it became query. Here Whitehead's view of the
rationality possible for religion may be taken very seriously: religion provides a coherent ordering of life directed toward conduct.
Here religion is the practical application of philosophy, no less
rational, no less query than philosophy. Religion is to philosophy
here as technology is to science, the *techne* inherent in the applications of philosophy. Here dogmas and doctrines are the impediments that yearnings for absolutes have imposed on the conduct
of life analogous to the presumptions that have impeded our acknowledgment of locality and inexhaustibility in philosophy. The
question with which we are presented by such a view is whether,
were we to abandon the absolutes inherent in dogmatic religion,
we would find ourselves with anything left that we might call
religious. Before undertaking this question, we may consider some
of the more proximate ways in which religion is to be understood
as practical judgment.

Religion is a practice along with the other practices I have considered: densely and materially located in historical circumstances,
influencing them and being influenced by them. One of the striking roles of religion, in practical terms, has been its concern with
sexuality, not only with procreation and reproduction, with relations to the human body, but with sexual roles and differentiations. Whatever position we may take on the issues that feminists
have brought to our attention concerning the masculinization of
God and the role of women in the hierarchy of their churches,
the practical influences of established religions on the role of

women and on their rights with respect to their bodies and their reproductive activities have been deep and pervasive. We may hazard the hypothesis that it could not be otherwise where the orderings of human experience that include matters of life and death, procreation and human feeling, are so dominated by established religions.

Religion is also practice in other senses I have considered. It serves other modes of life and judgment in ancillary roles, particularly in relation to different forms of practical judgment. Religion has composed the defining voice in many practical life arrangements, domestic certainly and public and political frequently. Modern Islamic implementations of doctrine into public and private life are an expression of a deeply fundamentalist tendency in many religions, imposing a monolithic doctrine on a multiplicity of forms of practice. I am speaking again of the oppressiveness of a given system of practice—in this case largely religious and dogmatic—where imposed upon other forms of practice and judgment. But the oppressiveness masks a more general truth: that religion may serve and control other practical human life activities, public and private. Religions have been the impetus to some of the most important liberating movements against oppression throughout the world.

The important questions for us concerning religion address the difference it makes, generically, in contrast with the oppressive or liberating roles it has played historically as an enduring component of human life and practice as well as the capacity of religion to be query. The first is the generic question of difference I have considered in relation to the different modes of query, supplemented by the question of whether religion is compatible with valor and charity. The generic answer is given by locality and inexhaustibility. There are many forms of query, each with its own mode of validation, each related to others. There is, then, a profound difference inherent in the heterogeneities of each mode of query in relation to others, expressed as the incommensurateness of any mode of validation from the standpoint of the others, manifested practically as the presence of the differentiations that define inexhaustibility.

In relation to religion, however, this question of difference plays a unique role. Incommensurateness belongs to religion in the impregnability of its doctrines, its emphasis on faith and dogma, and the typical role of authority in its rituals and other practices.

Religion, here, appears to be a site at which incommensurateness within reason passes into dogma. For there is apparently no part of religion that, subjected to rational interrogation unceasingly, would not be transformed into another form of query. Taking Whitehead's four factors of religious practice—ritual, emotion, belief, rationalization—we may say that each, subjected to query, would be absorbed into another mode: ritual into practical query, ethical or political; emotion into practical life in general; belief into science; rationalization into philosophy.[35] Historically, religion has resolved this tension through appeals to faith and authority, and has displayed incommensurateness on its surface.

One difference that religion has made, then, is that it expresses the incommensuratenesses of locality and inexhaustibility directly and transparently. A second difference, however, ironically, is that religion has typically manifested incommensuratenesses in absolute and dogmatic forms, entirely incompatible in doctrine with locality and inexhaustibility. A third difference, then, closely related to the second, is that religion has frequently, in some of its major forms, professed valor and charity while emphasizing the subordination of all finite things to a power greater than themselves. God's love partakes of all things, but they are each subservient to a higher good. Thus, we find in religion the most virulent of doctrinal clashes and the most insistent demands for uniformity and consensus, conjoined with a profound sense of valor entailing far-reaching charity and sacrifice. Religion appears, in this context, to be syndetic judgment carried too far, beyond its capacity to be supported by criticism. It affirms charity and valor separated from locality and inexhaustibility.

For religion to be rational, in the philosophic tradition, has meant conformity to evidence and to logical arguments, restriction to propositional judgment. Here belief and doctrine have been predominant. But religion is more than such beliefs and doctrines, and reason is more than propositional query. If we add to religion imperatives from other modes of judgment—in particular, the interrogation of the repetitive and ceremonial practices that typically constitute ritual, a continuing concern with the emotional side of experience, by emphasizing that emotions are judgmental, capable of reason,[36] and the demand for comprehensiveness and sensitivity to heterogeneity in experience, emotional as well as conceptual, practical as well as intellectual—it becomes far less plausible that any other form of query might replace religion. Although science is more deeply interrogative concerning evidence and justification than religion, it is less able to concern itself with the emotional and ceremonial side of human experience. Although art achieves as powerful and inspirational emotional qualities as religion, and contributes in remarkable ways to ceremony and ritual, it fails to influence conduct coherently and synthetically, but more frequently displays to us the discordance and variation inherent in local practices. Although philosophy, especially in its systematic works, attains a comprehensive vision of human experience, it tends to lose practicality, especially in relation to ceremony and ritual, tends to replace symbolism and mythology with arguments and proofs, tends to be discursively more than materially practical.

What such considerations suggest is that where practical query strives to attain comprehensiveness and coherence in vision and practice, especially in relation to the particularities—the solitariness—of local experiences, it will almost irresistibly become religious. This may be the reason why charity and sacrifice have always been found more within religion than philosophy or politics, and despite the fact that ethical and political query frequently lead to clashes with established religious doctrines. The prevailing condition of political query, to be the mode of practice whereby we manage those affairs of life and experience that are most urgent, most far-reaching, and most impenetrable and resistant to any other form of reason, places it in ongoing tension between established and traditional political forms and the demands that query imposes in any present. In this sense, religion is a primary form of political judgment, a major site where the tensions of political experience are enacted.

It is not, however, political query. Or rather, to be more accurate, it is situated intimately but singularly in the space in which political practices transpire. It is within political query, but is not political query itself and is not subject to it. It represents a synthesis of traditional doctrines joined with far-reaching ethical ideals. It is too doctrinal to be query, insufficiently interrogative of itself, and too ideal. Yet what it represents, the synthesis of ideality and tradition, forms the basis of any political query.

The question that we considered earlier now returns with renewed force, not only in relation to philosophy, but in relation to practical, especially political, query and potentially in relation to any mode of query. Can religion, with its doctrines and dogmas, be query; and, if so, would it remain religion if it ceased to be dogmatic, or would it be transformed into another form of query? I have suggested that particular religious doctrines stand in a divided relation within political query as practice and within philosophy conceptually and theoretically. Religion here plays the continuing role of the other within query. In this sense, once subjected to deep enough interrogation, religious doctrines would become philosophical and their implementation would be publicly moral or political. Such a transformation would entirely alter philosophy as it would religion.

What, however, of the view of religion, suggested earlier, that it is the practical implementation of philosophy—its technology? To this I add that philosophy has frequently been as dogmatic in its particular works as any religion. It is not so much the works of philosophy, however great, that compose its rationality, but the interplay of different works and systems, collectively, traditionally, and publicly. Similarly, it is not individual works of art that manifest artistic query, but art collectively, publicly and traditionally.

Such a viewpoint may be transferred to religion. Religions, in their individual manifestations, are frequently dogmatic and restrictive. But there are many religions and will be many more. From the standpoint of locality and inexhaustibility, there can be no superior coherent order to human life, only the many different orders that we are able to achieve through any of the forms of query, heterogeneous orders. The diversity and incommensurateness of modes of query engenders a syndetic imperative in two different forms. One we may characterize as theoretical and conceptual; the other is its practical implementation. The former is realized through philosophy; the latter, through religion. It is to be distinguished from political query by its relation to philosophy. Political query is the form in which influence takes precedence over any other form of validation. In religion, however, belief and faith are more important than influence. In religion, charity and sacrifice are present on the surface of religious life and experience, while they tend to be obscured in political query by the imminence of practical concerns. Here we may understand the atemporality of the doctrines of religion joined with the insistent temporality of religious practices as the displacement of religious attention from the urgency of immediate political demands to a remote, often infinite, future to leave room for charity and sacrifice.

In this context, religion is the implementation—the technology—that realizes the practical potentialities inherent within the syndetic side of philosophy, realizing, however, a unique syndetic validation, since it joins in practical terms emotion with theory, particularities of valor with the syntheses demanded by query. The difference that religion makes here is the practical as against the theoretical side of syndetic judgment—the realization of possibilities of conduct as contrasted with possibilities of discursive expression. Religion here is typically dogmatic—along with most other human activities, including philosophy—but can be query in its collectivity, many different religious viewpoints seen as mutually interrogative of ideal possibilities. Here religious "tolerance" or something stronger, exhilaration at religious plurality, is not merely a practical compromise that enables different faiths to coexist, but is an essential condition whereby religion may be query. Even where there are violent religious clashes, these may be understood to be political forces in conflict, open to political query. We take for granted that no religious doctrines may be beyond interrogation, at least practically if not conceptually, and that no doctrines be imposed coercively. More important is that the unavoidability of sacrifice not be taken to justify its excesses. We typically find in religious sacrifices confirmation of the terrors of sacrifice and the implementation of sacrifices to obscure them. In this way religion manifests another analogy with technology, the implicit pretense that it has attained comprehensiveness.

The analogy between technology and religion, representing the practical implementation of science and philosophy respectively, has another interesting ramification. Technology is potentially query—a form of political query—with the qualification that in many of its typical forms, it is blind and dogmatic, imposing exclusively technical solutions on inexhaustibly complex practical spheres. Similarly, religion is potentially a form of query with the qualification that it is frequently blind and dogmatic, imposing exclusively doctrinal solutions within complex practical spheres. Neither of these impositions and oppressions is inherent in the practice, which is why technology and religion are potentially important forms of query: they are capable of raising questions that cannot be raised in other forms. We cannot claim to be rational in the sense of intermodal query without acknowledging the capacity of technology to resolve practical difficulties in human experience and to transform human practices. Similarly, we cannot claim rationality without acknowledging the capacity of religion to resolve practical difficulties in human experience syndetically and to transform human practices. Nor can we claim rationality without acknowledging the charity that pertains more to the religious side of human experience than to any other, though too often in dogmatic terms. Religion is an important manifestation of the dividedness in reason and human being.

EVERYDAY EXPERIENCE

What would it mean for everyday experience to be rational, especially as practice? In one direction, this question concerns the development of wisdom, the subject of the final chapter: the enrichment of everyday lived practices in their complexities by query. In another direction, however, the question is misguided, for everyday experience is not rational though it is certainly practice—practical judgment but not practical query.

Query is distinguished from other forms of judgment by inventiveness and interrogation. Everyday experience is not typically so interrogative, but is pervaded by half-truths, dogmas, superstitions, and mundane mystiques. Everyday experience is not query, though it is deeply and irresistibly intermodal, but is a hodgepodge of different judgments with different modalities, permeated by incomplete validations. One of the striking aspects of psychoanalysis is the rich account it gives of this uncoordinated mixture of judgments that composes everyday experience.

Ordinary experience is certainly practice, as it is also propositional and fabricative. All the modes of judgment belong to it, while judgment and query apply to it, influence it. It is practical judgment in the several senses distinguished above: it is a practice, mediately situated within the conditions of human experience, influencing the future and being influenced by the past; it serves and influences other modes of judgment and query, is a source of artistic inventions and scientific inspirations; it makes an enormous difference simply in being the everyday experience it is; and, unique to it, it is the site at which all other practical differences are realized. It is in this last role that everyday experience finds itself unable to be query, since it is the site at which the heterogeneities of the modes of query come together.

That everyday experience is a practice, historically, temporally, and mediately situated amid power and desire, materially and densely, is so clear a condition and so thoroughly pervasive, that I need not defend it. More controversial is whether, amid its complex entanglements, everyday experience composes a practice, or is a hodgepodge of many and all. In the context of locality and inexhaustibility, every practice is inexhaustible, complexly entangled and mediately situated. Yet where science pursues its forms of query through a certain purification in method and form, as well as the intensification of certain technical proficiencies, everyday experience avoids such formalization and purification. Similarly, even within those forms of query that emphasize complexity and inexhaustibility, there is an intensification of certain forms of experience and interrogation that is essential to the further interrogations demanded by query. In everyday practice, there is little purification and formalization except as these enter from the other modes of query.

This suggests that everyday experience is not one practice, not even an inexhaustible practice, but a hodgepodge, a heterogeneous mixture of practices, joined more by circumstance and temporality than by interpenetration and conjunction. The mediateness of practical judgments entails that they will be densely entangled, materially and specifically. But among these entanglements are those toward which we have few rational resources: we cannot even begin to discern the requisite forms of interrogation and are largely at a loss for invention. Here, I suggest, we find ourselves situated in our everyday experiences, the confluence of the rational forms and activities we have been able to develop, together in ways that transcend our rational abilities.

Everyday experience, here, is where we confront inexhaustibility transparently and nakedly in marking the limits of any rational interrogation. The impulse toward intermodality and multimodality in judgment and query that enriches the modes and enhances their validation also undermines the coherence of everyday experience, the indeterminateness that is to be found on the other side of effective forms of query. Practically speaking, the more effective any practice of query may be, the more destabilizing it must be at some level of practical judgment—typically that of everyday experience.

Everyday experience is not practical judgment alone, for it includes every other mode of query, not least in the direct responsiveness that is required within some human beings' lived experience in order for any interrogations to proceed, but including the ramifications and transformations worked by any material practice. Science influences most people's lives in virtue of what it has contributed to human life. But it influences scientists' lives directly in their everyday activities and encounters. Thus, even the most effective of scientists—or artists and philosophers—may find themselves with disorganized and dissatisfying everyday, domestic lives, for it is within their own personal experiences that the heterogeneities among the modes of judgment and query are prominent.

Everyday experience is then not so much practice, though it is historically and mediately situated, but filled with multiple sites where heterogeneous practices intersect. Everyday experience is practical judgment in relation to any of the modes of judgment and query, influencing and being influenced by them—the source of inspirations and confusions. Everyday experience is also practical judgment in two more radical and important senses involving the generic site of heterogeneous human experiences. Everyday, ordinary personal and collective experience is the heterogeneous sphere within which the other activities in human life are realized. Whatever human beings do, in practice or any other form of judgment, is manifested somewhere in ordinary lived experience, personal and collective.

One way to characterize the importance of everyday experience is to suggest that it determines the ground for all the forms of rationality. There is a sense in which this is true, though it is badly stated, because everyday experience is more influenced by technical developments than conversely. Everyday experience is a pervasive and inescapable condition of all human judgments, in any mode. All influence human experience; all are influenced by the experiences of the human beings who participate in them. In this sense, the question of the difference that everyday lived experience makes, as practice, is a question of the differences that constitute human being. The answer, in the context of locality and inexhaustibility, is that these are inexhaustible differences and they cannot be more then locally delineated.

Practical judgment is the influence of the future by the exercise of human powers. The primary site where this transpires, at least from the standpoint of individual human beings, is within their everyday experiences. Publicly speaking, in terms of the practice of political query, influence is established through institutions—the state, market, corporations, military. Personally speaking, control is realized wherever it is in the personal experiences of individual participants.

Everyday experience, then, is where indeterminateness and lack of control are most directly and vividly experienced. And since by locality and inexhaustibility, there is no resolution that is more than locally proximate, everyday experience is always in danger of unraveling before us, displaying its terrifying side, the abyss on whose edges we constantly find ourselves. Indeed, though all joys and fulfillments are as much within everyday experience as are uncertainties and incommensuratenesses, the latter are the major inspiration to practical judgment.

Everyday experience is the site at which all the forms of judgment, especially practical judgment and query, realize themselves. It is a major—if not the primary—site at which the validation of practical judgment and query is represented. In this sense, everyday experience manifests the inescapable failures inherent in practical judgment, especially in its political forms. The question is what difference reason or query can make in relation to everyday experience, with its heterogeneities and conflicts. The only answer we can give is that of practical query in all its forms, especially political query. To heterogeneity and failure we bring whatever practical resources are available to us. Yet there is more to be said concerning the differences that practical query can make upon everyday experience. This is the question of how we are to live in the context of locality and inexhaustibility, and distinguish such everyday practicality from the sophisticated forms of query that inhabit the spiritual and cultural regions of human experience. It is a question of what we may call wisdom.

NOTES

1. See John R. Searle, *Speech Acts: An Essay in the Philosophy of Language* (London: Cambridge University Press, 1969), p. 16: "I am

using the hypothesis of language as rule-governed intentional behavior to explain the possibility of, not to provide evidence for, linguistic characterizations. The form that this hypothesis will take is that speaking a language is performing speech acts, acts such as making statements, giving commands, asking questions, making promises, and so on; and more abstractly, acts such as referring and predicating; and, secondly, that these acts are in general made possible by and are performed in accordance with certain rules for the use of linguistic elements."

See also Michel Foucault, "The Discourse on Language," trans. Rupert Swyer, *Archaeology of Knowledge*, trans. A. M. Sheriden-Smith (New York: Random House, 1972), p. 216: "I am supposing that in every society the production of discourse is at once controlled, selected, organised and redistributed according to a certain number of procedures, whose role is to avert its powers and its dangers, to cope with chance events, to evade its ponderous, awesome materiality."

We have two views here relating language to practice and rules. The first emphasizes the acts that discursive utterances perform, the second the powers that govern discursive utterances. The first offers a theory of language in terms of linguistic utterances; the second offers a theory of discourse as practice, distinguished from language.

See also Foucault, *Archaeology of Knowledge*, p. 88: "The statement is neither a syntagma, or a rule of construction, nor a canonic form of succession and permutation; it is that which enables such groups of signs to exist, and enables these rules or forms to become manifest. But although it enables them to exist, it does so in a special way—a way that must not be confused with the existence of signs as elements of a language (*langue*), or with the material existence of those marks that occupy a fragment of space or last for a variable length of time."

Three persistent motifs are implicated in this view of discourse—language, practice, and rules—along with the other major entanglements of practice—power, desire, and knowledge. I discuss these issues concerning language in my *Limits of Language*.

2. See the passage from Foucault in note 1, above.

3. See the discussion of ideology in chap. 2.

4. See Saussure, *Course in General Linguistics*, Part I.

5. See Derrida, *Of Grammatology*, for a detailed discussion of Saussure's privileging of speech over writing.

6. Saussure, *Course in General Linguistics*, p. 9: "*Langage* is the whole of human speech; *langue* is only a part, but the part essential to the science of language.

"Taken as a whole, speech is many-sided and heterogeneous; straddling several areas simultaneously—physical, physiological, and psychological—it belongs both to the individual and to society; we cannot put it into any category of human facts, for we cannot discover its unity.

"Language, on the contrary, is a self-contained whole and a principle of classification. As soon as we give language first place among the facts of speech, we introduce a natural order into a mass that lends itself to no other classification."

7. "[I]n language there are only differences. Even more important: a difference generally implies positive terms between which the differences is set up; but in language there are only differences *without positive terms*" (ibid., p. 120).

8. "Language is a system of signs that expresses ideas. . . . (ibid., p. 16).

9. "Whenever two illocutionary acts contain the same reference and predication, provided that the meaning of the referring expression is the same, I shall say the same proposition is expressed" (Searle, *Speech Acts*, p. 29).

10. Searle claims "that an adequate study of speech acts is a study of *langue*" (ibid., p. 17). Otherwise, language would be inseparable from the other practices that constitute lived experience. One would not have "speech acts" constituting a basis for language, but language situated amid human practices more generally, that is, entwined with desire and power along with truth.

11. See Searle's formulation of the principle of expressibility, in *Speech Acts*, p. 19: "whatever can be meant can be said." I add two qualifications, one "somehow," against any system of rules; the other that meaning is then profoundly and mediately entangled among the material conditions of discursive utterances. See my *Limits of Language*.

12. For such a view, see Noam Chomsky, *Cartesian Linguistics* (New York: Harper & Row, 1966).

13. "Linguistic theory is concerned primarily with an ideal speaker-listener, in a completely homogeneous speech-community, who knows its language perfectly and is unaffected by such grammatically irrelevant conditions as memory limitations, distractions, shifts of attention and interest, and errors (random or characteristic) in applying his knowledge of the language in actual performance. . . .

"We thus make a fundamental distiction between *competence* (the speaker-hearer's knowledge of his language) and *performance* (the actual use of language in concrete situations)" (ibid., pp. 3–4).

14. "[I]t is in principle possible for every speech act one performs or could perform to be uniquely determined by a given sentence (or set of sentences), given the assumption that the speaker is speaking literally and that the context is appropriate" (Searle, *Speech Acts*, p. 18). This notion of unique determination is a form of perfectibility.

15. Ibid., p. 19. See note 11, above.

16. See chap. 2, note 15.

17. See Kuhn, *Structure of Scientific Revolutions*; Rorty, *Philosophy and the Mirror of Nature*.

18. "What political status can you give to discourse if you see in it merely a thin transparency that shines for an instant at the limit of things and thoughts? Has not the practice of revolutionary discourse and scientific discourse in Europe over the past two hundred years freed you from this idea that words are wind, a external whisper, a beating of wings that one has difficulty in hearing in the serious matter of history?" (Foucault, *Archaeology of Knowledge*, p. 209).

19. "By correcting itself, by rectifying its errors, by clarifying its formulations, discourse does not necessarily undo its relations with ideology. The role of ideology does not diminish as rigour increases and error is dissipated . . . ." (ibid., p. 186).

20. *Philosophical Investigations*, trans. G. E. M. Anscombe (Oxford: Blackwell, 1963); see also Hilary Putnam, "Analyticity and Apriority: Beyond Wittgenstein and Quine," in *Studies in Metaphysics*, edd. Peter A. French and Theodore Edward Uehling et al., Midwest Studies in Philosophy 4 (Minneapolis: University of Minnesota Press, 1979), pp. 423–41.

21. This sense of prejudice is very different from Gadamer's, in *Truth and Method*, which does not explore deeply enough the exclusions and sacrifices of prejudice.

22. For example, in *Order of Things*, Foucault contrasts our causal scientific understanding with what he calls, in Merleau-Ponty's phrase, "the prose of the world," signatures and similitudes.

23. *Introduction to Metaphysics*, trans. Ralph Manheim (Garden City, N.Y.: Doubleday, 1961).

24. Heidegger, for example, emphasizes the revelation that is art: "The origin of the work of art—that is, the origin of both the creators and the preservers, which is to say of a people's historical existence, is art. This is so because art is by nature an origin: a distinctive way in which truth comes into being, that is, becomes historical" ("Origin of the Work of Art," p. 78).

He also claims that technology is a way in which truth comes into being. Nevertheless, "[b]ecause the essence of technology is nothing technological, essential reflection upon technology and decisive confrontation with it must happen in a realm that is, on the one hand, akin to the essence of technology and, on the other, fundamentally different from it.

"Such a realm is art" (Heidegger, "Question Concerning Technology," p. 317).

25. See my *Theory of Art* and "Sovereignty and Utility of the Work of Art." The notion of contrast comes from Whitehead, *Process and Reality.*

26. See Edward C. Banfield, *Democratic Muse: Visual Art and the Public Interest* (New York: Basic Books, 1984).

27. I would include that movement in which the fundamental structures of *Dasein* and *Sein* on the one hand, *différance* and the *arche-trace* on the other, may escape their dense and material situations.

28. See especially John Dewey, "The Need for a Recovery of Philosophy," in *Experience, Nature, and Freedom*, ed. Richard Bernstein (Indianapolis: Bobbs-Merrill, 1960), pp. 19–69; also Rorty, *Consequences of Pragmatism*, for a more iconoclastic reading.

29. See George Santayana, "Philosophical Heresy," in *Obiter Scripta*, edd. J. Buchler and B. Schwartz (New York: Scribners, 1936), pp. 94–107; and my *Metaphysical Aporia and Philosophical Heresy* (Albany: State University of New York Press, 1990).

30. Alfred North Whitehead, *Religion in the Making* (New York: Macmillan, 1926), p. 16: "and if you are never solitary, you are never religious. Collective enthusiasms, revivals, institutions, churches, rituals, bibles, codes of behaviour, are the trappings of religion, its passing forms. They may be useful, or harmful; they may be authoritatively ordained, or merely temporary expedients. But the end of religion is beyond all this" (p. 17).

31. Ibid., p. 18.

32. "Religion, so far as it receives external expression in human history, exhibits four factors or sides of itself. These factors are ritual, emotion, belief, rationalization. There is definite organized procedure, which is ritual; there are definite types of emotional expression; there are definitely expressed beliefs; and there is the adjustment of these beliefs into a system, internally coherent and coherent with other beliefs" (ibid., p. 18).

33. "Rational religion is religion whose beliefs and rituals have been reorganized with the aim of making it the central element in a coherent ordering of life—an ordering which shall be coherent both in respect to the elucidation of thought, and in respect to the direction of conduct towards a unified purpose commanding ethical approval" (ibid., p. 31).

34. "Religion should connect the rational generality of philosophy with the emotions and purposes springing out of existence in a particular society, in a particular epoch, and conditioned by particular antecedents. Religion is the translation of general ideas into particular thoughts, particular emotions, and particular purposes; it is directed to the end of stretching individual interest beyond its self-defeating particularity. Philosophy finds religion, and modifies it; and conversely religion is among the data of experience which philosophy must weave into its own

scheme. Religion is an ultimate craving to infuse into the insistent particularity of emotion that non-temporal generality which primarily belongs to conceptual thought alone" (Whitehead, *Process and Reality*,
pp. 15–16).

35. See notes 32–34, above.

36. See my *Inexhaustibility and Human Being*, chap. 4.

8

WISDOM

WHAT DOES A THEORY OF PRACTICAL JUDGMENT based on locality, inexhaustibility, and ergonality tell us about how to live and how to die? What does it tell us about what we should do, which practical judgments are good and which are not? If there were answers to such questions, they would compose wisdom. The questions then become, with suitable qualifications, what wisdom is congenial with inexhaustibility and locality? What practical query composes wisdom? If this question echoes Greek philosophy, it may be because it crosses cultural lines, though perhaps not all such lines.

The qualifications follow from the mediateness of practice, from locality. Wisdom can be neither a state nor a possession, but is constituted by the situated activities of practical query. As neither a state nor a possession, practical query belongs no more to individuals than to collectives; to institutions and governments no less than to human beings. It is practical reason, understood as unremitting interrogation, invention, and validation. The qualifications entail that we may not identify such query with individual judgments alone, that politics and other collective practices are to be regarded as rational and irrational, analogous in many ways to individual practices. Nevertheless, traditions of wise men and women embody our recognition that practical reason is embodied in individual examples of virtue, and, moreover, that individuals bear responsibilities for the good.

That wisdom should be reason in practice, individual or collective, flies in the face of the Western philosophic tradition in several ways. Not least is the privilege the tradition has bestowed upon individuality in practice, so that wisdom pertains to individual human beings and not to collectives and groups. I have appeared to follow that aspect of the tradition in emphasizing the importance of individual examples of virtue as paradigms of practical query. Yet collective practices can be as rational, belong as much to query, as individual practices. Moreover, collectives such as communities and governments also constitute paradigms of rational practice. Even so, individual agents face responsibilities for practice, for decisions in relation to the good, in special ways that reflect their roles as agents. The question confronts every human being as practical agent, at every moment of life, what can I, an individual human being, do in the context of the inexhaustible prospects of human locality? Even where we grant the materiality and rationality of collective practices, we must emphasize the perspectives of individual agents immersed within them. The danger is that we may imagine that such individuals possess and wield effective powers, either within or apart from collective milieux, while powers are dispersed and pervasive as well as inseparable from resistances. Even to raise questions of wisdom in the context of local practices seems to defy our understanding of the collectivities of practical judgment.

What may appear to involve little difference with the tradition is the association of wisdom with reason, individual or collective. Yet the view of reason developed here is untraditional. Reason is associated predominantly with no particular mode of judgment and validation, with propositional judgment and science, rule and principle, no more than with politics or art, practice or fabrication. Reason is an activity of thought and practice more than a state or possession. It is interrogation and invention directed toward fulfillment, involving many modes including modes that cannot even be anticipated. Practical reason is inexhaustible; consequently, wisdom too is inexhaustible.

What may be strange is the suggestion that wisdom is practical query and therefore interrogation and invention, not a confident knowledge of how to act and what to do. Of what value is a wisdom that asks but does not answer? Before responding to this question, I would remind ourselves of the Socratic principle that self-knowledge precedes any other kind of knowledge, since without knowing who and what we are—human beings, in natural and social surroundings—we cannot employ or evaluate any other knowledge. Here self-knowledge is close to wisdom, with the qualification that Socrates claims always to lack it and forever to seek it. This unceasing quest for self-knowledge may be associated with practical query with the qualification that this knowledge of self constitutes a basis for human practices that never become stable. No established knowledge of the self satisfies Socrates' maxim. Moreover, given his repeated denial that he possesses it, we may consider the possibility that there can be no form of human being or human practice—no self-knowledge—that constitutes stable norms for practical query. We have a self-knowledge whose pursuit is required for any other, proximate form of knowledge, yet no one can be said to possess self-knowledge.

An alternative is to associate self-knowledge with query on the one hand and with a particular perspective on query on the other. I have suggested that we may associate wisdom with a certain individual perspective on practical judgment, related to virtue. The danger is that wisdom will be regarded as the sole form of rational practice, and the rationality of collective practical judgments, of politics, will be neglected. The alternative is that wisdom, associated with Socrates' self-knowledge, is to be regarded as a limited perspective on practice, emphasizing the self as a practical agent within the multiple collectives that compose the conditions of mediateness. With the appropriate qualifications defining the rationality of collective practical judgments, we may then interpret wisdom and self-knowledge to be the forms of practice that constitute rational practical agents' perspectives on their collective surroundings. What should *I* do given my particular circumstances? Self-knowledge is the form of interrogation that constitutes the rationality of such individual practices. In both cases, I add the qualification that the most effective forms of practice are collective, not individual. Wisdom, then, is in part knowledge of how to act among and in relation to collectives, but it is constantly surpassed by individual and collective considerations and events. This incompleteness constitutes the inexpugnable innocence that surrounds wisdom, that it is never knowledgeable enough of the conflicting considerations that constitute the locales of political undertakings.

We may turn, now, to the second of the Socratic themes, that self-knowledge is not something that can be won or possessed, but engages us in inexhaustible interrogations. Self-knowledge, here, involves unending interrogations and inventions without stable resolution or fulfillment. It is a process that exhilarates and fulfills, but also endlessly threatens catastrophe, in its ongoing activities not in its results, though results are doubly relevant in the case of practical query, essential to it as query and as practice, concerned with consequences and outcomes.

Wisdom or self-knowledge, here, is practical query from the standpoint of individual practical agents and judges, in the contexts of their lives, face-to-face with others. It is individual practice based on unending practical interrogations. It is the unterminating interrogation of every past practice, though every such interrogation is situated amid the results of past practices and is densely and materially influenced by them. It acknowledges the dividedness of every practice and every human situation, constituted by power and desire.

That wisdom is from the perspectives of individual agents entails that it can never be more than a part of practical query, even a part that lacks effective powers. Offsetting this severe limitation is the intimate relation of wisdom to desire. Wisdom is that form of practical query situated mediately between power and intimacy, destined always to lack sufficient powers but capable of deeply interrogating the local conditions and excesses of desire. Wisdom therefore inhabits the juncture of practical activities that compose everyday experience. It seeks to control the uncontrollable, to render coherent and rational what is fundamentally incoherent and divided, to open divisions in what seems monolithic. Yet it is for all that inescapable, the personal and intimate reflection of the mediateness of every practical situation.

Wisdom is unending interrogation, practical query, not least because it and we are situated mediately among events and surroundings, between past and future, subject to past conditions and striving to influence the future. In this sense, there could be no state of wisdom, no termination of its powers, not within the irresistible temporality of human experience. Every action leads on to other actions; every undertaking is influenced by the past and influences the future. And beyond this temporality, there are the entanglements of human practices and experiences among other practices and experiences. Wisdom, as individual practical query, can have no fulfillment, but is finite, local, inexhaustible practical judgment.

CHARITY

Wisdom begins with charity—or rather, since in relation to mediateness, there is no beginning, wisdom is deeply and perva-

sively characterized by charity. Wisdom is founded on charity—
or rather, since in relation to locality, there are no foundations,
wisdom depends on and is moved by charity. Charity is the pervasive judgmental affirmation of inexhaustibility, everywhere and in
every being. It is awareness of the immeasurability of inexhaustible
beings, immeasurable not in being indefinite and indeterminate,
but in being incalculable, inexhaustible, transcending any determinate scale.

Inexhaustibility is the complementarity of determinateness and
indeterminateness, thoroughgoing and pervasive but also reflexive,
including itself. Inexhaustibility is in this sense included in self-
knowledge and self-awareness: every reflexive determination is inexhaustible, determinate in certain respects and indeterminate in
others, complementarily and conversely. As a result, the determinations that compose judgments, however valid and secure,
contain within themselves indeterminatenesses that, ignored, constitute neglect of charity.

To be an inexhaustible being is to be determinate and indeterminate, complementarily, but also, in relation to judgment, to be
judgeable in manifold ways, open indefinitely to further judgments and, generically, to further determinations inexhaustibly.
This inexhaustibility of potentialities of determination is valor: the
determinate but inexhaustible powers that pertain to any being.
To be, here, is to possess valor, that is, to be inexhaustible: determinate and indeterminate, local and excessive. To be is to be open
to material determinations, in particular through experience and
judgment, but to determinations that transcend any antecedent (or
subsequent) limits.

I have criticized the tradition in which things have been characterized by value rather than valor—by a metric of equivalences,
exchanges, and substitutions. Such a system of values is incompatible with charity, for it reduces things to a system of relations,
neglecting their inexhaustibility, repudiating their valor. The mark
of valor is inexhaustibility: the transcendence by any being, however transitory or trivial, of every particular determination, therefore an irresistible potentiality for openness and variation.[1]

Inexhaustibility and valor belong to things. Charity, sacrifice,
and valor belong to judgment. I have defined wisdom as pertaining
to personal perspectives concerned with and defined by individual
practical judgment—those perspectives that compose reason from

within the sphere of a practical agent. It follows that wisdom requires a certain personal attitude and relation toward things. This relation, which affirms the valor inherent in every being as such in virtue of its finiteness and inexhaustibility, is charity. It is an intimate relation bearing responsibility to the good.

It follows from inexhaustibility that there is no ultimate or comprehensive measure of the nature or worth of any being. Rather there are proximate determinations, each from within some perspective and judgment. It follows further that human being and practical judgments are involved in any such determination, though such determinations are also functions of multifarious external relations. "Man" is not the measure, for there is no measure. There are instead heterogeneous potentials for determination to be realized through judgment, inherent in past and future practices and in natural and human surroundings.

To be is to be valorous, filled with inexhaustible plenitude. Our practical response to this plenitude may be to recoil in horror, to seek to bring it under our control by constriction and even violence, or to affirm it through charity and to mourn its negativities in sacrifice. What the Western tradition has tended to do, except in occasional glimpses of alternatives, is to repudiate inexhaustibility, in one way or another, thereby to deny both the indeterminateness in every determination and the heterogeneous plenitude in every being. These denials have been theoretical and practical, but seldom fabricative or artistic, for art manifests inexhaustibility even in the context of explicit doctrines of absolutism and attenuation.

What, practically speaking, does charity mean? In general terms, it means a respect for whatever surrounds us, in and out of human experience, human or natural, for the hidden and unanticipatable potentialities inherent everywhere, in every thing, living or nonliving, present or still unrealized. It is a respect and awe before the miracle and majesty of being, that it is inexhaustible, that it transcends any work and any understanding. To be is to be inexhaustibly valorous—finitely and contingently. It is always to be more than, a surplus inherent in, any determinate manifestation of being. It is love for heterogeneity.

A second meaning of charity lies in the indeterminateness that pertains specifically to practical judgment, to human practical experience and human responses toward inexhaustibility. Practice is inescapably enmeshed in indeterminateness, including surprising developments into the future and uncontrollable determinants provided by the past. Practice is densely and specifically material in its influences and implications. In this respect, every practical judgment, however rational, confronts failure at every turn. In this respect, closer to sacrifice than charity, inexhaustibility entails that practice itself is inexhaustible, that is, always transcending any of its determinate intentions, always employing powers that escape knowledge and control.

Wisdom, then, in relation to charity lies in a pervasive and penetrating awe and modesty before the mystery of creation—the creation of natural and artificial beings as well as the creative powers possessed by human beings—and a pervasive though modest acknowledgment of the two sides of practical judgment: a continuing striving for control through the use of powers, joined with the inescapability of loss of control due to inexhaustibility. In this sense, wisdom bows before the inexhaustible plenitude of our natural surroundings and our own experiences. Wisdom is faced with the most fundamental of practical problems: given that whatever I do will be destructive, and that what will be destroyed is an inexhaustible plenitude (but that what will be produced will be another inexhaustible plenitude), given further, that whatever I do will escape my influence in inexhaustible ways, how can I act so as to work toward the good? Charity raises this inescapable question. The answer leads to sacrifice.

SACRIFICE

If wisdom begins with charity, though there is no beginning, then wisdom ends with sacrifice, though there is no end. Moreover, the end is very different from the beginning, for wisdom welcomes charity: without it there cannot be reason in practice, cannot be wisdom. Wisdom does not affirm, but despairs at sacrifice, and would do whatever it could to escape it. It is the tragic fate of sacrificial religions not to achieve this understanding, but to seek out sacrifices neglecting charity as if sacrifice might overcome itself. It is the evil within oppressive political régimes to oppose this understanding, and to impose violence and domination in the name of sacrifice. Yet just as charity belongs to inexhaustibility, sacrifice belongs to locality. And inexhaustibility and locality belong together. It follows that wisdom requires charity and sacrifice together: the one representing the inexhaustibility in locality; the other, the locality in inexhaustibility.

Sacrifice is the condition that there are no practices, no undertakings and powers, that can avoid the contingencies of mediate experiences. Among these contingencies are the conflicts and incompatibilities among heterogeneous things. The consequence for practice is that to exercise influence in certain respects is to lose control in others. Practical query cannot overcome this locality, the inevitability of loss. All it can do is to strive to transform failure and loss into a sacrifice pervaded by charity. Every being is inexhaustible, therefore an inexhaustible loss where loss cannot be avoided. Nevertheless, conversely, a loss can only be in certain respects, never altogether. What once endured, and does no longer, belongs historically to the locales it did. Charity is affirmation of the inexhaustible valor inherent in every being. Sacrifice is the local consequence of valor in relation to practice: the unavoidability of loss. The deepest difficulty of practice is that to seek sacrifice is to deny charity, and without charity, sacrifice is waste.

Certain forms of life keep their distance from sacrifice and charity through remote or universal voices—for example, the way in which astrophysics exercises dominion over the major cosmic events constituting our epoch. There is no charity here, and appears to be no sacrifice, because individual things are subsumed, despite their inexhaustibility, under generic patterns. Yet the very form of thought is sacrificial, excludes other forms of life and query as irrational. And other forms of life are unable to keep such a distance—for example, art expresses inexhaustibility through its imaginative fabrications and endless contrasts. Within the contrasts of art lie inexhaustible valors; within artistic creativity lie inexhaustible sovereign beings.

Practical judgment is deeply enmired within sacrifice and charity: the latter, its defining source; the former, the threat that defines the arduousness and terror of practical experience. To act is to produce consequences within whose spheres emerge achievements and failures. Practice here confronts charity and sacrifice as the conditions that make rational practice and wisdom possible and terrifying.

There are practices that produce violence and destruction without cognizance of charity. There are practices that produce destructive consequences out of malice and contempt, others that produce destruction oblivious to the pricelessness of what has been destroyed, still others that are not so oblivious, which recognize the goodness of surrounding things, but which deny their inexhaustibility. All these forms of violence and destruction lack wisdom because they lack a sense of charity. Without charity, failure is waste.

Wisdom begins in charity and finds itself faced with unavoidable sacrifices. But the sacrifices are meaningful as sacrifices only from within locales defined by charity, by inexhaustibility and locality. Wisdom is the inexhaustible awareness, endless judgment of the truth, that practical judgment is mediately situated among heterogeneous conditions. It is an awareness that can be overcome by neither the necessity of practice nor the inevitability of conflict. In the Western tradition, it has been represented as an ideal of fulfillment—the lion lying down with the lamb—so that all conflicts are overcome. This dream, that peace can replace the heterogeneity demanding sacrifice, is unreal; incompatible with finiteness, locality, and inexhaustibility; and unintelligible. It is incompatible with practical judgment. It is an ideal essential to charity.

Practical judgment, insofar as it becomes practical query, begins with charity enmeshed in mediate conditions, influenced by the past and influencing the future. There is no escape from mediateness; there is no escape from sacrifice. But there is an important step required for sacrifice: that the loss and failure it imposes depend on charity, on inexhaustibility. Only based on charity can a sacrificial practice hope to avoid waste.

Wisdom begins in charity in the sense that without it there can be no sense of sacrifice. And without understanding charity and sacrifice, one acts wastefully, unresponsive to the irreplaceable inexhaustibility of one's surroundings. What makes practical query possible is responsiveness to the inexhaustible things that surround us, in and out of experience, past and future. That responsiveness is charity. Here wisdom is the capacity to engage in practice faced with inexhaustible demands and inexhaustible losses. It is the capacity to transcend the despair Kierkegaard describes as infinite resignation:[2] to engage in practice despite sacrifice and loss, experiencing them profoundly and inexhaustibly. Such a capacity is unintelligible from the standpoint of deliberation, but this lack of intelligibility is inescapable in relation to a multiplicity of modes of judgment. Nevertheless, the capacity to engage in practical query despite inexhaustible sacrifices cannot produce the peace of mind attained by Kierkegaard's knight of faith.[3] Peace and wisdom do not belong together from the standpoint of local practices.

PEACE

In the tradition, one of its most beautiful and glorious themes, wisdom is allied with peace of mind.

> The ignorant man is not only agitated by external causes in many ways, and never enjoys true peace of soul, but lives also ignorant, as it were, both of God and of things, and as soon as he ceases to suffer ceases also to be. On the other hand, the wise man, in so far as he is considered as such, is scarcely ever moved in his mind, but, being conscious by a certain eternal necessity of himself, of God, and of things, never ceases to be, and always enjoys true peace of soul.[4]

Peace of soul here is associated with freedom, understanding, and being, but always through what Spinoza calls "eternal necessity." Finiteness and contingency can be overcome, in wisdom and peace of mind, only through an unbroken movement to timelessness and universality.

Similarly, even in Whitehead, where the finite and infinite are conjoined in God, peace is associated with the suprapersonal and infinite.

> I choose the term 'Peace' for that Harmony of Harmonies which calms destructive turbulence and completes civilization. . . .
> . . . Peace carries with it a surpassing of personality. There is an inversion of relative values. It is primarily a trust in the efficacy of Beauty. It is a sense that fineness of achievement is as it were a key unlocking treasures that the narrow nature of things would keep remote. There is thus involved a grasp of infinitude, an appeal beyond boundaries.[5]

In Spinoza and Whitehead, as well as Hegel, this infinite relation characterized as peace is inseparable from the finite contingencies that define it. The connection is more indirect than direct in Spinoza, a consequence of the insight that finite modes follow both from God and from each other. Peace of mind is eternity in duration. In Whitehead, however, peace is one of five qualities of civilization: Truth, Beauty, Adventure, Art, and Peace.[6] In Hegel too, the historical moments of its process are necessary to Spirit, and in Absolute Knowledge Spirit must abandon the universality of the pure notion for the externalizations in which it realizes itself— a relinquishment Hegel calls "sacrifice."[7]

Peace belongs traditionally to the universal, suprapersonal side of finiteness, even in those philosophers who most fully understand the nature of finiteness. The Stoic theme of the infinite remains intact with only minor revisions: that finite, changeable natural events beset and besiege us, may even, in Whitehead and Hegel, thrill and inspire us, but cannot fulfill that side of human yearnings which requires universality and, even more strongly, eternity and infinity.

There is, in terms of locality and inexhaustibility, no infinite and eternal necessity, and no peace of mind can be associated with it. There can be no peace that escapes from external influences, a consequence of the mediateness of locality. We are always enmeshed and entangled within circumstances and events, not simply conditions of our finiteness, but conditions of any local being whatever. It follows that peace of mind has no eternity with which to rest, no harmony of harmonies as its foundation, no absoluteness in the sum of finite moments.

There is, then, no positive peace, if this means a comprehensive harmony and universality or an escape from the vicissitudes of local events and conditions. There is, however, another kind of peace, closely allied with wisdom and practical reason, which follows from locality and inexhaustibility. It is not a movement from the finite to the infinite, but follows a different theme in the tradition. Whitehead speaks of the "surpassing of personality" and the "treasures that the narrow nature of things would keep remote." He associates these with universal ideals and infinity. I associate them instead with locality and inexhaustibility.

In all experience, but especially all practical judgment, we act from within milieux defined by local conditions. In one sense, there is no escape from this locality: it is a generic condition of being. In another sense, locality is not closure, and what we cannot escape from is not walled off from other locales. There is, in Whitehead's language, an unending adventure of the future in our practical experiences and what they will bring—novelty as well as responsibility. And there is the endless promise of inexhaustible treasures. The surpassing of personality may be regarded as an understanding, through all the modes of judgment, not merely theoretical or propositional judgment, that no locale is closed, but inexhaustibly involves other locales. The treasures that overcome narrowness may be regarded as the promises of inexhaustibility in every being, however narrow, in every finite condition, however circumscribed. There is a peace inherent in inexhaustibility, a peace inseparable from charity.

What kind of peace can this be, given that it confronts us with failure and sacrifice? In Whitehead's terms, it cohabits uneasily with anaesthesia as its twin, an absence of feeling that strives to overcome despair. Here Kierkegaard and Whitehead join hands, recognizing that finiteness, however inexhaustible it may be, threatens our composure and emotional fortitude to the point where we may maintain stability only by withdrawal. A peace of this nature may be possible and desirable, but it is not a positive peace, however wise we may to be achieve it.

Far more important, anaesthesia is unresponsiveness, and is incompatible with charity. The question then becomes how we can maintain charity, how we can be deeply and profoundly responsive to our surroundings, from within and without, and not be overcome by the weight of our impotence and despair. The question is how charity can be conjoined with sacrifice without abandoning hope. The question is how wisdom can bring peace.

My answer is that sacrifice belongs to charity, rather than composing its alien other. Charity presupposes inexhaustibility, and cannot be threatened by it. There is, in every sacrifice, the inception of inexhaustible promises of novelty and adventure. Charity, from the standpoint of practice, demands that we engage ourselves in the most demanding, interrogative, and inventive ways we can, taking whatever risks are necessary. The risks belong to practice and charity. To understand this involves a certain peace, not an escape from the terror and uncertainty of local practices, but not a withdrawal from them either. It is the peace of ideals, of pursuing the good.

For Kierkegaard's knight of infinite resignation, there are only ultimate moments and ultimate despair.[8] There is infinite despair, infinite resignation, before the infinite task of overcoming incommensurateness—the Sisyphean task of seeking the Absolute in vain. But that such a task is Sisyphean makes it neither self-contradictory nor hopeless, not where the temporality of practice is affirmed. Charity is absent in its material density and specificity—we may characterize it as a love for the particularities and materialities that belong to individual beings, love for heterogeneity. There is no absolute reconciliation of all contradictory moments; there is no ideal practice and no ideal fulfillment. But there are practices that achieve local fulfillments, and there is nothing higher than such fulfillment, nothing higher in human life than query.

Wisdom lies in the capacity to understand and pursue the good in multifarious ways within the material reality of sacrifice and loss. There are anaesthetic temptations on all sides of wisdom: to exclude certain beings and their qualities; to impose an arbitrary system of hierarchy; to become inured to the inevitability of destruction and violence, avoiding the charitability in sacrifice; to become resigned to the unavoidability of failure, no longer experiencing the charity in sacrifice; to despair infinitely at the absence of ideal fulfillment; to lapse into passivity before the greater powers of collective forces.

Wisdom consists in succumbing to none of these temptations, yet to maintain the presence of charity and sacrifice in individual practice. This means respecting things for their inexhaustible promise and seeking to preserve their heterogeneities while engaging in practices that will destroy them, filled with hope. It means respecting the necessity for practice and the positive qualities of practical validation while recognizing the inexhaustible losses that practice imposes. It means a peace that neither overcomes nor exists alongside of despair and resignation, not to mention anguish and terror. It means a peace that is found within and through them.

Wisdom consists in understanding the impossibility and the necessity of practical query. The impossibility lies in the unintelligibility of mediation among heterogeneous local beings. The necessity entails the unavoidability of practical validation, especially within the most daunting of political conditions. Indeed, politics more than individual practice makes the nature of peace and wisdom clear. For in politics, we confront issues of utmost practical magnitude, involving the lives and deaths of many people, many other living creatures, the future of our planet. There is reason in politics, political query, that so closely manifests the heterogeneities of practice and locality that it must be allied with political wisdom. But it cannot be identified with a wisdom inherent in ideal fulfillments, for there are no such political fulfillments. Rather, wisdom consists in the joint determination of ideal norms and the charity that overcomes their dominance. It lies in the rational hope and faith that there is such a thing as practical validation. It does not lie in any timeless ideals that would overcome the contingencies of political practices, even as it would be ideal.

To be wise, then, is to engage in practical query, with its complexity and inexhaustibility, and not to be defeated by it through anaesthesia. All such defeats consist in constriction and refusal of the inexhaustibility of practical deliberation, either by denying the magnitude and complexity of practical undertakings or by denying the possibility of practical validation given such complexities. There is a peace inherent in practical query that belongs to inexhaustibility—its positive side—accompanied by the profound realization that the positive side of inexhaustibility is inseparable from its destructiveness.

EMOTION

Closely allied with the Western tradition's view of the insecurities of daily life and its practices, and its identification of peace of mind with the stability of eternity, is its disjunction between reason and emotion, associating the former with stability and dependability, the latter with variability and uncertainty. The culmination of this tradition is found in Freud, where the uncontrollable powers of emotion are conjoined with self-deception, producing a destructive side to human life against which reason has few if any powers. What such views have in common is their expression of the almost irresistible sense we have that we are at the mercy of our emotions, over which we have little control: mere creatures buffeted by their powers, unable to attain peace and security. Emotions here constitute an impermeable obstacle to the implementation of practical powers.

What is lacking from such a picture is a sense of the reach of practical judgment within which our emotions are situated. For emotion is not uniquely beyond our capacities to control, but rather, exemplifies the generic fragility and insecurity of our practical powers. That reason should be more controllable than emotion is largely a myth, based on Western tradition's restricted sense of reason. That emotion is less rational than thought is similarly a myth, indebted to an analogous view of reason. Rather, we find our capacities in any mode of query greatly limited, but also exhilaratingly powerful, mirroring the insecurities of our emotional lives. There is no greater stability and security in science, for example, or philosophy, however rational or unemotional they may seem to be; moreover, the qualification is absurd, because emotion inhabits every sphere of human life. And there is certainly no greater security and permanence in politics, in any collective practical undertakings. Emotion is not the source of insecurity, but expresses locality and inexhaustibility: the finiteness of being and experience. Emotion is a major site where we encounter the uncertainties and promises of our practical powers. It is a pervasive condition of our practical activities.[9]

I have rejected the association of reason with permanence and timelessness. Reason is query, unterminating judgment, interrogation, and invention. Emotion is open to, part of query, along with every other form of human life, along with thought, movement, discourse, and argument. Within every form of human practice, separately and together, there are openings to interrogation, modes of validation, possibilities of invention, and there are closures, blindnesses to possibility, withdrawals from variation. Far more important, following Spinoza, we may say that there is no aspect of human life that is free from emotion; nor is it imaginable why such anaesthesia would be desirable. Emotion belongs to every human practice as the form in which practical judgment interrogates itself.

This connection between emotion and practice is intrinsic. Judgments of every kind, scientific or deliberative, are accompanied by and influenced by emotions. Emotions here function as influences and responses, as practical judgments. Emotions work within the temporality of practical judgments, directed from the past toward the future in terms of influences and consequences. In this sense, then, emotion is practice, but is not simply practical judgment. It is too pervasive for that. Rather, emotion is the form in which practical judgments interrogate their own conditions.[10]

I define emotion, after Spinoza, as the form in which practical judgment interrogates its powers, particularly to the extent that these powers are enhanced or diminished. In this sense, every practice is emotional, interrogates its powers and influences. The relation between power and desire may then be understood in a wider context than I have so far considered it: emotion joins desire as the field of practical interrogation in which our practical powers are at stake. Anger, joy, love, and hatred are among the recurrent forms in which we relate as practical agents to our surroundings and to other practical agents in terms of whether our powers are helped or hindered by them. For example, anger is the practical interrogation of and judgmental response to how other people or things hinder our practical powers; joy is exhilaration at our practical powers and what they have been able to accomplish; love is interrogation and affirmation of the positive ways in which people and things enrich and enhance our judgmental powers; hatred is the interrogation and affirmation of the ways in which people and things threaten our practical capacities. Emotion is the form in which we are made aware of and interrogate our practical powers.

If this is true, then the question of how emotion is related to reason is one of the most important of practical questions. It is not a question of how we can be freed from unwanted and destructive emotions, how we can overcome the sediments and warps in our feelings, how we can escape from debilitating desires, but is the question of how we can in practical judgment participate emotionally in the interrogations that practice demands to be query. Wisdom here is not a state of mind that overcomes emotion, but is emotion itself in its rational forms. It is essential that emotion be capable of reason and that reason include emotion as the interrogative form in which practice functions rationally. It is similarly essential that desire be joined with power (and emotion) in the rational interrogations that constitute practical query.

It follows that the peace of mind that one side of inexhaustibility bestows in wisdom includes the capacity of wisdom to be fully emotional and fully embodied. There is a peace that escapes from emotion and desire, culminating in anaesthesia, unresponsiveness and inattention. There is another peace, inseparable from the terrors of practice with its imposing responsibilities and the swell of powerful emotions, that is the realization of inexhaustibility in practice. Here we do not hope to escape from emotion and desire but recognize their importance to wisdom and practical query.

Wisdom here is reason in emotion and emotion in reason, inseparably. It is the capacity to interrogate practice through practice, therefore through emotion, unendingly. It is affirmation of reason in practical powers joined with the understanding that rational practical agents interrogate their practices emotionally.

We can now understand in a different way why peace and emotion join in practical query in relation to locality and inexhaustibility. The reason is that such a peace is not anaesthesia but inexhaustible interrogativeness. Desire and emotion are the explicit forms such interrogations take in practical contexts. Practice becomes wisdom, becomes query, only to the extent that it is open inexhaustibly to interrogation upon interrogation, the explicit form of which, in relation to our practical powers, is emotion joined with desire.

We may understand further the inseparability of our practical experiences from our bodies first and our sexualities second.[11] Practice is always located in relation to our body; more important, throughout human history, practice has been differentiated sexually. In traditional philosophic terms it is difficult to understand the importance of sexual differences to such practices as mathematics and philosophy, typically thought more suitable for men than women, typically to the detriment of women.

Within all practices are emotions that reflect complex interrogations of our powers and those of others. And these, joined with the body, frequently take sexual forms, closely related to power and desire. I do not mean here merely that we desire other people based on sexual differences, but that sexual differences take specific forms in relation to desire and emotion, in relation to practical judgment. Practice is as sexually divided as it is entwined with and divided by our bodies. And the explicit manifestation of such differentiations and interrelations is found in emotion and its twin, desire. In emotion and desire we find the interrogations that inhabit our practical powers; insofar as these are enhanced or diminished, they are expressed emotionally and realized bodily and sexually. This is no less true in relation to wisdom than to everyday practices, with the qualification that wisdom involves the understanding that practice—in the form of emotion and desire—

defines its own, if open, conditions and qualifications, and that sexual differences have traditionally been assigned a social force oppressive to women and indefensible from the standpoint of practical query.

LIFE

The questions to which wisdom provides answers are how we should live and how we should die. Such questions are complex and difficult, particularly to the extent that life is not one thing but inexhaustibly many, filled with many modes of judgment and query, surrounded by inexhaustibly heterogeneous things. The question of how to live addresses every mode of judgment, including propositional and fabricative judgment as well as practice. Yet the most obvious kind of answer that wisdom provides is a practical one of what we must do to influence the future in ways that will promote the good. Practice imposes itself here upon a multiplicity of judgmental modalities. More important, questions of life and death pertain especially to everyday lived experience, and not so much to specialized modes of query such as science, art, and philosophy, which exercise their own determinate constraints and which largely provide their own answers. Even so, these belong to lived experience through the lives of their participants.

The question of how to live, then, to which wisdom addresses itself, has multiple answers, depending on the context of life and practice that sets the terms. One kind of answer is that the best, most fulfilled human life is that of query, in its diverse modes. Reason in human life is not one; nor is there a superior mode of query, but possesses multiple forms and realizations. To Aristotle's argument that every action requires a single end, the good life, toward which it is directed, I respond that every judgment presupposes fulfillment, but that there are multifarious modes of judgment, and there is no supreme mode of reason under which the others are to be subsumed. Query is the fulfillment of judgment, through endless interrogation and invention; query is divided into heterogeneous modes, each unintelligible as query from the standpoint of the others. The fulfillment of human life is query: unremitting and inexhaustible interrogation, invention, and validation.

Yet to call the life of query wisdom strains this argument at several points. For one thing, wisdom pertains to practice more than to other modes of judgment and query, and pertains to individual more than to collective practice. For another, the practice of science, in its more specialized forms, is not regarded as wisdom, not only because it emphasizes propositional more than practical judgment, but because, in its specialization, it withdraws from the practical considerations that define the spheres of wisdom. This is true even though science is one of the most powerful of means whereby we influence the future. Again, wisdom pertains specifically to everyday practice more than to any of the particular modes of query.

The distinction between propositional query and wise practice can be interpreted in several different ways. One is that science offers us knowledge and not wisdom, that scientific understanding is alien to human fulfillment. Such a view betrays an inadequate understanding of query, of the intermodality of reason, and of the relation of query to lived experience. Even so, it embodies truths we should not neglect. A second interpretation is to return to the restrictions on wisdom with which I introduced my discussion: wisdom defines an individual-centered, practical perspective within a context of inexhaustible modes of collective practices. In particular, science is distinguishable from wisdom not only because it is more propositional than practice, and more specialized than everyday individual practical experiences, but because it is more collective than individual. It succeeds, as query, largely in its collective accomplishments rather than in individual contributions. In addition, third, science is but one of the modes of query, of immense importance, but which, given undue emphasis, can inhibit the intermodalities necessary to the life of reason. Science of itself is neither wisdom nor the life of reason. Nevertheless, there can be no life of reason, no wisdom, that neglects the contributions and activities of propositional query.

What we may say instead, in response to the collectivity in reason, is that the good life is the life of query, including science as well as art, philosophy, and practice, but that it includes many of these only in their fruits and activities, and not as practices engaged in by every human being. It would be unjustifiable, an unwarranted imposition, to demand that everyone contribute personally to the development of scientific query, interrogatively and

inventively. To the contrary, what wisdom demands is the incor-
poration and interrogation of the fruits of scientific query into
everyday practices. It demands an intermodality and multimodality in query that includes science, but not always the strictures of
scientific query in personal experience.

This qualification, that it would be extreme and unwarranted
to expect that human beings participate personally in science and
art, history and social theory, to the extent that they might contribute novel and significant judgments to the store of human experience, does not entail that the life of reason should be restricted
for most people to everyday rational practices. The qualification
may in part be required because many people have neither the
interest nor the ability to engage in productive scientific research
or artistic production; the qualification is far more significantly
required because there is no uniform model of human life and
practice within which every form of query has a particular role.
Because practice has multiple ends and modes, the life of reason
is exhibited in diverse and heterogeneous ways. It follows that
certain forms of productive query are of importance in many individual human lives only collectively, in their results and implications for everyday experience, and in relation to other forms of
query. It follows also that within each rational life there will be
variations by individual and by modality, always including intermodality and multimodality. In the life of reason are inexhaustibly
many pathways, but each is query, in its interrogations and its
multimodalities. The life of query is unremitting judgment upon
judgment, interrogative, inventive and validative, divided among
heterogeneous individuals and collectives into different modes. Included are the inexhaustible possibilities of collective interrogation
and invention that cannot be fulfilled within any individual human
life and practice.

The good life, the only fulfilled life possible for human beings,
is the life of query, individually divided into diverse modalities,
collectively pursuing unending interrogations and validations. In a
sense, this is the only wisdom of which human beings are capable,
individually and collectively. It is the wisdom that composes query
and its achievements. But there is a more restrictive and more
natural sense of wisdom, not incompatible with this more general
sense of reason in human life, that pertains to individual life and
practice. I have defined this sense of wisdom in terms of individual

practical perspectives. Wisdom is reason from the standpoint of individual agents engaged in practical judgments. In general, the question is how we should act in our everyday practices. The answer is given by and through query. The immediate question is how such a view of wisdom applies to everyday practice.

Perspectives defined by practical query are based on judgments defined by power and desire, directed into a future that forever escapes control and understanding. In the context of inexhaustibility and locality, wisdom is based on charity and sacrifice. In the present context I add our understanding of everyday experience. For everyday life and experience are not, like science and art, modes of query with intrinsic modes of validation inherent within them, not novel but specialized forms of intermodal query like psychoanalysis, but are complex intermixtures of modes of query and other judgments. Everyday experience could never be query alone, for it is the place where query meets less interrogative forms of judgment and practice. It is the site where the heterogeneities of judgment and experience join.

Everyday experience composes the spheres of individual and communal practices where the multiple modes of judgment and query meet in the heterogeneous experiences of individual human beings. It is not practice alone, but it is a hodgepodge of different modes of judgment. It is such a hodgepodge, such a heterogeneous mixture of modalities, whether or not new forms of intermodal query have been engendered within it. It is a complex mixture of modalities and activities, largely but not exclusively defined in terms of practices and consequences.

Wisdom here is individual practical query given the inexhaustibility of multiple modes of judgment and query that inhabit human experience and the heterogeneous variations that compose human life. How should we live?—as rationally as possible given that there is no mode of reason that takes precedence over the others, no mode of life that defines the guidelines for ordinary practices. Wisdom in life is practical query, given that where it typically functions, in everyday experience, life is filled with the complex entanglements of inexhaustibility and locality.

Wisdom in everyday experience focuses on individual practical agents pervaded by the complexities and heterogeneities of political practices. Ordinary life is not political to the extent that it is restricted to local experience, to the extent that it does not involve consequences of far-reaching importance to many people. However, the other side of this condition is that everyday life is the intersection of all the forms of more sophisticated experiences, including technical and emotional practices. We find in everyday practices the same complexities required in politics, the same sensitivities to inexhaustibility and locality, if without the supreme importance of typical political determinations. It follows that wisdom in everyday life is always more making do than following rules and principles, with the qualification that wisdom employs all the modes of query applicable within experience. I add that just as query cannot provide guarantees, but is the most interrogative and responsive constellation of human judgment, wisdom guarantees neither peace of mind nor fulfillment, guarantees neither contentment nor success in practice, confronts failure and loss at every turn.

DEATH

If wisdom in life is local practical query, then it is indistinguishable from wisdom in death. But the question of wisdom in death—how shall I die? rather than how shall I live?—reveals something more to wisdom in life than I have considered so far. For what death discloses is not unique to it, but expresses the irresistibility of limits and of the limits of limits. There is nothing absolute about death, no more than any other local condition. Even if human beings lived forever, they would not be able to accomplish everything or be able to be everywhere. And death does not establish absolute closure, does not terminate a person's being absolutely. For a person remains relevant in many ways into the future, in the memories of others, in influences upon the future, sometimes expanding in importance through time.[12] Nevertheless, we may be confident that every sphere of relevance has local limits, and that the ramifications of any person's life will reach an end, that every person will eventually cease to be relevant in some future, and humanity altogether will cease to matter someday and does not matter somewhere.

Finiteness is limitation together with openness: locality and inexhaustibility. The openness tends to obscure the materiality and specificity of limitation, tends to make us hopeful that somehow every limit may be overcome although overcoming requires limits and imposes others. Still, though human beings cannot fly like birds, they can fly. In every life, however wretched, hope remains that destructive conditions may be overcome. This is the positive side of hope, grounded in inexhaustibility, but deeply distorting our understanding of limits. For the materiality and density of practical conditions means not that every limit may be overcome, but that every limit has limits. We confront many limits in every-day experience with little possibility of modification for most people: our size, sexuality, athletic ability; our imaginativeness, historical circumstances, social mobility. Even so, some people find ways to change them. Far more important, poverty, crime, disease, and death can be given only partial remedy. What we are most able to do is to establish new limits, inexhaustibly, to the limits that surround us.

Death is not so much the unique manifestation of limits that cannot be overcome—for there are endless other such limits—but the most personal and terrifying manifestation. For this reason, death bears the symbolic role of expressing limits as such in a uniquely personal way. Death appears personal in a way that no other conditions are: others always share with me my poverty and my social milieux, but my death belongs to me and to no one else. Yet this description is misleading, for others share in one's death: one's family and friends, sometimes humanity more generally. Every person's death has a sphere of relevance, and perhaps the greatest tragedy is not death itself but a death that has no relevance for others. In addition, however, death is something we all share: our common fate.

A paradox is situated at the heart of one's death: that it is deeply personal yet of greater importance to others than oneself. We acknowledge this paradox in recognizing that we confront death more poignantly when others die, our parents and loved ones, the early and tragic deaths of children. Death reflects the inevitability of limits and the limits of those limits. We remember those who have died.

Death is most poignant when it is personal, but there are the deaths of nations and communities, families and dynasties, species of animals and plants, even the extinction of humanity altogether. The latter reveals, however, not the absolute nature of such an extinction, but that even after human life ceases, in some future, it will not, cannot, be altogether extinguished, in its continuing influences but, more important, in the locales to which it was relevant. There is no such thing as absolute extinction; there are no absolute junctures in the fabric of nature. There are the terminations that belong to the passage of time. Nevertheless, these terminations and limits exercise their material powers, sometimes terribly, sometimes sadly, at other times bringing renewed hope.

Wisdom in relation to death is wisdom in relation to life, enforcing our sense of the inescapable catastrophes and waste of practical experience. In whatever we do, there are possibilities of irremediable disasters, including our own deaths and the deaths of others. Death exhibits the fragility of human and other being, the omnipresence and proximity of catastrophic failures. The Western tradition in all its forms—metaphysical, epistemological, and utopian—has sought ways of ameliorating this catastrophic side of practice, if only by repudiating the scale on which it is measured, but more effectively by technological means that give greater influence over practical consequences. Yet although we have extended life expectancy in some countries by many years, although medical advances display great achievements at a political scale, we have pushed back only a bit the disastrous limits inherent in everyday practices. People suffer automobile and household accidents, heart attacks, AIDS, cancer, epidemics, chronic incapacities and devastating wars. There may be a remedy to any of these within the decade; we may extend human longevity from 70 to 170 years. Yet death is inevitable, along with aging, not simply in its biological term, but in the continuing presence of uncontrollable disasters.

Let us change the question before us. The question is how we should live and how we should die, as wisely as possible. What, in this context, can wisdom be? There is no answer to the question of how we should die wisely, for wisdom is a form of life, that of individual practical query. Rather, the question is what it is to live wisely given the imminence of death. Death, however, is no absolute, but the presence and sign of limits in being and of catastrophic failure in practice. Death imposes on wisdom continuing awareness of catastrophes in practice. Wisdom can neither ignore such disasters, as a utopian vision may suggest, nor can it minimize their destructions.

Death reveals the dark and terrifying, wasteful side of everyday practice, thereby the grim side of wisdom and practical query that offsets any illusory hope. No matter what we do, no matter how rational, no matter how wise, we will fail, sometimes disastrously. There is no escape in life or death from the importance of good fortune. Wisdom is not blind to such catastrophes, but includes them within its judgments. A wise person understands the limits inherent in wisdom itself.

There can be no peace that requires escape from limits. Instead, there is a peace of limits, an affirmation of limits and of the limits of limits. There is an illusory hope that any limit can be overcome and a more local and situated hope that every limit has its limits. This hope belongs to inexhaustibility in general and to wisdom in particular, that what we do will not be in vain because there are no absolute limits. There is present even within such a hope a despair at the limits there are, for some are terrifying. And death is among the most terrible of all the limits we face; however, for some people whose lives are filled with suffering, death is solace.

There are limits, but every limit is limited. It is impossible to avoid catastrophic failures, but every failure is open to local mediation through determinate practices. Wisdom lies at the intersection in everyday experience of these conditions of local practices. Death marks on the one hand the inevitability of waste and failure and the never-ending project of transforming death into life. While death is not the only catastrophic failure in human practices, it is so prominent and so irresistible that we may regard it as the predominant manifestation that forces us to the limits of all our practices: individual and collective, wise and foolish, everyday and technological. It is a condition that requires us to ask repeatedly whether we have after all succeeded in any practical query given that human beings continue to die and die prematurely as a result of our practices. It is wisdom's responsibility to resolve this question from within itself.

RESISTANCE

Wisdom is the knowledge and the capacity to engage in practical interrogation from the standpoint of an individual practical judge. It is, in this focus on agents and their judgments, but a part of practice. For practice includes collective and institutional under-

takings in which individual agents serve as minor elements. The
points at which individual members of a corporate structure may
pursue wisdom and achieve practical effectiveness in their corporate practices are relatively rare. That is what I mean by the dispersion of powers and the greater effectiveness of collective as against
individual powers. Wisdom offers no guarantees of efficacy, only
that questions are endlessly asked and alternatives explored.

The relative inefficacy of individual agents in collective practical
contexts requires supplementation by the pervasiveness of resistance. Power is dispersed and pervasive, as is resistance. Such dispersion entails that in collective and, especially, political contexts
there is no direct or even easily determinable relation between
individual undertakings and large-scale effectiveness. Wherever
there is power there is resistance, but there are no valid formulas
for such resistance; wisdom and rationality provide no formulas.
Power coexists with resistance as its odd term, as its divided other.
This means that there is resistance even where there is dominant
power, even where there is compromise and conciliation. Above
all, there is no particular form that resistance may or should take,
any more than there is an ideal form of power where power perme-
ates every practice.

The question remains, and it is all the more urgent, of what we
should do in contexts of oppression, what we should do to resist
and oppose injustice. The question remains, therefore, of what
wisdom can tell us in contexts of oppression, more generally, in
collective and large-scale political contexts. One answer, following
the darker line of thought, is that there is no connection whatever,
that there is even a fundamental misconception at the heart of the
view that an individual practical agent can define more or less
effective courses of action in the context of divided and dispersed
powers and resistances. To the contrary, there will be power and
resistance no matter what we do, so it does not greatly matter
what any individual chooses to do, or what any individual understands. What matters are the structures and patterns that coalesce
in and among individual activities.

Such a view is, politically speaking, largely correct. But it entails
not the emptiness of impotent unreason, but the importance of
wisdom in relation to resistance. Individual or private contexts of
practice share with politics locality and inexhaustibility. They face
in principle the inadequacies of every utopian ideal, the impover-

ishment of every principle, the losses in every practice. There is no significant difference in principle between the practical issues facing people whose lovers have been brutal, whose children have committed crimes, whose friends have betrayed their trust, whose loved ones suffer from incurable diseases, and the practical issues of war and peace. None can be given ideal resolution. None can escape the penalties of failure and the despair in sacrifice. None can do other than, more than, call forth unending practical interrogation and validation.

The relevant difference is not one of theory or principle but of practice. There is an enormous practical difference between concerns that affect humanity altogether, the life or death of our species, millions of people, and those that affect only local participants. That we may love the latter and be indifferent to the former does not affect the distinction between political and personal practices, though it may deeply affect what we may and want to do. That some practices have implications for human beings in general and over great regions of space and time requires that we undertake them very differently from more restricted practices.

Wisdom, here, is not the capacity to attain political success, for there are no guarantees or methods for achieving such success. Wisdom is not even the capacity to achieve practical success in more private contexts, but is rather practical query itself, based on locality and inexhaustibility, leading to charity and sacrifice. It is the enrichment of our practical sensibilities with the resources available through any of the modes of query. But it is most of all the practical understanding, realized in practical judgments themselves, of the sacrificial implications of practical conditions.

It follows that the distinctions in scale between public and private, political and restricted, contexts of practice must belong to wisdom, not so much constitutive of a special understanding that inhabits public, political scales, but, rather, embodied in a deep sensitivity to what is important and what is not that characterizes charity in its political forms. Here we may sadly note that the Western philosophic tradition has repeatedly neglected this distinction, in multiple ways. One way is by establishing ideals that are not able to support the subtle and complex distinctions required where humanity is at stake. Where moral ideals become too pure, too absolute, they entail that every compromise is immoral, expedient, while political practices always involve such compromises, and not by expediency. Rather, politics is where principles themselves demand compromise, not repudiation. A second way is by treating the movement from individual to political contexts as one of calculation, a movement from individual interests to consensus in terms of costs and benefits. Where value is defined in terms of individual interests, then politics becomes a calculus of benefits and losses. In literature, by way of contrast, there is constant oscillation around unresolvable tensions: in *Antigone*, for example, but also in the *Oresteia*, with its unsatisfactory resolution of the punishment of Orestes, and *Medea*; in *Lear* especially, but also in *Julius Caesar*; in *An Enemy of the People* but also in *Middlemarch*.

Wisdom consists not so much in political acumen, which we may identify with political query, largely because political virtues are more dispersed and pervasive than any individual practical reason can support; but, rather, wisdom, from the point of view of an individual practical agent, involves a deep and unrelenting sensitivity, based on charity, to the dangers in every local practical undertaking of the political measures that threaten it. The wise person does not substitute ideals for query, ethical principles for interrogation and invention, does not imagine that practice can escape sacrifice and failure, but remains open continuously to the novel and productive possibilities practice can unleash and the threat to every practice of profound failure. It is essential that we live private lives, essential to wisdom and to everyday fulfillments; but it is equally essential to wisdom that no sharp line be drawn between private and public ramifications. Wisdom reflects the permeability of every barrier between local practical contexts.

It follows that the political form of wisdom cannot be utopian, cannot rest on stable and unchallengeable ideals, but is rather resistance itself: resistance to oppression, injustice, domination, violence; resistance to waste. From the standpoint of an individual agent, this means sensitivity to the need for political practices and continual resistance to being dominated by them. We cannot attain justice or liberation, but we must endlessly oppose injustice and oppression.

LOCALITY AND INEXHAUSTIBILITY

I conclude that wisdom is the practical work of locality and inexhaustibility from the standpoint of an individual agent. When a person asks, What should I do? The answer, given by query, follows locality and inexhaustibility: first, in a deep sensitivity to inexhaustibility, in charity; then, second, in the locality of human being and practice, entailing sacrifice; moreover, third, in the inseparability of essential differences between intimate and political practices; then, fourth, in continuing resistance to violence and oppression. Wisdom is query in individual, local practice, based on charity and sacrifice, pervaded by an awareness of the urgency and importance of practices in their political forms.

We may ask, having come so far, whether wisdom is, after all, a good thing. If we are asking whether its possession guarantees success in practice, the answer is negative; if we are asking whether it contributes to success in practical validation, the answer is that it is all we have and the best we have, for it defines the only terms of interrogation and validation possible, but that it is divided into multifarious modes and forms, with no comprehensive unification.

Wisdom cannot guarantee success both because there are no guarantees and because failure, in the form of sacrifice, is always present in every undertaking. The question may then become is wisdom a good thing for those who possess it, does it make them happy or does it make them miserable? The answer is the same as the one we may give concerning locality and inexhaustibility. Do these enrich and enhance human experience, or do they confine and oppress us? The answer is that these are the pervasive conditions of human being and of being in general, and that oppression and enrichment belong to them. It is because of locality and inexhaustibility that we can invent, interrogate, succeed, in life or practice. It is also because of them that we fail, unendingly and inevitably. Success and failure are generic conditions of human experience.

Would we be better off if we were not capable of wisdom? If the question is whether would we suffer less if we did not know suffering, the answer is surely affirmative. But, suffering is not the worst thing there is; it belongs to life and practice as one of their moments. On the other side of suffering there is the exhilaration of interrogation and the fulfillment of judgment. Wisdom reflects the possibility that practice may be query. In this context, the question whether we would be better off, how we might be better off, is either unintelligible or belongs to query. It follows that we cannot intelligibly wonder whether wisdom is good or bad any more than we can wonder whether query is good or bad, for only in query can such wonder can have meaning. We can wonder from within practical query whether art has human value or whether science and technology contribute beneficently to human life. We can wonder from within propositional query whether practice is based on evidence and warrant, whether it can be justified by experimentation. We can wonder from within practical query whether wisdom is an alien moment in a largely political terrain of power and oppression. But we cannot wonder from within practical query whether practical query is good or bad.

The question becomes whether wisdom, from its individual perspective, is essential to practical query, and if so, to characterize its qualities. But I have done this as well as I can, if in general terms. Wisdom is unavoidable in practical query even where we recognize the inevitability of public practical considerations. It is the site where public and private scales of practice meet. It provides us with the complex mixture of affinities and terrors that inhabits most heterogeneous regions of locality and inexhaustibility. I may add as a final note that wisdom as practical query defines for us, as individual human beings, whatever we are practically capable of being, for it is the form of interrogation that constitutes whatever self-knowledge might be possible in terms of query. Yet wisdom is not omnipotence, and will frequently lack the powers necessary to make us joyful and contented. Alternatively, that we might be joyous and contented by wisdom, by practical query, is the greatest hope for human being.

NOTES

1. Foucault offers a striking description of valor in relations that do not become substitutive, that preserve a sense of inexhaustibility, in his account of the medieval view of manifold forms of resemblance: the "prose of the world."

"There are four of these that are, beyond doubt, essential.

"First of all, *convenientia*. . . . Those things are 'convenient' which come sufficiently close to one another to be in juxtaposition; their edge touch, their fringes intermingle, the extremity of the one also denotes the beginning of the other. . . . in this hinge between two things a resemblance appears. A resemblance that becomes double as soon as one attempts to unravel it: a resemblance of the place, the site upon which nature has placed the two things, and thus a similitude of properties; for in this natural container, the world, adjacency is not a exterior relation between things, but the sign of a relationship, obscure though it may be. . . .

"The second form of similitude is *aemulatio*: a sort of 'convenience' that has been freed from the law of place and is able to function, without motion, from a distance. . . . There is something in emulation of the reflection and the mirror: it is the means whereby things scattered through the universe can answer one another. . . .

"The third form of similitude is *analogy*. . . . In this analogy, *convenientia* and *aemulatio* are superimposed. Like the latter, it makes possible the marvellous confrontation of resemblances across space; but it also speaks, like the former, of adjacencies, of bonds and joints. . . .

"Lastly, the fourth form of resemblance is provided by the play of *sympathies*. . . . Sympathy is an instance of the *Same* so strong and so insistent that it will not rest content to be merely one of the forms of likeness; it has the dangerous power of *assimilating*, of rendering things identical to one another, of mingling them, of causing their individuality to disappear—and thus of rendering them foreign to what they were before. Sympathy transforms. It alters, but in the direction of identity. . . .

"That is why sympathy is compensated for by its twin, antipathy. Antipathy maintains the isolation of things and prevents their assimilation" (*Order of Things*, pp. 17–24).

To this inexhaustible play of resemblances and differences I add their manifestations: "There are no resemblances without signatures. The world of similarity can only be a world of signs. . . . the system of signatures reverses the relation of the visible to the invisible. Resemblance was the invisible form of that which, from the depths of the world, made things visible" (ibid., p. 26). The primary concern of these passages is with the epistemic figures that constitute knowledge and truth, which require resemblances and signs. But there is present also a remarkable account of inexhaustibility with no traces of substitution or equivalence, of the reduction of one pole of a similitude to the other. Rather, the play of resemblances is inexhaustible, a play that finds other local beings, some quite remote, in signs of the present. More important, within this play there remains an inexhaustible interplay of similarity and the inexhaustible presence of difference. There are similarities but there is neither exchange nor equivalence. Things reflect, answer, and transform themselves into each other, insofar as they are different, and this movement requires time and effect. There is valor but not a restricted economy of value. The system of relations that constitutes the prose of the world is one that reflects the inexhaustible valorousness of beings without compromising charity.

2. Søren Kierkegaard, *Fear and Trembling*, trans. W. Lowrie (Garden City, New York: Doubleday, 1954).

3. Ibid.

4. Spinoza, *Ethics*, V, Prop. XLII, note.

5. *Adventures of Ideas* (New York: Macmillan, 1933), p. 367.

6. Ibid., p. 353: "The Unity of Adventure includes among its components all individual realities, each with the importance of the personal or social fact to which it belongs. Such individual importance in the components belongs to the essence of Beauty. In this Supreme Adventure, the Reality which the Adventure transmutes into its Unity of Appearance, requires the real occasions of the advancing world each claiming its due share of attention. This Appearance, thus enjoyed, is the final Beauty with which the Universe achieves its justification. This Beauty has always within it the renewal derived from the Advance of the Temporal World" (ibid., p. 381).

7. "Absolute Knowledge contains within itself this necessity of relinquishing itself from the form of the pure notion, and necessarily involves the transition of the notion into consciousness. For Spirit that knows itself is, just for the reason that it grasps its own notion, immediate identity with itself; and this, in the distinction that it implies, is the certainty of what is immediate or is sense-consciousness—the beginning from which we started. . . .

". . . Knowledge is aware not only of itself, but also of the negative of itself, or its limit. Knowing its limit means knowing how to sacrifice itself. This sacrifice is the self-abandonment, in which Spirit sets forth, in the form of free fortuitous happening, its process of becoming Spirit, intuitively apprehending, outside it its pure self as Time, and likewise its existence as Space. This last form into which Spirit passes, *Nature*, is its living immediate process of development" (Hegel, *Philosophy of Mind*, pp. 806–807).

8. Kierkegaard, *Fear and Trembling*.

9. We find traces of this insight in Spinoza. "By emotion I understand the modifications of the body by which the power of acting of the body itself is increased, diminished, helped, or hindered, together with the ideas of these modifications" (*Ethics*, III, Def. III). Here emotion is associated pervasively with practice, not just with a part of it, a factor in all the powers of action of the body, all human practices. It is involved wherever human practical powers are enhanced or diminished. To this we may add Spinoza's view of reason in emotion. "If, therefore, we can be the adequate cause of any of these modifications, I understand the emotion to be an action, otherwise it is a passive state" (ibid.).

Spinoza appears to preserve the distinction between reason and emotion in the distinction between activity and passivity. The difference is that emotion itself may be rational where we are the adequate cause of a bodily modification. More precisely, while Spinoza follows the traditional association of reason with eternity, he by no means associates emotion with variability and reason with stability. Emotion is a pervasive ingredient of all human functioning, belonging to practical powers intrinsically, along with desire, capable therefore of reason and unreason.

10. See my *Inexhaustibility in Human Being*, chap. 4, for an extended discussion of this understanding.

11. See ibid.; also, my "Limits of Sexuality."

12. See my *Inexhaustibility and Human Being*, chap. 10.

BIBLIOGRAPHY

Aristotle. *The Basic Works of Aristotle*. Ed. Richard McKeon. New York: Random House, 1941.

Banfield, Edward C. *Democratic Muse: Visual Art and the Public Interest*. New York: Basic Books, 1984.

Barber, Benjamin R. "Deconstituting Politics: Robert Nozick and Philosophical Reductionism." In *The Frontiers of Political Theory*. Edd. Michael Freeman and David Robertson. Brighton, Sussex: Harvester, 1980. Pp. 23–46.

Beauvoir, Simone de. *The Ethics of Ambiguity*. Trans. Bernard Frechtman. New York: Philosophical Library, 1948.

Benjamin, Walter. "The Work of Art in the Age of Mechanical Reproduction." *Illuminations*. New York: Schocken, 1968. Pp. 217–51.

Bernstein, Richard J. *Beyond Objectivism and Relativism: Science, Hermeneutics, and Praxis*. Philadelphia: University of Pennsylvania Press, 1983.

Buchler, Justus. *Metaphysics of Natural Complexes*. New York: Columbia University Press, 1966.

Caulfield, Catherine. *In the Rain Forest*. London: Heinemann, 1985.

Chomsky, Noam. *Cartesian Linguistics*. New York: Harper & Row, 1966.

Collingwood, R. G. *The Principles of Art*. Oxford: Oxford University Press, 1938.

Cotta, Sergio. *Why Violence? A Philosophical Interpretation*. Trans. Giovanni Gullace. Gainesville: University of Florida Press, 1985.

Derrida, Jacques. *Of Grammatology*. Trans. Gayatri Spivak. Baltimore: The Johns Hopkins University Press, 1974.

———. "The Politics of Friendship." Trans. Gabriel Motzkin. *Journal of Philosophy*, 85, No. 11 (November 1988), 632–48.

Dessauer, Friedrich. *Philosophie der Technik: Das Problem der Realisierung*. Bonn: Cohen, 1927.

———. "Technology in its Proper Sphere." In *Philosophy and Technology*. Edd. Carl Mitcham and Robert Mackey. New York: Free Press, 1972. pp. 317–34.

Dewey, John. *Art as Experience*. New York: Minton, Balch, 1934.

———. *Experience and Nature*. 2nd ed. New York: Dover, 1929.

———. *Experience, Nature, and Freedom*. Ed. Richard Bernstein. Indianapolis: Bobbs-Merrill, 1960.

———. *Human Nature and Conduct*. New York: Holt, 1922.

———. "The Need for a Recovery of Philosophy." In *Experience, Nature, and Freedom*. Ed. Richard Bernstein. Indianapolis: Bobbs-Merril, 1960. Pp. 19–69.

———. *The Quest for Certainty*. New York: Minton, Balch, 1929.

———. *Theory of Valuation*. Chicago: The University of Chicago Press, 1939.

Ellul, Jacques. *The Technological Order*. Ed. Carl F. Stover. Detroit: Wayne State University Press, 1963.

———. "The Technological Order." In *Philosophy and Technology*. Edd. Carl Mitcham and Robert Mackey. New York: Free Press, 1972. Pp. 86–105.

———. *The Technological Society*. Trans. John Wilkinson. New York: Knopf, 1964.

The English Philosophers from Bacon to Mill. Ed. E. A. Burtt. New York: Modern Library, 1939.

Feibleman, James K. "Pure Science, Applied Science, and Technology: An Attempt at Definitions." In *Philosophy and Technology*. Edd. Carl Mitcham and Robert Mackey. New York: Free Press, 1972. Pp. 33–41.

———. *The Two-Story World*. Ed. Huntington Cairns. New York: Holt, Rinehart and Winston, 1966.

Foucault, Michel. *The Archaeology of Knowledge*. Trans. A. M. Sheridan Smith. New York: Random House, 1972.

———. *The Birth of the Clinic: An Archaeology of Medical Perception*. Trans. A. M. Sheridan-Smith. New York: Random House, 1973.

———. "The Discourse on Language." Trans. Rupert Swyer. The Archaeology of Knowledge. Trans. A. M. Sheriden Smith. New York: Random House, 1972. Pp. 215–37.

———. *The History of Sexuality*. I. *An Introduction*. Trans. Robert Hurley. New York: Random House, 1980.

———. *The Order of Things: An Archaeology of the Human Sciences*. New York: Vintage, 1973.

———. *Power/Knowledge*. Ed. Colin Gordon. New York: Pantheon, 1980.

Fraser, Nancy. "Foucault on Modern Power: Empirical Insights and Normative Confusions." *Praxis International*, 1, No. 3 (October 1981), 272–87.

Freud, Sigmund. "The Relation of the Poet to Day-dreaming." In *Collected Papers*. Trans. I. F. Grant Duff. New York: Basic Books, 1959. First published in *Neue Revue*, 1 (1908).

The Frontiers of Political Theory. Edd. Michael Freeman and David Robertson. Brighton, Sussex: Harvester, 1980.

Gadamer, Hans-Georg. *Truth and Method*. New York: Seabury, 1975.

Goodman, Nelson. *Languages of Art*. 2nd ed. Indianapolis: Hackett, 1976.

———. *Ways of Worldmaking*. Indianapolis: Hackett, 1978.

Habermas, Jürgen. *Communication and the Evolution of Society*. Trans. Thomas McCarthy. Boston: Beacon Press, 1979.

———. *The Legitimation Crisis*. Trans. Thomas McCarthy. Boston: Beacon, 1975.

Hegel, G. W. F. *Phenomenology of Mind*. Trans. J. B. Baillie. London: Allen & Unwin, 1910.

———. *The Science of Logic*. Trans. William Wallace. Oxford: Oxford University Press, 1873.

Heidegger, Martin. *Basic Writings*. Ed. D. F. Krell. New York: Harper & Row, 1977.

———. *Being and Time*. Trans. J. Macquarrie and E. Robinson. New York: Harper & Row, 1962.

———. *Discourse on Thinking*. Trans. J. A. Anderson and E. Hans Freund. New York: Harper & Row, 1966.

———. *Introduction to Metaphysics*. Trans. Ralph Manheim. Garden City, N.Y.: Doubleday, 1961.

———. "The Origin of the Work of Art." In *Poetry, Language, Thought*. Trans. A. Hofstadter. New York: Harper & Row, 1971. Pp. 238–317.

———. *Poetry, Language, Thought*. Trans. A. Hofstadter. New York: Harper & Row, 1971.

———. "The Question Concerning Technology." In *Basic Writings*. Trans. J. Macquarrie and E. Robinson. New York: Harper & Row, 1962. Pp. 287–317.

Horkheimer, Max. *Eclipse of Reason*. New York: Continuum, 1974.

Ihde, Don. *Technics and Praxis*. Boston: Reidel, 1979.

Illich, Ivan. *Tools for Conviviality*. New York: Harper & Row, 1973.

Jung, Carl G. "Psychology and Literature." *Modern Man in Search of a Soul*. Trans. W. S. Dell and C. F. Baynes. New York: Harcourt Brace Jovanovich, 1955. Pp. 152–72.

Jünger, Friedrich Georg. *The Failure of Technology*. Chicago: Regnery, 1956.

Kant, Immanuel. *Critique of Judgment*. Trans. J. H. Bernard. New York: Hafner, 1951.

———. *Fundamental Principles of the Metaphysics of Morals. Kant's* CRITIQUE OF PRACTICAL REASON *and Other Works on the Theory of Ethics*. Trans. T. K. Abbott. New York: Longmans, Green, 1879.

———. *Kant's* CRITIQUE OF PRACTICAL REASON *and Other Works on the Theory of Ethics*. Trans. T. K. Abbott. New York: Longmans, Green, 1879.

————. *Critique of Pure Reason.* Trans. Norman Kemp Smith. London: Macmillan, 1956.

Kierkegaard, Søren. *Fear and Trembling.* Trans. W. Lowrie. Garden City, New York: Doubleday, 1954.

Kuhn, Thomas S. *The Structure of Scientific Revolutions.* Chicago: The University of Chicago Press, 1962.

Kundera, Milan. "Man Thinks, God Laughs." Address on receiving the Jerusalem Prize for Literature on the Freedom of Man in Society. In *The New York Review of Books.* Trans. Linda Asher. June 13, 1985.

Langer, Susanne. *Feeling and Form.* New York: Scribner's, 1953.

Locke, John. *An Essay Concerning the True Original, Extent and end of Civil Government.* In *The English Philosophers from Bacon to Mill.* Ed. E. A. Burtt. New York: Modern Public Library, 1939. Pp. 403–503.

Malraux, André. *The Voices of Silence.* Trans. Stuart Gilbert. Princeton: Princeton University Press, 1953.

Merleau-Ponty, Maurice. "Eye and Mind." Trans. Carleton Dallery. *The Primacy of Perception.* Evanston: Northwestern University Press, 1964. Pp. 159–90.

Technology and Social Change. Ed. Emmanuel G. Mesthene. Indianapolis: Bobbs-Merrill, 1967.

————. "Technology and Wisdom." In *Philosophy and Technology.* Edd. Carl Mitcham and Robert Mackey. New York: Free Press, 1972. Pp. 109–115.

Nozick, Robert. *Anarchy, State, Utopia.* New York: Basic Books, 1974.

Peirce, Charles Sanders. "How to Make Our Ideas Clear." *Philosophical Writings of Peirce.* Ed. Justus Buchler. New York: Dover, 1955. Pp. 21–41.

————. "Logic as Semiotic: The Theory of Signs." *Philosophical Writings of Peirce.* Ed. Justus Buchler. New York: Dover, 1955. Pp. 98–119.

Philosophical Writings of Peirce. Ed. Justus Buchler. New York: Dover, 1955.

Philosophy and Technology. Edd. Carl Mitcham and Robert Mackey. New York: Free Press, 1972.

Polanyi, Michael. *Knowing and Being.* Chicago: The University of Chicago Press, 1969.

Putnam, Hilary. "Analyticity and Apriority: Beyond Wittgenstein and Quine." In *Studies in Metaphysics.* Edd. Peter A. French and Theodore Edward Uehling et al. Midwest Studies in Philosophy 4. Minneapolis: University of Minnesota Press, 1979. Pp. 423–41.

————. "How Not to Solve Ethical Problems." *The Lindley Lecture.* Lawrence: University of Kansas, 1983.

Rawls, John. *A Theory of Justice*. Cambridge: Harvard University Press, 1971.

Ricoeur, Paul. *Freud and Philosophy*. New Haven: Yale University Press, 1970.

Rorty, Richard. *Consequences of Pragmatism*. Minneapolis: University of Minnesota Press, 1982.

———. "Method, Social Science, and Social Hope." *Consequences of Pragmatism*. Minneapolis: University of Minnesota Press, 1982. Pp. 191–210.

———. *Philosophy and the Mirror of Nature*. Princeton: Princeton University Press, 1979.

Ross, Stephen David. *Inexhaustibility and Human Being: An Essay on Locality*. New York: Fordham University Press, 1989.

———. "The Inexhaustibility of Nature." *The Journal of Value Inquiry*, 7, No. 4 (Winter 1973), 241–53.

———. *Injustice and Restitution*. Albany: State University of New York Press, 1993.

———. *Learning and Discovery*. London and New York: Gordon and Breach, 1982.

———. *The Limits of Language*. New York: Fordham University Press, 1993.

———. "The Limits of Sexuality." *Philosophy and Social Cohesion*, 9, Nos. 3–4 (Spring 1984), 320–36.

———. *Metaphysical Aporia and Philosophical Heresy*. Albany: State University of New York Press, 1990.

———. *The Nature of Moral Responsibility*. Detroit: Wayne State University Press, 1973.

———. *Perspective in Whitehead's Metaphysics*. Albany: State University of New York, 1983.

———. *Philosophical Mysteries*. Albany: State University of New York Press, 1982.

———. *The Ring of Representation*. Albany: State University of New York Press, 1992.

———. "Skepticism, Holism, and Inexhaustibility." *Review of Metaphysics*, 35, No. 3 (March 1982), 527–56.

———. "The Soverignty and Utility of the Work of Art." *Journal of Aesthetics and Art Criticism*, 40, No. 2 (Winter 1981),-.

———. *A Theory of Art: Inexhaustibility by Contrast*. Albany: State University of New York Press, 1982.

———. *Transition to an Ordinal Metaphysics*. Albany: State University of New York Press, 1981.

Rotenstreich, Nathan. "Technology and Politics." In *Philosophy and Technology*. Edd. Carl Mitcham and Robert Mackey. New York: Free

Press, 1972. Pp. 151–60; from *International Philosophical Quarterly*, 7, No. 2 (June 1967) 197–212.

Samuelson, Paul A. *Functions of Economic Analysis*. Cambridge: Harvard University Press, 1947.

Santayana, George. *Obiter Scripta*. Ed. J. Buchler and B. Schwartz. New York: Scribner's, 1936.

———. "Philosophical Heresy." *Obiter Scripta*. Ed. J. Buchler and B. Schwartz. New York: Scribner's, 1936. Pp. 94–107.

Saussure, Ferdinand de. *Course in General Linguistics*. Trans. Wade Baskin. New York: McGraw-Hill, 1966.

Searle, John R. *Speech Acts: An Essay in the Philosophy of Language*. London: Cambridge University Press, 1969.

Singer, Peter. *Animal Liberation: A New Ethics for Our Treatment of Animals*. New York: Avon, 1975.

Skinner, B. F. *Walden Two*. New York: Macmillan, 1962.

Spinoza, Benedict de. *Ethics*. Ed. James Gutmann. New York: Hafner, 1949.

Walzer, Michael. "The Politics of Michael Foucault." *Dissent*, 4 (Fall 1983), 481–90.

Whitehead, Alfred North. *Adventures of Ideas*. New York: Macmillan, 1933.

———. *Process and Reality*. Corr. ed. Edd. D. R. Griffin and D. W. Sherburne. New York: Free Press, 1978.

———. *Religion in the Making*. New York: Macmillan, 1926.

———. *Science in the Modern World*. New York: Macmillan, 1925.

Wittgenstein, Ludwig. *Philosophical Investigations*. Trans. G. E. M. Anscombe. Oxford: Blackwell, 1963.

INDEX